DEMOCRACY
The God That Failed

DEMOCRACY
The God That Failed

**The Economics and Politics of
Monarchy, Democracy, and Natural Order**

Hans-Hermann Hoppe

Transaction Publishers
New Brunswick (U.S.A.) and London (U.K.)

Ninth paperback printing 2007

Copyright © 2001 by Transaction Publishers, New Brunswick, New Jersey.

This book is printed on acid-free paper that meets the American National Standard for Permanence of Paper for Printed Library Materials.

Library of Congress Catalog Number: 2001027380
ISBN: 978-0-7658-0088-6 (cloth); 978-0-7658-0868-4 (paper)
Printed in the United States of America

Library of Congress Cataloging-in-Publication Data

Hoppe, Hans-Hermann.
  Democracy—the god that failed: the economics & politics of monarchy, democracy & natural order / Hans-Hermann Hoppe.
      p. cm.
  Includes bibliographical references and index.
  ISBN 0-7658-0088-8 (cloth: alk. paper)—ISBN 0-7658-0868-4 (pbk. alk. paper)
  1. Economics—Political aspects. 2. Economics—Moral and ethical aspects. 3. Economic policy. 4. Monarchy. 5. Democracy. 6. Anarchy. 7. State, The—Economic aspects. I. Title.

HB74.P65 H66 2001
321.8-dc21   2001027380

Contents

Acknowledgments

M ost of the following studies have grown out of speeches delivered at various conferences sponsored by the Ludwig von Mises Institute and the Center for Libertarian Studies. Several of them have been published previously at different locations and in various translations. However, for the present occasion all of them have been systematically revised and substantially enlarged. I thank Llewellyn H. Rockwell Jr., president of the Ludwig von Mises Institute, and Burton S. Blumert, president of the Center for Libertarian Studies, for their continual support, financially and personally, in developing and elaborating the ideas presented here.

Others who afforded me a forum to express and test my ideas and thus contributed to the present work include Cristian Comanescu, Robert Nef, Gerard Radnitzky, Jiri Schwarz, Jesús Huerta de Soto, and Josef Sima. Thanks go to them, as well as to an anonymous benefactor for his ongoing financial support.

For many years I have been blessed with the friendship of Walter Block, David Gordon, Jeffrey Herbener, Guido Hülsmann, Stephan Kinsella, Ralph Raico, and Joseph Salerno. While none of them can be held responsible for any of my ideas, all of them, through suggestions and criticisms in countless conversations as well as their own scholarly writings, have exercised an indelible effect on my thinking.

Even more important has been the influence of Ludwig von Mises and Murray N. Rothbard. My intellectual debt to their work is notable and, I can only hope, has been dutifully and adequately acknowledged throughout the following studies. To Murray N. Rothbard, with whom I was fortunate to have been closely associated during the last decade of his life, I further owe a profound personal debt. His friendship, and his example of moral courage and of the ability to stay kind, and indeed cheerfully optimistic in the face even of seemingly overwhelming adversity, have deeply and lastingly affected my own conduct and outlook on life.

Last but not least, I thank my wife, Margaret Rudelich Hoppe, not just for assuming for more than twenty years now the thankless task of editing my English writings, but for always finding the time and energy, in between her work, household, and care for our two teenage children, to provide me with encouragement, comfort, and happiness.

Introduction

World War I marks one of the great watersheds of modern history. With its end the transformation of the entire Western world from monarchical rule and sovereign kings to democratic–republican rule and sovereign people that began with the French Revolution was completed. Until 1914, only three republics had existed in Europe—France, Switzerland, and after 1911, Portugal; and of all major European monarchies only the United Kingdom could be classified as a parliamentary system, i.e., one in which supreme power was vested in an elected parliament. Only four years later, after the United States had entered the European war and decisively determined its outcome, monarchies all but disappeared, and Europe along with the entire world entered the age of democratic republicanism.

In Europe, the militarily defeated Romanovs, Hohenzollerns, and Habsburgs had to abdicate or resign, and Russia, Germany, and Austria became democratic republics with universal—male and female—suffrage and parliamentary governments. Likewise, all of the newly created successor states with the sole exception of Yugoslavia adopted democratic republican constitutions. In Turkey and Greece, the monarchies were overthrown. And even where monarchies remained nominally in existence, as in Great Britain, Italy, Spain, Belgium, the Netherlands, and the Scandinavian countries, monarchs no longer exercised any governing power. Universal adult suffrage was introduced, and all government power was vested in parliaments and "public" officials.

The world-historic transformation from the *ancien régime* of royal or princely rulers to the new democratic–republican age of popularly elected or chosen rulers may be also characterized as that from Austria and the Austrian way to that of America and the American way. This is true for several reasons. First, Austria initiated the war, and America brought it to a close. Austria lost, and America won. Austria was ruled by a monarch—Emperor Franz Joseph—and America by a democratically elected president—Professor Woodrow Wilson. More importantly, however, World War I was not a traditional war fought over limited territorial objectives, but an ideological one; and Austria and America respectively were (and were perceived as such by the contending parties) the two countries that most clearly embodied the ideas in conflict with each other.[1]

World War I began as an old-fashioned territorial dispute. However, with the early involvement and the ultimate official entry into the war by the United States in April 1917, the war took on a new ideological dimension. The United States had been founded as a republic, and the democratic principle, inherent in the idea of a republic, had only recently been carried to victory as the result of the violent defeat and devastation of the secessionist Confederacy by the centralist Union government. At the time of World War I, this triumphant ideology of an expansionist democratic republicanism had found its very personification in then U.S. President Wilson. Under Wilson's administration, the European war became an ideological mission—to make the world safe for democracy and free of dynastic rulers. When in March 1917 the U.S.-allied Czar Nicholas II was forced to abdicate and a new democratic-republican government was established in Russia under Kerensky, Wilson was elated. With the Czar gone, the war had finally become a purely ideological conflict: of good against evil. Wilson and his closest foreign policy advisors, George D. Herron and Colonel House, disliked the Germany of the Kaiser, the aristocracy, and the military elite. But they hated Austria. As Erik von Kuehnelt-Leddihn has characterized the views of Wilson and the American Left, "Austria was far more wicked than Germany. It existed in contradiction of the Mazzinian principle of the national state, it had inherited many traditions as well as symbols from the Holy Roman Empire (double-headed eagle, black-gold colors, etc.); its dynasty had once ruled over Spain (another *bête noire*); it had led the Counter-Reformation, headed the Holy Alliance, fought against the *Risorgimento*, suppressed the Magyar rebellion under Kossuth (who had a monument in New York City), and morally supported the monarchical experiment in Mexico. Habsburg—the very name evoked memories of Roman Catholicism, of the Armada, the Inquisition, Metternich, Lafayette jailed at Olmütz, and Silvio Pellico in Brünn's Spielberg fortress. Such a state had to be shattered, such a dynasty had to disappear."[2]

---

[1]For a brilliant summary of the causes and consequences of World War I see Ralph Raico, "World War I: The Turning Point," in *The Costs of War: America's Pyrrhic Victories*, John V. Denson, ed. (New Brunswick, N.J.: Transaction Publishers, 1999).

[2]Erik von Kuehnelt-Leddihn, *Leftism Revisited: From de Sade to Pol Pot* (Washington, D.C.: Regnery, 1990), p. 210; on Wilson and Wilsonianism see further Murray N.

As an increasingly ideologically motivated conflict, the war quickly degenerated into a total war. Everywhere, the entire national economy was militarized (war socialism),[3] and the time-honored distinction between combatants and noncombatants and military and civilian life fell by the wayside. For this reason, World War I resulted in many more civilian casualties—victims of starvation and disease—than of soldiers killed on the battlefields. Moreover, due to the ideological character of the war, at its end no compromise peace but only total surrender, humiliation, and punishment was possible. Germany had to give up her monarchy, and Alsace-Lorraine was returned to France as before the Franco-Prussian War of 1870–71. The new German republic was burdened with heavy long-term reparations. Germany was demilitarized, the German Saarland was occupied by the French, and in the East large territories had to be ceded to Poland (West Prussia and Silesia). However, Germany was not dismembered and destroyed. Wilson had reserved this fate for Austria. With the deposition of the Habsburgs the entire Austrian–Hungarian Empire was dismembered. As the crowning achievement of Wilson's foreign policy, two new and artificial states: Czechoslovakia and Yugoslavia, were carved out of the former Empire. Austria herself, for centuries one of Europe's great powers, was reduced in size to its small German-speaking heartland; and, as another of Wilson's legacies, tiny Austria was forced to surrender its entirely German province of Southern Tyrolia—extending to the Brenner Pass—to Italy.

Since 1918 Austria has disappeared from the map of international power politics. Instead, the United States has emerged as the world's leading power. The American age—the *pax Americana*—had begun. The principle of democratic republicanism had triumphed. It was to triumph again with the end of World War II, and once more, or so it seemed, with the collapse of the Soviet Empire in the late 1980s and early 1990s. For some contemporary observers, the "End of History" has arrived. The American idea of universal and global democracy has finally come into its own.[4]

Rothbard, "World War I as Fulfillment: Power and the Intellectuals," *Journal of Libertarian Studies* 9, no. 1 (1989); Paul Gottfried, "Wilsonianism: The Legacy that Won't Die," *Journal of Libertarian Studies* 9, no. 2 (1990); idem, "On Liberal and Democratic Nationhood," *Journal of Libertarian Studies* 10, no. 1 (1991); Robert A. Nisbet, *The Present Age* (New York: Harper and Row, 1988).

[3]See Murray N. Rothbard, "War Collectivism in World War I," in *A New History of Leviathan*, Ronald Radosh and Murray N. Rothbard, eds. (New York: E.P. Dutton, 1972; Robert Higgs, *Crisis and Leviathan* (New York: Oxford University Press, 1987).

[4]See Francis Fukuyama, *The End of History and the Last Man* (New York: Avon Books, 1992).

Meanwhile, Habsburg–Austria and the prototypical pre-democratic Austrian experience assumed no more than historical interest. To be sure, it was not that Austria had not achieved any recognition. Even democratic intellectuals and artists from any field of intellectual and cultural endeavor could not ignore the enormous level of productivity of Austro-Hungarian and in particular Viennese culture. Indeed, the list of great names associated with late nineteenth and early twentieth century Vienna is seemingly endless.[5] However, rarely has this enormous intellectual and cultural productivity been brought in a systematic connection with the pre-democratic tradition of the Habsburg monarchy. Instead, if it has not been considered a mere coincidence, the productivity of Austrian-Viennese culture has been presented "politically correctly" as proof of the positive synergistic effects of a multiethnic society and of multiculturalism.[6]

However, at the end of the twentieth century increasing evidence is accumulating that rather than marking the end of history, the American system is itself in a deep crisis. Since the late 1960s or early 1970s, real wage incomes in the United States and in Western Europe have stagnated or even fallen. In Western Europe in particular, unemployment rates have been steadily edging upward and are currently exceeding ten percent. The public debt has risen everywhere to astronomical heights, in many cases exceeding a country's annual Gross Domestic Product.

---

[5]The list includes Ludwig Boltzmann, Franz Brentano, Rudolph Carnap, Edmund Husserl, Ernst Mach, Alexius Meinong, Karl Popper, Moritz Schlick, and Ludwig Wittgenstein among philosophers; Kurt Gödel, Hans Hahn, Karl Menger, and Richard von Mises among mathematicians; Eugen von Böhm-Bawerk, Gottfried von Haberler, Friedrich A. von Hayek, Carl Menger, Fritz Machlup, Ludwig von Mises, Oskar Morgenstern, Joseph Schumpeter, and Friedrich von Wieser among economists; Rudolph von Jhering, Hans Kelsen, Anton Menger, and Lorenz von Stein among lawyers and legal theorists; Alfred Adler, Joseph Breuer, Karl Bühler, and Sigmund Freud among psychologists; Max Adler, Otto Bauer, Egon Friedell, Heinrich Friedjung, Paul Lazarsfeld, Gustav Ratzenhofer, and Alfred Schütz among historians and sociologists; Hermann Broch, Franz Grillparzer, Hugo von Hofmannsthal, Karl Kraus, Fritz Mauthner, Robert Musil, Arthur Schnitzler, Georg Trakl, Otto Weininger, and Stefan Zweig among writers and literary critics; Gustav Klimt, Oskar Kokoschka, Adolf Loos, and Egon Schiele among artists and architects; and Alban Berg, Johannes Brahms, Anton Bruckner, Franz Lehar, Gustav Mahler, Arnold Schönberg, Johann Strauss, Anton von Webern, and Hugo Wolf among composers.

[6]See Allan Janik and Stephen Toulmin, *Wittgenstein's Vienna* (New York: Simon and Schuster, 1973); William M. Johnston, *The Austrian Mind: An Intellectual and Social History 1848–1938* (Berkeley: University of California Press, 1972); Carl E. Schorske, *Fin-de-Siècle Vienna: Politics and Culture* (New York: Random House, 1981).

Similarly, the social security systems everywhere are on or near the verge of bankruptcy. Further, the collapse of the Soviet Empire represented not so much a triumph of democracy as the bankruptcy of the idea of socialism, and it therefore also contained an indictment against the American (Western) system of democratic—rather than dictatorial—socialism. Moreover, throughout the Western hemisphere national, ethnic and cultural divisiveness, separatism and secessionism are on the rise. Wilson's multicultural democratic creations, Yugoslavia and Czechoslovakia, have broken apart. In the U.S., less than a century of full-blown democracy has resulted in steadily increasing moral degeneration, family and social disintegration, and cultural decay in the form of continually rising rates of divorce, illegitimacy, abortion, and crime. As a result of an ever-expanding list of nondiscrimination—"affirmative action"—laws and nondiscriminatory, multicultural, egalitarian immigration policies, every nook and cranny of American society is affected by government management and forced integration; accordingly, social strife and racial, ethnic, and moral-cultural tension and hostility have increased dramatically.

In light of these disillusioning experiences fundamental doubts concerning the virtues of the American system have resurfaced. What would have happened, it is being asked again, if in accordance with his reelection promise, Woodrow Wilson had kept the U.S. out of World War I? By virtue of its counterfactual nature, the answer to a question such as this can never be empirically confirmed or falsified. However, this does not make the question meaningless or the answer arbitrary. To the contrary, based on an understanding of the actual historical events and personalities involved, the question concerning the most likely alternative course of history can be answered in detail and with considerable confidence.[7]

If the United States had followed a strict noninterventionist foreign policy, it is likely that the intra-European conflict would have ended in late 1916 or early 1917 as the result of several peace initiatives, most notably by the Austrian Emperor Charles I. Moreover, the war would have been concluded with a mutually acceptable and face-saving compromise peace rather than the actual dictate. Consequently, Austria–Hungary, Germany, and Russia would have remained traditional monarchies instead of being turned into short-lived democratic

---

[7]For a contemporary collection of examples of "counterfactual history" see *Virtual History: Alternatives and Counterfactuals*, Niall Ferguson, ed. (New York: Basic Books, 1999).

republics. With a Russian Czar and a German and Austrian Kaiser in place, it would have been almost impossible for the Bolsheviks to seize power in Russia, and in reaction to a growing communist threat in Western Europe, for the Fascists and National Socialists to do the same in Italy and Germany.[8] Millions of victims of communism, national socialism, and World War II would have been saved. The extent of government interference with and control of the private economy in the United States and in Western Europe would never have reached the heights seen today. And rather than Central and Eastern Europe (and consequently half of the globe) falling into communist hands and for more than forty years being plundered, devastated, and forcibly insulated from Western markets, all of Europe (and the entire globe) would have remained integrated economically (as in the nineteenth century) in a world-wide system of division of labor and cooperation. World living standards would have grown immensely higher than they actually have.

Before the backdrop of this thought experiment and the actual course of events, the American system and the *pax Americana* appear—contrary to "official" history, which is always written by its victors, i.e., from the perspective of the proponents of democracy—to be nothing short of an unmitigated disaster; and Habsburg–Austria and the pre-democratic age appear most appealing.[9] Certainly, then, it would be worthwhile to take a systematic look at the historic transformation from monarchy to democracy.

---

[8]On the relationship between communism and the rise of fascism and national socialism see Ralph Raico, "Mises on Fascism, Democracy, and Other Questions," *Journal of Libertarian Studies* 12, no. 1 (1996); Ernst Nolte, *Der europäische Bürgerkrieg, 1917–1945. Nationalsozialismus und Bolschewismus* (Berlin: Propyläen, 1987).

[9]No less of an establishmentarian than George F. Kennan, writing in 1951, came indeed close to admitting as much:

> Yet, today, if one were offered the chance of having back again the Germany of 1913, a Germany run by conservative but relatively moderate people, no Nazis and no Communists, a vigorous Germany, united and unoccupied, full of energy and confidence, able to play a part again in the balancing-off of Russian power in Europe . . . well, there would be objections to it from many quarters, and it wouldn't make everybody happy; but in many ways it wouldn't be so bad, in comparison with our problem of today. Now, think what that means. When you tally up the total score of the two wars, in terms of their ostensible objectives, you find if there has been any gain at all, it is pretty hard to discern. (*American Diplomacy 1900–1950* [Chicago: University of Chicago Press, 1951], pp. 55–56)

While history will play an important role, the following is not the work of a historian, however, but of a political economist and philosopher. There are no new or unfamiliar data presented. Rather, insofar as a claim to originality is made, it is that the following studies contain new and unfamiliar *interpretations* of generally known and accepted facts; moreover, that it is the *interpretation of facts*, rather than the facts themselves, which are of central concern to the scientist and the subject of most contention and debate. One may, for instance, readily agree on the fact that in nineteenth-century America average living standards, tax rates, and economic regulations were comparatively low, while in the twentieth century living standards, taxes, and regulations were high. Yet were twentieth-century living standards higher *because* of higher taxes and regulations or *despite* higher taxes and regulations, i.e., would living standards be even higher if taxes and regulations had remained as low as they had been during the nineteenth century? Likewise, one may readily agree that welfare payments and crime rates were low during the 1950s and that both are now comparatively high. Yet has crime increased *because* of rising welfare payments or *despite* them, or have crime and welfare nothing to do with each other and is the relationship between the two phenomena merely coincidental? The facts do not provide an answer to such questions, and no amount of statistical manipulation of data can possibly change *this* fact. The data of history are logically compatible with any of such rival interpretations, and historians, insofar as they are just historians, have no way of deciding in favor of one or the other.

If one is to make a rational choice among such rival and incompatible interpretations, this is only possible if one has a *theory* at one's disposal, or at least a *theoretical proposition*, whose validity does *not* depend on historical experience but can be established *a priori*, i.e., once and for all by means of the *intellectual apprehension or comprehension of the nature of things*. In some circles this kind of theory is held in low esteem; and some philosophers, especially of the empiricist–positivist variety, have declared any such theory off-limits or even impossible. This is not a philosophical treatise devoted to a discussion of issues of epistemology and ontology. Here and in the following, I do not want to directly refute the empiricist–positivist thesis that there is no such thing as *a priori theory*, i.e., propositions which assert something about reality *and* can be validated independent of the outcome of any future experience.[10] It is only

---

[10]See on this subject Ludwig von Mises, *Theory and History: An Interpretation of Social and Economic Evolution* (Auburn, Ala.: Ludwig von Mises Institute, 1985);

appropriate, however, to acknowledge from the outset that I consider this thesis—and indeed the entire empiricist–positivist research program, which can be interpreted as the result of the application of the (egalitarian) principles of democracy to the realm of knowledge and research and has therefore dominated ideologically during most of the twentieth century,—as fundamentally mistaken and thoroughly refuted.[11] Here it suffices to present just a few examples of what is meant by *a priori theory*—and in particular to cite some such examples from the realm of the social sciences—in order to put any possible suspicion to rest and recommend my *theoretical approach* as intuitively plausible and in accordance with common sense.[12]

Examples of what I mean by *a priori theory* are: No material thing can be at two places at once. No two objects can occupy the same place. A straight line is the shortest line between two points. No two straight lines can enclose a space. Whatever object is red all over cannot be green (blue, yellow, etc.) all over. Whatever object is colored is also extended. Whatever object has shape has also size. If A is a part of B and B is a part of C, then A is a part of C. $4 = 3 + 1$. $6 = 2$ (33–30). Implausibly, empiricists must denigrate such propositions as mere linguistic–syntactic conventions without any empirical content, i.e., "empty" tautologies. In contrast to this view and in accordance with common sense, I understand the same propositions as asserting some simple but fundamental truths about the structure of reality. And in accordance with common sense, too, I would regard someone who wanted to "test" these propositions, or who reported "facts" contradicting or deviating from them, as confused. *A priori theory trumps and corrects experience* (and *logic overrules observation*), and *not vice-versa*.

---

idem, *The Ultimate Foundation of Economic Science: An Essay on Method* (Kansas City: Sheed Andrews and McMeel, 1978); Hans-Hermann Hoppe, *Kritik der kausalwissenschaftlichen Sozialforschung. Untersuchungen zur Grundlegung von Soziologie und Ökonomie* (Opladen: Westdeutscher Verlag, 1983); idem, *Economic Science and the Austrian Method* (Auburn, Ala.: Ludwig von Mises Institute, 1995).

[11]See Brand Blanshard, *Reason and Analysis* (LaSalle, Ind.: Open Court, 1964); also Arthur Pap, *Semantics and Necessary Truth* (New Haven, Conn.: Yale University Press, 1958); Saul Kripke, "Naming and Necessity," in *Semantics of Natural Language*, Donald Davidson and Gilbert Harman, eds. (New York: Reidel, 1972); and Paul Lorenzen, *Methodisches Denken* (Frankfurt/M.: Suhrkamp, 1968).

[12]Even a "good empiricist" would have to admit that, according to his own doctrine, he cannot possibly know *a priori* whether or not *a priori* theorems exist and may be used to decide between incompatible explanations of one and the same set of historical data; hence, he would have to adopt a wait-and-see attitude, too.

More importantly, examples of *a priori theory* also abound in the social sciences, in particular in the fields of political economy and philosophy: Human action is an actor's purposeful pursuit of valued ends with scarce means. No one can purposefully *not* act. Every action is aimed at improving the actor's subjective well-being above what it otherwise would have been. A larger quantity of a good is valued more highly than a smaller quantity of the same good. Satisfaction earlier is preferred over satisfaction later. Production must precede consumption. What is consumed now cannot be consumed again in the future. If the price of a good is lowered, either the same quantity or more will be bought than otherwise. Prices fixed below market clearing prices will lead to lasting shortages. Without private property in factors of production there can be no factor prices, and without factor prices cost-accounting is impossible. Taxes are an imposition on producers and/or wealth owners and reduce production and/or wealth below what it otherwise would have been. Interpersonal conflict is possible only if and insofar as things are scarce. No thing or part of a thing can be owned exclusively by more than one person at a time. Democracy (majority rule) is incompatible with private property (individual ownership and rule). No form of taxation can be uniform (equal), but every taxation involves the creation of two distinct and unequal classes of tax*payers* versus tax*receiver–consumers*. Property and property titles are distinct entities, and an increase of the latter without a corresponding increase of the former does not raise social wealth but leads to a redistribution of existing wealth.

For an empiricist, propositions such as these must be interpreted as either stating nothing empirical at all and being mere speech conventions, or as forever testable and tentative hypotheses. To us, as to common sense, they are neither. In fact, it strikes us as utterly disingenuous to portray these propositions as having no empirical content. Clearly, they state something about "real" things and events! And it seems similarly disingenuous to regard these propositions as hypotheses. Hypothetical propositions, as commonly understood, are statements such as these: Children prefer McDonald's over Burger King. The worldwide ratio of beef to pork spending is 2:1. Germans prefer Spain over Greece as a vacation destination. Longer education in public schools will lead to higher wages. The volume of shopping shortly before Christmas exceeds that of shortly after Christmas. Catholics vote predominantly "Democratic." Japanese save a quarter of their disposable income. Germans drink more beer than Frenchmen. The United States produces more computers than any other country. Most inhabitants of the U.S. are white and of European descent. Propositions such as these require the collection of historical data to be validated. And they must be continually reevaluated, because the asserted relationships are not *necessary* (but "contingent") ones; that is, because there is nothing *inherently* impossible, inconceivable, or plain wrong in assuming the opposite of the above: e.g., that children prefer Burger King to McDonald's, or Germans Greece to Spain, etc. This, however, is *not* the case with the former, theoretical propositions. To negate these propositions and assume, for instance, that a smaller quantity of a good might be preferred to a larger one of the same good, that what is being consumed now can possibly be consumed again in the future, or that cost-accounting could be accomplished also without factor prices, strikes one as absurd; and anyone engaged in "empirical research" and "testing" to determine which one of two contradictory propositions such as these does or does not hold appears to be either a fool or a fraud.

According to the approach adopted here, theoretical propositions like the ones just cited are accepted for what they apparently are: as statements about *necessary facts and relations*. As such, they can be *illustrated* by historical data, but historical data can neither *establish* nor *refute* them.[13] To the contrary. Even if historical experience is necessary in order to initially grasp a theoretical insight, this insight concerns facts and relations that extend and transcend logically beyond any particular historical experience. Hence, once a theoretical insight has been grasped it can be employed as a constant and permanent standard of "criticism," i.e., for the purpose of correcting, revising, and rejecting as well as of accepting historical reports and interpretations. For instance, based on theoretical insights it must be considered impossible that higher taxes and regulations can be the cause of higher living standards. Living standards can be higher only despite higher taxes and regulations. Similarly, theoretical insights can rule out reports such as that increased consumption has led to increased production (economic growth), that below-market-clearing (maximum) prices have resulted in unsold surpluses of goods, or that the absence of democracy has been responsible for the economic malfunctioning of socialism as nonsensical. As a matter

---

[13]To avoid any misunderstanding: To say that something is "necessary" (and can be recognized as such "*a priori*"), is *not* to claim that one is infallible. Mathematicians and logicians, too, claim to be concerned with necessary relations, and yet they do not claim to be infallible. Rather, what is claimed in this regard is only that in order to refute a *theoretical* proposition (in contrast to a hypothetical one) *another*, even more fundamental theoretical argument is required, just as another mathematical or logical proof or argument is required (and *not* "empirical evidence") in order to refute a mathematical or logical theorem.

of theory, only more saving and capital formation and/or advances in productivity can lead to increased production, only guaranteed above-market-clearing (minimum) prices can result in lasting surpluses, and only the absence of private property is responsible for the economic plight under socialism. And to reiterate, none of these insights requires further empirical study or testing. To study or test them is a sign of confusion.

When I noted earlier that this is not the work of a historian but of a political economist and philosopher, I obviously did not believe this to be a disadvantage. Quite to the contrary. As has been indicated, historians *qua* historians cannot rationally decide between incompatible interpretations of the same set of data or sequence of events; hence, they are unable to provide answers to most important social questions. The principal advantage that the political economist and philosopher has over the mere historian (and the benefits to be gained from the study of political economy and philosophy by the historian) is his knowledge of pure—*a priori*—social theory, which enables him to avoid otherwise unavoidable errors in the interpretation of sequences of complex historical data and present a theoretically corrected or "reconstructed," and a decidedly critical or "revisionist" account of history.

Based on and motivated by fundamental theoretical insights from both, political economy and political philosophy (ethics), in the following studies I propose the revision of three central—indeed almost mythical—beliefs and interpretations concerning modern history.

In accordance with elementary theoretical insights regarding the nature of private property and ownership versus "public" property and administration and of firms versus governments (or states), I propose first a revision of the prevailing view of traditional hereditary monarchies and provide instead an uncharacteristically favorable interpretation of monarchy and the monarchical experience. In short, monarchical government is reconstructed theoretically as privately-owned government, which in turn is explained as promoting future-orientedness and a concern for capital values and economic calculation by the government ruler. Second, equally unorthodox but by the same theoretical token, democracy and the democratic experience are cast in an untypically unfavorable light. Democratic government is reconstructed as publicly-owned government, which is explained as leading to present-orientedness and a disregard or neglect of capital values in government rulers, and the transition from monarchy to democracy is interpreted accordingly as civilizational decline.

Still more fundamental and unorthodox is the proposed third revision.

Despite the comparatively favorable portrait presented of monarchy, I am not a monarchist and the following is not a defense of monarchy. Instead, the position taken toward monarchy is this: *If* one must have a state, defined as an agency that exercises a compulsory territorial monopoly of ultimate decisionmaking (jurisdiction) and of taxation, then it is economically and ethically advantageous to choose monarchy over democracy. But this leaves the question open whether or not a state is necessary, i.e., if there exists an alternative to both, monarchy *and* democracy. History again cannot provide an answer to this question. By definition, there can be no such thing as an "experience" of counterfactuals and alternatives; and all one finds in modern history, at least insofar as the developed Western world is concerned, is the history of states and statism. Only theory can again provide an answer, for theoretical propositions, as just illustrated, concern necessary facts and relations; and accordingly, just as they can be used to rule certain historical reports and interpretations out as false or impossible, so can they be used to rule certain other things in as constructively possible, even if such things have never been seen or tried.

In complete contrast to the orthodox opinion on the matter, then, elementary social theory shows, and will be explained as showing, that no state as just defined can be justified, be it economically or ethically. Rather, every state, regardless of its constitution, is economically and ethically deficient. Every monopolist, including one of ultimate decisionmaking, is "bad" from the viewpoint of consumers. Monopoly is hereby understood in its classical meaning, as the absence of free entry into a particular line of production: only one agency, A, may produce X. Any such monopolist is "bad" for consumers because, shielded from potential new entrants into his line of production, the price for his product will be higher and the quality lower than otherwise. Further, no one would agree to a provision that allowed a monopolist of ultimate decisonmaking, i.e., the final arbiter and judge in every case of interpersonal conflict, to determine unilaterally (without the consent of everyone concerned) the price that one must pay for his service. The power to tax, that is, is ethically unacceptable. Indeed, a monopolist of ultimate decisionmaking equipped with the power to tax does not just produce less and lower quality justice, but he will produce more and more "bads," i.e., injustice and aggression. Thus, the choice between monarchy and democracy concerns a choice between two defective social orders. In fact, modern history provides ample illustration of the economic and ethical shortcomings of *all* states, whether monarchic or democratic.

Moreover, the same social theory demonstrates positively the possibility of an alternative social order free of the economic and ethical shortcomings of monarchy and democracy (as well as any other form of state). The term adopted here for a social system free of monopoly and taxation is "natural order." Other names used elsewhere or by others to refer to the same thing include "ordered anarchy," "private property anarchism," "anarcho-capitalism," "autogovernment," "private law society," and "pure capitalism."

Above and beyond monarchy and democracy, the following is concerned with the "logic" of a natural order, where every scarce resource is owned privately, where every enterprise is funded by voluntarily paying customers or private donors, and where entry into every line of production, including that of justice, police, and defense services, is free. It is in contrast to a natural order that the economic and ethical errors of monarchy are brought into relief. It is before the backdrop of a natural order that the still greater errors involved in democracy are clarified and that the historic transformation from monarchy to democracy is revealed as a civilizational decline. And it is because of the natural order's logical status as the theoretical answer to the fundamental problem of social order—of how to protect liberty, property, and the pursuit of happiness—that the following also includes extensive discussions of strategic matters and concerns, i.e., of the requirements of social change and in particular the radical transformation from democracy to natural order.

Regardless of the unorthodox interpretations and conclusions reached in the following studies, the theories and theorems used to do so are definitely *not* new or unorthodox. Indeed, if one assumes, as I do, that *a priori* social theory and theorems exist, then one should also expect that most of such knowledge is old and that theoretical progress is painstakingly slow. This indeed appears to be the case. Hence, even if my conclusions may seem radical or extreme, as a theoretician I am decidedly a conservative. I place myself in an intellectual tradition that stretches back at least to the sixteenth-century Spanish Scholastics and that has found its clearest modern expression in the so-called Austrian School of Economics: the tradition of pure social theory as represented above all by Carl Menger, Eugen von Böhm-Bawerk, Ludwig von Mises, and Murray N. Rothbard.[14]

---

[14]See Murray N. Rothbard, *Economic Thought Before Adam Smith: An Austrian Perspective on the History of Economic Thought* (Cheltenham, U.K.: Edward Elgar,

At the outset, I noted Habsburg–Austria and the United States of America as the countries associated most closely with the old monarchical regime and the new and current democratic–republican era, respectively. Here we encounter Habsburg–Austria again and discover another reason why the following studies also may be called *An Austrian View of the American Age*. The Austrian School of economics ranks among the most outstanding of the many intellectual and artistic traditions originating in pre-World War I Austria. As one of the many results of the destruction of the Habsburg Empire, however, the school's third generation, led by Ludwig von Mises, was uprooted in Austria and on the European continent and, with Mises's emigration to New York City in 1940, exported to the United States of America. And it would be in America where Austrian social theory has taken root most firmly, owing in particular to the work of Mises's outstanding American student, Murray N. Rothbard.

The following studies are written from the vantage point of modern Austrian social theory. Throughout, the influence of Ludwig von Mises and even more of Murray N. Rothbard is noticeable. The elementary theorems of political economy and philosophy, which are employed here for the purpose of reconstructing history and proposing a constructive alternative to democracy, have found their most detailed treatment in Mises's and Rothbard's principal theoretical works.[15] As well, many of the subjects discussed in the following have also been dealt with in their many applied works. Furthermore, the following studies share with Mises and especially Rothbard a fundamental and robust antistatist and pro-private property, and free enterprise position.

This notwithstanding, the following studies can in two regards claim originality. On the one hand, they provide for a more profound understanding of modern political history. In their applied works, Mises and Rothbard discussed most of the twentieth century's central economic and political issues and events: socialism versus capitalism, monopoly versus competition, private versus public property, production and trade versus taxation, regulation, and redistribution, etc.; and both gave detailed accounts of the rapid growth of state power during the

---

1995); idem, *Classical Economics: An Austrian Perspective on the History of Economic Thought* (Cheltenham, U.K.: Edward Elgar, 1995); also *Fifteen Great Austrian Economists*, Randall Holcombe, ed. (Auburn, Ala.: Ludwig von Mises Institute, 1999).

[15]Ludwig von Mises, *Human Action: A Treatise on Economics*, Scholar's Edition (Auburn, Ala.: Ludwig von Mises Institute, [1949] 1999); Murray N. Rothbard, *Man, Economy, and State: A Treatise on Economic Principles* (Auburn, Ala.: Ludwig von Mises Institute, [1962] 1993).

twentieth century and explained its economically and morally deleterious consequences. However, while they have proven exceptionally perceptive and farsighted in these endeavors (especially in comparison to their empiricist–positivist counterparts), neither Mises nor Rothbard made a systematic attempt to search for a cause of the decline of classical-liberal thought and laissez-faire capitalism and the concomitant rise of anticapitalist political ideologies and statism during the twentieth century. Certainly, they did not think of democracy as being such a cause. In fact, although aware of the economic and ethical deficiencies of democracy, both Mises and Rothbard had a soft spot for democracy and tended to view the transition from monarchy to democracy as progress. In contrast, I will explain the rapid growth of state power in the course of the twentieth century lamented by Mises and Rothbard as the systematic outcome of democracy and the democratic mindset, i.e., the (erroneous) belief in the efficiency and/or justice of public property and popular (majority) rule.

On the other hand, based on this deeper, "revisionist" understanding of modern history, the following studies arrive also at a "better"—clearer and more acute—understanding of the constructive alternative to the democratic *status quo*, i.e., a natural order. There are detailed explanations regarding the operation of a natural order as a state-less social system with freely financed insurance agencies serving as competitive providers of law and order. And there are equally detailed discussions of strategic matters. In particular, there are detailed discussions specifically of secession and of privatization as the primary vehicles and means by which to overcome democracy and establish a natural order.

Each of the following chapters is self-contained and can be read separately. While this implies some thematic overlap across chapters, they combine into a progressing and expanding theoretical whole. With these studies I wish to promote in particular the tradition of Austrian social theory and contribute to its reputation as not only a bastion of truth but also as inspiring, exciting, and refreshing. And by the same token but more generally, I wish to promote and contribute to the tradition of grand social theory, encompassing political economy, political philosophy and history and including normative as well as positive questions. An appropriate term for this sort of intellectual endeavor would seem to be sociology. But while the term sociology has been sometimes used in this meaning, under the dominant influence of the empiricist–positivist philosophy the term has acquired an altogether different meaning and reputation. According to the empiricist doctrine, normative questions are not "scientific" questions at all, and there exists no such thing as *a priori* theory. That pretty much rules out grand social theory from the outset as "unscientific." Accordingly, most of what passes nowadays as sociology is not only just plain false but also irrelevant and dull. In distinct contrast, the following studies are everything a good positivist claims one cannot and shall not be: interdisciplinary, theoretically oriented, and dealing with both positive-empirical *and* normative questions. I hope to demonstrate by example that this is the right approach as well as the more interesting one.

Hans-Hermann Hoppe
Las Vegas, Nevada
September 2000

1

On Time Preference, Government, and the Process of Decivilization

TIME PREFERENCE

In acting, an actor invariably aims to substitute a more satisfactory for a less satisfactory state of affairs and thus demonstrates a preference for more rather than fewer goods. Moreover, he invariably considers when in the future his goals will be reached, i.e., the time necessary to accomplish them, as well as a good's duration of serviceability. Thus, he also demonstrates a universal preference for earlier over later goods, and for more over less durable ones. This is the phenomenon of time preference.[1]

Every actor requires some amount of time to attain his goal, and since man must always consume something and cannot entirely stop consuming while he is alive, time is always scarce. Thus, *ceteris paribus*, present or earlier goods are, and must invariably be, valued more highly than future or later ones. In fact, if man were not constrained by time preference and if the only constraint operating on him were that of preferring more over less, he would invariably choose those production processes which yielded the largest output per input, regardless of the length of time needed for these methods to bear fruit. He would always save and never consume. For instance, instead of making a fishing net first, Crusoe would have begun constructing a fishing trawler—as it is the economically most efficient method of catching fish. That no one,

---

[1]See on the following in particular Ludwig von Mises, *Human Action: A Treatise on Economics*, Scholar's Edition (Auburn, Ala.: Ludwig von Mises Institute, 1998), chaps. 18 and 19; also William Stanley Jevons, *Theory of Political Economy* (New York: Augustus M. Kelley, 1965); Eugen von Böhm-Bawerk, *Capital and Interest*, 3 vols. (South Holland, Ill.: Libertarian Press, 1959); Richard von Strigl, *Capital and Production* (Auburn, Ala.: Ludwig von Mises Institute, 2001); Frank Fetter, *Capital, Interest, and Rent* (Kansas City: Sheed Andrews and McMeel, 1977); Murray N. Rothbard, *Man, Economy, and State*, 2 vols. (Los Angeles: Nash, 1970).

including Crusoe, can act in this way makes it evident that man cannot but "value fractions of time of the same length in a different way according as they are nearer or remoter from the instant of the actor's decision." "What restricts the amount of saving and investment is time preference."[2]

Constrained by time preference, man will only exchange a present good for a future one if he anticipates thereby increasing his amount of future goods. The rate of time preference, which is (and can be) different from person to person and from one point in time to the next, but which can never be anything but positive for everyone, simultaneously determines the height of the premium which present goods command over future ones as well as the amount of savings and investment. The market rate of interest is the aggregate sum of all individual time-preference rates reflecting the social rate of time preference and equilibrating social savings (i.e., the supply of present goods offered for exchange against future goods) and social investment (i.e., the demand for present goods thought capable of yielding future returns).

No supply of loanable funds can exist without previous savings, i.e., without abstaining from a possible consumption of present goods (an excess of current production over current consumption). And no demand for loanable funds would exist if no one perceived an opportunity to employ present goods productively, i.e., to invest them so as to produce a future output that would exceed current input. Indeed, if all present goods were consumed and none invested in time-consuming production methods, the interest rate would be infinitely high, which, anywhere outside of the Garden of Eden, would be tantamount to leading a mere animal existence, i.e., eking out a primitive subsistence living by encountering reality with nothing but one's bare hands and a desire for instant gratification.

A supply of and a demand for loanable funds only arise—and this is the human condition—if it is recognized first that indirect (more roundabout, lengthier) production processes yield a larger or better output per input than direct and short ones.[3] Second, it must be possible, by means of savings, to accumulate the amount of present (consumption) goods

---

[2]Mises, *Human Action*, pp. 483 and 491.

[3]To be sure, not all lengthier production processes are more productive than shorter ones, but under the assumption that man, constrained by time preference, will invariably (and at all times) select the shortest conceivable methods of producing some given output, any increase in output then can—praxeologically—only be achieved if the production process is lengthened, given constant technology.

needed to provide for all those wants whose satisfaction during the prolonged waiting time is deemed more urgent than the increment in future well-being expected from the adoption of a more time-consuming production process.

So long as these conditions are fulfilled, capital formation and accumulation will set in and continue. Land and labor (the originary factors of production), instead of being supported by and engaged in instantaneously gratifying production processes, are supported by an excess of production over consumption and employed in the production of capital goods. Capital goods have no value except as intermediate products in the process of turning out final (consumer) goods later, and insofar as the production of final products is more productive with than without them, or, what amounts to the same thing, insofar as he who possesses and can produce with the aid of capital goods is nearer in time to the completion of his ultimate goal than he who must do without them. The excess in value (price) of a capital good over the sum expended on the complementary originary factors required for its production is due to this time difference and the universal fact of time preference. It is the price paid for buying time, for moving closer to the completion of one's ultimate goal rather than having to start at the very beginning. For the same reason, the value of the final output must exceed the sum spent on its factors of production (the price paid for the capital good and all complementary labor services).

The lower the time-preference rate, the earlier the onset of the process of capital formation, and the faster the roundabout structure of production will be lengthened. Any increase in the accumulation of capital goods and the roundaboutness of the production structure in turn raises the marginal productivity of labor. This leads to either increased employment or wage rates, or even if the labor supply curve should become backward sloping with increased wage rates, to a higher wage total. Supplied with an increased amount of capital goods, a better paid population of wage earners will produce an overall increased—future—social product, thus also raising the real incomes of the owners of capital and land.

FACTORS INFLUENCING TIME PREFERENCE AND THE PROCESS OF CIVILIZATION

Among the factors influencing time preference one can distinguish between external, biological, personal, and social or institutional ones.

External factors are events in an actor's physical environment whose outcome he can neither directly nor indirectly control. Such events affect time preference only if and insofar as they are expected. They can be of two kinds. If a positive event such as manna falling from heaven is expected to happen at some future date, the marginal utility of future goods will fall relative to that of present ones. The time-preference rate will rise and consumption will be stimulated. Once the expected event has occurred and the larger supply of future goods has become a larger supply of present goods, the reverse will happen. The time-preference rate will fall, and savings will increase.

On the other hand, if a negative event such as a flood is expected, the marginal utility of future goods rises. The time-preference rate will fall and savings will increase. After the event, with a reduced supply of present goods, the time-preference rate will rise.[4]

Biological processes are technically within an actor's reach, but for all practical purposes and in the foreseeable future they too must be regarded as a given by an actor, similar to external events.

It is a given that man is born as a child, that he grows up to be an adult, that he is capable of procreation during part of his life, and that he ages and dies. These biological facts have a direct bearing on time preference. Because of biological constraints on their cognitive development, children have an extremely high time-preference rate. They do not possess a clear concept of a personal life expectancy extending over a lengthy period of time, and they lack full comprehension of production as a mode of indirect consumption. Accordingly, present goods and immediate gratification are highly preferred to future goods and delayed gratification. Savings–investment activities are rare, and the periods of production and provision seldom extend beyond the most immediate future. Children live from day to day and from one immediate gratification to the next.[5]

In the course of becoming an adult, an actor's initially extremely high time-preference rate tends to fall. With the recognition of one's life

---

[4]If it is expected that nothing at all can be done about the impending losses of future goods such that no present attempt to mitigate these losses through compensatory savings (or insurance) appears possible because such savings would be destroyed as well, the time-preference rate will immediately rise, and it will remain high after the event.

[5]On the high time preference of children as well as on biological (racial) and cultural factors modifying it see Walter Mischel, "Preference for Delayed Reinforcement: An Experimental Study of a Cultural Observation," *Journal of Abnormal and Social Psychology* 56 (1958); idem, "Preference for Delayed Reinforcement and Social Responsibility,: *Journal of Abnormal and Social Psychology* 62 (1961); idem, "Father-Absence and Delay of Gratification: Cross-Cultural Comparisons," *Journal of Abnormal and Social Psychology* 63 (1961).

expectancy and the potentialities of production as a means of indirect consumption, the marginal utility of future goods rises. Saving and investment are stimulated, and the periods of production and provision are lengthened.

Finally, becoming old and approaching the end of one's life, one's time-preference rate tends to rise. The marginal utility of future goods falls because there is less of a future left. Savings and investments will decrease, and consumption—including the nonreplacement of capital and durable consumer goods—will increase. This old-age effect may be counteracted and suspended, however. Owing to the biological fact of procreation, an actor may extend his period of provision beyond the duration of his own life. If and insofar as this is the case, his time-preference rate can remain at its adult-level until his death.

Within the constraints imposed by external and biological factors, an actor sets his time-preference rate in accordance with his subjective evaluations. How high or low this rate is and what changes it will undergo in the course of his lifetime depend on personal psychological factors. One man may not care about anything but the present and the most immediate future. Like a child, he may only be interested in instant or minimally delayed gratification. In accordance with his high time preference, he may want to be a vagabond, a drifter, a drunkard, a junkie, a daydreamer, or simply a happy-go-lucky kind of guy who likes to work as little as possible in order to enjoy each and every day to the fullest. Another man may worry about his and his offspring's future constantly and, by means of savings, may want to build up a steadily growing stock of capital and durable consumer goods in order to provide for an increasingly larger supply of future goods and an ever longer period of provision. A third person may feel a degree of time preference somewhere in between these extremes, or he may feel different degrees at different times and therefore choose still another lifestyle-career.[6]

---

[6]In contrast to the widespread recognition of the phenomenon of time preference by economists, in particular those of the "Austrian School," amazingly little attention has been paid to it by sociologists and political scientists. For a notable exception see Edward Banfield, *The Unheavenly City Revisited* (Boston: Little, Brown, 1974), esp. chap. 3. Banfield identifies time preference as the underlying cause for the persistent distinction between social classes and cultures, in particular between the "upper class" and the "lower class." Whereas members of the former are characterized by future-orientation, self-discipline, and a willingness to forego present gratification in exchange for a better future, members of the "lower class" are characterized by their present-orientation and hedonism.

However, no matter what a person's original time-preference rate or what the original distribution of such rates within a given population, once it is low enough to allow for any savings and capital or durable consumer-goods formation at all, a tendency toward a fall in the rate of time preference is set in motion, accompanied by a "process of civilization."[7]

The saver exchanges present (consumer) goods for future (capital) goods with the expectation that these will help produce a larger supply of present goods in the future. If he expected otherwise he would not save. If these expectations prove correct, *and if everything else remains the same*, the marginal utility of present goods relative to that of future ones will fall. His time-preference rate will be lower. He will save and invest more than in the past, and his future income will be still higher, leading to yet another reduction in his time-preference rate. Step by step, the time-preference rate approaches zero—without ever reaching it. In a monetary economy, as a result of his surrender of present money, a saver expects to receive a higher real-money income later. With a higher income, the marginal utility of present money falls relative to future money, the savings proportion rises, and future monetary income will be even higher.

If [the lower class individual] has any awareness of the future, it is of something fixed, fated, beyond his control: things happen *to* him, he does not *make* them happen. Impulse governs his behavior, either because he cannot discipline himself to sacrifice a present for a future satisfaction or because he has no sense of the future. He is therefore radically improvident. . . . He works only as he must to stay alive, and drifts from one unskilled job to another, taking no interest in his work. . . . He is careless with his things . . . and, even when nearly new, they are likely to be permanently out of order for lack of minor repairs. His body, too, is a thing "to be worked out but not repaired." (Banfield, *The Unheavenly City*, pp. 61–62)

Phenomena typically associated with the "lower class," such as family breakdown, promiscuity, venereal disease, alcoholism, drug addiction, violence, crime, high infant mortality, and low life expectancy, all have a common cause in high time preference. Their cause is not unemployment or low income. Rather, notes Banfield, causation is, if anything, the other way around: lasting unemployment and persistently low incomes likewise are the effects of an underlying high time preference.

As another important exception to the general neglect of the phenomenon of time preference at the hands of noneconomists see T. Alexander Smith, *Time and Public Policy* (Knoxville: University of Tennessee Press, 1988).

[7]For a detailed empirical, socio-psychological description of the phenomenon of the "process of civilization" see also Norbert Elias, *Über den Prozess der Zivilisation* (Frankfurt/M., 1968); English edition, *The Civilizing Process: A History of Manners* (New York: Urizen Books, 1978).

Moreover, in an exchange economy, the saver–investor also contributes to a lowering of the time-preference rate of nonsavers. With the accumulation of capital goods, the relative scarcity of labor services increases, and wage rates, *ceteris paribus*, will rise. Higher wage rates imply a rising supply of present goods for previous nonsavers. Thus, even those individuals who were previously nonsavers will see their personal time-preference rates fall.

In addition, as an indirect result of the increased real incomes brought about through savings, nutrition and health care improve, and life expectancy tends to rise. In a development similar to the transformation from childhood to adulthood, with a higher life expectancy more distant goals are added to an individual's present value scale. The marginal utility of future goods relative to that of present ones increases, and the time-preference rate declines further.[8]

Simultaneously, the saver–investor initiates a "process of civilization." In generating a tendency toward a fall in the rate of time preference, he—and everyone directly or indirectly connected to him through a network of exchanges—matures from childhood to adulthood and from barbarism to civilization.

In building up an expanding structure of capital and durable consumer goods, the saver–investor also steadily expands the range and horizon of his plans. The number of variables under his control and taken into account in his present actions increases. Accordingly, this increases the number and time horizons of his predictions concerning future events. Hence, the saver–investor is interested in acquiring and steadily improving upon his knowledge concerning an increasing number of variables and their interrelationships. Yet once he has acquired or improved his own knowledge and verbalized or displayed it in action, such knowledge becomes a "free good," available for imitation and utilization by others for their own purposes. Thus, by virtue of the saver's saving, even the most present-oriented person will be gradually transformed from a barbarian to a civilized man. His life ceases to be short, brutish, and nasty, and becomes longer, increasingly refined, and comfortable.

Figure 1 provides a graphic illustration of the phenomena of time preference and the process of civilization. It relates individual time-preference

---

[8]To avoid any sort of misunderstanding, it must be made clear that the mere fact of a longer life has no impact on time preference. Rather, it is only the individual's personal knowledge—the subjective expectation—of this fact, that leads to a fall in a person's degree of time preference.

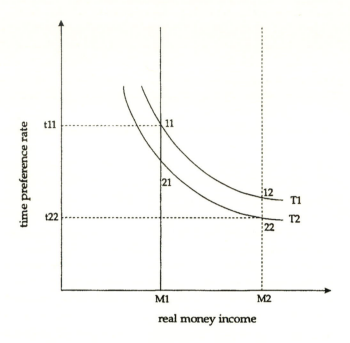

Figure 1
Time Preferences and the Process of Civilization

rates (the height of the premium of a specified present good over the same good at a specified later date which induces a given individual to engage in intertemporal exchange) on the vertical axis to the individual's *real* money income (his supply of present money) on the horizontal. In accordance with the law of marginal utility, each individual time-preference curve, such as T1 or T2, slopes downward as the supply of present money increases. The process of civilization is depicted by a movement from point 11—with a time preference rate of t11—to point 22—with a time preference rate of t22. This movement is the composite result of two interrelated changes. On the one hand, it involves a movement along T1 from point 11 to 12, representing the fall in the time-preference rate that results if an individual with a *given* personality possesses a larger supply of present goods. On the other hand, there is a movement from point 12 to 22. This change from a higher to a lower time-preference curve—with real income assumed to be given—represents the *changes* in personality as they occur during the transition from childhood to adulthood, in the course of rising life-expectancies, or as the result of an advancement of knowledge.

TIME PREFERENCE, PROPERTY, CRIME, AND GOVERNMENT

The actual amount of present goods allocated to the production of future goods depends on the one hand on a person's technical knowledge. For instance, without the knowledge of how to build a fishing net, Crusoe obviously could not have begun to exchange present goods for future ones, that is, to save and invest. On the other hand, given a person's technical knowledge, the amount of saving depends solely on his supply of present goods and his time-preference schedule. The smaller his supply of present goods and the higher his time-preference schedule, the higher his effective time-preference rate and the lower his actual savings will be.

In the beginning of humanity, there was only "land" (nature-given resources and obstacles) and "labor" (human bodies). Strictly speaking, the only *given* supply of any good is that of body-time. The supply of all other goods—be they perishable or durable consumer goods such as berries or caves, or indirectly useful goods (production factors), such as berry bushes and their surrounding land—is not "given." It is the result of someone's prior action; of the appropriation (homesteading) of nature by a specific individual. The facts and laws of nature and human biology are "givens," of course, and nature as such may be generous or skimpy. But only through an individual's act of appropriation is nature turned into a supply of goods. It is even more obvious that the supply of all *produced* goods is not "given." Be they consumer goods, which have been stored, conserved or made more durable, or produced factors of production (capital goods), they are all the outcome of the activities of specific individuals. Finally, technical knowledge is also not a "given." That one potato saved today can yield ten potatoes one year from now may be a fact of nature, but one must first have a potato. Yet even if one did and one were perfectly willing to invest it for this return or an even lower one, such a fact would be irrelevant unless the person in question knew the laws of potato growing.

Thus, neither the supply of present goods nor technology is given or fixed. Rather, they are artifacts, created with the intention of improving their appropriator–producer's well-being. These expectations can turn out right or wrong, and rather than securing a profit for the actor, his actions may result in a loss. But no one would spend any time picking berries unless he expected the berries to be edible. No one would appropriate a berry bush unless he thought that this would enhance his berry harvest. No one would want to learn about any fact or law of nature unless he anticipated that such knowledge would help him improve his circumstances.

In a social context, an individual's supply of appropriated and produced goods, his time-preference schedule, and hence his effective time-preference rate may also be affected by the actions–and the expectations regarding these actions—of others.[9]

The tendency toward a fall in the time-preference rate and the accompanying process of civilization will proceed so long—as has so far been tacitly assumed to be the case—as no one interferes with another's acts of nature-appropriation and production. So long as this is the case and each person is respected by everyone else as the owner of his supply of body-time and whatever goods he has appropriated and produced such that everyone may enjoy, unmolested by others, all present and future benefits to be derived from these goods, the existence of more than one person either leaves the tendency toward a fall in the time-preference rate unchanged, or it even accelerates and reinforces the very process. The former is the case if and insofar as A appropriates a previously unowned, nature-given good, or if he transforms such a good into a different one without causing any physical damage to the goods owned by another person B. A's supply of present goods, or the value of such goods for A, is increased, and hence, *ceteris paribus*, his time-preference rate will fall. Because A's acts have no impact on the supply of goods owned by B, B's time-preference rate remains unaffected. Furthermore, the tendency will actually be accelerated insofar as A and B, based on the mutual recognition of each other's property, engage in voluntary trade or cooperation and even without any such exchange insofar as they merely observe each other's activities and copy each other's knowledge. For any voluntary trade or cooperation between A and B increases—*ex ante*—the supply and/or the value attached to the supply of the goods of *both* parties (otherwise it would not take place), and hence the time-preference rate of both A *and* B will fall. Moreover, by learning facts and laws from one another, such as that there are potatoes, that potatoes can be eaten, or that one's present potato may yield ten future ones, the tendency toward a fall in the rate of time preference spreads from one person to another.

However, if violations of property rights occur and the goods appropriated or produced by A are stolen, damaged or expropriated by B, or if B restricts the uses that A is permitted to make of his goods in any way

---

[9]See on the following Rothbard, *Man, Economy, and State*, pp. 147–59; see also idem, *Power and Market* (Kansas City: Sheed Andrews and McMeel, 1977); Hans-Hermann Hoppe, *A Theory of Socialism and Capitalism* (Boston: Kluwer, 1989); idem, *The Economics and Ethics of Private Property* (Boston: Kluwer, 1993).

(apart from not being allowed to cause any physical damage to the property of B), then the tendency toward a fall in the rate of time preference will be disturbed, halted, or even reversed.

The violations of property rights—and the effect they have on the process of civilization—can be of two kinds. They can take the form of criminal activities (including negligent behavior), or they can take the form of institutional or governmental interference.

The characteristic mark of criminal invasions of property rights is that such activities are considered illegitimate or unjust not only by the victim, but by property owners in general (and possibly even by the criminal himself). Hence, the victim is considered to be entitled to defend himself if need be by retaliatory force, and he may punish and/or exact compensation from the offender.

The impact of crime is twofold. On the one hand, criminal activity reduces the supply of the goods of the victimized appropriator–producer –exchanger, thereby raising his effective time-preference rate (his time-preference schedule being given). On the other hand, insofar as individuals perceive a risk of future victimization they will accordingly reallocate their resources. They will build walls and fences, install locks and alarm systems, design or buy weapons, and purchase protection and insurance services. The existence of crime thus implies a setback in the process toward a fall in the rate of time preference as far as actual victims are concerned, and it leads to expenditures—by actual *and* potential victims—which would be considered wasteful without the existence of crime.[10]

Therefore, crime or a change in its rate has the same type of effect on time preference as the occurrence or a changed frequency of "natural" disasters. Floods, storms, heat waves, and earthquakes also reduce their victims' supplies of present goods and thus increase their effective time-preference rate. And the perceived risk-change of natural disasters also leads to resource reallocations and expense adjustments—such as the construction of dams, irrigation systems, dikes, shelters, or the purchase of earthquake insurance—which would be unnecessary without these natural risks.

More importantly, however, because actual and potential victims are permitted to defend, protect, and insure themselves against both social disasters such as crime as well as natural ones, the effect of these on time preference is temporary and unsystematic. Actual victims will

---

[10]See also Gordon Tullock, "The Welfare Costs of Tariffs, Monopolies, and Theft," *Western Economic Journal* 5 (1967).

save or invest a smaller amount of goods because they are poorer. And the altered risk perceptions among actual and potential victims shape the *direction* of their future actions. But as long as physical protection and defense are permitted, the existence of social or of natural disasters does not imply that the time-preference *degree* of actual or potential victims —their degree of *future*-orientation—will be systematically changed.[11] After taking account of the damage and redirecting one's activities, the tendency toward a fall in the rate of time preference and the attending process of civilization will resume its previous path. In its course, both the protection against crime and natural disasters can be expected to undergo continual improvement.[12]

Matters fundamentally change and the process of civilization is permanently derailed whenever property-rights violations take the form of government interference, however. The distinctive mark of government violations of private property rights is that contrary to criminal activities they are considered legitimate not only by the government agents who engage in them, but by the general public as well (and in rare instances possibly even by the victim). Hence, in these cases a victim may *not* legitimately defend himself against such violations.[13]

---

[11]In terms of Figure 1 above: Social and natural disasters alike imply a movement upward and to the left on a given time-preference curve—insofar as actual victims are concerned. But they do not imply a change in a person's character structure, i.e., a shift from a lower to a higher time-preference curve. Such a shift occurs in the presence of government disasters, however.

[12]On the evolution and efficiency of systems of competitive law courts and privately provided defense and law enforcement see Gustave de Molinari, *The Production of Security* (New York: Center for Libertarian Studies, 1977); William C. Wooldridge, *Uncle Sam the Monopoly Man* (New Rochelle, N.Y.: Arlington House, 1970); Murray N. Rothbard, *For A New Liberty* (New York: Macmillan, 1978); Hoppe, *The Economics and Ethics of Private Property*; Morris and Linda Tannehill, *The Market for Liberty* (New York: Laissez Faire Books, 1984); Terry Anderson and P.J. Hill, "The American Experiment in Anarcho-Capitalism: The Not So Wild, Wild West," *Journal of Libertarian Studies* (1980); Bruce L. Benson, "Guns for Protection, and other Private Sector Responses to the Government's Failure to Control Crime," *Journal of Libertarian Studies* (1986); idem, *The Enterprise of Law: Justice Without the State* (San Francisco: Pacific Research Institute, 1990); Roger D. McGrath, *Gunfighters, Highwaymen, and Vigilantes: Violence on the Frontier* (Berkeley: University of California Press, 1984); idem, "Treat Them to a Good Dose of Lead," *Chronicles* (January 1994).

[13]On the theory of the state see besides the works cited in footnote 9 above Franz Oppenheimer, *The State* (New York: Vanguard Press, 1914); idem, *System der Soziologie*, vol. 2, *Der Staat* (Stuttgart: Gustav Fischer, 1964); Alexander Rüstow, *Freedom and Domination* (Princeton, N.J.: Princeton University Press, 1980); Charles Tilly, "War Making and State Making as Organized Crime," in *Bringing the State*

The imposition of a government tax on property or income violates a property or income producer's rights as much as theft does. In both cases the appropriator–producer's supply of goods is diminished against his will and without his consent. Government money or "liquidity" creation involves no less a fraudulent expropriation of private-property owners than the operations of a criminal counterfeiter gang. Moreover, any government regulation as to what an owner may or may not do with his property—beyond the rule that no one may physically damage the property of others and that all exchange and trade with others must be voluntary and contractual—implies a "taking" of somebody's property on a par with acts of extortion, robbery, or destruction. But taxation, the government's provision of liquidity, and government regulations—unlike their criminal counterparts—are considered legitimate, and the victim of government interference—unlike the victim of a crime—is *not* entitled to physical defense and protection of his property.

Because of their legitimacy, then, government violations of property rights affect individual time preferences systematically differently and much more profoundly than does crime. Like crime, government interference with private-property rights reduces someone's supply of present goods and thus raises his effective time-preference rate. Yet government offenses—unlike crime—simultaneously raise the time-preference *degree* of actual and potential victims because they also imply a reduction in the supply of *future* goods (a reduced rate of return on investment). Crime, because it is illegitimate, occurs only intermittently—the robber disappears from the scene with his loot and leaves his victim alone. Thus, crime can be dealt with by increasing one's demand for protection goods and services (relative to that for nonprotection goods) so as to restore or even increase one's future rate of investment return and make it less likely that the same or a different robber will succeed a second time with the same or a different victim. In contrast, because they are legitimate, governmental property-rights violations are continual. The offender does not disappear into hiding but stays around, and the victim does not "arm" himself but must (at least he is generally expected to) remain defenseless.[14] Consequently future property-rights violations, rather than becoming less frequent, become institutionalized. The rate,

---

Back In, Peter B. Evans, Dietrich Rueschemeyer, and Theda Skocpol, eds. (Cambridge: Cambridge University Press, 1985); Richard Epstein, *Takings: Private Property and the Power of Eminent Domain* (Cambridge, Mass.: Harvard University Press, 1985).

[14]Lysander Spooner, *No Treason: The Constitution of No Authority* (Larkspur, Colo.: Pine Tree Press, 1966) writes:

regularity, and duration of future victimization increases. Instead of by improved protection, the actual and potential victims of government property-rights violations—as demonstrated by their continued defenselessness *vis-à-vis* their offenders—respond by associating a permanently higher risk with all future production and systematically adjusting their expectations concerning the rate of return on all future investment downward.

Competing with the tendency toward a falling rate of time preference, another opposing tendency comes into operation with the existence of government. By simultaneously reducing the supply of present *and* (expected) future goods, governmental property-rights violations not only raise time-preference rates (with given schedules) but also time-preference schedules. Because appropriator–producers are (and see themselves as) defenseless against future victimization by government agents, their expected rate of return on productive, future-oriented actions is reduced all-around, and accordingly all actual and potential victims become more present-oriented.

As will be explained in the course of the following section, if government property-rights violations take their course and grow extensive

○

The government does not, indeed, waylay a man in a lonely place, spring upon him from the roadside, and holding a pistol to his head, proceed to rifle his pockets. But the robbery is none the less a robbery on that account; and it is far more dastardly and shameful.

The highwayman takes solely upon himself the responsibility, danger, and crime of his own act. He does not pretend that he has a rightful claim to your money, or that he intends to use it for your own benefit. He does not pretend to be anything but a robber. He has not acquired impudence enough to profess to be merely a "protector," and that he takes men's money against their will, merely to enable him to "protect" those infatuated travelers, who feel perfectly able to protect themselves, or do not appreciate his peculiar system of protection. He is too sensible a man to make such professions as these. Furthermore, having taken your money, he leaves you, as you wish him to do. He does not persist in following you on the road, against your will; assuming to be your rightful "sovereign," on account of the "protection" he affords you. He does not keep "protecting" you, by commanding you to bow down and serve him; by requiring you to do this, and forbidding you to do that; by robbing you out of more money as often as he finds it for his interest or pleasure to do so; and by branding you as a rebel, a traitor, and an enemy to your country, and shooting you down without mercy, if you dispute his authority, or resist his demands. He is too much of a gentleman to be guilty of such impostures, and insults, and villainies as these. In short, he does not, in addition to robbing you, attempt to make you either his dupe or his slave. (p. 17)

enough, the natural tendency of humanity to build an expanding stock of capital and durable consumer goods and to become increasingly more farsighted and provide for ever-more distant goals may not only come to a standstill, but may be reversed by a tendency toward decivilization: formerly provident providers will be turned into drunks or daydreamers, adults into children, civilized men into barbarians, and producers into criminals.

GOVERNMENT, GOVERNMENT GROWTH, AND THE PROCESS OF DECIVILIZATION: FROM MONARCHY TO DEMOCRACY

Every government, and that means every agency that engages in continual, institutionalized property-rights violations (expropriations), is by its nature a territorial monopolist. There can be no "free entry" into the business of expropriations; otherwise, soon nothing would be left that could be expropriated, and any form of *institutionalized* expropriation would thus become impossible. Under the assumption of self-interest, every government will use this monopoly of expropriation to its own advantage—in order to maximize its wealth and income. Hence every government should be expected to have an inherent tendency toward growth. And in maximizing its own wealth and income by means of expropriation, every government represents a constant threat to the process of civilization—of falling time preferences and increasingly wider and longer provision—and an expanding source of decivilizing forces.

However, not every government prospers equally and produces decivilizing forces of the same strength. Different forms of government lead to different degrees of decivilization. Nor is every form of government, and every sequence of government forms, equally probable.

Given that all expropriation creates victims and victims cannot be relied upon to cooperate while being victimized, an agency that *institutionalizes* expropriation must have legitimacy. A majority of the nongovernmental public must regard the government's actions as just or at least as fair enough not to be resisted so as to render the victim defenseless.[15]

---

[15]On the fundamental importance of favorable public opinion for the exercise of government power see the classic treatment by Etienne de la Boétie, *The Politics of Obedience: The Discourse of Voluntary Servitude* (New York: Free Life Editions, 1975), with an introduction by Murray N. Rothbard; see also David Hume, "The First Principles of Government" in *Essays: Moral, Political, and Literary* (Oxford: Oxford University Press, 1971). Thus, Hume writes:

Nothing appears more surprising to those who consider human affairs with a philosophical eye, than the easiness with which the many are governed by

Yet acquiring legitimacy is not an easy task. For this reason, it is not likely, for instance, that a single world government could initially arise. Instead, all governments must begin territorially small. Nor is it likely, even for as small a population as that of a clan, a tribe, a village, or a town, that a government will initially be democratic, for who would not rather trust a specific known individual—especially in as sensitive a matter as that of a territorial monopoly of expropriation—than an anonymous, democratically elected person? Having to begin small, the original form of government is typically that of *personal* rule: of *private* ownership of the governmental apparatus of compulsion (monarchy).[16]

In every society of any degree of complexity, specific individuals quickly acquire elite status as a result of having diverse talents. Owing to achievements of superior wealth, wisdom, bravery, or a combination thereof, particular individuals command respect, and their opinions and judgments possess natural authority. As an outgrowth of this authority, members of the elite are most likely to succeed in establishing a legitimate territorial monopoly of compulsion, typically via the monopolization of judicial services (courts and legislation) and law enforcement (police).[17] And because they owe their privileged position to

---

the few, and the implicit submission, with which men resign their own sentiments and passions to those of their rulers. When we inquire by what means this wonder is effected we shall find, that as Force is always on the side of the governed, the governors have nothing to support them but opinion. It is, therefore, on opinion only that government is founded, and this maxim extends to the most despotic and most military governments, as well as to the most free and popular. The sultan of Egypt, or the emperor of Rome, might drive his harmless subjects, like brute beasts, against their sentiment and inclination. But he must, at least, have led his mamalukes or praetorian bands, like men, by their opinions. (*Essays*, p. 19)

See also Mises, *Human Action*, pp. 863–64.

[16]On the lengthy historical process of the acquisition of government power, and the primacy of monarchical rule, see Bertrand de Jouvenel, *Sovereignty: An Inquiry into the Political Good* (Chicago: University of Chicago Press, 1957), esp. chap. 10; idem, *On Power: The Natural History of its Growth* (New York: Viking, 1949); idem, "The Principate" in idem, *The Nature of Politics* (New York: Schocken Books, 1987); Rüstow, *Freedom and Domination*, esp. pp. 101–05.

[17]On the ubiquity of natural authority see de Jouvenel, *Sovereignty*, chap. 2.

All that was needed [for the formation of associations] was that some one man should feel within him a natural ascendancy and should then inspire others with trust in himself. . . . when we can see every day associations forming all around us, why should we imagine them forming in the distant past in some different way? What makes leaders, now as always, is natural ascendancy—authority as such. We see them arising under our very eyes whenever there is a rescue to organize or a fire to put out. (pp. 31–32)

their personal elitist character and achievements, they will consider themselves and be regarded by their fellows as the monopoly's *personal owner*. Democratic rule—in which the government apparatus is considered "public" property administered by regularly elected officials who do *not* personally own and are not viewed as owning the government but as its temporary *caretakers* or *trustees*—typically only follows personal rule and private government ownership. Because masses or majorities cannot possibly possess any natural authority (this being a personal, individual trait), democratic governments can acquire legitimacy only unnaturally—most typically through war or revolution. Only in activities such as war and revolution do masses act in concert and do victory and defeat depend on mass effort. And only under exceptional circumstances such as these can mass majorities gain the legitimacy needed to transform government into *public* property.

These two forms of government—private or public ownership of government (monarchy or democracy)—have systematically different effects on social time preference and the attendant process of civilization, and with the transition from personal (monarchical) to democratic (public) rule in particular, contrary to conventional wisdom, the decivilizing forces inherent in any form of government are systematically strengthened.[18]

The defining characteristic of private government ownership and the reason for a personal ruler's relatively lower degree of time preference (as compared to criminals and democratic governments) is that the expropriated resources and the monopoly privilege of future expropriation are individually *owned*. The expropriated resources are added to the ruler's private estate and treated as if they were a part of it, and the

---

And on the transition from authority to power, de Jouvenel goes on to say:

Power, however, is something very different from authority. The distinguishing mark of the latter is that it is exercised only over those who voluntarily accept it: if the rulers have authority over only a part of their subjects, they may receive from that part a strength sufficient to subject the others to their power.... Authority ends where voluntary assent ends. There is in every state a margin of obedience which is won only by the use of force or the threat of force: it is this margin which breaches liberty and demonstrates the failure of authority. Among free peoples it is a very small margin, because there authority is very great. (pp. 32–33)

[18]See on the following also the literature on the "tragedy of the commons," e.g., *Managing The Commons*, Garrett Hardin and John Baden, eds. (San Francisco: W.H. Freeman, 1977). See also Mancur Olson, "Dictatorship, Democracy, and Development," *American Political Science Review* 87, no. 3 (1993).

monopoly privilege of future expropriation is attached as a title to this estate and leads to an instant increase in its present value ("capitalization" of monopoly profit). Most importantly, as the private owner of the government estate, the ruler is entitled to pass his possessions on to his personal heir. He may sell, rent, or give away part or all of his privileged estate (and privately pocket the receipts from the sale or rental), and he may personally appoint or dismiss every administrator and employee of his estate.[19]

The institution of private government ownership systematically shapes the incentive structure confronting the ruler and distinctly influences his conduct of government affairs. Assuming no more than self-interest, the ruler tries to maximize his total wealth, i.e., the present value of his estate *and* his current income. He would *not* want to increase current income at the expense of a more than proportional drop in the present value of his assets. Furthermore, because acts of current income acquisition invariably have repercussions on present asset values

---

[19]According to this characterization of monarchy, present-day "monarchies" such as Great Britain, the Netherlands, Belgium, Sweden, Norway, Denmark, or Spain are clearly monarchies in name only. In fact, they represent examples of what is here and in the following referred to as democracies. The term "monarchy," as here defined, applies instead most appropriately to the form of government that characterized Europe through the end of the eighteenth century: the *ancien régime*—whence, stimulated by the American and in particular the French Revolution and in a process that was not completed until after the end of World War I, monarchies were gradually transformed into democracies.

Indeed, monarchy and democracy can be conceived of analytically as representing the two endpoints of a continuum, with various possible forms of government located at greater or lesser distances from one or the other extreme. Elective monarchies as they existed for periods of time in Poland, Bohemia, and Hungary, for instance, are obviously less monarchic than are hereditary monarchies. Likewise, "constitutional" monarchies are less monarchic than preconstitutional ones. And "parliamentary" monarchies may well have to be placed closer to a democracy than to a monarchy, or, with universal suffrage, they may be no monarchy at all. On the other hand, while a republican form of government implies by definition that the government apparatus is not privately but publicly owned (by "the people"), and a republic thus possesses an inherent tendency to gravitate toward the adoption of universal suffrage, i.e., democratic republicanism, not all republics are in fact equally close to democracy. For example, an aristocratic "republic" such as that of the Dutch United Provinces before 1673 (when William of Orange was elected hereditary *stadtholder*) may actually have to be classified as a quasi-monarchy rather than a democracy.

On the distinction between monarchy, republic, and democracy and their various historical manifestations see Erik von Kuehnelt-Leddihn, *Leftism Revisited: From de Sade and Marx to Hitler and Pol Pot* (Washington, D.C.: Regnery Gateway, 1990).

(reflecting the value of all future expected asset earnings discounted by the rate of time preference), private ownership in and of itself leads to economic calculation and thus promotes farsightedness.

While this is true of private ownership generally, in the special case of private ownership of *government* it implies a distinct moderation with respect to the ruler's drive to exploit his monopoly privilege of expropriation, for acts of expropriation are by their nature parasitic upon prior acts of production by the nongovernmental public. Where nothing has first been produced, nothing can be expropriated, and where everything has been expropriated, all future production will come to a shrieking halt. Hence, a private owner of government (a king) would avoid taxing his subjects so heavily as to reduce his future earning potential to the extent that the present value of his estate (his kingdom) would actually fall, for instance. Instead, to preserve or even enhance the value of his personal property, he would systematically restrain himself in his taxing policies, for the lower the degree of taxation, the more productive the subject population will be, and the more productive the population, the higher the value of the ruler's parasitic monopoly of expropriation will be. He will use his monopolistic privilege, of course. He will not *not* tax. But as the government's private owner, it is in his interest to draw—parasitically—on a growing, increasingly productive and prosperous nongovernment economy, as this would—always and without any effort on his part—also increase his own wealth and prosperity. Tax rates would thus tend to be low.[20]

Further, it is in a personal ruler's interest to use his monopoly of law (courts) and order (police) for the enforcement of the pre-established private property law. With the sole exception of himself (for the nongovernment public and all of its internal dealings, that is), he will want to enforce the principle that all property and income should be acquired productively and/or contractually, and accordingly, he will want to threaten all private rule-transgressions as crimes with punishment. The less *private* crime there is, the more private wealth there will be and the higher will be the value of the *ruler's* monopoly of taxation and expropriation. In

---

[20]Carlo M. Cipolla, *Before the Industrial Revolution: European Society and Economy, 1000-1700* (New York: W.W. Norton, 1980), p. 48, concludes: "All in all, one must admit that the portion of income drawn by the public sector most certainly increased from the eleventh century onward all over Europe, but it is difficult to imagine that, apart from particular times and places, the public power ever managed to draw more than 5 to 8 percent of national income." He notes further that this portion was not systematically exceeded until the second half of the nineteenth century. See also the two following notes.

fact, a private ruler will not want to lean exclusively on *tax* revenue to finance his own expenditures. Rather, he will also want to rely on productive activities and allocate part of his estate to the production and provision of "normal" goods and services, with the purpose of earning its owner a "normal" (market) *sales* revenue.[21]

Moreover, private ownership of government implies moderation for yet another systematic reason. All private property is by definition exclusive property. He who owns property is entitled to exclude

---

[21] On the recognition of the pre-existing private-property law by monarchs see Bertrand de Jouvenel, *Sovereignty*, esp. chaps. 10 and 11.

The attitude of the sovereign toward rights is expressed in the oath of the first French kings: "I will honor and preserve each one of you, and I will maintain for each the law and justice pertaining to him." When the king was called "debtor for justice," it was no empty phrase. If his duty was *suum cuique tribuere*, the *suum* was a fixed datum. It was not the case of rendering to each what, in the plenitude of his knowledge, he thought would be best for him, but what belonged to him according to custom. Subjective rights were not held on the precarious tenure of grant but were freehold possessions. The sovereign's right also was a freehold. It was a subjective right as much as the other rights, though of a more elevated dignity, but it could not take the other rights away. (pp. 172–73)

de Jouvenel later goes on to say:

The much-cited anecdote of Frederick the Great and the miller of Sans-Souci faithfully represents the ancient state of affairs. The king's rights have incomparably greater scope than those of the miller; but as far as the miller's right goes it is as good as the king's; on his own ground, the miller is entitled to hold off the king. Indeed there was a deep-seated feeling that all positive rights stood or fell together; if the king disregarded the miller's title to his land, so might the king's title to his throne be disregarded. The profound if obscure concept of legitimacy established the solidarity of all rights. (p. 189)

And on the funding of kings, de Jouvenel notes that:

State expenditures, as we now call them, were thought of in feudal times as the king's own expenditures, which he incurred by virtue of his station. When he came into his station, he simultaneously came into an "estate" (in the modern sense of the word); i.e., he found himself endowed with property rights ensuring an income adequate to "the king's needs." It is somewhat as if a government of our own times were expected to cover its ordinary expenditures from the proceeds of state-owned industries. (p. 178)

However, it remains worth emphasizing that any monopolization of law and order still implies higher prices and/or lower product quality than those prevailing under competitive conditions, and that even a king will still employ his monopoly of punishment to his own advantage: by shifting increasingly from the principle of restituting and compensating the victim of a rights violation to that of compensating himself, the king. See on this Bruce L. Benson, "The Development of Criminal Law and Its Enforcement," *Journal des Economistes et des Etudes Humaines* 3 (1992).

everyone else from its use and enjoyment, and he is at liberty to choose with whom, if anyone, he is willing to share in its usage. Typically, a private-property owner will include his family and exclude all others. The property becomes family property with him as the head of the family, and every nonfamily person will be excluded from using family property, except as invited guests or as paid employees or contractors. In the case of government, this exclusive character of private property takes on a special meaning. In this case it implies that everyone but the ruler and his family is excluded from benefiting from nonproductively acquired property and income. Only the ruling family—and to a minor extent its friends, employees, and business partners—shares in the enjoyment of tax revenues and can lead a parasitic life. The position as head of government—and of the government estate—is typically passed on within the ruling family, such that no one outside the king's family can realistically hope to become the next king. While entrance into the ruling family might not be closed entirely, it is highly restrictive. It might be possible to become a family member through marriage. However, the larger the ruling family, the smaller each member's share in the government's total confiscations will be. Hence, marriage typically will be restricted to members of the ruler's extended family. Only in exceptional cases will a member of the ruling family marry a complete "outsider"; even if this occurs, a family member by marriage will not normally become the head of the ruling family.

Owing to these restrictions regarding entrance into government and the exclusive status of the individual ruler and his family (as king and nobles), private-government ownership (monarchism) stimulates the development of a clear "class consciousness" on the part of the governed public and promotes opposition and resistance to any expansion of the government's power to tax. A clear-cut distinction between the few rulers and the many ruled exists, and there is little or no risk or chance of a person's moving from one class to the other. Confronted with an almost insurmountable barrier to "upward" mobility, solidarity among the ruled—their mutual identification as actual or potential victims of government violations of property rights—is strengthened, and the ruling class's risk of losing its legitimacy as a result of increased taxation is accordingly heightened.[22]

---

[22]Bertrand de Jouvenel writes: "A man of our time cannot conceive the lack of real power which characterized the medieval king, from which it naturally followed that in order to secure the execution of a decision he needed to involve other leaders whose say-so reinforced his own." Bertrand de Jouvenel, "On the Evolution of Forms of Government" in idem, *The Nature of Politics*, p. 113. Elsewhere, de Jouvenel noted:

In fact, the class consciousness among the ruled exerts a moderating effect not only on the government's internal policies, but also on its conduct of external affairs. Every government must be expected to pursue an expansionist foreign policy. The larger the territory and the greater the population over which a monopoly of confiscation extends, the better off those in charge of this monopoly will be. Because only one monopoly of expropriation can exist in any given territory, this expansionary tendency must be expected to go hand in hand with a tendency toward centralization (with ultimately only one, worldwide government remaining). Moreover, because centralization implies reduced opportunities for interterritorial migration—of voting with one's feet against one's government and in favor of another—the process of intergovernmental competition, of expansive elimination, should be expected to generate simultaneous tendencies toward increasingly higher rates of government expropriation and taxation.[23]

The king could not exact contributions, he could only solicit "subsidies." It was stressed that his loyal subjects granted him help of their free will, and they often seized this occasion to stipulate conditions. For instance, they granted subsidies to John the Good (of France), subject to the condition that he should henceforth refrain from minting money which was defective in weight. In order to replenish his Treasury, the king might go on a begging tour from town to town, expounding his requirements and obtaining local grants, as was done on the eve of the Hundred Years' War; or he might assemble from all parts of the country those whose financial support he craved. It is a serious mistake to confuse such an assembly with a modern sitting of parliament, though the latter phenomenon has arisen from the former. The Parliament is sovereign and may exact contributions. The older assemblies should rather be thought of as a gathering of modern company directors agreeing to turn over to the Exchequer a part of their profits, with some trade union leaders present agreeing to part with some of their unions' dues for public purposes. Each group was called on for a grant, and each was thus well placed to make conditions. A modern parliament could not be treated like that, but would impose its will by majority vote. (*Sovereignty*, pp. 178–79)

See also Douglass C. North and Robert P. Thomas, *The Rise of the Western World: A New Economic History* (Cambridge: Cambridge University Press, 1973), p. 96.

[23]On political decentralization—"political anarchy"—as a constraint on government power and a fundamental reason for the evolution of markets and capitalism, as well as on the tendency toward political centralization—expansive elimination—and the accompanying tendency toward an increase in governments' taxing and regulatory powers see Jean Baechler, *The Origins of Capitalism* (New York: St. Martin's Press, 1976), esp. chap. 7; Hoppe, *The Economics and Ethics of Private Property*, esp. chaps. 3 and 4; idem, "Migrazione, centralismo e secessione nell'Europa contemporanea," *Biblioteca della libertà* 118 (1992); idem, "Nationalism and Secession,"

However, a privately-owned government significantly affects the form and pace of this process. Owing to its exclusive character and the correspondingly developed class consciousness of the ruled, government attempts at territorial expansion tend to be viewed by the public as the ruler's private business, to be financed and carried out with his own personal funds. The added territory is the king's, and so he, not the public, should pay for it. Consequently, of the two possible methods of enlarging his realm, war and military conquest or contractual acquisition, a private ruler tends to prefer the latter. It must not be assumed that he is opposed to war, for he may well employ military means if presented with an opportunity. But war typically requires extraordinary resources, and since higher taxes and/or increased conscription to fund a war perceived by the public as somebody else's will encounter immediate popular resistance and thus pose a threat to the government's internal legitimacy, a personal ruler will have to bear all or most of the costs of a military venture himself. Accordingly, he will generally prefer the second, peaceful option as the less costly one. Instead of through conquest, he will want to advance his expansionist desires through land purchases or, even less costly and still better, through a policy of intermarriage between members of different ruling families. For a monarchical ruler, then, foreign policy is in large measure family and marriage policy, and territorial expansion typically proceeds via the contractual conjunction of originally independent kingdoms.[24]

Chronicles (November 1993); also Nathan Rosenberg and Luther E. Birdzell, *How the West Grew Rich* (New York: Basic Books, 1986).

[24] As a prominent example of this type of foreign policy, the case of the Habsburgs of Austria may be cited, whose conduct has been characterized by the motto "*bella gerunt alii; tu, felix Austria, nubes.*" Maximilian I (1493–1519)

> married the heiress of the dukes of Burgundy, who, over the past century, had acquired a number of provinces in the western extremities of the [Holy Roman] Empire—the Netherlands and the Free County of Burgundy, which bordered upon France. Maximilian by this marriage had a son Philip, whom he married to Joanna, heiress to Ferdinand and Isabella of Spain. Philip and Joanna produced a son Charles. Charles combined the inheritances of his four grandparents: Austria from Maximilian, the Netherlands and Free County from Mary of Burgundy, Castile and Spanish America from Isabella, Aragon and its Mediterranean and Italian possessions from Ferdinand. In addition, in 1519, he was elected Holy Roman Emperor and so became the symbolic head of all Germany. (Robert R. Palmer and Joel Colton, *A History of the Modern World* [New York: Alfred Knopf, 1992], p. 74)

On the limited and moderate character of monarchical wars see the discussion on democratic warfare below.

In contrast to the internal and external moderation of a monarchy, a democratic (publicly owned) government implies increased excess, and the transition from a world of kings to one of democratically-elected presidents must be expected to lead to a systematic increase in the intensity and extension of government power and a significantly strengthened tendency toward decivilization.

A democratic ruler can use the government apparatus to his personal advantage, but he does not own it. He cannot sell government resources and privately pocket the receipts from such sales, nor can he pass government possessions on to his personal heir. He owns the *current use* of government resources, but not their capital value. In distinct contrast to a king, a president will want to maximize not total government wealth (capital values and current income) but current income (regardless and at the expense of capital values). Indeed, even if he wished to act differently, he *could not*, for as public property, government resources are unsaleable, and without market prices economic calculation is *impossible*. Accordingly, it must be regarded as unavoidable that public-government ownership results in continual capital consumption. Instead of maintaining or even enhancing the value of the government estate, as a king would do, a president (the government's temporary caretaker or trustee) will use up as much of the government resources as quickly as possible, for what he does not consume *now*, he may *never* be able to consume. In particular, a president (as distinct from a king) has no interest in not ruining his country. For why would he *not* want to increase his confiscations if the advantage of a policy of moderation—the resulting higher capital value of the government estate—cannot be reaped privately, while the advantage of the opposite policy of higher taxes—a higher current income—*can* be so reaped? For a president, unlike for a king, moderation offers only disadvantages.[25]

---

[25]On the nature of public ownership and its inherent irrationality see also Rothbard, *Power and Market*, pp. 172–84; Hoppe, *A Theory of Socialism and Capitalism*, chap. 9.

The fundamental difference between private ownership of government (and low time preference) and public ownership of government (and high time preference) may be further illustrated by considering the institution of slavery, and contrasting the case of private slave ownership, as it existed for instance in antebellum America, with that of public slave ownership, as it existed for instance in the former Soviet Union and its Eastern European empire.

Just as privately owned slaves were threatened with punishment if they tried to escape, in all of the former Soviet empire emigration was outlawed and punished as a criminal offense, if necessary, by shooting those who tried to run away. Moreover,

Moreover, with public instead of private government ownership the second reason for moderation is also gone: the clear and developed class-consciousness of the ruled. There can never be more than one supreme ruler, whether king or president. Yet while entrance into the position of king and a promotion to the rank of nobility is systematically restricted under a monarchy, in a publicly owned government, anyone, in theory, can become a member of the ruling class—or even president. The distinction between the rulers and the ruled is blurred, and the class-consciousness of the ruled becomes fuzzy. The illusion even arises that such a distinction no longer exists: that with a democratic government no one is ruled by anyone but everyone instead rules himself. Indeed, it is largely due to this illusion that the transition from monarchy to democracy could be interpreted as progress and, hence, as deserving public support. Accordingly, public resistance against government

---

anti-loafing laws existed everywhere, and governments could assign any task and all rewards and punishments to any citizen. Hence the classification of the Soviet system as slavery. Unlike a private slave owner, however, Eastern-European slave owners—from Lenin to Gorbachev—could not sell or rent their subjects in a labor market and privately appropriate the receipts from the sale or rental of their "human capital." Hence the system's classification as public (or socialist) slavery.

Without markets for slaves and slave labor, matters are worse, not better, for the slave, for without prices for slaves and their labor, a slave owner can no longer rationally allocate his "human capital." He cannot determine the scarcity value of his various, heterogeneous pieces of human capital, and he can neither determine the opportunity-cost of using this capital in any given employment, nor compare it to the corresponding revenue. Accordingly, permanent misallocation, waste, and "consumption" of human capital results.

The empirical evidence indicates as much. While it occasionally happened that a private slave owner killed his slave, which is the ultimate "consumption" of human capital, socialist slavery in Eastern Europe resulted in the murder of millions of civilians. Under private slave ownership the health and life expectancy of slaves generally increased. In the Soviet Empire healthcare standards steadily deteriorated and life expectancies actually declined in recent decades. The level of practical training and education of private slaves generally rose. That of socialist slaves fell. The rate of reproduction among privately-owned slaves was positive. Among the slave populations of Eastern Europe it was generally negative. The rates of suicide, self-incapacitation, family breakups, promiscuity, "illegitimate" births, birth defects, venereal disease, abortion, alcoholism, and dull or brutish behavior among private slaves were high. But all such rates of "human capital consumption" were higher still for the socialist slaves of the former Soviet Empire. Similarly, while morally senseless and violent behavior among privately owned slaves occurred after their emancipation, the brutalization of social life in the aftermath of the abolition of socialist slavery has been far worse, revealing an even greater degree of moral degeneration. See also Hans-Hermann Hoppe's "Note on Socialism and Slavery" in *Chronicles* (August 1993): 6.

power is systematically weakened. While expropriation and taxation before may have appeared clearly oppressive and evil to the public, they seem much less so, mankind being what it is, once anyone may freely enter the ranks of those who are at the receiving end.

Consequently, taxes will increase, be it directly in the form of higher tax rates or indirectly in that of increased governmental money "creation" (inflation). Likewise, government employment and the ratio of government employees ("public servants") to private employees tends to rise, attracting and promoting individuals with high degrees of time preference and low and limited farsightedness.[26]

-----

[26]As Bertrand de Jouvenel explains:

From the twelfth to the eighteenth century governmental authority grew continuously. The process was understood by all who saw it happening; it stirred them into incessant protest and to violent reaction. In later times its growth has continued at an accelerated pace, and its extension has brought a corresponding extension of war. And now we no longer understand the process, we no longer protest, we no longer react. The quiescence of ours is a new thing, for which Power has to thank the smoke-screen in which it has wrapped itself. Formerly it could be seen, manifest in the person of the king, who did not disclaim being the master he was, and in whom human passions were discernible. Now, masked in anonymity, it claims to have no existence of its own, and to be but the impersonal and passionless instrument of the general will—but that is clearly a fiction—today as always Power is in the hands of a group of men who control the power house. All that has changed is that it has now been made easy for the ruled to change the personnel of the leading wielders of Power. Viewed from one angle, this weakens Power, because the wills which control a society's life can, at the society's pleasure, be replaced by other wills, in which it feels more confidence. But by opening the prospect of Power to all the ambitious talents, this arrangement makes the extension of Power much easier. Under the "ancien régime," society's moving spirits, who had, as they knew, no chance of a share in Power, were quick to denounce its smallest encroachment. Now, on the other hand, when everyone is potentially a minister, no one is concerned to cut down an office to which he aspires one day himself, or to put sand in a machine which he means to use himself when his turn comes. Hence it is that there is in the political circles of a modern society a wide complicity in the extension of power. (*On Power*, pp. 9–10)

In fact, during the entire monarchical age until the second half of the nineteenth century, which represents the turning point in the historical process of demonarchization and democratization beginning with the French Revolution and ending with World War I, the tax burden rarely exceeded 5 percent of national product (see also footnote 20 above). Since then it has increased constantly. In Western Europe it stood at 15 to 20 percent of national product after World War I, and in the meantime it has risen to around 50 percent. Likewise, during the entire monarchical age, until the latter half of the nineteenth century, government employment rarely exceeded 2

The combination of these interrelated factors—"public" ownership of the government plus free entry into it—significantly alters a government's conduct of both its internal and its external affairs. Internally, the government is likely to exhibit an increased tendency to incur debt. While a king is by no means opposed to debt, he is constrained in this "natural" inclination by the fact that as the government's private owner, he and his heirs are considered personally liable for the payment of all government debts (he can literally go bankrupt, or be forced by creditors to liquidate government assets). In distinct contrast, a presidential government caretaker is not held liable for debts incurred during his tenure of office. Rather, his debts are considered "public," to be repaid by future (equally nonliable) governments. If one is not held personally liable for one's debts, however, the debt load will rise, and present government consumption will be expanded at the expense of future government consumption. In order to repay a rising public debt, the level of future taxes (or monetary inflation) imposed on a future public will have to increase. And with the expectation of a higher future-tax burden, the nongovernment public also becomes affected by the incubus of rising time-preference degrees, for with higher future-tax rates, present consumption and short-term investment are rendered relatively more attractive as compared to saving and long-term investment.[27]

---

percent of the labor force. Since then it has increased steadily, and today it typically is 15 to 20 percent. See for details Peter Flora, *State, Economy, and Society in Western Europe 1815–1975: A Data Handbook* (London: Macmillan, 1983), vol. 1, chaps. 5 and 8.

[27]The difficulties encountered by monarchical rulers in securing loans are notorious (see also footnote 22 above); and kings typically had to pay above-average rates of interest reflecting their comparatively high default risk. See on this North and Thomas, *The Rise of the Western World*, p. 96. In contrast, democratic governments, as they came into full bloom with the end of World War I, have indeed demonstrated a constant tendency toward deficit-financing and increasing debts. Today, the "national debts" in Western Europe and the "Western World" rarely amount to less than 30 percent of national product and frequently exceed 100 percent.

Likewise, and directly related, the monarchical world was generally characterized by the existence of a commodity money—typically gold or silver—and with the establishment of a single, integrated world market in the course of the seventeenth and eighteenth centuries, by an international gold standard. A commodity money standard makes it difficult for a government to inflate the money supply. By monopolizing the mint and engaging in systematic "coin clipping" (currency depreciation), kings did their best to enrich themselves at the expense of the public. But as much as they tried, they did not succeed in establishing monopolies of pure fiat currencies: of irredeemable national paper monies that can be created virtually out of thin air, at practically no cost. No particular individual, not even a king, could be trusted with an extraordinary monopoly such as this! It was only under conditions

More importantly still, the government's conduct as the monopolist of law and order will undergo a systematic change. As explained above, a king will want to enforce the preexisting private property law, and notwithstanding his own exceptional status *vis-à-vis* some of its key provisions, he, too, will assume and accept private-property notions for himself and his possessions (at least insofar as *international* king-to-king relations are concerned). He does not create new law but merely occupies a privileged position within an existing, all-encompassing system of private law. In contrast, with a "publicly" owned and administered government a new type of "law" emerges: "public" law, which exempts government agents from personal liability and withholds "publicly owned" resources from economic management. With the establishment of "public law" (including constitutional and administrative law) not merely as law but as a "higher" law, a gradual erosion of private law ensues; that is, there is an increasing subordination and displacement of private law by and through public law.[28]

---

of democratic republicanism in the aftermath of World War I that the gold standard was abolished and at long last replaced with a worldwide system of irredeemable national paper monies in 1971. Since then, the supply of money and credit has increased dramatically. A seemingly permanent "secular" tendency toward inflation and currency depreciation has come into existence. Government deficit financing has turned into a mere banking technicality, and interest rates—as an indicator of the social rate of time preference—which had continuously declined for centuries and by the end of the nineteenth century had fallen to around 2 percent, have since exhibited a systematic upward tendency.

See also Murray N. Rothbard, *What Has Government Done to Our Money?* (Auburn, Ala.: Ludwig von Mises Institute, 1992); idem, *The Mystery of Banking* (New York: Richardson and Snyder, 1983); on the history of interest rates Sidney Homer and Richard Sylla, *A History of Interest Rates* (New Brunswick, N.J.: Rutgers University Press, 1991), esp. chap. 23, pp. 553–58.

[28]In fact, although undermined by the Renaissance and the Protestant Revolutions, throughout the monarchical age the notion prevailed that kings and their subjects were ruled by a single, universal law—"a code of rules anterior to and co-existent with the sovereign—rules which were intangible and fixed" (de Jouvenel, *Sovereignty*, p. 193). Law was considered something to be discovered and recognized as eternally "given," not something to be "made." It was held "that law could not be legislated, but only applied as something that had always existed," (Bernhard Rehfeld, *Die Wurzeln des Rechts* [Berlin 1951], p. 67). Indeed, as late as the beginning of the twentieth century, Albert V. Dicey (*Lectures on the Relation Between Law and Public Opinion in England During the Nineteenth Century* [London: Macmillan, 1903]) could still maintain that as for Great Britain, public or administrative law, as distinct from private law, did not exist: government agents, in their relationship with private citizens, were still regarded as bound by the same rules and subject to the same laws as any private citizen. It is again only after World War I, under

Rather than upholding private law among the nongovernment public and exploiting its legal monopoly solely for the purpose of redistributing wealth and income from civil society onto itself, a government "ruled" by public law will also employ its power increasingly for the purpose of legislation, i.e., for the creation of new, "positive" civil law, with the intent of redistributing wealth and income *within* civil society. For as a government's caretaker (not owner) it is of little or no concern that any such redistribution can only reduce future productivity. Confronted with popular elections and free entry into government, however, the advocacy and adoption of redistributive policies is predestined to become the very prerequisite for anyone wanting to attain or retain a government caretaker position. Accordingly, rather than representing a "consumption state" (as the typical monarchy does), with public government ownership, complementing and reinforcing the overall tendency toward rising taxes (and / or inflation), government employment and debt, the state will become increasingly transformed into a "welfare state."[29] And contrary to its typical portrayal as a "progressive" development, with this transformation the virus of rising degrees of time

---

democratic republicanism, that public agents achieve "immunity" from the provisions of private law, and that a view such as the leading socialist legal-theorist Gustav Radbruch's found general acceptance: that

> for an individualistic order of public law, the state, is only the narrow protective belt surrounding private law and private property. In contrast, for a social [democratic republican] order of law private law is to be regarded only as a provisional and constantly decreasing range of private initiative, temporarily spared within the all-comprehensive sphere of public law. (*Der Mensch im Recht* [Göttingen: Vandenhoeck, 1957], p. 40)

In the meantime,

> in our own day we are used to having our rights modified by the sovereign decisions of legislators. A landlord no longer feels surprised at being compelled to keep a tenant; an employer is no less used to having to raise the wages of his employees in virtue of the decrees of Power. Nowadays it is understood that our subjective rights are precarious and at the good pleasure of authority. (de Jouvenel, *Sovereignty*, p. 189)

On the distinction between law and legislation see also Bruno Leoni, *Freedom and the Law* (Princeton, N.J.: D. Van Nostrand, 1961); Friedrich A. Hayek, *Law, Legislation, and Liberty* (Chicago: University of Chicago Press, 1973), vol. 1, chaps. 4 and 6.

[29]Until the end of the nineteenth century, the bulk of public spending—often more than 50 percent—typically went to financing the army (which, assuming government expenditures to be 5 percent of national product, amounted to military expenditures of 2.5 percent of national product). The rest went to government administration. Welfare spending or "public charity" played almost no role. In contrast, under democratic republicanism military expenditures have typically risen to 5–10 percent of national product. But with public expenditures making up 50

preference will be planted in the midst of civil society, and a self-accelerating process of decivilization will be set in motion.[30]

The legislatively-enacted redistribution of income and wealth within civil society can essentially take on three forms. It can take the form of simple transfer payments, in which income and/or wealth is taken from Peter (the "haves") and doled out to Paul (the "have-nots"). It can take the form of "free" or below-cost provision of goods and services (such as education, health care, or infrastructure) by government, in which income and/or wealth is confiscated from one group of individuals—the taxpayers—and handed out to another, nonidentical one—the users of the respective goods and services. Or it can take the form of business and/or consumer regulations or "protection laws" (such as price controls, tariffs, or licensing requirements), whereby the wealth of the members of one group of businessmen or consumers is increased at the expense of a corresponding loss for those of another "competing" group (by imposing legal restrictions on the use which the latter are permitted to make of their private properties).

Regardless of its specific form, however, any such redistribution has a two-fold effect on civil society. First, the mere act of legislating—of

---

percent of national product, military expenditures now only represent 10 to 20 percent of total government spending. The bulk of public spending, typically more than 50 percent of total expenditures—and 25 percent of the national product—now is eaten up by public-welfare spending. See also Cipolla, *Before the Industrial Revolution*, pp. 54–55; Flora, *State, Economy, and Society in Western Europe*, chap. 8.

[30]Most important among the policies affecting social time preference is the introduction of "social security" legislation, as it was introduced during the 1880s in Bismarck's Germany and then became universal throughout the Western world in the aftermath of World War I. By relieving an individual of the task of having to provide for his own old age, the range and the temporal horizon of private provisionary action will be reduced. In particular, the value of marriage, family, and children will fall because they are less needed if one can fall back on "public" assistance. Indeed, since the onset of the democratic–republican age, all indicators of "family dysfunction" have exhibited a systematic upward tendency: the number of children has declined, the size of the endogenous population has stagnated or even fallen, and the rates of divorce, illegitimacy, single parenting, singledom, and abortion have risen. Moreover, personal-savings rates have begun to stagnate or even decline rather than rise proportionally or even over-proportionally with rising incomes. See Allan C. Carlson, *Family Questions: Reflections on the American Social Crises* (New Brunswick, N.J.: Transaction Publishers, 1992); idem, "What Has Government Done to Our Families?" *Essays in Political Economy* 13 (Auburn, Ala.: Ludwig von Mises Institute, 1991); Bryce J. Christensen, "The Family vs. the State," *Essays in Political Economy* 14 (Auburn, Ala.: Ludwig von Mises Institute, 1992); also Joseph A. Schumpeter, *Capitalism, Socialism, and Democracy* (New York: Harper, 1942), chap. 14.

democratic lawmaking—increases the degree of uncertainty. Rather than being immutable and hence predictable, law becomes increasingly flexible and unpredictable. What is right and wrong today may not be so tomorrow. The future is thus rendered more haphazard. Consequently, all-around time-preference degrees will rise, consumption and short-term orientation will be stimulated, and at the same time the respect for all laws will be systematically undermined and crime promoted (for if there is no immutable standard of "right," then there is also no firm definition of "crime").[31]

---

[31]On the relationship between time preference and crime see James Q. Wilson and Richard J. Herrnstein, *Crime and Human Nature* (New York: Simon and Schuster, 1985), pp. 49–56 and 416–22; Edward C. Banfield, *The Unheavenly City Revisited*; idem, "Present-Orientedness and Crime," in *Assessing the Criminal: Restitution, Retribution, and the Legal Process*, Randy E. Barnett and John Hagel, eds. (Cambridge, Mass.: Ballinger, 1977). While high time preference is by no means equivalent with crime—it also may find expression in such perfectly legal forms as personal recklessness, insensitivity, rudeness, unreliability, or untrustworthiness—a systematic relationship between them still exists, for in order to earn a market income a certain minimum of planning, patience, and sacrifice is required: one must first work for a while before one gets paid. In contrast, specific criminal activities such as murder, assault, rape, robbery, theft, and burglary require no such discipline: the reward for the aggressor is tangible and immediate, but the sacrifice—possible punishment—lies in the future and is uncertain. Accordingly, if the degree of social time preference is increased, it can be expected that the frequency of aggressive activities will rise. As Banfield explains:

> The threat of punishment at the hands of the law is unlikely to deter the present-oriented person. The gains that he expects from the illegal act are very near to the present, whereas the punishment that he would suffer—in the unlikely event of his being both caught and punished—lies in a future too distant for him to take into account. For the normal person there are of course risks other than the legal penalty that are strong deterrents: disgrace, loss of job, hardship for wife and children if one is sent to prison, and so on. The present-oriented person does not run such risks. In his circle it is taken for granted that one gets "in trouble" with the police now and then; he need not fear losing his job since he works intermittently or not at all, and as for his wife and children, he contributes little or nothing to their support and they may well be better off without him. (*The Unheavenly City Revisited*, pp. 140–41)

On the magnitude of the increase in criminal activity brought about by the operation of democratic republicanism in the course of the last hundred years as a consequence of steadily increased legislation and an ever-expanding range of "social," as opposed to private, responsibilities—see McGrath, *Gunfighters, Highwaymen, and Vigilantes*, esp. chap. 13. Comparing crime in some of the wildest places of the American "Wild West" (two frontier towns and mining camps in California and

Second, any income or wealth redistribution within civil society implies that the recipients are made economically better off without having produced either more or better goods or services, while others are made worse off without their having produced quantitatively or qualitatively less. Not producing, not producing anything worthwhile, or not correctly predicting the future and the future exchange-demand for one's products thus becomes relatively more attractive (or less prohibitive) as compared to producing something of value and predicting the future exchange-demand correctly. Consequently—and regardless of the specific legislative intent, be it to "help" or "protect" the poor, the unemployed, the sick, the young or the old, the uneducated or the stupid, the farmers, steelworkers or truckers, the uninsured, the homeless, whites or blacks, the married or unmarried, those with children or those without, etc.,—there will be more people producing less and displaying poor foresight, and fewer people producing more and predicting well. For if individuals possess even the slightest control over the criteria that "entitle" a person to be either on the receiving or on the "giving" end of the redistribution, they increasingly will shift out of the latter roles and into the former. There will be more poor, unemployed, uninsured, uncompetitive, homeless, and so on, than otherwise. Even if such a shift is not possible, as in the case of sex-, race-, or age-based income or wealth redistribution, the incentive to be productive and farsighted will still be

---

Nevada) to that of some of the wilder places of the present age, McGrath ("Treat Them to a Good Dose of Lead," pp. 17–18) sums up thus by stating that the frontier towns of Bodie and Aurora actually suffered rarely from robbery . . . today's cities, such as Detroit, New York, and Miami, have 20 times as much robbery per capita. The United States as a whole averages three times as much robbery per capita as Bodie and Aurora. Burglary and theft were also of infrequent occurrence in the mining towns. Most American cities today average 30 or 40 times as much burglary and theft per capita as Bodie and Aurora. The national rate is ten times higher. . . . There were no reported cases of rape in either Aurora or Bodie. . . . Today, a rape occurs every five minutes. . . . More than 4,100 of them occur in Los Angeles county alone. . . . The rape rate in the United States per 100,000 inhabitants is 42. . . . [Violence, including homicide, was frequent in Bodie and Aurora] but the men involved were both young, healthy, armed, and willing. . . . Yes, men (and some women) went about armed and male combatants killed each other, mostly in fights where there were somewhat "even chances." On the other hand, the young, the old, the female, and those who chose not to drink in saloons and display reckless bravado were rarely the victims of crime or violence. Moreover, dirty, low-down scoundrels got their just dessert. . . . In the early 1950s the city of Los Angeles averaged about 70 murders a year. Today the city averages more than 90 murders a month. . . . In 1952 there were 572 rapes reported to the LAPD. In 1992 there were 2,030 reported. During the same years robbery increased from a reported total of 2,566 to 39,508, and auto theft from 6,241 to 68,783.

reduced. There may not be more men or women, or whites or blacks, at least not immediately. However, because the members of the privileged sex, race, or age group are awarded an unearned income, they have less of an incentive to earn one in the future, and because the members of the discriminated sex, race, or age group are punished for possessing wealth or having produced an income, they, too, will be less productive in the future. In any case, there will be less productive activity, self-reliance and future-orientation, and more consumption, parasitism, dependency and shortsightedness. That is, the very problem that the redistribution was supposed to cure will have grown even bigger. Accordingly, the cost of maintaining the existing level of welfare distribution will be higher now than before, and in order to finance it, even higher taxes and more wealth confiscation must be imposed on the remaining producers. The tendency to shift from production to nonproduction activities will be further strengthened, leading to continuously rising time-preference rates and a progressive decivilization—infantilization and demoralization—of civil society.[32]

In addition, with public ownership and free entry into a democratic–republican government, the foreign policy changes as well. All governments are expected to be expansionary, as explained above, and there is no reason to assume that a president's expansionary desires will be smaller than a king's. However, while a king may satisfy this desire through marriage, this route is essentially precluded for a president. He does not own the government controlled territory; hence, he cannot contractually combine separate territories. And even if he concluded inter-government treaties, these would not possess the status of contracts but constitute at best only temporary pacts or alliances, because as agreements concerning publicly-owned resources, they could be revoked at any time by other future governments. If a democratic ruler and a democratically elected ruling elite want to expand their territory and hence their tax base, then only a military option of conquest and domination is open to them. Hence, the likelihood of war will be significantly increased.[33]

---

[32]On the "logic" of government interventionism—its counterproductivity, inherent instability, and "progressive" character—see Ludwig von Mises, *Critique of Interventionism* (New Rochelle, N.Y.: Arlington House, 1977); see also idem, *Human Action*, part 6: "The Hampered Market Economy."

For empirical illustrations of the decivilizing and demoralizing effects of redistributive policies see Banfield, *The Unheavenly City Revisited;* Charles Murray, *Losing Ground* (New York: Basic Books, 1984).

[33]Prior to and long after the onset of the democratic–republican transformation of Europe with the French (and the American) Revolution, most prominent social

Moreover, not only the likelihood but also the form of war will change. Typically, monarchical wars arise out of disputes over inheritances brought on by a complex network of interdynastic marriages and the irregular but constant extinction of certain dynasties. As violent inheritance disputes, monarchical wars are characterized by territorial objectives. They are not ideologically motivated quarrels but disputes over tangible properties. Moreover, since they are interdynastic property disputes, the public considers war the king's private affair, to be financed and executed with his own money and military forces. Further, as private conflicts between different ruling families the public expects and the kings feel compelled to recognize a clear distinction between combatants and noncombatants and to target their war efforts specifically against each other and their respective private property. As late as the eighteenth century, notes military historian Michael Howard,

> on the continent commerce, travel, cultural and learned intercourse went on in wartime almost unhindered. The wars were the king's wars. The role of the good citizen was to pay his taxes, and sound political economy dictated that he should be left alone to make the money out of

philosophers—from Montesquieu, Rousseau, Kant, Say, to J.S. Mill—had essentially contended "That it was only the ruling classes [the king, the nobility] who wanted war, and that 'the people,' if only they were allowed to speak for themselves, would opt enthusiastically for peace." Michael Howard, *War and the Liberal Conscience* (New Brunswick, N.J.: Rutgers University Press, 1978), chaps. 1 and 2, p. 45. Indeed, Immanuel Kant, in his *Perpetual Peace* (1795), claimed a republican constitution to be the prerequisite for perpetual peace. For under a republican constitution,

> when the consent of the citizens is necessary to decide whether there shall be war or not, nothing is more natural than that, since they would have to decide on imposing all of the hardships of war onto themselves, they will be very hesitant to begin such an evil adventure. In contrast, under a constitution where the subject is not a citizen, which is thus not republican, it is the easiest thing in the world, because the sovereign is not a citizen of the state but its owner, his dining, hunting, castles, parties, etc., will not suffer in the least from the war, and he can thus go to war for meaningless reasons, as if it were a pleasure trip. (*Gesammelte Werke in zwölf Bänden*, Wilhelm Weischedel, ed. [Frankfurt/M.: Suhrkamp, 1964], vol. 11, pp. 205f.)

In fact the opposite is true: the substitution of a republic for a monarchy does not imply less government power, or even self-rule. It implies the replacement of bad private-government administration by worse public-government administration. On the illusionary character of Kant's and others' views to the contrary and the "positive" historical correlation between democracy and increased militarization and war, see Michael Howard *War in European History* (New York: Oxford University Press, 1976); John F.C. Fuller, *War and Western Civilization 1832–1932* (Freeport, N.Y.: Books for Libraries, 1969); idem, *The Conduct of War, 1789–1961* (New York: Da Capo Press, 1992); also Ekkehard Krippendorff, *Staat und Krieg* (Frankfurt/M.: Suhrkamp, 1985).

which to pay those taxes. He was required to participate neither in the decision out of which wars arose nor to take part in them once they broke out, unless prompted by a spirit of youthful adventure. These matters were *arcana regni*, the concern of the sovereign alone.[34]

In fact, writes Guglielmo Ferrero of the eighteenth century,

war became limited and circumscribed by a system of precise rules. It was definitely regarded as a kind of single combat between the two armies, the civil population being merely spectators. Pillage, requisitions, and acts of violence against the population were forbidden in the home country as well as in the enemy country. Each army established depots in its rear in carefully chosen towns, shifting them as it moved about; . . . Conscription existed only in a rudimentary and sporadic form, . . . Soldiers being scarce and hard to find, everything was done to ensure their quality by a long, patient and meticulous training, but as this was costly, it rendered them very valuable, and it was necessary to let as few be killed as possible. Having to economize their men, generals tried to avoid fighting battles. The object of warfare was the execution of skillful maneuvers and not the annihilation of the adversary; a campaign without battles and without loss of life, a victory obtained by a clever combination of movements, was considered the crowning achievement of this art, the ideal pattern of perfection.[35] . . . It was avarice and calculation that made war more humane. . . . [W]ar became a kind of game between sovereigns. A war was a game with its rules and its stakes—a territory, an inheritance, a throne, a treaty. The loser

---

[34]Howard, *War in European History*, p. 73. For a similar assessment see Fuller, *The Conduct of War*:

So completely was civil life divorced from war that, in his *A Sentimental Journey through France and Italy*, Laurence Sterne relates that during the Seven Years' War [1756–1763] he left London for Paris with so much precipitation that "it never entered my mind that we were at war with France," and that on his arrival in Dover it suddenly occurred to him he was without a passport. However, this did not impede his journey, and when he arrived at Versailles, the Duke of Choiseul, French Foreign Minister, had one sent to him. In Paris he was cheered by his French admirers, and in Frontignac was invited to theatricals by the English colony. (pp. 22–23)

[35]See on this also Fuller, *The Conduct of War*, chap. 1. Fuller here (p. 23) quotes Daniel Defoe to the effect that often "armies of fifty thousand men of a side stand at bay within view of one another, and spend a whole campaign in dodging, or, as it is genteely called, observing one another, and then march off into winter quarters"; and similarly, Sir John Fontescue is quoted with the observation that

To force an enemy to consume his own supply was much, to compel him to supply his opponents was more, to take up winter-quarters in his territory was very much more. Thus to enter an enemy's borders and keep him marching backwards and forwards for weeks without giving him a chance of striking a blow, was in itself no small success. (p. 25)

paid, but a just proportion was always kept between the value of the stake and the risks to be taken, and the parties were always on guard against the kind of obstinacy which makes a player lose his head. They tried to keep the game in hand and to know when to stop.[36]

In contrast, democratic wars tend to be total wars. In blurring the distinction between the rulers and the ruled, a democratic republic strengthens the identification of the public with a particular state. Indeed, while dynastic rule promotes the identification with one's own family and community and the development of a "cosmopolitan" outlook and attitude,[37] democratic republicanism inevitably leads to

---

[36]Guglielmo Ferrero, *Peace and War* (Freeport, N.Y.: Books for Libraries Press, 1969), pp. 5–7. See also Fuller, *The Conduct of War*, pp. 20–25; idem, *War and Western Civilization*, pp. 26–29; Howard, *War in European History*, chap. 4; Palmer and Colton, *A History of the Western World*, pp. 274–75. In the eighteenth century, they note,

> never had war been so harmless, . . . This was one reason why governments went to war so lightly. On the other hand governments also withdrew from war much more easily than in later times. Their treasuries might be exhausted, their trained soldiers used up; only practical and rational questions were at stake; there was no war hysteria or pressure of mass opinion; the enemy of today might be the ally of tomorrow. Peace was almost as easy to make as war. Peace treaties were negotiated, not imposed. So the eighteenth century saw a series of wars and treaties, more wars, treaties, and rearrangements of alliances, all arising over much the same issues, and with exactly the same powers present at the end as at the beginning. (Ibid.)

[37]As the result of marriages, bequests, inheritances, etc., royal territories were often discontiguous, and kings frequently came to rule linguistically and culturally distinct populations. Accordingly, they found it in their interest to speak several languages: universal ones such as Latin, and then French, as well as local ones such as English, German, Italian, Russian, Dutch, Czech, etc. (See Malcolm Vale, "Civilization of Courts and Cities in the North, 1200–1500," in *Oxford History of Medieval Europe*, George Holmes, ed. [Oxford: Oxford University Press, 1988], pp. 322–23.) Likewise the small social and intellectual elites were usually proficient in several languages and thereby demonstrated their simultaneously local and supra-local, or cosmopolitan–intellectual orientation. This cosmopolitan outlook came to bear in the fact that throughout the monarchical age until 1914, Europe was characterized by a nearly complete freedom of migration. "A man could travel across the length and breadth of the Continent without a passport until he reached the frontiers of Russia and the Ottoman Empire. He could settle in a foreign country for work or leisure without formalities except, occasionally, some health requirements. Every currency was as good as gold" (A.J.P. Taylor, *From Sarajevo to Potsdam* [New York: Harcourt, Brace and World, 1966], p. 7). In contrast, today in the age of democratic republicanism, it has become unthinkable that one might be ruled by a "foreigner," or that states could be anything but contiguously extended territories. States are defined by their citizens, and citizens in turn are defined by their state passports. International migration is strictly regulated and controlled. Political rulers and the intellectual elite, far more numerous now, are increasingly ignorant of foreign

nationalism, i.e., the emotional identification of the public with large, anonymous groups of people, characterized in terms of a common language, history, religion and/or culture and in contradistinction to other, foreign nations. Interstate wars are thus transformed into national wars. Rather than representing "merely" violent dynastic property disputes, which may be "resolved" through acts of territorial occupation, they become battles between different ways of life, which can only be "resolved" through cultural, linguistic, or religious domination and subjugation (or extermination). It becomes more and more difficult for members of the public to remain neutral or to extricate themselves from all personal involvement. Resistance against higher taxes to fund a war is increasingly considered treachery or treason. Conscription becomes the rule, rather than the exception. And with mass armies of cheap and hence easily disposable conscripts fighting for national supremacy (or against national suppression) backed by the economic resources of the entire nation, all distinctions between combatants and noncombatants fall by the wayside, and wars become increasingly brutal. "Once the state ceased to be regarded as 'property' of dynastic princes," notes Michael Howard,

> and became instead the instrument of powerful forces dedicated to such abstract concepts as Liberty, or Nationality, or Revolution, which enabled large numbers of the population to see in that state the embodiment of some absolute Good for which no price was too high, no sacrifice too great to pay; then the "temperate and indecisive contests" of the rococo age appeared as absurd anachronisms.[38]

---

languages. It is no coincidence that of all the members of the European Parliament, only Otto von Habsburg, the current family head of the former Habsburg rulers, speaks all of the parliament's official business languages.

For a prominent, highly apologetic historical treatment of the transition from cosmopolitanism to nationalism in nineteenth-century Germany, see Friedrich Meinecke, *Cosmopolitanism and the National State* (Princeton, N.J.: Princeton University Press, 1970).

[38]Howard, *War in European Civilization*, pp. 75–76. See also Marshal Ferdinand Foch, *The Principles of War* (Chapham and Hall, 1918):

> A new era had begun, the era of national wars, of wars which were to assume a maddening pace; for those wars were destined to throw into the fight all the resources of the nation; they were to set themselves the goal, not of a dynastic interest, not the conquest or possession of a province, but the defense or propagation of philosophical ideas in the first place, next of principles of independence, of unity, of nonmaterial advantages of various kinds. Lastly, they staked upon the issue the interests and fortune of every individual private. Hence the rise of passions, that is elements of force, hitherto in the main unused. (p. 30)

In distinct contrast to the limited warfare of the *ancien régime*, then, the new era of democratic–republican warfare, which began with the French Revolution and the Napoleonic wars, which is further exhibited during the nineteenth century by the American War of Southern Independence, and which reaches its apex during the twentieth century with World War I and World War II and continues to the present, is the era of total war. As William A. Orton has summarized it:

> Nineteenth-century wars were kept within bounds by the tradition, well recognized in international law, that civilian property and business were outside the sphere of combat. Civilian assets were not exposed to arbitrary distraint or permanent seizure, and apart from such territorial and financial stipulations as one state might impose on another, the economic and cultural life of the belligerents was generally allowed to continue pretty much as it had been. Twentieth-century practice has changed all that. During both World Wars limitless lists of contraband coupled with unilateral declarations of maritime law put every sort of commerce in jeopardy, and made waste paper of all

---

Similarly concludes Fuller (*War and Western Civilization*, pp. 26–27):

> The influence of the spirit of nationality, that is of democracy, on war was profound, . . . [it] emotionalized war and, consequently, brutalized it; . . . In the eighteenth century wars were largely the occupation of kings, courtiers and gentlemen. Armies lived on their depots, they interfered as little as possible with the people, and as soldiers were paid out of the king's privy purse they were too costly to be thrown away lightly on massed attacks. The change came about with the French Revolution, sansculottism replaced courtiership, and as armies became more and more the instruments of the people, not only did they grow in size but in ferocity. National armies fight nations, royal armies fight their like, the first obey a mob—always demented, the second a king—generally sane. . . . All this developed out of the French Revolution, which also gave to the world conscription—herd warfare, and the herd coupling with finance and commerce has begotten new realms of war. For when once the whole nation fights, then is the whole national credit available for the purposes of war.

And on the effects of conscription in particular, Fuller notes (*Conduct of War*, pp. 33 and 35):

> Conscription changed the basis of warfare. Hitherto soldiers had been costly, now they were cheap; battles had been avoided, now they were sought, and however heavy were the losses, they could rapidly be made good by the muster-roll. . . . From August [of 1793, when the parliament of the French republic decreed universal compulsory military service] onward, not only was war to become more and more unlimited, but finally total. In the fourth decade of the twentieth century life was held so cheaply that the massacre of civilian populations on wholesale lines became as accepted a strategic aim as battles were in previous wars. In 150 years conscription had led the world back to tribal barbarism.

precedents. The close of the first war was marked by a determined and successful effort to impair the economic recovery of the principal losers, and to retain certain civilian properties. The second war has seen the extension of that policy to a point at which international law in war has ceased to exist. For years the Government of Germany, so far as its arm could reach, had based a policy of confiscation on a racial theory that had no standing in civil law, international law, nor Christian ethics; and when the war began, that violation of the comity of nations proved contagious. Anglo-American leadership, in both speech and action, launched a crusade that admitted of neither legal nor territorial limits to the exercise of coercion. The concept of neutrality was denounced in both theory and practice. Not only enemy assets and interests, but the assets and interests of any parties whatsoever, even in neutral countries, were exposed to every constraint the belligerent powers could make effective; and the assets and interests of neutral states and their civilians, lodged in belligerent territories or under belligerent control, were subjected to practically the same sort of coercion as those of enemy nationals. Thus "total war" became a sort of war that no civilian community could hope to escape; and "peace loving nations" will draw the obvious inference.[39]

RETROSPECTIVE AND PROSPECTS

The process of civilization set in motion by individual saving, investment, and the accumulation of durable consumer goods and capital goods—of gradually falling time preferences and an ever widening and lengthening range and horizon of private provisions—may be temporarily upset by crime. But because a person is permitted to defend himself against crime, the existence of criminal activities does not alter the direction of the process. It merely leads to more defense spending and less nondefense spending.

Instead, a change in direction—stagnating or even rising time preferences—can be brought about only if property-rights violations become *institutionalized*; i.e., in the environment of a government. Whereas all governments must be assumed to have a tendency toward internal growth as well as territorial expansion (political centralization), not all forms of government can be expected to be equally successful in their endeavors. If the government is privately owned (under monarchical rule), the incentive structure facing the ruler is such that it is in his self-interest to be relatively farsighted and to engage only in moderate taxation and warfare. The speed of the process of civilization will be slowed

---

[39]William A. Orton, *The Liberal Tradition: A Study of the Social and Spiritual Conditions of Freedom* (Port Washington, N.Y.: Kennikat Press, 1969), pp. 251–52.

down systematically. However, the decivilizing forces arising from monarchical rule may be expected to be insufficiently strong to overcome the fundamental, countervailing tendency toward falling time-preference rates and ever-expanding ranges of private provisions. Rather, it is only when a government is *publicly* owned (under democratic–republican rule) that the decivilizing effects of government can be expected to grow strong enough to actually halt the civilizing process, or even to alter its direction and bring about an opposite tendency toward decivilization: capital consumption, shrinking planning horizons and provisions, and a progressive infantilization and brutalization of social life.

Retrospectively, in light of these theoretical conclusions much of modern European and Western history can be rationally reconstructed and understood. In the course of one and a half centuries—beginning with the American and French Revolutions and continuing to the present—Europe, and in its wake the entire western world, has undergone an epochal transformation. Everywhere, monarchical rule and sovereign kings were replaced by democratic–republican rule and sovereign "peoples."[40]

The first direct attack by republicanism and popular sovereignty on the monarchical principle was repelled with the military defeat of Napoleon and the restoration of Bourbon rule in France. As a result of the Napoleonic experience, republicanism was widely discredited during much of the nineteenth-century. "Republicanism was still thought to be violent—bellicose in its foreign policy, turbulent in its political workings, unfriendly to the church, and socialistic or at least equalitarian in its view of property and private wealth."[41] Still, the democratic–republican spirit of the French Revolution left a permanent imprint. From the restoration of the monarchical order in 1815 until the outbreak of World War I in 1914, popular political participation and representation was systematically expanded all across Europe. Everywhere the franchise

---

[40]On the historical significance and the revolutionary character of this transformation see Guglielmo Ferrero, *Peace and War*, esp. pp. 155ff; idem, *Macht* (Bern: A. Francke, 1944); Robert R. Palmer and Joel Colton, *A History of the Modern World*, esp. chaps. 14 and 18; also Reinhard Bendix, *Kings or People* (Berkeley: University of California Press, 1978).

On the intellectual debate on the idea of popular sovereignty, and universal suffrage, in particular in Great Britain, see Elie Halevy, *The Growth of Philosophical Radicalism* (Boston: Beacon Press, 1955), esp. pp. 120–50.

[41]Palmer and Colton, *A History of the Modern World*, p. 606.

was successively widened, and the powers of popularly elected parliaments were gradually increased.[42]

Nonetheless, although increasingly emasculated, the principle of monarchical government remained dominant until the cataclysmic events of World War I. Before the war only two republics existed in Europe: Switzerland and France. Only four years later, after the United States government had entered the European war and decisively determined its outcome, monarchies had all but disappeared, and Europe had turned to democratic republicanism. With the involvement of the U.S., the war took on a new dimension. Rather than being an old-fashioned territorial dispute, as was the case before 1917, it turned into an ideological war. The U.S. had been founded as a republic, and the democratic principle in particular, inherent in the idea of a republic, had only recently been carried to victory as the result of the violent defeat and devastation of the secessionist Confederacy by the centralist Union government. At the time of World War I, this triumphant ideology of expansionist democratic–republicanism had found its very personification in then-U.S. President Woodrow Wilson. Under Wilson's administration the European war became an ideological mission—to make the world safe for democracy and free of dynastic rulers.[43] Hence, the defeated Romanovs, Hohenzollerns, and Habsburgs had to abdicate or resign, and Russia, Germany, and Austria became democratic republics with universal—male and female—suffrage and parliamentary governments. Likewise, all of the newly created successor states—Poland, Finland, Estonia, Latvia, Lithuania, Hungary, and Czechoslovakia adopted democratic–republican constitutions, with Yugoslavia as the only exception. In Turkey and Greece, the monarchies were overthrown. And even where monarchies remained in existence, as in Great Britain, Italy, Spain, Belgium, the Netherlands, and the Scandinavian countries, monarchs no longer exercised any governmental power. Everywhere, universal adult suffrage was introduced, and all government power was invested in parliaments and "public" officials.[44]

---

[42]For the details of this process see Flora, *State, Economy, and Society in Western Europe*, chap. 3.

[43]On the U.S. war involvement see Fuller, *The Conduct of War*, chap. 9; on the role of Woodrow Wilson in particular, see Murray N. Rothbard, "World War I as Fulfillment: Power and the Intellectuals," *Journal of Libertarian Studies* 9, no. 1 (1989); Paul Gottfried, "Wilsonianism: The Legacy that Won't Die," *Journal of Libertarian Studies* 9, no. 2 (1990).

[44]Interestingly, the Swiss republic, which was the first country to firmly establish the institution of universal suffrage for males above the age of 20 (1848), was the last to expand the suffrage also to women (1971).

A new era—the democratic–republican age under the aegis of a domi-
nating U.S. government—had begun.

From the perspective of economic theory, the end of World War I can
be identified as the point in time at which private-government ownership was completely replaced by public government ownership, and
from which a tendency toward rising degrees of social time preference,
government growth, and an attending process of decivilization should
be expected to have taken off. Indeed, as indicated in detail above, such
has been the grand underlying theme of twentieth century Western history.[45] Since 1918, practically all indicators of high or rising time preferences have exhibited a systematic upward tendency: as far as
government is concerned, democratic republicanism produced communism (and with this public slavery and government sponsored mass
murder even in peacetime), fascism, national socialism and, lastly and
most enduringly, social democracy ("liberalism").[46] Compulsory military service has become almost universal, foreign and civil wars have
increased in frequency and in brutality, and the process of political centralization has advanced further than ever. Internally, democratic republicanism has led to permanently rising taxes, debts, and public
employment. It has led to the destruction of the gold standard, unparalleled paper-money inflation, and increased protectionism and migration controls. Even the most fundamental private law provisions have
been perverted by an unabating flood of legislation and regulation. Simultaneously, as regards civil society, the institutions of marriage and
family have been increasingly weakened, the number of children has
declined, and the rates of divorce, illegitimacy, single parenthood, singledom, and abortion have increased. Rather than rising with rising
incomes, savings rates have been stagnating or even falling. In comparison to the nineteenth century, the cognitive prowess of the political and
intellectual elites and the quality of public education have declined. And

---

[45]On the worldwide growth of statism since World War I see Paul Johnson, *Modern Times: The World from the Twenties to the Eighties* (New York: Harper and Row,
1983); on U.S. government growth, and its relation to war, see Robert Higgs, *Crisis
and Leviathan: Critical Episodes in the Growth of American Government* (New York:
Oxford University Press, 1987).

[46]On the common historical roots of Soviet communism, and of fascism and
national socialism as "tyrannies" (literally: "arbitrary powers, the holders of which
claim to use it for the people and in fact appeal to the people, for support")—in
World War I, and on the "primary" character of the former and the "derivative" of
the latter, see Elie Halevy, *The Era of Tyrannies* (Garden City, N.Y.: Anchor Books,
1965).

the rates of crime, structural unemployment, welfare dependency, parasitism, negligence, recklessness, incivility, psychopathy, and hedonism have increased.

Ultimately, the course of human history is determined by ideas, whether they are true or false. Just as kings could not exercise their rule unless public opinion accepted their rule as legitimate, so democratic rulers are equally dependent on public opinion to sustain their political power. It is public opinion, therefore, that must change if we are to prevent the process of decivilization from running its full course. And just as monarchy was once accepted as legitimate but is today considered to be an unthinkable solution to the current social crisis, it is not inconceivable that the idea of democratic rule might someday be regarded as morally illegitimate and politically unthinkable. Such a delegitimation is a necessary precondition to avoiding ultimate social catastrophe. It is not government (monarchical or democratic) that is the source of human civilization and social peace but private property, and the recognition and defense of private property rights, contractualism, and individual responsibility.

2

On Monarchy, Democracy, and the Idea of Natural Order

THEORY:
THE COMPARATIVE ECONOMICS
OF PRIVATE AND PUBLIC GOVERNMENT OWNERSHIP

A government is a territorial monopolist of compulsion—an agency which may engage in continual, institutionalized property rights violations and the exploitation—in the form of expropriation, taxation and regulation—of private property owners. Assuming no more than self-interest on the part of government agents, all governments must be expected to make use of this monopoly and exhibit a tendency toward *increased* exploitation.[1] However, not every form of government can be expected to be equally successful in this endeavor or to go about it in the same way. Rather, in light of elementary economic theory, the conduct of government and the effects of government policy on civil society can be expected to be systematically different, depending on whether the government apparatus is owned privately or publicly.[2]

The defining characteristic of private government ownership is that the expropriated resources and the monopoly privilege of future expropriation are individually *owned*. The appropriated resources are added to the ruler's private estate and treated as if they were a part of it, and the monopoly privilege of future expropriation is attached as a title to this

---

[1]On the theory of the state see Murray N. Rothbard, *For A New Liberty* (New York: Macmillan, 1978); idem, *The Ethics of Liberty* (New York: New York University Press, 1998); idem, *Power and Market* (Kansas City: Sheed Andrews and McMeel, 1977); Hans-Hermann Hoppe, *Eigentum, Anarchie und Staat* (Opladen: Westdeutscher Verlag, 1987); idem, *A Theory of Socialism and Capitalism* (Boston: Kluwer, 1989); idem, *The Economics and Ethics of Private Property* (Boston: Kluwer, 1993); also Albert J. Nock, *Our Enemy, the State* (Delevan, Wisc.: Hallberg Publishing, 1983); Franz Oppenheimer, *The State* (New York: Vanguard Press, 1914); idem, *System der Soziologie*, vol., *Der Staat* (Stuttgart: Gustav Fischer, 1964).

[2]See on the following also chaps. 1, 3, and 13.

estate and leads to an instant increase in its present value ('capitalization' of monopoly profit). Most importantly, as private owner of the government estate, the ruler is entitled to pass his possessions onto his personal heir; he may sell, rent, or give away part or all of his privileged estate and privately pocket the receipts from the sale or rental; and he may personally employ or dismiss every administrator and employee of his estate.

In contrast, with a publicly owned government the control over the government apparatus lies in the hands of a trustee, or caretaker. The caretaker may use the apparatus to his personal advantage, but he does not own it. He cannot sell government resources and privately pocket the receipts, nor can he pass government possessions onto his personal heir. He owns the *current use* of government resources, but not their capital value. Moreover, while entrance into the position of a private owner of government is restricted by the owner's personal discretion, entrance into the position of a caretaker–ruler is open. Anyone, in principle, can become the government's caretaker.

From these assumptions two central, interrelated predictions can be deduced: (1) A private government owner will tend to have a systematically longer planning horizon, i.e., his degree of time preference will be lower, and accordingly, his degree of economic exploitation will tend to be less than that of a government caretaker; and (2), subject to a higher degree of exploitation the nongovernmental public will also be comparatively more present-oriented under a system of publicly-owned government than under a regime of private government ownership.

(1) A private government owner will predictably try to maximize his total wealth; i.e., the present value of his estate *and* his current income. He will *not* want to increase his current income at the expense of a more than proportional drop in the present value of his assets, and because acts of current income acquisition invariably have repercussions on present asset values (reflecting the value of all future—expected—asset earnings discounted by the rate of time preference), private ownership in and of itself leads to economic calculation and thus promotes farsightedness. In the case of the private ownership of *government*, this implies a distinct moderation with respect to the ruler's incentive to exploit his monopoly privilege of expropriation, for acts of expropriation are by their nature parasitic upon prior acts of production on the part of the nongovernmental public. Where nothing has first been produced, nothing can be expropriated; and where everything is expropriated, all future production will come to a shrieking halt. Accordingly, a private

government owner will want to avoid exploiting his subjects so heavily, for instance, as to reduce his future earnings potential to such an extent that the present value of his estate actually falls. Instead, in order to preserve or possibly even enhance the value of his personal property, he will systematically restrain himself in his exploitation policies. For the lower the degree of exploitation, the more productive the subject population will be; and the more productive the population, the higher will be the value of the ruler's parasitic monopoly of expropriation. He will use his monopolistic privilege, of course. He will not *not* exploit. But as the government's private owner, it is in his interest to draw parasitically on a growing, increasingly productive and prosperous nongovernment economy as this would effortlessly also increase his own wealth and prosperity—and the degree of exploitation thus would tend to be low.

Moreover, private ownership of government implies moderation and farsightedness for yet another reason. All private property is by definition exclusive property. He who owns property is entitled to exclude everyone else from its use and enjoyment; and he is at liberty to choose with whom, if anyone, he is willing to share in its usage. Typically, he will include his family and exclude all others, except as invited guests or as paid employees or contractors. Only the ruling family—and to a minor extent its friends, employees and business partners—share in the enjoyment of the expropriated resources and can thus lead a parasitic life. Because of these restrictions regarding entrance into government and the exclusive status of the individual ruler and his family, private government ownership stimulates the development of a clear "class consciousness" on the part of the nongovernment public and promotes the opposition and resistance to any expansion of the government's exploitative power. A clear-cut distinction between the (few) rulers on the one hand and the (many) ruled on the other exists, and there is little risk or hope of anyone of either class ever falling or rising from one class to the other. Confronted with an almost insurmountable barrier in the way of upward mobility, the solidarity among the ruled—their mutual identification as actual or potential victims of governmental property rights violations—is strengthened, and the risk to the ruling class of losing its legitimacy as the result of increased exploitation is heightened.[3]

In distinct contrast, the caretaker of a publicly owned government will try to maximize not total government wealth (capital values and

---

[3]See also Bertrand de Jouvenel, *On Power: The Natural History of its Growth* (New York: Viking, 1949), esp. pp. 9–10.

current income) but current income (regardless, and at the expense, of capital values). Indeed, even if the caretaker wishes to act differently, he *cannot*, for as public property government resources are unsaleable, and without market prices economic calculation is *impossible*. Accordingly, it must be regarded as unavoidable that public government ownership will result in continual capital consumption. Instead of maintaining or even enhancing the value of the government estate, as a private owner would tend to do, a government's temporary caretaker will quickly use up as much of the government resources as possible, for what he does not consume *now*, he may *never* be able to consume. In particular, a care-taker—as distinct from a government's private owner—has no interest in not ruining his country. For why should he *not* want to increase his exploitation, if the advantage of a policy of moderation—the resulting higher capital value of the government estate—can*not* be reaped pri-vately, while the advantage of the opposite policy of increased exploita-tion—a higher current income—*can* be so reaped? To a caretaker, unlike to a private owner, moderation has only disadvantages.[4]

In addition, with a publicly owned government anyone in principle can become a member of the ruling class or even the supreme power. The distinction between the rulers and the ruled as well as the class con-sciousness of the ruled become blurred. The illusion even arises that the distinction no longer exists: that with a public government no one is ruled by anyone, but everyone instead rules himself. Accordingly, pub-lic resistance against government power is systematically weakened. While exploitation and expropriation before might have appeared plainly oppressive and evil to the public, they seem much less so, man-kind being what it is, once anyone may freely enter the ranks of those who are at the receiving end. Consequently, not only will exploitation increase, whether openly in the form of higher taxes or discretely as increased governmental money "creation" (inflation) or legislative regulation. Likewise, the number of government employees ("public servants") will rise absolutely as well as relatively to private employ-ment, in particular attracting and promoting individuals with high de-grees of time preference, and limited farsightedness.

---

[4]See Rothbard, *Power and Market*, pp. 188–89; also *Managing the Commons*, Garret Hardin and John Baden, eds. (San Francisco: W.H. Freeman, 1977); and Mancur Olson, "Dictatorship, Democracy, and Development," *American Political Science Re-view* 87, no. 3 (1993).

(2) In contrast to the right of self-defense in the event of a criminal attack, the victim of government violations of private property rights may not legitimately defend himself against such violations.[5]

The imposition of a government tax on property or income violates a property owner's and income producer's rights as much as theft does. In both cases the owner–producer's supply of goods is diminished against his will and without his consent. Government money or "liquidity" creation involves no less a fraudulent expropriation of private property owners than the operations of a criminal counterfeiting gang. As well, any government regulation as to what an owner may or may not do with his property—beyond the rule that no one may physically damage the property of others and that all exchange and trade be voluntary and contractual—implies the "taking" of somebody's property, on a par with acts of extortion, robbery, or destruction. But taxation, the government's provision for liquidity, and government regulations, unlike their criminal equivalents, are considered legitimate, and the victim of government interference, unlike the victim of a crime, is *not* entitled to physically defend and protect his property.

Owing to their legitimacy, then, government violations of property rights affect individual time preferences in a systematically different and much more profound way than does crime. Like crime, all government interference with private property rights reduces someone's supply of present goods and thus raises his effective time preference rate. However, government offenses—unlike crime—simultaneously raise the time preference *degree* of actual and potential victims because they also imply a reduction in the supply of *future* goods (a reduced rate of return on investment). Crime, because it is illegitimate, occurs only intermittently—the robber disappears from the scene with his loot and leaves his victim alone. Thus, crime can be dealt with by increasing one's demand for protective goods and services (relative to that for nonprotection goods) so as to restore or even increase one's future rate of investment return and make it less likely that the same or a different robber will succeed a second time. In contrast, because they are legitimate, governmental property rights violations are continual. The offender does not disappear into hiding but stays around, and the victim does not arm himself but must (at least he is generally expected to) remain defenseless. The actual and potential victims of government property rights violations—as demonstrated by their continued defenselessness

---

[5]In addition to the works quoted in note 1 above, see Lysander Spooner, *No Treason: The Constitution of No Authority* (Larkspur, Colo.: Pine Tree Press, 1966), p. 17.

vis-à-vis their offenders—respond by associating a permanently higher risk with all future production and systematically adjusting their expectations concerning the rate of return on all future investment downward. By simultaneously reducing the supply of present *and* expected future goods, governmental property rights violations not only raise time preference *rates* (with given schedules) but also time preference *schedules.* Because owner–producers are (and see themselves as) defenseless against future victimization by government agents, their expected rate of return on productive, future-oriented actions is reduced all-around, and accordingly, all actual and potential victims become more present-oriented.[6]

Moreover, because the degree of exploitation is comparatively higher under a publicly owned government, this tendency toward present-orientation will be significantly more pronounced if the government is publicly owned than if it is owned privately.[7]

APPLICATION:
THE TRANSITION FROM
MONARCHY TO DEMOCRACY (1789–1918)

Hereditary monarchies represent the historical example of privately owned governments, and democratic republics that of publicly owned governments.

Throughout most of its history, mankind, insofar as it was subject to any government control at all, was under monarchical rule. There were exceptions: Athenian democracy, Rome during its republican era until 31 B.C., the republics of Venice, Florence, and Genoa during the Renaissance period, the Swiss cantons since 1291, the United Provinces from 1648 until 1673, and England under Cromwell from 1649 until 1660. Yet these were rare occurrences in a world dominated by monarchies. With the exception of Switzerland, they were short-lived phenomena. Constrained by monarchical surroundings, all older republics satisfied the open entry condition of public property only imperfectly, for while a

---

[6]On the phenomenon and theory of time preference see in particular Ludwig von Mises, *Human Action: A Treatise on Economics,* Scholar's Edition (Auburn, Ala.: Ludwig von Mises Institute, 1998), chaps. 18 and 19; also William Stanley Jevons, *Theory of Political Economy* (New York: Augustus M. Kelley, 1965); Eugen von Böhm-Bawerk, *Capital and Interest,* 3 vols. (South Holland, Ill.: Libertarian Press, 1959); Frank Fetter, *Capital, Interest, and Rent* (Kansas City: Sheed Andrews and McMeel, 1977); Murray N. Rothbard, *Man, Economy, and State,* 2 vols. (Auburn, Ala.: Ludwig von Mises Institute, 1993).

[7]See also chaps. 1, 3, and 13.

republican form of government implies by definition that the government is not privately but publicly owned, and a republic can thus be expected to possess an inherent tendency toward the adoption of universal suffrage, in all of the earlier republics, entry into government was limited to relatively small groups of "nobles."

With the end of World War I, mankind truly left the monarchical age.[8] In the course of one and a half centuries since the French Revolution, Europe, and in its wake the entire world, have undergone a fundamental transformation. Everywhere, monarchical rule and sovereign kings were replaced by democratic–republican rule and sovereign "peoples."

The first assault of republicanism and the idea of popular sovereignty on the dominating monarchical principle was repelled with the military defeat of Napoleon and the restoration of Bourbon rule in France; and as a result of the revolutionary terror and the Napoleonic wars, republicanism was widely discredited for much of the nineteenth century. However, the democratic–republican spirit of the French Revolution left a permanent imprint. From the restoration of the monarchical order in 1815 until the outbreak of World War I in 1914, all across Europe popular political participation and representation was systematically expanded. The franchise was successively widened and the powers of popularly elected parliaments increased everywhere.[9]

From 1815 to 1830, the right to vote in France was still severely restricted under the restored Bourbons. Out of a population of some 30 million, the electorate included only France's very largest property owners—about 100,000 people (less than one-half of one percent of the population above the age of twenty). As a result of the July Revolution of 1830, the abdication of Charles X and the coronation of the Duke of Orleans, Louis Philippe, the number of voters increased to about 200,000. As a result of the revolutionary upheavals of 1848, France again turned republican, and universal and unrestricted suffrage for all male citizens above the age of twenty-one was introduced. Napoleon III was elected by nearly 5.5 million votes out of an electorate of more than 8 million.

---

[8]See on this Guglielmo Ferrero, *Peace and War* (Freeport, N.Y.: Books for Libraries Press, 1969), esp. chap. 3; idem, *Macht* (Bern: A. Francke, 1944); Erik von Kuehnelt-Leddihn, *Leftism Revisited* (Washington D.C.: Henry Regnery, 1990); Reinhard Bendix, *Kings or People* (Berkeley: University of California Press, 1978).

[9]For a detailed documentation see Peter Flora, *State, Economy, and Society in Western Europe 1815–1975* (Frankfurt/M.: Campus, 1983), vol. 1, chap. 3; also Robert R. Palmer and Joel Colton, *A History of the Modern World* (New York: Alfred Knopf, 1992), esp. chaps. 14 and 18.

In the United Kingdom, after 1815 the electorate consisted of some 500,000 well-to-do property owners (about 4 percent of the population above age 20). The Reform Bill of 1832 lowered the property owner requirements and extended the franchise to about 800,000. The next extension, from about 1 million to 2 million, came with the Second Reform Bill of 1867. In 1884 property restrictions were relaxed even further and the electorate increased to about 6 million (almost a third of the population above age 20 and more than three-fourths of all male adults).

In Prussia, as the most important of the thirty-nine independent German states recognized after the Vienna Congress, democratization set in with the revolution of 1848 and the constitution of 1850. The lower chamber of the Prussian parliament was hence elected by universal male suffrage. However, until 1918 the electorate remained stratified into three estates with different voting powers. For example, the wealthiest people—those who contributed a third of all taxes—elected a third of the members of the lower house. In 1867 the North German Confederation, including Prussia and twenty-one other German states, was founded. Its constitution provided for universal unrestricted suffrage for all males above the age of twenty-five. In 1871, after the victory over Napoleon III, the constitution of the North German Confederation was essentially adopted by the newly founded German Empire. Out of a total population of around 35 million, nearly 8 million people (or about a third of the population over twenty) elected the first German *Reichstag*.

After Italy's political unification under the leadership of the Kingdom of Sardinia and Piedmont in 1861, the vote was only given to about 500,000 people out of a population of some 25 million (about 3.5 percent of the population above age twenty). In 1882, the property requirements were relaxed, and the minimum voting age was lowered from twenty-five to twenty-one years. As a result, the Italian electorate increased to more than 2 million. In 1913, almost universal and unrestricted suffrage for all males above thirty and minimally restricted suffrage for males above twenty-one was introduced, raising the number of Italian voters to more than 8 million (more than 40 percent of the population above twenty).

In Austria, restricted and unequal male suffrage was introduced in 1873. The electorate, composed of four classes or *curiae* of unequal voting powers, totaled 1.2 million voters out of a population of about 20 million (10 percent of the population above twenty). In 1867 a fifth *curia* was added. Forty years later the *curia* system was abolished, and universal and equal suffrage for males above age twenty-four was adopted, bringing the number of voters close to 6 million (almost 40 percent of the population above twenty).

Russia had elected provincial and district councils—*zemstvos*—since 1864; and in 1905, as a fallout of its lost war against Japan, it created a parliament—the *Duma*—which was elected by near universal, although indirect and unequal, male suffrage. As for Europe's minor powers, universal or almost universal and equal male suffrage has existed in Switzerland since 1848, and was adopted between 1890 and 1910 in Belgium, the Netherlands, Norway, Sweden, Spain, Greece, Bulgaria, Serbia, and Turkey.

Although increasingly emasculated, the monarchical principle dominated until the cataclysmic events of World War I. Before 1914, only two republics existed in Europe—France and Switzerland. And of all major European monarchies, only the United Kingdom could be classified as a parliamentary system; that is, one in which supreme power was vested in an elected parliament. Only four years later, after the United States—where the democratic principle implied in the idea of a republic had only recently been carried to victory as a result of the destruction of the secessionist Confederacy by the centralist Union government[10]—had entered the European war and decisively determined its outcome, monarchies had all but disappeared, and Europe turned to democratic republicanism.[11]

In Europe, the defeated Romanovs, Hohenzollerns, and Habsburgs had to abdicate or resign, and Russia, Germany, and Austria became democratic republics with universal—male and female—suffrage and parliamentary governments. Likewise, all of the newly created successor states—Poland, Finland, Estonia, Latvia, Lithuania, Hungary, and Czechoslovakia (with the sole exception of Yugoslavia)—adopted democratic–republican constitutions. In Turkey and Greece, the monarchies were overthrown. Even where monarchies remained nominally in existence, as in Great Britain, Italy, Spain, Belgium, the Netherlands, and

---

[10]On the aristocratic (*undemocratic*) character of the early U.S., see Lord Acton, "Political Causes of the American Revolution" in idem, *The Liberal Interpretation of History* (Chicago: University of Chicago Press, 1967); also, Chris Woltermann, "Federalism, Democracy and the People," *Telos* 26, no. 1 (1993).

[11]On the U.S. war involvement see John F.C. Fuller, *The Conduct of War* (New York: Da Capo, 1992), chap. 9; on the role of Woodrow Wilson, and his policy of wanting to "make the world safe for democracy," see Murray N. Rothbard, "World War I as Fulfillment: Power and the Intellectuals," *Journal of Libertarian Studies* 9, no. 1 (1989); Paul Gottfried, "Wilsonianism: The Legacy that Won't Die," *Journal of Libertarian Studies* 9, no. 2 (1990); Kuehnelt-Leddihn, *Leftism Revisited*, chap. 15.

the Scandinavian countries, monarchs no longer exercised any govern-ing power. Universal adult suffrage was introduced, and all govern-ment power was invested in parliaments and "public" officials.[12] A new world order—the democratic–republican age under the aegis of a domi-nating U.S. government—had begun.

EVIDENCE AND ILLUSTRATIONS:
EXPLOITATION AND PRESENT-ORIENTEDNESS UNDER
MONARCHY AND DEMOCRATIC REPUBLICANISM

From the viewpoint of economic theory, the end of World War I can be identified as the point in time at which private government owner-ship was completely replaced by public government ownership, and whence a systematic tendency toward increased exploitation—govern-ment growth—and rising degrees of social time preference—present-orientedness—can be expected to take off. Indeed, such has been the grand, underlying theme of post-World War I Western history: With some forebodings in the last third of the nineteenth century in conjunc-tion with an increased emasculation of the *ancien régimes*, from 1918 onward practically all indicators of governmental exploitation and of rising time preferences have exhibited a systematic upward tendency.

Indicators of Exploitation

There is no doubt that the amount of *taxes* imposed on civil society increased during the monarchical age.[13] However, throughout the entire period, the *share* of government revenue remained remarkably stable and low. Economic historian Carlo M. Cipolla concludes,

> All in all, one must admit that the portion of income drawn by the public sector most certainly increased from the eleventh century on-ward all over Europe, but it is difficult to imagine that, apart from particular times and places, the public power ever managed to draw more than 5 to 8 percent of national income.

And he then goes on to note that this portion was not systematically exceeded until the second half of the nineteenth century.[14] In feudal times, observes Bertrand de Jouvenel,

---

[12]Interestingly, the Swiss Republic, which had been the first country to establish universal male suffrage (in 1848), was the last to expand suffrage also to women (in 1971). Similarly, the French Republic, where universal male suffrage had existed since 1848, extended the franchise to women only in 1945.

[13]See Hans Joachim Schoeps, *Preussen. Geschichte eines Staates* (Frankfurt/M.: Ullstein, 1981), p. 405 on data for England, Prussia, and Austria.

[14]Carlo M. Cipolla, *Before the Industrial Revolution: European Society and Economy, 1000–1700* (New York: W.W. Norton, 1980), p. 48.

state expenditures, as we now call them, were thought of . . . as the king's own expenditures, which he incurred by virtue of his station. When he came into his station, he simultaneously came into an "estate" [in the modern sense of the word]; i.e., he found himself endowed with property rights ensuring an income adequate to "the king's needs." It is somewhat as if a government of our own times were expected to cover its ordinary expenditures from the proceeds of state-owned industries.[15]

In the course of the political centralization during the sixteenth and seventeenth centuries, additional sources of government revenue had been opened up: customs, excise duties, and land taxes. However, up until the mid-nineteenth century of all Western European countries only the United Kingdom, for instance, had an income tax (from 1843 on). France first introduced some form of income tax in 1873, Italy in 1877, Norway in 1892, the Netherlands in 1894, Austria in 1898, Sweden in 1903, the U.S. in 1913, Switzerland in 1916, Denmark and Finland in 1917, Ireland and Belgium in 1922, and Germany in 1924.[16] Yet even at the time of the outbreak of World War I, total government expenditure as a percentage of Gross Domestic Product (GDP) typically had not risen above 10 percent and only rarely, as in the case of Germany, exceeded 15 percent. In striking contrast, with the onset of the democratic republican age, total government expenditures as a percentage of GDP typically increased to

---

[15]Bertrand de Jouvenel, *Sovereignty: An Inquiry into the Political Good* (Chicago: University of Chicago Press, 1957), p. 178. "The king," de Jouvenel goes on to explain,

> could not exact contributions, he could only solicit "subsidies." It was stressed that his loyal subjects granted him help of their own free will, and they often seized this occasion to stipulate conditions. For instance, they granted subsidies to John the Good [of France], subject to the condition that he should henceforth refrain from minting money that was defective in weight. . . . In order to replenish his Treasury, the king might go on a begging tour from town to town, expounding his requirements and obtaining local grants, as was done on the eve of the Hundred Years' War; or he might assemble from all parts of the country those whose financial support he craved. It is a serious mistake to confuse such an assembly with a modern sitting parliament, though the latter phenomenon has arisen from the former. The Parliament is sovereign and may exact contributions. The older assemblies should rather be thought of as a gathering of modern company directors agreeing to turn over to the Exchequer a part of their profits, with some trade union leaders present agreeing to part with some of their unions' dues for public purposes. Each group was called on for a grant, and each was thus well placed to make conditions. A modern parliament could not be treated like that, but would impose its will by majority vote. (pp. 178–79)

[16]See Flora, *State, Economy, and Society in Western Europe*, vol. 1, pp. 258–59.

20 to 30 percent in the course of the 1920s and 1930s, and by the mid-1970s had generally reached 50 percent.[17]

There is also no doubt that total *government employment* increased during the monarchical age. But until the very end of the nineteenth century, government employment rarely exceeded 3 percent of the total labor force. Royal ministers and parliamentarians typically did not receive publicly funded salaries but were expected to support themselves out of their private incomes. In contrast, with the advances of the process of democratization, they became salaried officials; and since then government employment has continually increased. In Austria, for instance, government employment as a percentage of the labor force increased from less than 3 percent in 1900 to more than 8 percent in the 1920s and almost 15 percent by the mid-1970s. In France it rose from 3 percent in 1900 to 4 percent in 1920 and about 15 percent in the mid-1970s. In Germany it grew from 5 percent in 1900 to close to 10 percent by the mid-1920s to close to 15 percent in the mid-1970s. In the United Kingdom it increased from less than 3 percent in 1900 to more than 6 percent in the 1920s and again close to 15 percent by the mid-1970s. The trend in Italy and almost everywhere else was similar, and by the mid-1970s only in small Switzerland was government employment still somewhat less than 10 percent of the labor force.[18]

A similar pattern emerges from an inspection of *inflation* and data on the *money supply*. The monarchical world was generally characterized by the existence of a *commodity* money—typically silver or gold—and at long last, after the establishment of a single integrated world market in the course of the seventeenth and eighteenth centuries, by an international gold standard. A commodity money standard makes it difficult, if not impossible, for a government to inflate the money supply. In monopolizing the mint and engaging in "coin-clipping," kings did their best to enrich themselves at the expense of the public. There also had been attempts to introduce an irredeemable fiat currency. Indeed, the history of

---

[17]Ibid, chap. 8. Predictably, government expenditures typically rose during war times. However, the pattern described above applies to war times as well. In Great Britain, for instance, during the height of the Napoleonic Wars government expenditures as a percentage of GDP climbed to almost 25 percent. In contrast, during World War I it reached almost 50 percent, and during World War II it rose to well above 60 percent. See ibid., pp. 440–41.

[18]Ibid, chap. 5. In fact, the current share of government employment of about 15 percent of the labor force must be considered systematically *under*estimated, for apart from excluding all military personnel it also excludes the personnel in hospitals, welfare institutions, social insurance agencies, and nationalized industries.

the Bank of England, for instance, from its inception in 1694 onward was one of the periodic suspension of specie payment—in 1696, 1720, 1745, and from 1797 until 1821. But these fiat money experiments, associated in particular with the Bank of Amsterdam, the Bank of England, and John Law and the Banque Royale of France, had been regional curiosities which ended quickly in financial disasters such as the collapse of the Dutch "Tulip Mania" in 1637 and the "Mississippi Bubble" and the "South Sea Bubble" in 1720. As hard as they tried, monarchical rulers did not succeed in establishing monopolies of *pure fiat currencies*, i.e., of irredeemable government paper monies, which can be created virtually out of thin air, at practically no cost. No particular individual, not even a king, could be trusted with an extraordinary monopoly such as this

It was only under conditions of democratic republicanism—of anonymous and impersonal rule—that this feat was accomplished. During World War I, as during earlier wars, the belligerent governments had gone off the gold standard. Everywhere in Europe, the result was a dramatic increase in the supply of paper money. In defeated Germany, Austria, and Soviet Russia in particular, hyperinflationary conditions ensued in the immediate aftermath of the war. Unlike earlier wars, however, World War I did not conclude with a return to the gold standard. Instead, from the mid-1920s until 1971, and interrupted by a series of international monetary crises, a pseudo gold standard—the gold exchange standard—was implemented. Essentially, only the U.S. would redeem dollars in gold (and from 1933 on, after going off the gold standard domestically, only to foreign central banks). Britain would redeem pounds in dollars (or, rarely, in gold bullion rather than gold coin), and the rest of Europe would redeem their currencies in pounds. Consequently, and as a reflection of the international power hierarchy which had come into existence by the end of World War I, the U.S. government now inflated paper dollars on top of gold, Britain inflated pounds on top of inflating dollars, and the other European countries inflated their paper currencies on top of inflating dollars or pounds (and after 1945 only dollars). Finally, in 1971, with ever larger dollar reserves accumulated in European central banks and the imminent danger of a European "run" on the U.S. gold reserves, even the last remnant of the international gold standard was abolished. Since then, and for the first time in history, the entire world has adopted a pure fiat money system of freely fluctuating government paper currencies.[19]

---

[19]See also Murray N. Rothbard, *What Has Government Done to Our Money?* (Auburn, Ala.: Ludwig von Mises Institute, 1990); Henry Hazlitt, *From Bretton Woods*

As a result, from the beginning of the democratic–republican age—initially under a pseudo gold standard and at an accelerated pace since 1971 under a government paper money standard—a seemingly permanent secular tendency toward inflation and currency depreciation has existed.

During the monarchical age with commodity money largely outside of government control, the "level" of prices had generally fallen and the purchasing power of money increased, except during times of war or new gold discoveries. Various price indices for Britain, for instance, indicate that prices were substantially lower in 1760 than they had been hundred years earlier; and in 1860 they were lower than they had been in 1760.[20] Connected by an international gold standard, the development in other countries was similar.[21] In sharp contrast, during the democratic–republican age, with the world financial center shifted from Britain to the U.S. and the latter in the role of international monetary trend setter, a very different pattern emerged. Before World War I, the U.S. index of wholesale commodity prices had fallen from 125 shortly after the end of the War between the States, in 1868, to below 80 in 1914. It was then lower than it had been in 1800.[22] In contrast, shortly after World War I, in 1921, the U.S. wholesale commodity price index stood at 113. After World War II, in 1948, it had risen to 185. In 1971 it was 255, by 1981 it reached 658, and in 1991 it was near 1,000. During only two decades of irredeemable fiat money, the consumer price index in the U.S. rose from 40 in 1971 to 136 in 1991, in the United Kingdom it climbed from 24 to 157, in France from 30 to 137, and in Germany from 56 to 116.[23]

Similarly, during more than seventy years, from 1845 until the end of World War I in 1918, the British money supply had increased about

---

to World Inflation (Chicago: Regnery, 1984); Hans-Hermann Hoppe, "Banking, Nation States, and International Politics: A Sociological Reconstruction of the Present Economic Order," *Review of Austrian Economics* 4 (1990); idem, "How is Fiat Money Possible? or, The Devolution of Money and Credit," *Review of Austrian Economics* 7, no. 2 (1994).

[20]See B.R. Mitchell, *Abstract of British Historical Statistics* (Cambridge: Cambridge University Press, 1962), pp. 468ff.

[21]B.R. Mitchell, *European Historical Statistics 1750–1970* (New York: Columbia University Press, 1978), pp. 388ff.

[22]1930 = 100; see Ron Paul and Lewis Lehrmann, *The Case for Gold: A Minority Report to the U.S. Gold Commission* (Washington, D.C.: Cato Institute, 1982), p. 165f.

[23]1983 = 100; see *Economic Report of the President* (Washington D.C.: Government Printing Office, 1992).

six-fold.[24] In distinct contrast, during the seventy-three years from 1918 until 1991, the U.S. money supply increased more than sixty-four-fold

In addition to taxation and inflation, a government can resort to *debt* in order to finance its current expenditures. As with taxation and inflation, there is no doubt that government debt increased in the course of the monarchical age. However, as predicted theoretically, in this field monarchs also showed considerably more moderation and farsightedness than democratic–republican caretakers.

Throughout the monarchical age, government debts were essentially war debts. While the total debt thereby tended to increase over time, during peacetime at least monarchs characteristically *reduced* their debts. The British example is fairly representative. In the course of the eighteenth and nineteenth centuries, government debt increased. It was 76 million pounds after the Spanish War in 1748, 127 million after the Seven Years' War in 1763, 232 million after the American War of Independence in 1783, and 900 million after the Napoleonic Wars in 1815. Yet during each peacetime period—from 1727–1739, from 1748–1756, and from 1762–1775, total debt actually decreased. From 1815 until 1914, the British national debt fell from a total of 900 to below 700 million pounds.

In striking contrast, since the onset of the democratic–republican age British debt has only increased, in war *and* in peace. In 1920 it was 7.9

---

[24]See Mitchell, *Abstract of British Historical Statistics*, p. 444f.

[25]See Milton Friedman and Anna Schwartz, *A Monetary History of the United States, 1867–1960* (Princeton, N.J.: Princeton University Press, 1963), pp. 704–22; and *Economic Report of the President, 1992*.

A remarkable distinction between the monarchical and the democratic–republican age also exists regarding the development and recognition of monetary theory. The early theoretician of fiat money and credit John Law, having had his turn at monetary reform from 1711–1720, secretly left France and sought refuge in Venice, where he died impoverished and forgotten. In distinct contrast, John Law's twentieth-century successor, John Maynard Keynes, who bore responsibility for the demise of the classical gold standard during the post-World War I era, and who left behind the Bretton Woods system which collapsed in 1971, was honored during his lifetime and is still honored today as the world's foremost economist. (If nothing else, Keynes's personal philosophy of hedonism and present-orientation, which is summarized in his famous dictum that "in the long run we are all dead," indeed sums up the very spirit of the democratic age.) Similarly, Milton Friedman, who bears much responsibility for the post-1971 monetary order and thus for the most inflationary peacetime period in all of human history, is hailed as one of the great economists. See further on this Joseph T. Salerno, "Two Traditions in Modern Monetary Theory: John Law and A.R.J. Turgot," *Journal des Economistes et des Etudes Humaines* 2, no. 2/3 (1991).

billion pounds, in 1938 8.3 billion, in 1945 22.4 billion, in 1970 34 billion, and since then it has skyrocketed to more than 190 billion pounds in 1987.[26] Likewise, U.S government debt has increased through war and peace. Federal government debt after World War I, in 1919, was about 25 billion dollars. In 1940 it was 43 billion, and after World War II, in 1946, it stood at about 270 billion. By 1970 it had risen to 370 billion, and since 1971, under a pure fiat money regime, it has literally exploded. In 1979 it was about 840 billion, and in 1985 more than 1.8 trillion. In 1988 it reached almost 2.5 trillion, by 1992 it exceeded 3 trillion dollars, and presently it stands at approximately 6 trillion dollars.[27]

Finally, the same tendency toward increased exploitation and present-orientation emerges upon examination of government *legislation and regulation*. During the monarchical age, with a clear-cut distinction between the ruler and the ruled, the king and his parliament were held to be *under* the law. They applied preexisting law as judge or jury. They did not make law. Writes Bertrand de Jouvenel:

> The monarch was looked on only as judge and not as legislator. He made subjective rights respected and respected them himself; he found

---

[26]See Sidney Homer and Richard Sylla, *A History of Interest Rates* (New Brunswick, N.J.: Rutgers University Press, 1991), pp. 188 and 437.

[27]See Jonathan Hughes, *American Economic History* (Glenview, Ill.: Scott, Foresman, 1990), pp. 432, 498, and 589.

Furthermore, constrained by a commodity money standard, monarchs were unable to "monetize" their debt. When the king sold bonds to private financiers or banks, under the gold standard this had no effect on the total money supply. If the king spent more as a consequence, others would have to spend less. Accordingly, lenders were interested in correctly assessing the risk associated with their loans, and kings typically paid interest rates substantially above those paid by commercial borrowers. See Homer and Sylla, *A History of Interest Rates*, p. 84 and pp. 5, 99, 106, and 113f. In contrast, under the gold exchange standard with only a very indirect tie of paper money to gold, and especially under a pure fiat money regime with no tie to gold at all, government deficit financing is turned into a mere banking technicality. Currently, by selling its debt to the banking system, governments can in effect create new money to pay for their debt. When the treasury department sells bonds to the commercial banking system, the banks do not pay for these bonds out of their existing money deposits; assisted by open-market purchases by the government owned central bank, they create additional demand deposits out of thin air. The banking system does not spend less as a consequence of the government spending more. Rather, the government spends more, and the banks spend (loan) as much as before. In addition, they earn an interest return on their newly acquired bond holdings. See Murray N. Rothbard, *The Mystery of Banking* (New York: Richardson and Snyder, 1983), esp. chap. 11. Accordingly, there is little hesitation on the part of banks to purchase government bonds even at below market interest rates, and rising government debt and increased inflation thus goes hand in hand.

these rights in being and did not dispute that they were anterior to his authority. . . . Subjective rights were not held on the precarious tenure of grant but were freehold possessions. The sovereign's right also was a freehold. It was a subjective right as much as the other rights, though of a more elevated dignity, but it could not take the other rights away. . . . Indeed, there was a deep-seated feeling that all positive rights stood or fell together; if the king disregarded (a private citizen's) title to his land, so might the king's title to his throne be disregarded. The profound if obscure concept of legitimacy established the solidarity of all rights. No change in these rights could be effected without the consent of their holders.[28]

To be sure, the monopolization of law administration led to higher prices and/or lower product quality than those that would have prevailed under competitive conditions, and in the course of time kings employed their monopoly increasingly to their own advantage. For instance, in the course of time kings had increasingly employed their monopoly of law and order for a perversion of the idea of punishment. The primary objective of punishment originally had been the restitution and compensation of the *victim* of a rights violation by the offender. Under monarchical rule, the objective of punishment had increasingly shifted to compensating the *king*, instead.[29] However, while this practice implied an expansion of government power, it did not involve any redistribution of wealth and income within civil society, nor did it imply that the king himself was exempt from the standard provisions of private law. Private law was still supreme. And indeed, as late as the beginning of the twentieth century, A.V. Dicey could still maintain that as for Great Britain, for instance, legislative law—public law—as distinct from pre-existing law—private law—did not exist. The law governing the relationships between private citizens was still considered fixed and immutable, and government agents in their relationship with private citizens were regarded as bound by the same laws as any private citizen.[30]

In striking contrast, under democracy, with the exercise of power shrouded in anonymity, presidents and parliaments quickly came to rise

---

[28]De Jouvenel, *Sovereignty*, pp. 172–73 and 189; see also Fritz Kern, *Kingship and Law in the Middle Ages* (Oxford: Blackwell 1948), esp. p. 151; Bernhard Rehfeld, *Die Wurzeln des Rechts* (Berlin, 1951), esp. p. 67.

[29]See Bruce L. Benson, "The Development of Criminal Law and Its Enforcement," *Journal des Economistes et des Etudes Humaines* 3, no. 1 (1992).

[30]See Albert V. Dicey, *Lectures on the Relation Between Law and Public Opinion in England During the Nineteenth Century* (London: Macmillan, 1903); also Friedrich A. Hayek, *Law, Legislation, and Liberty* (Chicago: University of Chicago Press, 1973), vol. 1, chaps. 4 and 6.

above the law. They became not only judge but legislator, the creator of "new" law.[31] Today, notes Jouvenel,

> we are used to having our rights modified by the sovereign decisions of legislators. A landlord no longer feels surprised at being compelled to keep a tenant; an employer is no less used to having to raise the wages of his employees in virtue of the decrees of Power. Nowadays it is understood that our subjective rights are precarious and at the good pleasure of authority.[32]

In a development similar to the democratization of money—the substitution of government paper money for private commodity money and the resulting inflation and increased financial uncertainty—the democratization of law and law administration has led to a steadily growing flood of legislation. Presently, the number of legislative acts and regulations passed by parliaments in the course of a single year is in the tens of thousands, filling hundreds of thousands of pages, affecting all aspects of civil and commercial life, and resulting in a steady depreciation of all law and heightened legal uncertainty. As a typical example, the 1994 edition of the *Code of Federal Regulations* (CFR), the annual compendium of all U.S. federal government regulations currently in effect, consists of a total of 201 books, occupying about 26 feet of library shelf space. The Code's index alone is 754 pages. The Code contains regulations concerning the production and distribution of almost everything imaginable: from celery, mushrooms, watermelons, watchbands, the labeling of incandescent light bulbs, hosiery, parachute jumping, iron and steel manufacturing, sexual offenses on college campuses to the cooking of onion rings made out of diced onions, revealing the almost totalitarian power of a democratic government.[33]

Indicators of Present-Orientedness

The phenomenon of social time preference is somewhat more elusive than that of expropriation and exploitation, and it is more

---

[31]See Robert Nisbet, *Community and Power* (New York: Oxford University Press, 1962), pp. 110–11.

[32]Bertrand de Jouvenel, *Sovereignty*, p. 189; see also Nisbet, *Community and Power*, chap. 5:

> The king may have ruled at times with a degree of irresponsibility that few modern governmental officials can enjoy, but it is doubtful whether, in terms of effective powers and services, any king of even the seventeenth-century "absolute monarchies" wielded the kind of authority that now inheres in the office of many a high-ranking official in the democracies. (p. 103)

[33]See Donald Boudreaux, "The World's Biggest Government," *Free Market* (November 1994).

•

complicated to identify suitable indicators of present-orientation. More-over, some indicators are less direct—"softer"—than those of exploitation. But all of them point in the same direction and together provide as clear an illustration of the second theoretical prediction: that democratic rule also promotes short-sightedness (present-orientation) within civil society.[34]

The most direct indicator of social time preference is the rate of *interest*. The interest rate is the ratio of the valuation of present goods as compared to future goods. More specifically, it indicates the premium at which present money is traded against future money. A high interest rate implies more "present-orientedness" and a low rate of interest implies more "future-orientation." Under normal conditions—that is under the assumption of increasing standards of living and real money incomes—the interest rate can be expected to fall and ultimately approach, yet never quite reach, zero, for with rising real incomes, the marginal utility of present money falls relative to that of future money, and hence under the *ceteris paribus* assumption of a *given* time preference *schedule* the interest *rate* must fall. Consequently, savings and investment will increase, future real incomes will be still higher, and so on.

In fact, a tendency toward falling interest rates characterizes mankind's suprasecular trend of development. Minimum interest rates on 'normal safe loans' were around 16 percent at the beginning of Greek financial history in the sixth century B.C., and fell to 6 percent during the Hellenistic period. In Rome, minimum interest rates fell from more than 8 percent during the earliest period of the Republic to 4 percent during the first century of the Empire. In thirteenth-century Europe, the lowest interest rates on 'safe' loans were 8 percent. In the fourteenth century they came down to about 5 percent. In the fifteenth century they fell to 4 percent. In the seventeenth century they went down to 3 percent. And at the end of the nineteenth century minimum interest rates had further declined to less than 2.5 percent.[35]

This trend was by no means smooth. It was frequently interrupted by periods, sometimes as long as centuries, of rising interest rates. However, such periods were associated with major wars and revolutions such as the Hundred Years' War during the fourteenth century, the Wars of Religion from the late sixteenth to the early seventeenth century, the American and French Revolutions and the Napoleonic Wars

---

[34]See also T. Alexander Smith, *Time and Public Policy* (Knoxville: University of Tennessee Press, 1988).

[35]See Homer and Sylla, *A History of Interest Rates*, pp. 557–58.

from the late eighteenth to the early nineteenth century, and the two World Wars in the twentieth century. Furthermore, whereas high or rising minimum interest rates indicate periods of generally low or declining living standards, the overriding opposite tendency toward low and falling interest rates reflects mankind's overall progress—its advance from barbarism to civilization. Specifically, the trend toward lower interest rates reflects the rise of the Western World, its peoples' increasing prosperity, farsightedness, intelligence, and moral strength, and the unparalleled height of nineteenth-century European civilization.

With this historical backdrop and in accordance with economic theory, then, it should be expected that twentieth-century interest rates would be still *lower* than nineteenth-century rates. Indeed, only two possible explanations exist why this is *not* so. The first possibility is that twentieth century real incomes did not exceed, or even fell below, nineteenth-century incomes. However, this explanation can be ruled out on empirical grounds, for it seems fairly uncontroversial that twentieth-century incomes are in fact higher. Then only the second explanation remains. If real incomes are higher but interest rates are not lower, then the *ceteris paribus* clause can no longer be assumed true. Rather, the social time preference *schedule* must have shifted upward. That is, the character of the population must have changed. People on the average must have lost in moral and intellectual strength and become more present-oriented. Indeed, this appears to be the case.

From 1815 onward, throughout Europe and the Western World minimum interest rates steadily declined to a historic low of well below 3 percent on the average at the turn of the century. With the onset of the democratic–republican age this earlier tendency came to a halt and seems to have changed direction, revealing twentieth century Europe and the U.S. as declining civilizations. An inspection of the lowest decennial average interest rates for Britain, France, the Netherlands, Belgium, Germany, Sweden, Switzerland, and the U.S., for instance, shows that during the entire post-World War I era interest rates in Europe were never as low as or lower than they had been during the second half of the nineteenth century. Only in the U.S., in the 1950s, did interest rates ever fall below late nineteenth-century rates. Yet this was only a short-lived phenomenon, and even then U.S. interest rates were not lower than they had been in Britain during the second half of the nineteenth century. Instead, twentieth-century rates were significantly *higher* than nineteenth century rates universally, and if anything they have exhibited a *rising* tendency.[36] This conclusion does not substantially change, even

---

[36]See ibid., pp. 554–55.

when it is taken into account that modern interest rates, in particular since the 1970s, include a systematic inflation premium. After adjusting recent nominal interest rates for inflation in order to yield an estimate of *real* interest rates, contemporary interest rates still appear to be significantly higher than they were one-hundred years ago. On the average, minimum long-term interest rates in Europe and the U.S. nowadays seem to be well above 4 percent and possibly as high as 5 percent—that is above the interest rates of seventeenth-century Europe and as high or higher than fifteenth-century rates. Likewise, current U.S. savings rates of around 5 percent of disposable income are no higher than they were more than three hundred years ago in a much poorer seventeenth-century England.[37]

Parallel to this development and reflecting a more specific aspect of the same underlying phenomenon of high or rising social time preferences, indicators of *family disintegration*—"dysfunctional families"—have exhibited a systematic increase.

Until the end of the nineteenth century, the bulk of government spending—typically more than 50 percent—went to financing the military. Assuming government expenditures to be then about 5 percent of the national product, this amounted to military expenditures of 2.5 percent of the national product. The remainder went to government administration. Welfare spending or "public charity" played almost no role. Insurance was considered to be in the province of individual responsibility, and poverty relief seen as the task of voluntary charity. In contrast, as a reflection of the egalitarianism inherent in democracy, from the beginning of the democratization in the late nineteenth century onward came the collectivization of individual responsibility. Military expenditures have typically risen to 5–10 percent of the national product in the course of the twentieth century. But with public expenditures currently making up 50 percent of the national product, military expenditures now only represent 10–20 percent of total government spending. The bulk of public spending—typically more than 50 percent of total expenditures (or 25 percent of the national product)—is now eaten up by public welfare spending: by compulsory government "insurance" against illness, occupational injuries, old age, unemployment, and an ever expanding list of other disabilities.[38]

---

[37]See Cipolla, *Before the Industrial Revolution*, p. 39.

[38]See ibid., pp. 54–55; Flora, *State, Economy, and Society in Western Europe*, chap. 8 and p. 454.

Consequently, by increasingly relieving individuals of the responsibility of having to provide for their own health, safety, and old age, the range and temporal horizon of private provisionary action have been systematically reduced. In particular, the value of marriage, family, and children have fallen, since one can fall back on "public" assistance. Thus, since the onset of the democratic–republican age the number of children has declined, and the size of the endogenous population has stagnated or even fallen. For centuries, until the end of the nineteenth century, the birth rate was almost constant: somewhere between 30 to 40 per 1,000 population (usually somewhat higher in predominantly Catholic and lower in Protestant countries). In sharp contrast, during the twentieth century birthrates all over Europe and the U.S. have experienced a dramatic decline—down to about 15 to 20 per 1,000.[39] At the same time, the rates of divorce, illegitimacy, single parenting, singledom, and abortion have steadily increased, while personal savings rates have begun to stagnate or even fall rather than rise proportionally or even over-proportionally with rising incomes.[40]

Moreover, as a consequence of the depreciation of law resulting from legislation and the collectivization of responsibility effected in particular by social security legislation, the rate of *crimes* of a serious nature, such as murder, assault, robbery, and theft, has also shown a systematic upward tendency.

In the "normal" course of events—that is with rising standards of living—it would be expected that the protection against social disasters such as crime would undergo continual improvement, just as one would expect the protection against natural disasters such as floods, earthquakes and hurricanes to become progressively better. Indeed, throughout the Western world this appears to have been the case by and large—until recently, during the second half of the twentieth century, when crime rates began to climb steadily upward.[41]

---

[39]See Mitchell, *European Historical Statistics 1750–1970*, pp. 16ff.

[40]See Allan C. Carlson, *Family Questions: Reflections on the American Social Crises* (New Brunswick, N.J.: Transaction Publishers, 1988); idem, *The Swedish Experiment in Family Politics* (New Brunswick, N.J.: Transaction Publishers, 1990); idem, "What Has Government Done to Our Families?" *Essays in Political Economy* 13 (Auburn, Ala.: Ludwig von Mises Institute, 1991); Charles Murray, *Losing Ground* (New York: Basic Books, 1984); for an early diagnosis see Joseph A. Schumpeter, *Capitalism, Socialism, and Democracy* (New York: Harper, 1942), chap. 14.

[41]See James Q. Wilson and Richard J. Herrnstein, *Crime and Human Nature* (New York: Simon and Schuster, 1985), pp. 408–09; on the magnitude of the increase in criminal activity brought about by democratic republicanism and welfarism in the

To be sure, there are a number of factors other than increased irresponsibility and shortsightedness brought on by legislation and welfare that may contribute to crime. Men commit more crimes than women, the young more than the old, blacks more than whites, and city dwellers more than villagers.[42] Accordingly, changes in the composition of the sexes, age groups, races, and the degree of urbanization could be expected to have a systematic effect on crime. However, all of these factors are relatively stable and thus cannot account for any systematic change in the long-term downward trend of crime rates. As for European countries, their populations were and are comparatively homogeneous; and in the U.S., the proportion of blacks has remained stable. The sex composition is largely a biological constant; and as a result of wars, only the proportion of males has periodically fallen, thus actually reinforcing the "normal" trend toward falling crime rates. Similarly, the composition of age groups has changed only slowly; and due to declining birth rates and higher life expectancies the average age of the population has actually increased, thus helping to depress crime rates still further. Finally, the degree of urbanization began to increase dramatically from about 1800 onward. A period of rising crime rates during the early nineteenth century can be attributed to this initial spurt of urbanization.[43] Yet after a period of adjustment to the new phenomenon of urbanization, from the mid-nineteenth century onward, the countervailing tendency toward falling crime rates took hold again, despite the fact that the process of rapid urbanization continued for about another hundred years. And when crime rates began to move systematically upward, from the mid-twentieth century onward, the process of increasing urbanization had actually come to a halt.

It thus appears that the phenomenon of rising crime rates cannot be explained other than with reference to the process of democratization: by a rising degree of social time preference, an increasing loss of individual responsibility, intellectually and morally, and a diminished respect for all law—moral relativism—stimulated by an unabated flood of

---

course of the last hundred years see also Roger D. McGrath, *Gunfighters, Highwaymen, and Vigilantes* (Berkeley: University of California Press, 1984), esp. chap. 13; idem, "Treat Them to a Good Dose of Lead," *Chronicles* (January 1994).

[42]See J. Philippe Rushton, *Race, Evolution, and Behavior* (New Brunswick, N.J.: Transaction Publishers, 1995); Michael Levin, *Why Race Matters* (Westport, Conn.: Praeger, 1998).

[43]See Wilson and Herrnstein, *Crime and Human Nature*, p. 411.

legislation.[44] Of course, "high time preference" is by no means equivalent with "crime." A high time preference can also find expression in such perfectly lawful activities as recklessness, unreliability, poor manners, laziness, stupidity, or hedonism. Nonetheless, a systematic relationship between high time preference and crime exists, for in order to earn a market income a certain minimum of planning, patience, and sacrifice is required. One must first work for a while before one gets paid. In contrast, most serious criminal activities such as murder, assault, rape, robbery, theft, and burglary require no such discipline. The reward for the aggressor is immediate and tangible, whereas the sacrifice—possible punishment—lies in the future and is uncertain. Consequently, if the social degree of time preference were increased, it would be expected that the frequency in particular of these forms of aggressive behavior would rise—as they in fact did.[45]

---

[44]Essentially the same conclusion is also reached by ibid., pp. 414–15:

As a society becomes more egalitarian in its outlook, it becomes skeptical of claims that the inputs of some persons are intrinsically superior to those of others, and thus its members become more disposed to describe others' output as unjustly earned. There can be little doubt, we think, that the trend of thought in modern nations has been toward more egalitarian views, buttressed in some instances by the rising belief among disadvantaged racial, ethnic, and religious minorities that the deference they once paid need be paid no longer; on the contrary, now the majority group owes them something as reparations for past injustices. Of course, persons can acquire more egalitarian or even more reparations-seeking views without becoming more criminal. But at the margin, some individuals—perhaps those impulsive ones who value the products of an affluent society—find that value suddenly enhanced when they allow themselves to be persuaded that the current owner of a car has no greater (i.e., no more just) claim to it than they do.... Data on changes in internalized inhibitions against crime are virtually nonexistent. . . . [However,] one tantalizing but isolated fact may suggest that internalized inhibitions have in fact changed, at least in some societies. Wolpin finds that in England the ratio of murderers who committed suicide before being arrested to all convicted murderers fell more or less steadily from about three out of four in 1929 to about one in four in 1967.

[45]On the relationship between high time preference and crime see also Edward C. Banfield, *The Unheavenly City Revisited* (Boston: Little, Brown, 1974), esp. chaps. 3 and 8; idem, "Present-Orientedness and Crime," in *Assessing the Criminal*, Randy E. Barnett and John Hagel, eds. (Cambridge, Mass.: Ballinger, 1977). Explains Banfield (*The Unheavenly City Revisited*, pp. 140–41):

The threat of punishment at the hands of the law is unlikely to deter the present-oriented person. The gains he expects from the illegal act are very near to the present, whereas the punishment that he would suffer—in the unlikely event of his being both caught and punished—lies in a future too

CONCLUSION:
MONARCHY, DEMOCRACY, AND THE IDEA OF NATURAL ORDER

From the vantage point of elementary economic theory and in light of historical evidence, then, a revisionist view of modern history results. The Whig theory of history, according to which mankind marches continually forward toward ever higher levels of progress, is incorrect. From the viewpoint of those who prefer less exploitation over more and who value farsightedness and individual responsibility above short-sightedness and irresponsibility, the historic transition from monarchy to democracy represents not progress but civilizational decline. Nor does this verdict change if more or other indicators are included. Quite to the contrary. Without question the most important indicator of exploitation and present-orientedness *not* discussed above is *war*. Yet if this indicator were included the relative performance of democratic republican government appears to be even worse, not better. In addition to increased exploitation and social decay, the transition from monarchy to democracy has brought a change from limited warfare to total war, and the twentieth century, the age of democracy, must be ranked also among the most murderous periods in all of history.[46]

---

distant for him to take into account. For the normal person there are of course risks other than the legal penalty that are strong deterrents: disgrace, loss of job, hardship for wife and children if one is sent to prison, and so on. The present-oriented person does not run such risks. . . . he need not fear losing his job since he works intermittently or not at all, and for his wife and children, he contributes little or nothing to their support and they may well be better off without him.

See also Wilson and Herrnstein, *Crime and Human Nature*, pp. 416–22. Wilson and Herrnstein report of indicators for young persons becoming increasingly "more present-oriented and thus more impulsive than those who grew up earlier." There is some evidence that this is true. In 1959, Davids, Kidder, and Reich administered to a group of institutionalized male and female delinquents in Rhode Island various tests (completing a story, telling the interviewer whether they would save or spend various sums of money if given to them) designed to measure their time orientation. The results showed them to be markedly more present-oriented than were comparable nondelinquents. Fifteen years later, essentially the same tests were given to a new group of institutionalized delinquents in the same state and of the same age. This group was much more present-oriented and thus much less willing to delay gratification (by, for example, saving rather than spending the money) than the earlier group of delinquents. Moreover, the more recent group frequently mentioned spending the gift money on drugs (nobody suggested that in 1959) and never mentioned giving it to somebody else (several had said they would do so in 1959), p. 418.

[46]On the contrast between monarchical and democratic warfare see Fuller, *The Conduct of War*, esp. chaps. 1 and 2; idem, *War and Western Civilization* (Freeport, N.Y.:

Thus, inevitably two final questions arise. The current state of affairs can hardly be "the end of history." What can we expect? And what can we do? As for the first question, the answer is brief. At the end of the twentieth century, democratic republicanism in the U.S. and all across the Western world has apparently exhausted the reserve fund that was inherited from the past. For decades, until the 1990s boom, real incomes have stagnated or even fallen.[47] The public debt and the cost of social security systems have brought on the prospect of an imminent economic meltdown. At the same time, societal breakdown and social conflict have risen to dangerous heights. If the tendency toward increased exploitation and present-orientedness continues on its current path, the Western democratic welfare states will collapse as the East European socialist peoples' republics did in the late 1980s. Hence one is left with the second question: What can we do *now*, in order to prevent the process of civilizational decline from running its full course to an economic and social catastrophe?

Above all, the idea of democracy and majority rule must be delegitimized. Ultimately, the course of history is determined by *ideas*, be they true or false. Just as kings could not exercise their rule unless a majority of public opinion accepted such rule as legitimate, so will democratic rulers not last without ideological support in public opinion.[48] Likewise, the transition from monarchical to democratic rule must be explained as fundamentally nothing but a *change* in public opinion. In fact, until the end of World War I, the overwhelming majority of the public in Europe accepted monarchical rule as legitimate.[49] Today, hardly anyone would do so. On the contrary, the idea of monarchical government is

---

Books for Libraries, 1969); Michael Howard, *War in European History* (Oxford: Oxford University Press, 1978), esp. chap. 6; idem, *War and the Liberal Conscience* (New Brunswick, N.J.: Rutgers University Press, 1978); de Jouvenel, *On Power*, chap. 8; William A. Orton, *The Liberal Tradition* (Port Washington, Wash.: Kennikat Press, 1969), pp. 25ff.; Ferrero, *Peace and War*, chap. 1; see also chap. 1 above.

[47]For a revealing analysis of U.S. data see Robert Batemarco, "GNP, PPR, and the Standard of Living," *Review of Austrian Economics* 1 (1987).

[48]On the relation between government and public opinion see the classic expositions by Etienne de la Boétie, *The Politics of Obedience: The Discourse of Voluntary Servitude* (New York: Free Life Editions, 1975); David Hume, *Essays: Moral, Political, and Literary* (Oxford: Oxford University Press, 1963), esp. Essay 4: "Of the First Principles of Government."

[49]As late as 1871, for instance, with universal male suffrage, the National Assembly of the French Republic contained only about 200 republicans out of more than 600 deputies. And the restoration of a monarchy was only prevented because the supporters of the Bourbons and the Orleans stalemated each other.

considered laughable. Consequently, a return to the *ancien régime* must be regarded as impossible. The legitimacy of monarchical rule appears to have been irretrievably lost. Nor would such a return be a genuine solution. For monarchies, whatever their relative merits, *do* exploit and *do* contribute to present-orientedness as well. Rather, the idea of democratic–republican rule must be rendered equally if not more laughable, not in the least by identifying it as the source of the ongoing process of decivilization.

But at the same time, and still more importantly, a positive *alternative* to monarchy *and* democracy—the idea of a natural order—must be delineated and understood. On the one hand, this involves the recognition that it is not exploitation, either monarchical or democratic, but private property, production, and voluntary exchange that are the ultimate sources of human civilization. On the other hand, it involves the recognition of a fundamental sociological insight (which incidentally also helps identify precisely where the historic opposition to monarchy went wrong): that the maintenance and preservation of a private property based exchange economy requires as its sociological presupposition the existence of a voluntarily acknowledged natural elite—*a nobilitas naturalis.*[50]

The natural outcome of the voluntary transactions between various private property owners is decidedly nonegalitarian, hierarchical, and elitist. As the result of widely diverse human talents, in every society of any degree of complexity a few individuals quickly acquire the status of an elite. Owing to superior achievements of wealth, wisdom, bravery or a combination thereof, some individuals come to possess "natural authority," and their opinions and judgments enjoy widespread respect. Moreover, because of selective mating and marriage and the laws of civil and genetic inheritance, positions of natural authority are more likely than not passed on within a few noble families. It is to the heads of these families with long-established records of superior achievement, farsightedness, and exemplary personal conduct that men turn with their conflicts and complaints against each other, and it is these very leaders of the natural elite who typically act as judges and peacemakers, often free of charge, out of a sense of obligation required and expected of a person of authority or even out of a principled concern for civil justice, as a privately produced "public good."[51]

---

[50]See also Wilhelm Röpke, *A Humane Economy* (Indianapolis, Ind.: Liberty Fund, 1971), pp. 129–36; de Jouvenel, *On Power*, chap. 17.

[51]See also Marvin Harris, *Cannibals and Kings: The Origins of Culture* (New York: Vintage Books, 1977), pp. 104ff., on the private provision of public goods by "big men."

In fact, the endogenous origin of a monarchy (as opposed to its exogenous origin *via* conquest)[52] can only be understood against the background of a prior order of natural elites. The small but decisive step in
the transition to monarchical rule—the original sin—consisted precisely
in the *monopolization* of the function of judge and peacemaker. The step
was taken once a single member of the voluntarily acknowledged natural elite—the king—insisted, against the opposition of other members of
the social elite, that all conflicts within a specified territory be brought
before him and conflicting parties no longer choose any other judge or
peacekeeper but him. From this moment on, law and law enforcement
became more expensive: instead of being offered free of charge or for a
voluntary payment, they were financed with the help of a compulsory
tax. At the same time, the quality of law deteriorated: instead of upholding the pre-existing law and applying universal and immutable principles of justice, a monopolistic judge, who did not have to fear losing
clients as a result of being less than impartial in his judgments, could
successively alter the existing law to his own advantage.

It was to a large extent the inflated price of justice and the perver-
sions of ancient law by the kings which motivated the historical opposition to monarchy. However, confusion as to the causes of this
phenomenon prevailed. There were those who recognized correctly that
the problem lay with *monopoly*, not with elites or nobility.[53] But they
were far outnumbered by those who erroneously blamed it on the elitist
character of the rulers instead, and who accordingly strove to maintain
the monopoly of law and law enforcement and merely replace the king
and the visible royal pomp by the "people" and the presumed modesty
and decency of the "common man." Hence the historic success of democracy.

Ironically, the monarchy was then destroyed by the same social
forces that kings had first stimulated when they began to exclude competing natural authorities from acting as judges. In order to overcome

---

[52]For a comparative evaluation of theories of the endogenous versus the exogenous origin of government and a historical critique of the latter as incorrect or incomplete see Wilhelm Mühlmann, *Rassen, Ethnien, Kulturen* (Neuwied:
Luchterhand, 1964), pp. 248–319, esp. pp. 291–96.

For proponents of theories of the exogenous origin of government see Friedrich
Ratzel, *Politische Geographie* (Munich, 1923); Oppenheimer, *Der Staat*; Alexander
Rüstow, *Freedom and Domination* (Princeton, N.J.: Princeton University Press, 1976).

[53]See, for instance, Gustave de Molinari, *The Production of Security* (New York:
Center for Libertarian Studies, 1977), published originally in French in 1849.

their resistance, kings typically aligned themselves with the people, the common man.[54] Appealing to the always popular sentiment of envy, kings promised the people cheaper and better justice in exchange and at the expense of taxing—cutting down to size—their own betters (that is, the kings' competitors). When the kings' promises turned out to be empty, as was to be predicted, the same egalitarian sentiments which they had previously courted now focused and turned against them. After all, the king himself was a member of the nobility, and as a result of the exclusion of all other judges, his position had become only more elevated and elitist and his conduct only more arrogant. Accordingly, it appeared only logical then that kings, too, should be brought down and that the egalitarian policies, which monarchs had initiated, be carried through to their ultimate conclusion: the monopolistic control of the judiciary by the common man.

Predictably, as explained and illustrated in detail above, the democratization of law and law enforcement—the substitution of the people for the king—made matters only worse, however. The price of justice and peace has risen astronomically, and all the while the quality of law has steadily deteriorated to the point where the idea of law as a body of universal and immutable principles of justice has almost disappeared from public opinion and has been replaced by the idea of law as legislation (government-*made* law). At the same time, democracy has succeeded where monarchy only made a modest beginning: in the ultimate destruction of the natural elites. The fortunes of great families have dissipated, and their tradition of culture and economic independence, intellectual farsightedness, and moral and spiritual leadership has been forgotten. Rich men still exist today, but more frequently than not they

---

[54]See on this Henri Pirenne, *Medieval Cities* (Princeton, N.J.: Princeton University Press, 1974). "The clear interest of the monarchy," writes Pirenne,

> was to support the adversaries of high feudalism. Naturally, help was given whenever it was possible to do so without becoming obligated to these [city] middle classes who in arising against their lords fought, to all intents and purposes, in the interests of royal prerogatives. To accept the king as arbitrator of their quarrel was, for the parties in conflict, to recognize his sovereignty. The entry of the burghers upon the political scene had as a consequence the weakening of the contractual principle of the Feudal State to the advantage of the principle of the authority of the Monarchical State. It was impossible that royalty should not take count of this and seize every chance to show its good-will to the communes which, without intending to do so, labored so usefully in its behalf. (pp. 179–80)

See also ibid., p. 227f. and de Jouvenel, *On Power*, chap. 17.

owe their fortune now directly or indirectly to the state. Hence, they are often more dependent on the state's continued favors than people of far lesser wealth. They are typically no longer the heads of long established leading families but *nouveaux riches*. Their conduct is not marked by special virtue, dignity, or taste but is a reflection of the same proletarian mass-culture of present-orientedness, opportunism, and hedonism that the rich now share with everyone else; consequently, their opinions carry no more weight in public opinion than anyone else's.

Hence, when democratic rule has finally exhausted its legitimacy the problem faced will be significantly more difficult than when kings lost their legitimacy. Then, it would have been sufficient to abolish the king's monopoly of law and law enforcement and replace it with a natural order of competing jurisdictions, because remnants of natural elites who could have taken on this task still existed. Now, this will no longer suffice. If the monopoly of law and law enforcement of democratic governments is dissolved, there appears to be no other authority to whom one can turn for justice, and chaos would seem to be inevitable. Thus, in addition to advocating the abdication of democracy, it is now of central strategic importance that at the same time ideological support be given to all decentralizing or even secessionist social forces. In other words, the tendency toward political centralization that has characterized the Western world for many centuries, first under monarchical rule and then under democratic auspices, must be systematically reversed.[55] Even if as a result of a secessionist tendency a new government, whether democratic or not, should spring up, territorially smaller governments and increased political competition will tend to encourage moderation as regards exploitation. In any case, only in small regions, communities or districts will it be possible again for a few individuals, based on the popular recognition of their economic independence, outstanding professional achievement, morally impeccable personal life, and superior judgment and taste, to rise to the rank of natural, voluntarily acknowledged authorities and lend legitimacy to the idea of a natural order[56] of

---

[55]On the political economy of political centralization, and the rationale of decentralization and secession see Hans-Hermann Hoppe, "The Economic and Political Rational for European Secessionism," in *Secession, State, and Liberty*, David Gordon, ed. (New Brunswick, N.J.: Transaction Publishers, 1998); Jean Baechler, *The Origins of Capitalism* (New York: St. Martin's Press, 1976), esp. chap. 7; see also chap. 5 below.

[56]"In a sound society," writes Wilhelm Röpke,

leadership, responsibility, and exemplary defense of the society's guiding norms and values must be the exalted duty and unchallengeable right of a minority that forms and is willingly and respectfully recognized as the apex

competing judges and overlapping jurisdictions—an "anarchic" private law society—as the answer to monarchy *and* democracy.

---

of a social pyramid hierarchically structured by performance. Mass society ... must be counteracted by individual leadership—not on the part of original geniuses or eccentrics or will-o'-the wisp intellectuals, but, on the contrary, on the part of people with courage to reject eccentric novelty for the sake of the 'old truths' which Goethe admonishes us to hold on to and for the sake of historically proved, indestructible, and simple human values. In other words, we need the leadership of ... "ascetics of civilization," secularized saints as it were, who in our age occupy a place which must not for long remain vacant at any time and in any society. That is what those have in mind who say that the "revolt of the masses" must be countered by another revolt, the "revolt of the elite." ... What we need is true *nobilitas naturalis*. No era can do without it, least of all ours, when so much is shaking and crumbling away. We need a natural nobility whose authority is, fortunately, readily accepted by all men, an elite deriving its title solely from supreme performance and peerless moral example and invested with the moral dignity of such a life. Only a few from every stratum of society can ascend into this thin layer of natural nobility. The way to it is an exemplary and slowly maturing life of dedicated endeavor on behalf of all, unimpeachable integrity, constant restraint of our common greed, proved soundness of judgment, a spotless private life, indomitable courage in standing up for truth and law, and generally the highest example. This is how the few, carried upward by the trust of the people, gradually attain to a position above the classes, interests, passions, wickedness, and foolishness of men and finally become the nation's conscience. To belong to this group of moral aristocrats should be the highest and most desirable aim, next to which all the other triumphs of life are pale and insipid.... No free society, least of all ours, which threatens to degenerate into mass society, can subsist without such a class of censors. The continued existence of our free world will ultimately depend on whether our age can produce a sufficient number of such aristocrats of public spirit. (*A Humane Economy*, pp. 130–31)

3

On Monarchy, Democracy, Public Opinion, and Delegitimation

I

It is appropriate to begin with a few observations on Ludwig von Mises, and his idea of a free society.

"The program of liberalism," wrote Mises,

> if condensed into a single word, would have to read: *property*, that is, private ownership of the means of production (for in regard to commodities ready for consumption, private property is a matter of course and is not disputed even by the socialists and communists). All the other demands of liberalism result from this fundamental demand.[1]

Based on private property, Mises explained, the emergence of society—human cooperation was the result of the natural diversity of people and property and the recognition that work performed under division of labor is more productive than work performed in self-sufficient isolation. He explained:

> If and as far as labor under the division of labor is more productive than isolated labor, and if and as far as man is able to realize this fact, human action itself tends toward cooperation and association; . . . Experience teaches that this condition higher productivity achieved under division of labor is present because its cause the inborn inequality of men and the inequality in the geographical distribution of the natural factors of production is real. Thus we are in a position to comprehend the course of social evolution.[2]

If the emergence of society human cooperation under division of labor can be explained as the result of self-interested action, it is also true that, mankind being what it is, murderers, robbers, thieves, thugs, and

---

[1]Ludwig von Mises, *Liberalism: In the Classical Tradition* (Irvington-on-Hudson, N.Y.: Foundation for Economic Education, 1985), p. 19.

[2]Ludwig von Mises, *Human Action: A Treatise on Economics* (Chicago: Regnery, 1966), pp. 160–61.

con-artists will always exist, and life in society will be intolerable unless they are threatened with physical punishment. "The liberal understands quite well," wrote Mises,

> that without resort to compulsion, the existence of society would be endangered and that behind the rules of conduct whose observance is necessary to assure peaceful human cooperation must stand the threat of force if the whole edifice of society is not to be continually at the mercy of any one of its members. One must be in a position to compel the person who will not respect the lives, health, personal freedom, or private property of others to acquiesce in the rules of life in society. This is the function that the liberal doctrine assigns to the state: the protection of property, liberty, and peace.[3]

If this is accepted, how is a government to be organized so as to assure that it will in fact do what it is supposed to do: protect pre-existing private property rights? In view of what I shall say later on in favor of the institution of monarchy, Mises's liberal opposition to the *ancien régime* of absolute kings and princes is worth noting here. Kings and princes were privileged personae. Almost by definition, they stood opposed to the liberal idea of the unity and universality of law. Thus, Mises stated, the liberal theory of the state is hostile to princes.

> The princely state has no natural boundaries. To be an increaser of his family estate is the ideal of the prince; he strives to leave his successor more land than he inherited from his father. To keep on acquiring new possessions until one encounters an equally strong or stronger adversary—that is the striving of kings.... Princes regard countries no differently from the way an estate owner regards his forests, meadows, and fields. They sell them, they exchange them (e.g., "rounding off" boundaries); and each time rule over the inhabitants is transferred also. ... Lands and peoples are, in the eyes of princes, nothing but objects of princely ownership; the former form the basis of sovereignty, the latter the appurtenances of landownership. From the people who live in "his" land the prince demands obedience and loyalty; he regards them almost as his property.[4]

---

[3]Mises, *Liberalism*, p. 37.

[4]Ludwig von Mises, *Nation, State, and Economy: Contributions to the Politics and History of Our Time* (New York: New York University Press, 1983), pp. 32–33. Further, Mises notes,

> [t]he princely state strives restlessly for expansion of its territory and for increase in the number of its subjects. On the one hand it aims at the acquisition of land and fosters immigration; on the other hand it sets the strictest penalties against emigration. The more land and the more subjects,

As Mises rejected a princely state as incompatible with the protection of private property rights, what was to be substituted for it? His answer was democracy and democratic government. However, Mises's definition of democratic government is fundamentally different from its colloquial meaning. Mises grew up in a multinational state and was painfully aware of the antiliberal results of majority rule in ethnically mixed territories.[5] Rather than majority rule, to Mises democracy meant literally "self-determination, self-government, self-rule,"[6] and accordingly, a democratic government was an essentially voluntary membership organization in that it recognized each of its constituents' unrestricted right to secession. "Liberalism," explained Mises,

> forces no one against his will into the structure of the state. Whoever wants to emigrate is not held back. When a part of the people of a state wants to drop out of the union, liberalism does not hinder it from doing so. Colonies that want to become independent need only do so. The nation as an organic entity can be neither increased nor reduced by changes in states; the world as a whole can neither win nor lose from them.[7]

> The right of self-determination in regard to the question of membership in a state thus means: whenever the inhabitants of a particular territory, whether it be a single village, a whole district, or a series of adjacent districts, make it known, by a freely conducted plebiscite, that they no longer wish to remain united to the state to which they belong at the time, their wishes are to be respected and complied with. This is the only feasible and effective way of preventing revolutions and international wars. . . . If it were in any way possible to grant this right of

---

the more revenue and the more soldiers. Only in the size of the state does assurance of its preservation lie. Smaller states are always in danger of being swallowed up by larger ones. (p. 39)

[5]"In polyglot territories," Mises writes, "the application of the majority principle leads not to the freedom of all but to the rule of the majority over the minority. . . . Majority rule signifies . . . for a part of the people . . . not popular rule but foreign rule" (ibid., pp. 55 and 50). Under the special circumstances of Habsburg–Austria as a multinational and yet fundamentally German state, the application of majoritarian principles would not only promote the dissolution of the Empire. In particular, whether the Empire was dissolved or not, democracy would systematically work against the Germans and ultimately lead to German "national suicide" (p. 117). This, according to Mises, was the "tragic position" of the German liberals in Austria (p. 115). "Democratization in Austria was identical with de-Germanization" (p. 126).

[6]Ibid., p. 46.

[7]Ibid., pp. 39–40.

self-determination to every individual person, it would have to be done.[8]

Hence, Mises's answer as to how to assure that a government will protect property rights is through the threat of unlimited secession and its own characteristic of voluntary membership.

II

I do not wish to further investigate Mises's idea of democratic government here but to turn instead to the modern definition of democracy and the question of its compatibility with the foundation of liberalism: that of private property and its protection.

It might be argued that Mises's definition of democratic government was applicable to the U.S. until 1861. Until then, it was generally held that the right to secession existed and that the Union was nothing but a voluntary association of independent states. However, after the crushing defeat and devastation of the secessionist Confederacy by Lincoln and the Union, it was clear that the right to secede no longer existed and that democracy meant absolute and unlimited majority rule. Nor does it appear that any state since that time has met Mises's definition of democratic government. Instead, like their American model, all modern democracies are compulsory membership organizations.

It is all the more surprising that Mises never subjected this modern model of democracy to the same systematic analysis that he had applied to princely government. To be sure, no one has been more farsighted regarding the destructive effects of modern governments' social and

---

[8]Mises, *Liberalism*, pp. 109–10. The objections Mises has against unlimited secession are solely technical in nature (economies of scale, etc.). Thus, for instance, Mises admits having difficulties imagining "in a nationally mixed city to create two police forces, perhaps a German and a Czech, each of which could take action only against members of its own nationality." *Nation, State, and Economy*, p. 53. On the other hand, Mises notes that

the political ideas of modern times allow the continued existence of small states more secure today than in earlier centuries. . . . There can be no question of a test of economic self-sufficiency in the formation of states at a time when the division of labor embraces broad stretches of land, whole continents, indeed the whole world. It does not matter whether the inhabitants of a state meet their needs directly or indirectly by production at home; what is important is only that they can meet them at all. . . . Even at the time when the state structure was unified, they [seceding inhabitants] did not obtain [their imported] goods for nothing but only for value supplied in return, and this value in return does not become greater when the political community has fallen apart. . . . The size of a state's territory therefore does not matter. (pp. 81–82)

economic policies than Mises, and no one has recognized more clearly the dramatic increase of state power in the course of the twentieth century, but Mises never connected these phenomena systematically with modern compulsory democracy. Nowhere did he suggest that the decline of liberalism and the dominance of anticapitalist political ideologies in this century of socialism, social democracy, democratic capitalism, social market economics or whatever other label has been attached to various antiliberal programs and policies finds its systematic explanation in majoritarian democracy itself.

What I propose to do here is to fill in the gap left by Mises and provide an analysis of the logic of majoritarian democracy, thereby making modern history—our age—intelligible and predictable.

III

Without the right to secession, a democratic government is, economically speaking, a compulsory territorial monopolist of protection and ultimate decisionmaking (jurisdiction) and is in this respect indistinguishable from princely government. Just as princes did not allow secession, so it is outlawed under democracy. Furthermore, as implied in the position of a compulsory monopolist, both democratic government as well as princes possess the right to tax. That is, both are permitted to determine unilaterally, without consent of the protected, the sum that the protected must pay for their own protection.

From this common classification as compulsory monopolies, a fundamental similarity of both princely and democratic government can be deduced[9]: Under monopolistic auspices, the price of justice and protection will continually rise and the quantity and quality of justice and protection fall. *Qua* expropriating property protector, a tax-funded protection agency is a contradiction in terms and will inevitably lead to more taxes and less protection. Even if, as liberals advocate, a government limited its activities exclusively to the protection of pre-existing property rights, the further question of how much protection to produce arises. Motivated (as everyone is) by self-interest and the disutility of

---

[9]On the economic theory of monopoly see Murray N. Rothbard, *Man, Economy, and State: A Treatise on Economic Principles*, 2 vols. (Auburn, Ala.: Ludwig von Mises Institute, 1993), chap. 10; on the monopolistic production of security in particular see idem, *For A New Liberty* (New York: Collier, 1978), chaps. 12 and 14; Gustave de Molinari, *The Production of Security* (New York: Center for Libertarian Studies, 1977); Morris and Linda Tannehill, *The Market for Liberty* (New York: Laissez Faire Books, 1984); and Hans-Hermann Hoppe, *The Private Production of Defense* (Auburn, Ala.: Ludwig von Mises Institute, 1998).

labor but with the unique power to tax, a government agent's response will invariably be the same: To maximize expenditures on protection, and conceivably almost all of a nation's wealth can be consumed by the cost of protection, and at the same time to minimize the actual production of protection. The more money one can spend and the less one must work to produce, the better off one will be.

Moreover, a monopoly of jurisdiction will inevitably lead to a steady deterioration in the quality of protection. If one can appeal exclusively to government for justice, justice will be distorted in favor of government, constitutions and appeals courts notwithstanding. Constitutions and appeals courts are government constitutions and agencies, and any limitations on government action they might provide are invariably decided by agents of one and the same institution. Predictably, the definition of property and protection will continually be altered and the range of jurisdiction expanded to the government's advantage.

IV

While they are both inconsistent with the protection of life and property, princely and democratic government are also different in one fundamental respect. The decisive difference lies in the fact that entry into a princely government is systematically restricted by the prince's personal discretion, while under democracy entry into and participation in government is open to everyone on equal terms. Anyone not just a hereditary class of nobles is permitted to become a government official and exercise any government function, all the way up to that of prime minister or president.

Typically, this distinction between restricted versus free entry into government and the transition from princely to democratic government has been interpreted as an advance toward liberalism: from a society of status and privilege to one of equality before the law. But this interpretation rests on a fundamental misunderstanding. From a classical-liberal point of view, democratic government must be considered worse than and a regression from princely government.

Free and equal entry into government democratic equality is something entirely different from and incompatible with the classical-liberal concept of one universal law, equally applicable to everyone, everywhere, and at all times. Liberalism, Mises noted, "strives for the greatest possible unification of law, in the last analysis for world unity of law."[10] However, free entry into government does not accomplish *this* goal. To

---

[10]Mises, *Nation, State, and Economy*, p. 38.

the contrary, the objectionable inequality of the higher law of princes versus the subordinate law of ordinary subjects is preserved under democracy in the separation of public versus private law and the supremacy of the former over the latter. Under democracy, everyone is equal insofar as entry into government is open to all on the same terms. In a democracy no *personal* privileges or privileged persons exist. However, *functional* privileges and privileged functions exist. As long as they act in an official capacity, democratic government agents are governed and protected by public law and thereby occupy a privileged position *vis-à-vis* persons acting under the mere authority of private law (most fundamentally in being permitted to support their own activities by taxes imposed on private law subjects). Privileges, discrimination, and protectionism do not disappear. To the contrary. Rather than being restricted to princes and nobles, privileges, discrimination, and protectionism can be exercised by and accorded to everyone.

Predictably, under democratic conditions the tendency of every compulsory monopoly to increase prices and decrease quality is strengthened. As a hereditary monopolist, a prince regards the territory and people under his jurisdiction as his personal property and engages in the monopolistic exploitation of his "property." Under democracy, exploitation does not disappear. Even though everyone is permitted to enter government, this does not eliminate the distinction between the rulers and the ruled. Government and the governed are not one and the same person. Instead of a prince who considers the country his private property, a temporary and interchangeable caretaker is put in monopolistic charge. The caretaker does not own the country, but as long as he is in office he is permitted to use it to his and his protégés' advantage. He owns its current use, *usufruct,* but not its capital stock. This does not eliminate exploitation. Rather, it makes exploitation less calculating and carried out with little or no regard to the capital stock. In other words, it is shortsighted.[11]

Both hereditary princes and democratic caretakers can increase their current spending by means of higher taxes. However, a prince tends to avoid increasing taxes if this leads to capital consumption—a drop in the present discounted value of the capital stock of which he is the owner. In contrast, a caretaker shows no such reluctance. While he

---

[11]On this and the following see Murray N. Rothbard, *Power and Market: Government and the Economy* (Kansas City: Sheed Andrews and McMeel, 1977), chap. 5; and Hans-Hermann Hoppe, "The Political Economy of Monarchy and Democracy, and the Idea of a Natural Order," *Journal of Libertarian Studies* 11, no. 2 (1995).

owns the present tax-revenue, he does not own the capital stock from which it is derived—others do. Accordingly, under democratic conditions taxation increases far beyond its level under princely rule.

In addition, both princes and caretakers can increase their current spending by means of debt, and endowed with the power to tax, both tend to incur more debt than would private citizens. However, whereas a prince assumes a liability against his personal property whenever he borrows from (sells bonds to) the nongovernment public (hence the present value of his property falls), a democratic caretaker is free of any such consideration. He can enjoy all the benefits of higher current spending, while the liability and concurrent drop in property values falls upon others. Accordingly, government debt is higher and increases faster under democratic conditions than under princely rule.

Finally, both princes and caretakers can use their compulsory monopoly power to gain control over the money supply, so both can also increase their own present spending by inflating the supply of money. However, a prince who inflates the money supply will weigh two factors: his immediate enrichment *and* the fact that, as the inevitable result of a larger money supply, the future purchasing power of money and of his own future taxes will be lower. Unlike a prince, a democratic caretaker is concerned only with his immediate enrichment, for he does not own current *and* future tax revenues. He only owns the present tax revenue, so he is solely concerned with the present purchasing power of money. By increasing the money supply, he can increase his present purchasing power, while the attendant lower purchasing power of money and tax receipts must be born in the future by others. Accordingly, money inflation will also be more prevalent under democratic conditions than under princely rule.

V

Moreover, with free entry into and participation in government, the perversion of justice and protection (law and order) will proceed even faster. The notion of universal and immutable human rights and in particular of property rights essentially disappears and is replaced by that of law as government-made legislation and rights as government-given grants.[12]

---

[12]On the fundamental distinction between law and legislation see Bruno Leoni, *Freedom and the Law* (Indianapolis: Liberty Fund, 1991); Friedrich A. Hayek, *Law, Legislation and Liberty*, 2 vols. (Chicago: University of Chicago Press, 1973), vol. 1: *Rules and Order*; Murray N. Rothbard, *The Ethics of Liberty* (New York: New York University Press, 1998).

Rather than just redistributing income and wealth from civil society onto government by means of taxation, deficit financing, and money inflation, both hereditary princes and democratic caretakers can also use their monopoly of jurisdiction for the redistribution of income and wealth *within* civil society. The incentives faced in this regard by princes and caretakers are distinctly different, however.

It is instructive to take another look at princely government. As regards redistribution, princes face two disincentives. The first is a logical one. Even though a prince ranks above everyone else, his rights, too, are private rights, albeit of a somewhat elevated kind. If a prince takes the property of one person and distributes it to another, he undermines the principle on which his own position and security *vis-à-vis* other princes rests.[13] Second, from an economic point of view, all general income and wealth redistribution from the "haves" of something to the "have-nots" is counterproductive and reduces the overall value of the territory. This is not to say that princes abstain from redistributive policies entirely, but their policies take a distinctly different form. On the one hand, they must appear in accordance with the idea of *private* property rights; on the other hand, they should *increase* future productivity and hence the country's present value. Accordingly, princes typically grant *personal* rather than group privileges; they award privileges to haves instead of have-nots, and they attend to so called "social problems" by reallocating labor cultivation, acculturation, and colonization policies rather than redistributing income and wealth.

In contrast, a democratic caretaker faces no logical obstacle to the redistribution of private property. Rather than involving himself with the preservation and improvement of capital values, he will be concerned primarily with the protection and advancement of his own position against the competition of new government entrants.

This type of caretaker's legitimacy does not rest on the legitimacy of private property. It rests on the legitimacy of "social" or "public" property. Thus, if he takes property from one person and gives it to another, as a caretaker he does not contradict his own ideological foundation. Rather, he affirms the supremacy of the different principle of social ownership. Consequently, under democratic conditions private law—the law of property and contract underlying civil society—disappears as an independent domain of law and is absorbed by an all-encompassing

[13]See also Bertrand de Jouvenel, *Sovereignty: An Inquiry into the Political Good* (Chicago: University of Chicago Press, 1957), pp. 172–73, 189.

public—government made—law (legislation). As the German socialist legal theorist Gustav Radbruch noted, from the perspective of a democratic caretaker "private law is to be regarded only as a provisional and constantly decreasing range of private initiative, temporarily spared within the all-comprehensive sphere of public law."[14] Ultimately, all property is public property. Each established private property right is only provisionally valid and may be altered in accordance with a caretaker's unilateral determination of the requirements of "public safety" and "social security."

Second and more specifically, because caretakers do not own the country's capital stock, the counterproductive effects of income and wealth redistribution are of little or no concern. However, the long-term repercussions of redistributive measures are unimportant to them, while their immediate and short-term effects are not. A caretaker is always under the pressure of political competition from others seeking to replace him. Given the rules of democratic government—of one-man-one-vote and majority rule—a caretaker, whether to secure his present position or advance to another, must award or promise to award privileges to *groups* rather than particular individuals, and given that there always exist more have-nots than haves of everything worth having, his redistribution will be egalitarian rather than elitist. Accordingly, as the result of democratic competition the character structure of society will be progressively deformed.

For one, regardless of the criteria on which it is based, all redistribution involves "taking" from an original owner and/or producer—the "haver" of something—and "giving" to another nonowner and/or nonproducer—the "nonhaver" of this thing. The incentive to be an original owner or producer of the thing in question is reduced, and the incentive to be a nonowner and nonproducer is raised. Consequently, the number of havers and producers declines and that of nonhavers and nonproducers rises. And since it is presumably something *good* that is being redistributed—of which the haver-producers have too much and the nonhaver-nonproducers too little, this change implies quite literally that the relative number of bad or not-so-good people and bad or not-so-good personal characteristics and habits will continually rise, and life in society will become increasingly less pleasant. Rather than colonization, cultivation, and acculturation, democracy will bring about social degeneration, corruption, and decay.

---

[14]Gustav Radbruch, *Der Mensch im Recht* (Göttingen: Vandenhoeck, 1927), p. 40.

Moreover, free competition is not always good. Free competition in the production of goods is good, but free competition in the production of bads is not. Free competition in the torturing and killing of innocents, or free competition in counterfeiting or swindling, for instance, is not good; it is worse than bad. It has already been explained why government as a compulsory membership organization endowed with the power of ultimate decisionmaking and taxation must be considered a bad, at least from a liberal viewpoint. It requires a second look to realize that democratic competition is indeed worse than bad.

In every society, as long as mankind is what it is, people who covet another man's property will exist.[15] Some people are more afflicted by this sentiment than others. But people usually learn not to act on such feelings or even feel ashamed for entertaining them. Generally only a few individuals are unable to successfully suppress their desire for others' property, and they are treated as criminals by their fellow men and repressed by physical punishment. Under princely rule, only one single person—the prince—can possibly act on the desire for another man's property, and it is this which makes him a potential danger and a "bad." Apart from the already noted logical and economic disincentives, however, a prince is further restrained in his redistributive desires by the circumstance that all members of society have learned to regard the taking and redistributing of another man's property as shameful and immoral and accordingly watch a prince's every action with utmost suspicion. In distinct contrast, by freeing up entry into government, everyone is permitted to openly express his desire for other men's property. What was formerly regarded as immoral and accordingly suppressed is now considered a legitimate sentiment. Everyone may openly covet everyone else's property, as long as he appeals to democracy; and everyone may act on his desire for another man's property, provided that he finds entrance into government. Hence, under democracy everyone becomes a threat.

Consequently, under democratic conditions the popular, if immoral and anti-social, desire for other men's property is systematically strengthened. Every demand is legitimate, if it is proclaimed publicly under the special protection of "freedom of speech." Everything can be said and claimed, and everything is up for grabs. Not even the seemingly most secure private property right is exempt from redistributive demands. Worse, subject to mass elections, those members of society

---

[15]See on this Helmut Schoeck, *Envy: A Theory of Social Behavior* (New York: Harcourt, Brace and World, 1970).

with little or no moral inhibition against taking another man's property, habitual amoralists who are most talented in assembling majorities from a multitude of morally uninhibited and mutually incompatible popular demands, efficient demagogues, will tend to gain entrance in and rise to the top of government. Hence, a bad situation becomes even worse.[16]

Historically, the selection of a prince was through the accident of his noble birth, and his only personal qualification was typically his up-bringing as a future prince and preserver of the dynasty and its status and possessions. This did not assure that a prince would not be bad and dangerous, of course. However, it is worth remembering that any prince who failed in his primary duty of preserving the dynasty—who wrecked or ruined the country, caused civil unrest, turmoil and strife, or otherwise endangered the position of the dynasty—faced the immedi-ate risk of either being neutralized or assassinated by another member of his own family. In any case, however, even if the accident of birth and his upbringing could not preclude that a prince might be bad and danger-ous, at the same time the accident of a noble birth and a princely educa-tion also did not preclude that he might be a harmless dilettante or even a good and moral person. In contrast, the selection of government rulers by means of popular elections makes it practically impossible that any good or harmless person could ever rise to the top. Prime ministers and presidents are selected for their proven efficiency as morally uninhibi-ted demagogues. Thus, democracy virtually assures that *only* bad and dangerous men will ever rise to the top of government[17]; indeed, as the

---

[16]See also Hans-Hermann Hoppe, *Eigentum, Anarchie und Staat. Studien zur Theo-rie des Kapitalismus* (Opladen: Westdeutscher Verlag, 1987), pp. 182ff.

[17]Politicians, notes H.L. Mencken with his characteristic wit,

seldom if ever get there [into public office] by merit alone, at least in democratic states. Sometimes, to be sure, it happens, but only by a kind of miracle. They are chosen normally for quite different reasons, the chief of which is simply their power to impress and enchant the intellectually underprivileged. . . . Will any of them venture to tell the plain truth, the whole truth and nothing but the truth about the situation of the country, foreign or domestic? Will any of them refrain from promises that he knows he can't fulfill—that no human being *could* fulfill? Will any of them utter a word, however obvious, that will alarm and alienate any of the huge pack of morons who cluster at the public trough, wallowing in the pap that grows thinner and thinner, hoping against hope? Answer: maybe for a few weeks at the start. . . . But not after the issue is fairly joined, and the struggle is on in earnest. . . . They will all promise every man, woman and child in the country whatever he, she or it wants. They'll all be roving the land looking for chances to make the rich poor, to remedy the irremediable, to succor the

result of free political competition and selection, those who rise will become *increasingly* bad and dangerous individuals, yet as temporary and interchangeable caretakers they will only rarely be assassinated.

VI

After more than a century of compulsory democracy, the predictable results are before our very eyes. The tax load imposed on property owners and producers makes the economic burden even of slaves and serfs seem moderate in comparison. Government debt has risen to breathtaking heights. Gold has been replaced by government manufactured paper as money, and its value has continually dwindled. Every detail of private life, property, trade, and contract is regulated by ever higher mountains of paper laws (legislation). In the name of social, public or national security, our caretakers "protect" us from global warming and cooling and the extinction of animals and plants, from husbands and wives, parents and employers, poverty, disease, disaster, ignorance, prejudice, racism, sexism, homophobia, and countless other public enemies and dangers. And with enormous stockpiles of weapons of aggression and mass destruction they "defend" us, even outside of the U.S., from ever new Hitlers and all suspected Hitlerite sympathizers.

However, the only task a government was ever supposed to assume—of protecting our life and property—our caretakers do not perform. To the contrary, the higher the expenditures on social, public, and national security have risen, the more our private property rights have been eroded, the more our property has been expropriated, confiscated, destroyed, and depreciated, and the more we have been deprived of the very foundation of all protection: of personal independence, economic strength, and private wealth. The more paper laws have been produced,

---

unsuccorable, to unscramble the unscrambleable, to dephlogisticate the undephlogisticable. They will all be curing warts by saying words over them, and paying off the national debt with money that no one will have to earn. When one of them demonstrates that twice two is five, another will prove that it is six, six and a half, ten, twenty, *n*. In brief, they will divest themselves from their character as sensible, candid and truthful men, and become simply candidates for office, bent only on collaring votes. They will all know by then, even supposing that some of them don't know it now, that votes are collared under democracy, not by talking sense but by talking nonsense, and they will apply themselves to the job with a hearty yo-heave-ho. Most of them, before the uproar is over, will actually convince themselves. The winner will be whoever promises the most with the least probability of delivering anything. (*A Mencken Chrestomathy* [New York: Vintage Books, 1982], pp. 148–51)

the more legal uncertainty and moral hazard has been created, and law-lessness has displaced law and order. And while we have become ever more helpless, impoverished, threatened, and insecure, our rulers have become increasingly more corrupt, dangerously armed, and arrogant.

At this point, the question of the future of liberalism arises. It is appropriate to return to my beginning: to Ludwig von Mises and the idea of a liberal social order. Like Etienne de la Boétie and David Hume before him, Mises recognized that the power of every government, whether of princes or caretakers, benevolent men or tyrants, rests ulti-mately on opinion rather than physical force. The agents of government are always only a small proportion of the total population under their control, whether under princely or democratic rule. Even smaller is the proportion of central government agents. But this implies that a govern-ment, and in particular a central government, cannot possibly impose its will upon the entire population, unless it finds widespread support and voluntary cooperation within the nongovernmental public. As La Boétie put it:

> He who thus domineers over you . . . has indeed nothing more than the power that you confer upon him to destroy you. Where has he acquired enough eyes to spy upon you, if you do not provide them yourselves? How can he have so many arms to beat you with, if he does not borrow them from you? The feet that trample down your cities, where does he get them if they are not your own? How does he have any power over you except through you? How would he dare assail you if he had no cooperation from you? What would he do to you if you yourself did not connive with the thief who plunders you, if you were not accomplices of the murderer who kills you, if you were not traitors to yourselves? You sow your crops in order that he may ravage them, you install and furnish your homes to give him goods to pillage; you rear your daugh-ters that he may gratify his lust; you bring up your children in order that he may confer upon them the greatest privilege he knows to be led into his battles, to be delivered to butchery, to be made the servants of his greed and the instruments of his vengeance; you yield your bodies unto hard labor in order that he may indulge in his delights and wal-low in his filthy pleasures; you weaken yourselves in order to make him the stronger and mightier to hold you in check.[18]

However, if the power of every government rests only on opinion and consensual cooperation, then, as Mises's foremost student and our other intellectual master, Murray N. Rothbard, explained in his introduction to

---

[18]Etienne de la Boétie, *The Politics of Obedience: The Discourse of Voluntary Servitude* (New York: Free Life Editions, 1975), p. 52.

La Boétie's sixteenth century treatise, it also follows that each government can be brought down by a mere change of opinion and the exercise of sheer will power. "For if tyranny really rests on mass consent, then the obvious means for its overthrow is simply mass *withdrawal* of that consent."[19] That is, in order to strip government of its powers and repair it to the status of a voluntary membership organization (as before 1861), it is not necessary to take it over, to engage in violent battle against it, or even to lay hands on one's rulers. In fact, to do so would only reaffirm the principle of compulsion and aggressive violence underlying the current system and inevitably lead to the replacement of one government or tyrant by another. To the contrary, it is only necessary that one decide to withdraw from the compulsory union and reassume one's right to self protection. Indeed, it is essential that one proceed in no other way than by peaceful secession and noncooperation.[20]

If this advice seems at first naive (what difference does it make if you or I decide to secede from the Union?), its status as a genuine strategy of social revolution becomes apparent once the full implications of an act of personal secession are spelled out. The decision to secede involves that one regard the central government as illegitimate, and that one accordingly treat it and its agents as an outlaw agency and "foreign" occupying forces. That is, if compelled by them, one complies, out of prudence and for no other reason than self-preservation, but one does nothing to support or facilitate their operations. One tries to keep as much of one's property and surrender as little tax money as possible. One considers all federal law, legislation and regulation null and void and ignores it whenever possible. One does not work or volunteer for the central government, whether its executive, legislative, or judicial branch, and one does not associate with anyone who does (and in particular not with those high up in the hierarchy of caretakers). One does not participate in

---

[19]Ibid., p. 15.

[20]Rothbard explains in his introduction to La Boétie (ibid., p. 17):

It was a medieval tradition to justify tyrannicide of unjust rulers who break the divine law, but La Boétie's doctrine, though non-violent, was in the deepest sense far more radical. For while the assassination of a tyrant is simply an isolated individual act *within* an existing political system, mass civil disobedience, being a direct act on the part of large masses of people, is far more revolutionary in launching a transformation of the system itself. It is also more elegant and profound in theoretical terms, flowing immediately as it does from La Boétie's insight about power necessarily resting on popular consent; for then the remedy to power is simply to withdraw that consent.

central government politics and contributes nothing to the operation of the federal political machinery. One does not contribute to any national political party or political campaign, nor to any organization, agency, foundation, institute, or think-tank cooperating with or funded by any branch of the federal Leviathan or anyone living or working in or near Washington D.C.

Instead, with as much of one's property as can possibly be secured from the hands of government one begins to provide for one's own protection and adopts a new systematic twofold investment strategy. On the one hand, just as the existence of private crime requires an appropriate defense such as locks, guns, gates, guards, and insurance, so the existence of government requires specific defense measures: that one invest in such forms and at such locations which withdraw, remove, hide, or conceal one's wealth as far as possible from the eyes and arms of government. But defensive measures are not sufficient. In order to gain full protection of one's property from the reaches of government, it is necessary not to remain isolated in one's decision to secede. Not everyone must follow one's example, of course. Indeed, it is not even necessary that a majority of the entire population do so. It is necessary, however, that at least a majority of the population at many separate localities do so, and to reach this critical level of *mass* withdrawal it is essential to complement one's defensive measures with an offensive strategy: to invest in an ideological campaign of delegitimizing the idea and institution of democratic government among the public.

The mass of people, as La Boétie and Mises recognized, always and everywhere consists of "brutes," "dullards," and "fools," easily deluded and sunk into habitual submission. Thus today, inundated from early childhood with government propaganda in public schools and educational institutions by legions of publicly certified intellectuals, most people mindlessly accept and repeat nonsense such as that democracy is self-rule and government is of, by, and for the people. Even if they can see through this deception, most still unquestioningly accept democratic government on account of the fact that it provides them with a multitude of goods and benefits. Such "fools," observed La Boétie, do not realize that they are "merely recovering a portion of their own property, and that their ruler could not have given them what they were receiving without having first taken it from them."[21] Thus, every social revolution will necessarily have to begin with just a few uncommon men: the natural elite.

---

[21]Ibid., p. 70.

This is how La Boétie describes this elite and its role:

There are always a few, better endowed than others, who feel the weight of the yoke and cannot restrain themselves from attempting to shake it off: these are the men who never become tamed under subjection and who always, like Ulysses on land and sea constantly seeking the smoke of his chimney, cannot prevent themselves from peering about for their natural privileges and from remembering their ancestors and their former ways. These are in fact the men who, possessed of clear minds and farsighted spirit, are not satisfied, like the brutish mass, to see only what is at their feet, but rather look about them, behind and before, and even recall the things of the past in order to judge those of the future, and compare both with their present condition. These are the ones who, having good minds of their own, have further trained them by study and learning. Even if liberty had entirely perished from the earth, such men would invent it. For them slavery has no satisfaction, no matter how well disguised.[22]

Just as there can be no revolution without a liberal-libertarian elite, however, so can there also be no revolution without some form of mass participation. That is, the elite cannot reach its own goal of restoring private property rights and law and order unless it succeeds in communicating its ideas to the public, openly if possible and secretly if necessary, and awakening the masses from their subservient slumber by arousing, at least temporarily, their natural instinct of wanting to be free. As Mises put it: "The flowering of human society depends on two factors: the intellectual power of outstanding men to conceive sound social and economic theories, and the ability of these or other men to make these ideologies palatable to the majority."[23]

Hence, the decision by members of the elite to secede from and not cooperate with government must always include the resolve of engaging in, or contributing to, a continuous ideological struggle, for if the power of government rests on the widespread acceptance of false indeed absurd and foolish ideas, then the only genuine protection is the systematic attack of these ideas and the propagation and proliferation of true ones. Yet just as one must be always cautious and careful regarding one's material investments, it is equally important that one be eternally vigilant and selective in one's ideological investments.

In particular, in this endeavor it is not sufficient to merely criticize or support critics and criticisms of specific government policies or personalities, for even if correct and popular, such criticism does not penetrate

---

[22]Ibid., p. 65.

[23]Mises, *Human Action*, p. 864.

to the root of the problem. In the terminology of the "New Left," it is "immanent to the system" and thus harmless from the point of view of government. Accordingly, any support given to such efforts, however well-intended, is at best wasteful and at worst further increases the power of government. Rather, while criticisms and critics of government may *start* with specific policies or personalities, or even if they *must* do so to attract mass attention, everything and everyone worth supporting will have to go further. Every critic and criticism deserving of support must proceed to explain each and every particular government failing as symptomatic of an underlying flaw in the very idea of government itself (and of democratic government in particular). In other words, no critic or criticism is worthy of anyone's support unless it exposes as intellectual fraud the two pillars on which all government power rests: the belief that the protection of private property, unique among all goods, necessitates a compulsory monopoly (a nonvoluntary membership organization), and that private property and protection are best secured if entry into this monopoly of law and order is free and its directors are elected democratically.

In fact, there must never be even the slightest wavering in one's commitment to uncompromising ideological radicalism ("extremism"). Not only would anything less be counterproductive, but more importantly, *only* radical—indeed, radically simple—ideas can possibly stir the emotions of the dull and indolent masses. And nothing is more effective in persuading the masses to cease cooperating with government than the constant and relentless exposure, desanctification, and ridicule of government and its representatives as moral and economic frauds and impostors: as emperors without clothes subject to contempt and the butt of all jokes.

If and only if the members of the natural liberal-libertarian elite have fully grasped this lesson and begin to act accordingly will liberalism have a future. Only then will they have done what La Boétie advised us all to do:

> Resolve to serve no more, and you are at once freed. I do not ask that you place hands upon the tyrant to topple him over, but simply that you support him no longer; then you will behold him, like a great Colossus whose pedestal has been pulled away, fall of his own weight and break into pieces.[24]

---

[24]La Boétie, *The Politics of Obedience*, pp. 52–53.

4

On Democracy, Redistribution, and the Destruction of Property

Imagine a world government, democratically elected according to the principle of one-man-one-vote on a worldwide scale. What would the probable outcome of an election be? Most likely, we would get a Chinese–Indian coalition government. And what would this government most likely decide to do in order to satisfy its supporters and be reelected? The government would probably find that the so-called Western world had far too much wealth and the rest of the world, in particular China and India, far too little, and that a systematic wealth and income redistribution would be necessary.[1] Or imagine that in your own country the right to vote were expanded to seven year olds. While the government would not likely be staffed of children, its policies would most definitely reflect the "legitimate concerns" of children to have "adequate and "equal" access to "free" french fries, lemonade, and videos.[2]

With these "thought experiments" in mind, there can be no doubt about the consequences which resulted from the process of democratization that began in Europe and the U.S. in the second half of the

---

[1] The combined population of China and India is around 2.2 billion (of a current world population of about 6 billion). By contrast, the combined population of Western Europe and North America is approximately 700 million.

[2] During the mid-nineteenth century the average life-expectancy in Western Europe and North America was approximately forty years. At that time, apart from being restricted exclusively to males as well as by significant minimum property requirements, the franchise was restricted by a minimum age requirement of typically twenty-five years (in some places such as the United Kingdom and Sweden the requirement was as low as twenty-one years, and in others such as France and Denmark it was as high as thirty years). Nowadays, while the average life-expectancy in Western Europe and North America has risen to well above seventy years, the franchise extends everywhere to males and females, all property requirements have been abolished, and the minimum voting age has been generally lowered to eighteen years. If the original "maturity" requirements had been maintained, the minimum age should have been raised instead: from on the average twenty-five years to about fifty years!

nineteenth century and has come to fruition since the end of World War I. The successive expansion of the franchise and finally the establishment of universal adult suffrage did *within* each country what a world democracy would do for the entire globe: it set in motion a seemingly permanent tendency toward wealth and income redistribution.[3]

One-man-one-vote combined with "free entry" into government democracy implies that every person and his personal property comes within reach of and is up for grabs by everyone else. A "tragedy of the commons" is created.[4] It can be expected that majorities of "have-nots" will relentlessly try to enrich themselves at the expense of minorities of "haves." This is not to say that there will be only one class of have-nots and one class of haves, and that the redistribution will occur uniformly from the rich onto the poor. To the contrary. While the redistribution from rich to poor will always play a prominent role, it would be a sociological blunder to assume that it will be the sole or even the predominant form of redistribution.[5] After all, the "permanently" rich and the "permanently" poor are usually rich or poor for a reason. The rich are characteristically bright and industrious, and the poor typically dull, lazy, or

---

[3]As a rough indicator of this tendency one may want to relate successive expansions of the electorate during the late nineteenth and early twentieth century to the rise of the socialist and social-democratic voter turnout (and the parallel decline of classical liberal parties). A few examples will have to suffice here. (1) *Germany*: For the years 1871, 1903, and 1919, the total number of votes cast was 4.1, 9.5, and 30.5 million respectively; the socialist voter turnout was 3, 32, and 46 percent respectively; the liberal voter turnout was 46, 22, and 23 percent respectively. (2) *Italy*: For the years 1895, 1913, and 1919, the total number of votes was 1.3, 5.1, and 5.8 million respectively; the socialist voter turnout was 7, 18, and 32 percent respectively; the liberal voter turnout was 80, 56, and 35 percent respectively. (3) *United Kingdom*: For the years 1906, and 1918, the total number of votes was 7.3, and 21.4 million respectively; the socialist voter turnout was 5, and 21 percent respectively; the liberal voter turnout was 49, and 25 percent respectively. (4) *Sweden*: For the years 1905, 1911, and 1921, the total number of votes cast was 0.2, 0.6, and 1.7 million respectively; the socialist voter turnout was 9, 28, and 36 percent respectively; the liberal voter turnout was 45, 40, and 19 percent respectively. (5) *Netherlands*: For the years 1888, 1905, and 1922, the total votes cast was 0.3, 0.8, and 3.3 million respectively; the socialist voter turnout was 3, 17, and 27 percent respectively; the liberal voter turnout was 40, 28, and 9 percent respectively.

[4]The "tragedy of the commons" refers to the overutilization, waste, or depletion of resources held in common (as publicly owned goods). See *Managing the Commons*, Garrett Hardin and John Baden, eds. (San Francisco: W.H. Freeman, 1977).

[5]See on this Joseph A. Pechman, "The Rich, the Poor, and the Taxes They Pay," *Public Interest* (Fall 1969); Murray N. Rothbard, *For A New Liberty* (New York: Collier, 1978), pp. 157–62.

both.[6] It is not very likely that dullards, even if they make up a majority, will systematically outsmart and enrich themselves at the expense of a minority of bright and energetic individuals. Rather, most redistribution will take place *within* the group of the "non-poor," and frequently it will actually be the better-off who succeed in having themselves subsidized by the worse-off. Consider, for example, the almost universal practice of offering a "free" university education, whereby the working class, whose children rarely attend universities, pay through taxation for the education of middle-class children![7] Moreover, it can be expected that there will be many competing groups and coalitions trying to gain at the expense of others. There will be various changing criteria defining what it is that makes one person a "have" (deserving to be looted) and another a "have-not" (deserving to receive the loot). At the same time, individuals will be members of a multitude of groups of "haves" and/or "have-nots," losing on account of one of their characteristics

---

[6]See on this Edward C. Banfield, *The Unheavenly City Revisited* (Boston: Little, Brown, 1974), esp. chap. 3. Typically, Banfield explains, poverty is merely a transitory phase, restricted to the early stage in a person's working career. "Permanent" poverty, by contrast, is caused by specific cultural values and attitudes: a person's present-orientedness or, in economic terms, its high degree of time preference (which is highly correlated with low intelligence, and both of which appear to have a common genetic basis). Whereas the former—temporarily-poor-yet-upward-moving—individual is characterized by future-orientation, self-discipline, and a willingness to forego present gratification in exchange for a better future, the latter—permanently poor—individual is characterized by present-orientation and hedonism. Writes Banfield:

If [the latter] has any awareness of the future, it is of something fixed, fated, beyond his control: things happen to him, he does not make them happen. Impulse governs his behavior, either because he cannot discipline himself to sacrifice a present for a future satisfaction or because he has no sense of the future. He is therefore radically improvident. . . . He works only as he must to stay alive, and drifts from one unskilled job to another, taking no interest in his work. . . . He is careless with his things . . . and, even when nearly new, they are likely to be permanently out of order for lack of minor repairs. His body, too, is a thing "to be worked out but not repaired." (pp. 61–62)

[7]See on this Armen Alchian, "The Economic and Social Impact of Free Tuition," in idem, *Economic Forces at Work* (Indianapolis, Ind.: Liberty Fund, 1977); Rothbard, *For A New Liberty*, chap. 7. Other examples involving this type of redistribution are farm subsidies, favoring in particular large wealthy farmers, minimum wages, favoring higher paid skilled (and unionized) workers at the expense of unskilled (and nonunionized) workers, and, of course, all forms of "business protection" laws (protective tariffs), favoring wealthy owners of corporations at the expense of the mass of comparatively poor consumers.

and gaining on account of another, with some individuals ending up net-losers and others net-winners of redistribution.

The recognition of democracy as a machinery of popular wealth and income redistribution in conjunction with one of the most fundamental principles in all of economics that one will end up getting more of whatever it is that is being subsidized provides the key to understanding the present age.[8]

All redistribution, regardless of the criterion on which it is based, involves "taking" from the original owners and/or producers (the "havers" of something) and "giving" to nonowners and nonproducers (the "nonhavers" of something). The incentive to be an original owner or producer of the thing in question is reduced, and the incentive to be a non-owner and non-producer is raised. Accordingly, as a result of subsidizing individuals because they are poor, there will be more poverty. By subsidizing people because they are unemployed, more unemployment will be created. Supporting single mothers out of tax funds will lead to an increase in single motherhood, "illegitimacy," and divorce.[9] In outlawing child labor, income is transferred from families with children to childless persons (as a result of the legal restriction on the supply of labor, wage rates will rise). Accordingly, the birthrate will fall. On the other hand, by subsidizing the education of children, the opposite effect is created. Income is transferred from the childless and those with few children to those with many children. As a result the birthrate will increase. Yet then the value of children will again fall, and birthrates will decline as a result of the so-called social security system, for in subsidizing retirees (the old) out of taxes imposed on current income earners (the young), the institution of a family—the intergenerational bond between parents, grandparents, and children—is systematically weakened. The old need no longer rely on the assistance of their children if they have made no provision for their own old age, and the young (with typically less accumulated wealth) must support the old (with typically more accumulated wealth) rather than the other way around, as is typical within families. Parents' wish for children, and childrens' wish for parents will decline, family breakups and dysfunctional families

---

[8]On the economics of redistribution see Ludwig von Mises, *Socialism: An Economic and Sociological Analysis* (Indianapolis, Ind.: Liberty Fund, 1981), esp. chap. 34; Murray N. Rothbard, *Power and Market: Government and the Economy* (Kansas City: Sheed Andrews and McMeel, 1977), pp. 169ff.; idem, *For A New Liberty*, chap. 8.

[9]For a detailed empirical investigation of these and numerous related issues see Charles Murray, *Losing Ground* (New York: Basic Books, 1984).

will increase, and provisionary action—saving and capital formation—will fall, while consumption rises.[10]

As a result of subsidizing the malingerers, the neurotics, the careless, the alcoholics, the drug addicts, the Aids-infected, and the physically and mentally "challenged" through insurance regulation and compulsory health insurance, there will be more illness, malingering, neuroticism, carelessness, alcoholism, drug addiction, Aids infection, and physical and mental retardation.[11] By forcing noncriminals, including the victims of crime, to pay for the imprisonment of criminals (rather than making criminals compensate their victims and pay the full cost of their own apprehension and incarceration), crime will

---

[10]Concerning the effect of "social security," compulsory school attendance laws and the prohibition of child labor on the progressive destruction of families see Allan C. Carlson, *What Has Government Done to Our Families?* (Auburn, Ala.: Ludwig von Mises Institute, 1991); also Bryce J. Christensen, *The Family vs. the State* (Auburn, Ala.: Ludwig von Mises Institute, 1992).

[11]For one of the earliest, most profound, and most farsighted analyses of this see Mises, *Socialism*, pp. 429–32 and 438–41. Writing in the early 1920s, Mises described the effects of "social insurance" as follows:

> By weakening or completely destroying the will to be well and able to work, social insurance creates illness and inability to work; it produces the habit of complaining. . . . In short, it is an institution which tends to encourage disease, not to say accidents, and to intensify considerably the physical and psychic results of accidents and illnesses. As a social institution it makes a people sick bodily and mentally or at least helps to multiply, lengthen, and intensify disease. (p. 432)

Moreover, Mises proceeds to the heart of the matter and explains why insurance against most health and accident risks, and in particular against the risk of unemployment, is economically *impossible*:

> The value of health and accident insurance becomes problematic by reason of the possibility that they insured person may himself bring about, or at least intensify, the condition insured against. But in the case of unemployment insurance, the condition insured against can never develop unless the insured persons so will. . . . Unemployment is a problem of wages, not work. It is just as impossible to insure against unemployment as it would be to insure against, say, the unsaleability of commodities. . . . Unemployment insurance is definitely a misnomer. There can never be any statistical foundation for such an insurance. (p. 439)

On the logic of risk and insurance see further Ludwig von Mises, *Human Action: A Treatise on Economics*, Scholar's Edition (Auburn, Ala.: Ludwig von Mises Institute, 1998), chap. 6; on the dysgenic consequences of social "insurance" see Seymour W. Itzkoff, *The Road to Equality: Evolution and Social Reality* (Westport, Conn.: Praeger, 1992); idem, *The Decline of Intelligence in America* (Westport, Conn.: Praeger, 1994).

increase.[12] By forcing businessmen, through "affirmative action" ("non-discrimination") programs, to employ more women, homosexuals, blacks, or other "minorities" than they would like to, there will be more employed minorities, and fewer employers and fewer male, heterosexual, and white employment.[13] By compelling private land owners to subsidize ("protect") "endangered species" residing on their land through environmental legislation, there will be more and better-off animals, and fewer and worse-off humans.[14]

Most importantly, by compelling private property owners and/or market income earners (producers) to subsidize "politicians," "political parties," and "civil servants" (politicians and government employees do not *pay* taxes but are *paid* out of taxes),[15] there will be less wealth

---

[12]On crime and punishment see Murray N. Rothbard, *The Ethics of Liberty* (New York: New York University Press, 1998), chap. 13; *Assessing the Criminal*, Randy E. Barnett and John Hagel, eds. (Cambridge, Mass.: Ballinger, 1977); *Criminal Justice? The Legal System vs. Individual Responsibility*, Robert J. Bidinotto, ed. (Irvington-on Hudson, N.Y.: Foundation for Economic Education, 1994).

[13]On the law and economics of "affirmative action" and discrimination see Richard A. Epstein, *Forbidden Grounds* (Chicago: University of Chicago Press, 1992); *Discrimination, Affirmative Action, and Equal Opportunity*, Walter Block and Michael Walker, eds. (Vancouver: Fraser Institute, 1982).

[14] On conservation and environmentalism see Murray N. Rothbard, "Conservation in the Free Market," in idem, *Egalitarianism as a Revolt Against Nature and Other Essays* (Washington, D.C.: Libertarian Review Press, 1974); idem, *Power and Market*, pp. 63–70; idem, "Law, Property Rights, and Air Pollution," in idem, *The Logic of Action Two* (Cheltenham, U.K.: Edward Elgar, 1997); Llewellyn Rockwell, Jr., *The Anti-Environmentalist Manifesto* (Burlingame, Calif.: Center for Libertarian Studies, 1993).

[15]See on this Rothbard, *Power and Market*, chap. 2, and pp. 84ff. To recognize this important truth it is only necessary to raise the question "What would happen if all taxes were abolished?" Would this imply, for instance, that everyone's income would increase from net (after-tax) income to gross (before-tax) income? The answer is clearly "no." For something is currently done with the taxes collected. They are used, for instance, to pay the salaries of government employees. Their salaries could not possibly rise if taxes were abolished. Rather, their salaries would fall to zero, which demonstrates that they are not paying any taxes at all. As Rothbard explains: "If a bureaucrat receives a salary of $ 5,000 a year and pays $ 1,000 in 'taxes' to the government, it is quite obvious that he is simply receiving a salary of $ 4,000 and pays no taxes at all. The heads of government have simply chosen a complex and misleading accounting device to make it appear that he pays taxes in the same way as any other men making the same income" (ibid., p. 278, also p. 142). Once this has been understood it becomes obvious why certain groups such as school teachers and university professors are almost always and uniformly in favor of higher taxes. They are not thereby generously accepting a greater burden imposed on themselves. Instead, higher taxes are the means by which they increase their own tax-financed

formation, fewer producers and less productivity, and ever more waste, "parasites" and parasitism.

Businessmen (capitalists) and their employees cannot earn an income unless they produce goods or services which are sold in markets. The buyers' purchases are voluntary. By buying a good or service, the buyers (consumers) demonstrate that they *prefer* this good or service over the sum of money that they must surrender in order to acquire it. In contrast, politicians, parties, and civil servants produce nothing which is sold in markets. No one *buys* government "goods" or "services." They are produced, and costs are incurred to produce them, but they are not sold and bought. On the one hand, this implies that it is impossible to determine their value and find out whether or not this value justifies their costs. Because no one buys them, no one actually demonstrates that he considers government goods and services worth their costs, and indeed, whether or not anyone attaches any value to them at all. From the viewpoint of economic theory, it is thus entirely illegitimate to assume, as is always done in national income accounting, that government goods and services are worth what it costs to produce them, and then to simply *add* this value to that of the "normal," privately produced (bought and sold) goods and services to arrive at gross domestic (or national) product, for instance. It might as well be assumed that government goods and services are worth nothing, or even that they are not "goods" at all but "bads," and hence, that the cost of politicians and the entire civil service should be *subtracted* from the total value of privately produced goods and services. Indeed, to assume *this* would be far more justified. For on the other hand, as to its practical implications, the subsidizing of politicians and civil servants amounts to a subsidy to "produce" with little or no regard for the well-being of one's alleged consumers, and with much or sole regard instead for the well-being of the "producers," i.e., the politicians and civil servants. Their salaries remain the same, whether their output satisfies consumers or not. Accordingly, as a result of the expansion of "public" sector employment, there will be increasing laziness, carelessness, incompetence, disservice, maltreatment, waste, and even destruction—and at the same time ever more arrogance, demagoguery, and lies ("we work for the public good").[16]

---

salaries. On the issue of taxpayers versus tax-consumers (or tax-eaters) see also John C. Calhoun, *A Disquisition on Government* (New York: Liberal Arts Press, 1953), pp. 16–18.

[16]On the fundamental errors involved in the standard national income accounting procedures, and a constructive alternative, see Murray N. Rothbard, *America's*

After less than one hundred years of democracy and redistribution, the predictable results are in. The "reserve fund" that was inherited from the past is apparently exhausted. For several decades (since the late 1960s or the early 1970s), real standards of living have stagnated or even fallen in the West.[17] The "public" debt and the cost of the existing social security and health care system have brought on the prospect of an imminent economic meltdown.[18] At the same time, almost every form of undesirable behavior unemployment, welfare dependency, negligence, recklessness, incivility, psychopathy, hedonism, and crime has increased, and social conflict and societal breakdown have risen to dangerous heights.[19] If current trends continue, it is safe to say that the Western welfare state (social democracy) will collapse just as Eastern (Russian-style) socialism collapsed in the late 1980s.

However, economic collapse does not automatically lead to improvement. Matters can become worse rather than better. What is necessary besides a crisis are ideas—correct ideas—and men capable of understanding and implementing them once the opportunity arises. Ultimately, the course of history is determined by ideas, be they true or false, and by men acting upon and being inspired by true or false ideas. The current mess is also the result of ideas. It is the result of the overwhelming acceptance, by public opinion, of the idea of democracy. As long as this acceptance prevails, a catastrophe is unavoidable, and there can be no hope for improvement even after its arrival. On the other hand, as soon as the idea of democracy is recognized as false and vicious—and ideas can, in principle, be changed almost instantaneously—a catastrophe can be avoided.

Great Depression (Kansas City: Sheed and Ward, 1975), pp. 296–304; idem, *Power and Market*, pp. 199–202.

[17]For an instructive study using Rothbard's suggestions for an alternative method of national income accounting see Robert Batemarco, "GNP, PPR, and the Standard of Living," *Review of Austrian Economics* 1 (1987).

[18]For a summary overview see Victoria Curzon Price, "The Mature Welfare State: Can It Be Reformed?" in *Can The Present Problems of Mature Welfare States Such as Sweden Be Solved?* Nils Karlson, ed. (Stockholm: City University Press, 1995), esp. pp. 15–19.

[19]In the U.S., for instance, between 1960 and 1990 the murder rate doubled, rape rates quadrupled, the robbery rate increased five-fold, and the likelihood of becoming the victim of an aggravated assault increased by 700 percent. See on this Seymour Itzkoff, *The Decline of Intelligence in America*; Roger D. McGrath, "Treat Them to a Good Dose of Lead," *Chronicles* (January 1994).

The central task of those wanting to turn the tide and prevent an outright breakdown is the "delegitimation" of the idea of democracy as the root cause of the present state of progressive "decivilization." To this purpose, one should first point out that it is difficult to find many proponents of democracy in the history of political theory. Almost all major thinkers had nothing but contempt for democracy. Even the Founding Fathers of the U.S., nowadays considered the model of a democracy, were strictly opposed to it. Without a single exception, they thought of democracy as nothing but mob-rule. They considered themselves to be members of a 'natural aristocracy,' and rather than a democracy they advocated an aristocratic republic.[20] Furthermore, even among the few theoretical defenders of democracy such as Rousseau, for instance, it is almost impossible to find anyone advocating democracy for anything but extremely small communities (villages or towns). Indeed, in small communities where everyone knows everyone else personally, most people must acknowledge that the position of the "haves" is typically based on their superior personal achievement just as the position of the "have-nots" finds its typical explanation in their personal deficiencies and inferiority. Under these circumstances, it is far more difficult to get

---

[20]See on this Erik von Kuehnelt-Leddihn, *Leftism Revisited* (Washington D.C.: Regnery Gateway, 1990), esp. chap. 6. Of the American founders, Alexander Hamilton was a monarchist. Likewise, the Governor of Pennsylvania, Robert Morris, had strong monarchist leanings. George Washington expressed his profound distaste of democracy in a letter of September 30, 1798, to James McHenry. John Adams was convinced that every society grows aristocrats as inevitably as a field of corn will grow some large ears and some small. In a letter to John Taylor he insisted, like Plato and Aristotle, that democracy would ultimately evolve into despotism, and in a letter to Jefferson he declared that "democracy will envy all, contend with all, endeavor to pull down all, and when by chance it happens to get the upper hand for a short time, it will be revengeful, bloody and cruel." James Madison, in a letter to Jared Parks, complained of the difficulty "of protecting the rights of property against the spirit of democracy." And even Thomas Jefferson, probably the most "democratic" of the Founders, confessed in a letter to John Adams that he considered

> the natural aristocracy . . . as the most precious gift of nature, for the instruction, the trusts and governments of society. And indeed, it would have been inconsistent in creation to have formed men for the social state, and not have provided virtue and wisdom enough to manage the concerns of society. May we not even say that that form of government is best, which provides most effectually for a pure selection of these natural *aristoi* into the offices of government?

Characterizing the general attitude of the founders, then, the most appropriate pronouncement is that of John Randolph of Roanoke: "I am an aristocrat: I love liberty, I hate equality."

away with trying to loot other people and their personal property to one's advantage. In distinct contrast, in large territories encompassing millions or even hundreds of millions of people, where the potential looters do not know their victims, and *vice versa*, the human desire to enrich oneself at another's expense is subject to little or no restraint.[21]

More importantly, it must be made clear again that the idea of democracy is *immoral* as well as *uneconomical*. As for the moral status of majority rule, it must be pointed out that it allows for A and B to band together to rip off C, C and A in turn joining to rip off B, and then B and C conspiring against A, and so on. This is not justice but a moral outrage, and rather than treating democracy and democrats with respect, they should be treated with open contempt and ridiculed as moral frauds.[22]

---

[21]Rousseau's *Social Contract*, which appeared in 1762, was actually meant to be a theoretical commentary on the political situation in his hometown of Geneva, then an independent city state of less than 30,000 inhabitants ruled, in effect, by a tiny hereditary oligarchy of the heads of Geneva's leading aristocratic families in control of the Small Council and the Council of the Two Hundred. Rousseau's appeal to the "people" and "popular sovereignty" was intended as an attack on this oligarchy, but by no means as a defense of direct democracy and universal political participation as it is nowadays understood. Rather, what Rousseau had in mind when he wrote in support of the "sovereign people" were merely the members of Geneva's other political body, the Grand Council, which was made up of some 1,500 members and included besides Geneva's upper aristocratic crust also its lower hereditary aristocracy.

[22]Fortunately, despite the relentless propaganda spread by government funded and controlled school teachers—such as "democracy means that we all rule ourselves"—as well as by celebrated Nobel laureates such as James Buchanan and his "public choice" school of economics—such as "governments are voluntary institutions just as firms" (James M. Buchanan and Gordon Tullock, *The Calculus of Consent* [Ann Arbor: University of Michigan Press, 1962], p. 19)— there is still enough common sense left, both in *academia* as well as among the general public, to find a sympathetic ear for such criticisms. As for *academia*, an economist as prominent as Joseph A. Schumpeter would note regarding views such as Buchanan's that "the theory which construes taxes on the analogy of club dues or the purchase of the service of, say, a doctor only proves how far removed this part of the social sciences is from scientific habits of minds" (Joseph A. Schumpeter, *Capitalism, Socialism, and Democracy* [New York: Harper, 1942], p. 198). And as far as the general public is concerned, one can find consolation in the remarks of the great American journalist and writer H.L. Mencken, who wrote:

> The average man, whatever his errors otherwise, at least sees clearly that government is something lying outside him and outside the generality of his fellow men—that it is a separate, independent, and hostile power, only partly under his control, and capable of doing him great harm. . . . Is it a fact of no significance that robbing the government is everywhere regarded a crime of less magnitude than robbing an individual, or even a corporation? . . . When a private citizen is robbed, a worthy man is deprived

On the other hand, as for the economic quality of democracy, it must be stressed relentlessly that it is not democracy but private property, production, and voluntary exchange that are the ultimate sources of human civilization and prosperity. In particular, contrary to widespread myths, it needs to be emphasized that the lack of democracy had essentially nothing to do with the bankruptcy of Russian-style socialism. It was not the selection principle for politicians that constituted socialism's problem. It was politics and political decisionmaking as such. Instead of each private producer deciding independently what to do with particular resources, as under a regime of private property and contractualism, with fully or partially socialized factors of production each decision requires someone else's permission. It is irrelevant to the producer how those giving permission are chosen. What matters to him is that permission must be sought at all. As long as this is the case, the incentive of producers to produce is reduced and impoverishment will ensue. Private property is as incompatible with democracy as it is with any other form of political rule.[23] Rather than democracy, justice as well as economic efficiency require a pure and unrestricted private property society an "anarchy of production" in which no one rules anybody, and all producers' relations are voluntary and thus mutually beneficial.[24]

Lastly, as for strategic considerations, in order to approach the goal of a non-exploitative social order, i.e., private property anarchy, the idea of majoritarianism should be turned against democratic rule itself. Under any form of governmental rule, including a democracy, the "ruling

---

of the fruits of his industry and thrift; when the government is robbed, the worst that happens is that certain rogues and loafers have less money to play with than they had before. The notion that they had earned that money is never entertained; to most sensible men it would seem ludicrous. They are simply rascals who, by accident of law, have a somewhat dubious right to a share in the earnings of their fellow men. When that share is diminished by private enterprise the business is, on the whole, far more noble than not." (*A Mencken Chrestomathy* [New York: Vintage Books, 1949], pp. 146–47; see also H. L. Mencken, *Notes on Democracy* (New York: Knopf, 1926).

[23]See on this Hans-Hermann Hoppe, *A Theory of Socialism and Capitalism* (Boston: Kluwer, 1989); idem, "Desocialization in a United Germany," *Review of Austrian Economics* 5, no. 2 (1991); Murray N. Rothbard, "The End of Socialism and the Calculation Debate Revisited," in idem, *The Logic of Action One* (Cheltenham, U.K.: Edward Elgar, 1997); idem, "How and How Not To Desocialize," *Review of Austrian Economics* 6, no. 1 (1992).

[24]See on this Rothbard, *The Ethics of Liberty*; Hans-Hermann Hoppe, *The Economics and Ethics of Private Property* (Boston: Kluwer, 1993) esp. part 2; also Anthony de Jasay, *Choice, Contract, Consent: A Restatement of Liberalism* (London: Institute of Economic Affairs, 1991).

class" (politicians and civil servants) represents only a small proportion of the total population. While it is possible that one hundred parasites may lead a comfortable life on the products of one thousand hosts, one thousand parasites cannot live off of one hundred hosts. Based on the recognition of this fact, it would appear possible to persuade a majority of the voters that it is adding insult to injury to let those living off of other peoples' taxes have a say in how high these taxes are, and to thus decide, democratically, to take the right to vote away from all government employees and everyone who receives government benefits, whether they are welfare recipients or government contractors.

In addition, in conjunction with this strategy it is necessary to recognize the overwhelming importance of secession and secessionist movements. If majority decisions are "right," then the largest of all possible majorities, a world majority and a democratic world government, must be considered ultimately "right,"[25] with the consequences predicted at the outset of this chapter. In contrast, secession always involves the breaking away of smaller from larger populations. It is thus a vote against the principle of democracy and majoritarianism. The further the process of secession proceeds to the level of small regions, cities, city districts, towns, villages, and ultimately individual households and voluntary associations of private households and firms, the more difficult it will become to maintain the current level of redistributive policies. At the same time, the smaller the territorial units, the more likely it will be that a few individuals, based on the popular recognition of their economic independence, outstanding professional achievement, morally impeccable personal life, superior judgment, courage, and taste, will rise to the rank of natural, voluntarily acknowledged elites and lend legitimacy to the idea of a natural order of competing (non-monopolistic) and freely (voluntarily) financed peacekeepers, judges, and overlapping jurisdictions as exists even now in the arena of international trade and travel. A pure private law society—as the answer to democracy and any other form of political (coercive) rule.[26]

---

[25]See on this also Murray N. Rothbard, *Power and Market*, pp. 189ff.

[26]On the law and economics of secession see *Secession, State and Liberty*, David Gordon, ed. (New Brunswick, N.J.: Transaction Publishers, 1998), with essays by Donald W. Livingston, Stephen Yates, Scott Boykin, Murray N. Rothbard, Clyde N. Wilson, Joseph R. Stromberg, Thomas DiLorenzo, James Ostrowski, Hans-Hermann Hoppe, Pierre Desrochers and Eric Duhaime, and Bruce L. Benson; also Hans-Hermann Hoppe, "The Western State as a Paradigm: Learning From History," *Politics and Regimes: Religion and Public Life* 30 (1997); Robert W. McGee, "Secession Reconsidered," *Journal of Libertarian Studies* 11, no. 1 (1994).

5
On Centralization and Secession

A state is a territorial monopolist of compulsion—an agency which may engage in continual, institutionalized property rights violations and the exploitation—in the form of expropriation, taxation, and regulation—of private property owners.[1] Assuming no more than self-interest on the part of government agents, all states (governments) can be expected to make use of this monopoly and thus exhibit a tendency toward *increased* exploitation. On the one hand, this means increased domestic exploitation (and internal taxation). On the other hand, and this aspect in particular will be of interest in the following, it means territorial expansionism. States will always try to enlarge their exploitation and tax base. In doing so, however, they will come into conflict with other, competing states. The competition between states qua territorial monopolists of compulsion is by its very nature an eliminative competition. That is, there can be only one monopolist of exploitation and taxation in any given area; thus, the competition between different states can be expected to promote a tendency toward increased political centralization and ultimately one single world state.

A glance at Western history suffices to illustrate the validity of this conclusion. At the beginning of this millenium, for instance, Europe consisted of thousands of independent political units. Now, only several dozen such units remain. To be sure, decentralizing forces also existed. There was the progressive disintegration of the Ottoman Empire from the sixteenth century until after World War I and the establishment of

---

[1]On the theory of the state see Murray N. Rothbard, *For A New Liberty* (New York: Macmillan, 1978); idem, *The Ethics of Liberty* (New York: New York University Press, 1998); idem, *Power and Market* (Kansas City: Sheed Andrews and McMeel, 1977); Hans-Hermann Hoppe, *Eigentum, Anarchie und Staat* (Opladen: Westdeutscher Verlag, 1987); idem, *A Theory of Socialism and Capitalism* (Boston: Kluwer, 1989); idem, *The Economics and Ethics of Private Property* (Boston: Kluwer, 1993); also Albert J. Nock, *Our Enemy, the State* (Delevan, Wisc.: Hallberg Publishing, 1983); Franz Oppenheimer, *The State* (New York: Vanguard Press, 1914); idem, *System der Soziologie*, Vol.2: *Der Staat* (Stuttgart: G. Fischer, 1964); Anthony de Jasay, *The State* (Oxford: Blackwell, 1985).

modern Turkey. The discontiguous Habsburg Empire was gradually dismembered from the time of its greatest expansion under Charles V until it disappeared and modern Austria was founded in 1918. And only recently, before our very eyes, the former Soviet Empire disintegrated. There are now more than a dozen independent states on the soil of the former Soviet Union. The former Yugoslavia consists now of Slovenia, Croatia, Serbia, Macedonia, and Bosnia. And the Czechs and the Slovaks have split and formed independent countries. However, the overriding tendency was in the opposite direction. For instance, during the second half of the seventeenth century, Germany consisted of some 234 countries, 51 free cities, and 1,500 independent knightly manors. By the early nineteenth century, the total number of the three had fallen to below 50, and by 1871 unification had been achieved. The scenario in Italy was similar. Even small states have a history of expansion and centralization. Switzerland began in 1291 as a confederation of three independent cantonal states. By 1848 it was a single (federal) state with some two dozen cantonal provinces.

Moreover, from a global perspective, mankind has come closer than ever before to the establishment of a world government. Even before the dissolution of the Soviet Empire, the United States had attained hegemonical status over Western Europe (most notably over West Germany) and the Pacific rim countries (most notably over Japan)—as indicated by the presence of American troops and military bases, by the NATO and SEATO pacts, by the role of the American dollar as the ultimate international reserve currency and of the U.S. Federal Reserve System as the "lender" or "liquidity provider" of last resort for the entire Western banking system, and by institutions such as the International Monetary Fund (IMF), the World Bank, and the recently established World Trade Organization (WTO).[2] In addition, under American hegemony the political integration of Western Europe has steadily advanced. With the recent establishment of a European Central Bank and a European Currency (EURO), the European Community is near completion. At the

---

[2]On the role of "fiat" (paper) money, central banking, and international (interstate) monetary cooperation as a vehicle of political unification and an instrument of economic imperialism, i.e., the exploitation of "peripheral" by "dominant" states, see Hans-Hermann Hoppe, "Banking, Nation States, and International Politics: A Sociological Reconstruction of the Present Economic Order," in idem, *The Economics and Ethics of Private Property*; Jörg Guido Hülsmann, "Political Unification: A Generalized Progression Theorem," *Journal of Libertarian Studies* 13, no. 1 (1977); also Murray N. Rothbard, *Wall Street, Banks, and American Foreign Policy*, (Burlingame, Calif.: Center for Libertarian Studies, 1995). See also notes 18 and 19 below.

same time, with the North American Free Trade Agreement (NAFTA) a significant step toward the political integration of the American continent has been taken. In the absence of the Soviet Empire and its military threat, the United States has emerged as the world's sole and undisputed military superpower and its "top cop."

According to the orthodox view, centralization is generally a "good" and progressive movement, whereas disintegration and secession, even if sometimes unavoidable, represent an anachronism. It is assumed that larger political units—and ultimately a single world government—imply wider markets and hence increased wealth. As evidence of this, it is pointed out that economic prosperity has increased dramatically with increased centralization. However, rather than reflecting any truth, this orthodox view is more illustrative of the fact that history is typically written by its victors. Correlation or temporal coincidence do not prove causation. In fact, the relationship between economic prosperity and centralization is very different from and indeed almost the opposite of what orthodoxy alleges.[3]

Political integration (centralization) and economic (market) integration are two completely different phenomena. Political integration involves the territorial expansion of a state's power of taxation and property regulation (expropriation). Economic integration is the extension of the interpersonal and interregional division of labor and market participation.[4] In principle, in taxing and regulating private property owners and market income earners, all governments are counterproductive. They *reduce* market participation and the formation of economic wealth.[5] Once the existence of a government has been assumed, however, no direct relationship between territorial size and economic integration exists. Switzerland and Albania are both small countries, but

---

[3]On the following see Jean Baechler, *The Origins of Capitalism* (New York: St.Martin's Press, 1976), esp. chap. 7; Hans-Hermann Hoppe, "The Economic and Political Rationale for European Secessionism," in *Secession, State, and Liberty*, David Gordon, ed. (New Brunswick, N.J.: Transaction Publishers, 1998); also Eric L. Jones, *The European Miracle* (Cambridge: Cambridge University Press, 1981); Nathan Rosenberg and L.E. Birdzell, *How the West Grew Rich* (New York: Basic Books, 1986); David S. Landes, *The Wealth and Poverty of Nations* (New York: Norton, 1998).

[4]On the the emergence of division of labor and economic integration see Ludwig von Mises, *Human Action: A Treatise on Economics*, Scholar's Edition (Auburn, Ala.: Ludwig von Mises Institute, 1998), chap. 8; Murray N. Rothbard, "Freedom, Inequality, Primitivism, and the Division of Labor," in idem, *Egalitarianism as a Revolt Against Nature and Other Essays* (Auburn, Ala.: Ludwig von Mises Institute, 2000).

[5]See on this Rothbard, *Power and Market*.

Switzerland exhibits a high degree of economic integration, whereas Albania does not. Both the U.S. and the former Soviet Union are large. Yet while there is much division of labor and market participation in the U.S., there was almost no economic integration in the Soviet Union, where virtually no private capital ownership existed.[6] Centralization, then, can go hand in hand with either economic progress or retrogression. Progress results whenever a less taxing and regulating government expands its territory at the expense of a more exploitative one. If the reverse occurs, centralization implies economic disintegration and retrogression.

However, there is a highly important indirect relationship between size and economic integration. A central government ruling over large-scale territories—and even less so a single world government—cannot come into existence *ab ovo*. Instead, all institutions with the power to tax and regulate owners of private property must start out small. Smallness contributes to moderation, however. A small government has many close competitors, and if it taxes and regulates its own subjects visibly more than its competitors, it is bound to suffer from the emigration of labor and capital and a corresponding loss of future tax revenue. Consider a single household, or a village, as an independent territory, for instance. Could a father do to his son, or a mayor to his village, what the government of the Soviet Union did to its subjects (i.e., deny them any right to private capital ownership) or what governments all across Western Europe and the U.S. do to their citizens (i.e., expropriate up to 50 percent of their productive output)? Obviously not. There would either be an immediate revolt and the government would be overthrown, or emigration to another nearby household or village would ensue.[7]

---

[6]See on this ibid.

[7]Political competition, then, is a far more effective device for limiting a government's natural desire to expand its exploitative powers than are internal constitutional limitations. Indeed, the attempts of some public choice theorists and of "constitutional economics" to design liberal model constitutions must strike one as hopelessly naive. For constitutional courts, and supreme court judges, are part and parcel of the government apparatus whose powers they are supposed to limit. Why in the world should they want to constrain the power of the very organization that provides them with jobs, money, and prestige? To assume so is not only theoretically inconsistent, i.e., incompatible with the assumption of self-interest. The assumption is also without any historical foundation. Despite the explicit limitation of the power of the central government contained in the Tenth Amendment of the U.S. Constitution, for instance, it has been the interpretation by the U.S. Supreme Court, which has rendered the amendment essentially null and void. Similarly, despite the constitutional guarantee of private property by the (West) German constitution, for

Contrary to orthodoxy, then, precisely the fact that Europe possessed a highly decentralized power structure composed of countless independent political units explains the origin of capitalism—the expansion of market participation and of economic growth—in the Western world.[8] It is not by accident that capitalism first flourished under conditions of extreme political decentralization: in the northern Italian city states, in southern Germany, and in the secessionist Low Countries (Netherlands).

The competition among small states for taxable subjects brings them into conflict with each other. As a result of interstate conflicts, historically drawn out over the course of centuries, a few states succeed in expanding their territories, while others are eliminated or incorporated. Which states win in this process of eliminative competition depends on many factors, of course, but in the long run, the decisive factor is the relative amount of economic resources at a government's disposal.[9] Through taxation and regulation, governments do not positively contribute to the creation of economic wealth. Instead, they parasitically draw on existing wealth. However, they can influence the amount of existing wealth negatively. Other things being equal, the lower the tax

---

instance, the German supreme court, after the German reunification in 1990, declared all communist expropriations prior to the founding of the East German state in 1949 "valid." Thus, more than 50 percent of former East Germany's land used for agriculture were appropriated by the (West) German state (rather than being returned to the original private owners, as required by a literal interpretation of the constitution).

[8]The importance of international "anarchy" for the rise of European capitalism has been justly emphasized by Jean Baechler. Thus, he writes in *The Origins of Capitalism*:

"The constant expansion of the market, both in extensiveness and in intensity, was the result of an absence of a political order extending over the whole of Western Europe." (p. 73) "The expansion of capitalism owes its origin and *raison d'etre* to political anarchy. . . . Collectivism and state management have only succeeded in school textbooks." (p. 77)

All power tends toward the absolute. If it is not absolute, this is because some kind of limitations have come into play. . . . those in the position of power at the center ceaselessly tried to erode these limitations. They have never succeeded, and for the reason that also seems to me to be tied to the international system: a limitation of power to act externally and the constant threat of foreign assault [the two characteristics of a multi-polar system] imply that power is also limited internally and must rely on autonomous centers of decisionmaking and so may use them only sparingly. (p. 78)

[9]See on this Paul Kennedy, *The Rise and Fall of the Great Powers: Economic Change and Military Conflict from 1500 to 2000* (New York: Vintage Books, 1987).

and regulation burden imposed by a government on its domestic economy, the larger its population tends to grow (due to internal reasons as
well as immigration factors), and the larger the amount of domestically
produced wealth on which it can draw in its conflicts with neighboring
competitors. For this reason centralization is frequently progressive.
States which tax and regulate their domestic economies little—liberal
states—tend to defeat and expand their territories at the expense of non-
liberal ones.[10] This accounts for the outbreak of the "Industrial Revolution" in centralized England and France. It explains why in the course of
the nineteenth century Western Europe came to dominate the rest of the
world (rather than the other way around), and why this colonialism was
generally progressive. Furthermore, it explains the rise of the U.S. to the
rank of superpower in the course of the twentieth century.

However, the further the process of more liberal governments de-
feating less liberal ones proceeds—i.e., the larger the territories, the
fewer and more distant the remaining competitors, and thus the more
costly international migration—the lower a government's incentive to
continue in its domestic liberalism will be. As one approaches the limit
of a One World state, all possibilities of voting with one's feet against a
government disappear. Wherever one goes, the same tax and regulation
structure applies. Thus relieved of the problem of emigration, a fundamental rein on the expansion of governmental power is gone. This explains developments of the twentieth century: with World War I, and
even more so with World War II, the U.S. attained hegemony over Western Europe and became heir to its vast colonial empires. A decisive step
in the direction of global unification was taken with the establishment of
a *pax Americana*. And indeed, throughout the entire period the U.S.,
Western Europe, and most of the rest of the world have suffered from a
steady and dramatic growth of government power, taxation, and regulatory expropriation.[11]

---

[10]See on this Hans-Hermann Hoppe, "Marxist and Austrian Class Analysis," in
idem, *The Economics and Ethics of Private Property*; idem, "Banking, Nation States, and
International Politics"; on the requirement of a liberal market economy, i.e., domestic laissez-faire, for the successful conduct of war see Ludwig von Mises, *Nationalök-
onomie. Theorie des Handelns und Wirtschaftens* (Munich: Philosophia Verlag, 1980),
part 6, chap. 9; idem, *Interventionism: An Economic Analysis* (Irvington-on-Hudson,
N.Y.: Foundation for Economic Education, 1998), chap. 6; on the contrary tendency
of states to use wars as pretexts for the destruction of domestic laissez-faire and the
implementation of increasingly interventionist or socialist economic systems see
Robert Higgs, *Crisis and Leviathan* (New York: Oxford University Press, 1987).

[11]On this theme see also Paul Johnson, *Modern Times* (New York: Harper and
Row, 1983); Robert Nisbet, *The Present Age* (New York: Harper and Row, 1988).

In light of social and economic theory and history, then, a case for secession can be made.[12]

Initially, secession is nothing more than a shifting of control over the nationalized wealth from a larger, central government to a smaller, regional one. Whether this leads to more or less economic integration and prosperity depends largely on the new regional government's policies. However, the act of secession in itself has a positive impact on production, for one of the most important reasons for secession is typically the belief on the part of the secessionists that they and their territory are being exploited by others. The Slovenes felt, and rightly so, that they were being robbed systematically by the Serbs and the Serbian-dominated central Yugoslavian government; the Baltic people resented the fact that they had to pay tribute to the Russians and the Russian-dominated government of the Soviet Union.[13] By virtue of secession, hegemonic domestic relations are replaced by contractual—mutually beneficial—foreign relations. Instead of forced integration there is voluntary separation. Forced integration, as also illustrated by measures such as busing, rent controls, affirmative action, antidiscrimination laws and, as will be explained shortly, "free immigration," invariably creates tension, hatred, and conflict. In contrast, voluntary separation leads to harmony and peace.[14] Under forced integration any mistake can be blamed on a "foreign" group or culture and all success claimed as one's own; hence, there is little reason for any culture to learn from another. Under a regime of "separate but equal," one must face up to the reality not only of cultural diversity but in particular of visibly different ranks of cultural advancement. If a secessionist people wishes to improve or maintain its position *vis-à-vis* a competing one, nothing but discriminative learning

---

[12]On the following see also *Secession, State, and Liberty*, Gordon, ed.; Robert McGee, "Secession Reconsidered," *Journal of Libertarian Studies* 11, no. 1 (1994); Ludwig von Mises, *Liberalism: In the Classical Tradition* (Irvington-on-Hudson, N.Y.: Foundation for Economic Education, 1985), esp. pp. 108–10.

[13]Similarly, one of the decisive reasons for the attempt by the Southern Confederacy to secede from the American Union was the Morrill Tariff Act of 1861, which imposed a 47 percent tax on the value of all imported goods. At the time, the American South exported three-fourths of its agricultural output and imported in turn most of its manufactured goods from abroad. In effect, the tariff meant that the South was forced to pay higher taxes that went to the North to subsidize inefficient northern manufacturers and industrial workers.

[14]See on this Murray N. Rothbard, "Nations by Consent: Decomposing the Nation-State," in *Secession, State, and Liberty*, David Gordon, ed.; Ludwig von Mises, *Nation, State, and the Economy* (New York: New York University Press, 1983), esp. pp. 31–77; also chap. 7 below.

will help. It must imitate, assimilate, and, if possible, improve upon the skills, traits, practices, and rules characteristic of more advanced societies, and it must avoid those characteristic of less advanced societies. Rather than promoting a downward leveling of cultures as under forced integration, secession stimulates a cooperative process of cultural selection and advancement.[15]

Moreover, while everything else depends on the new regional government's domestic policies and no direct relationship between size and economic integration exists, there is an important indirect connection. Just as political centralization ultimately tends to promote economic disintegration, so secession tends to advance integration and economic development. First, secession always involves the breaking away of a smaller from a larger population and is thus a vote against the principle of democracy and majoritarian rule in favor of private, decentralized ownership. More importantly, secession always involves increased opportunities for interregional migration, and a secessionist government is immediately confronted with the threat of emigration. To avoid the loss in particular of its most productive subjects, it comes under increased pressure to adopt comparatively liberal domestic policies by allowing more private property and imposing a lower tax and regulation burden

---

[15]Egalitarian propaganda notwithstanding, enormous differences with respect to the degree of cultural advancement exist, for instance, in former Yugoslavia between Slovenes, Croats, Serbs, and Kosovo-Albanians and/or Catholics, Orthodox, and Muslims; or in the former Soviet Union between Latvians, Estonians, Lithuanians, Germans, Poles, Ukrainians, Russians, Georgians, Rumanians, Armenians, Chechens, Aszerbaijanis, Turkmenis, Kazaks, and so on. The immediate result of the political separation of these culturally distinct people will simply be an increased variety of governments and forms of social organization. It will have to be expected further, however, that some of these newly independent governments and their social policies will be worse (from the point of view of economic integration and prosperity) than those that would have prevailed if the former central government had remained in power, while others will turn out to be better. For instance, it may well be worse for Aszerbaijanis to be ruled by a native government than by one made up of Russians, or for Kosovo-Albanians to fall into the hands of some of their own rather than those of a Serbian government. At the same time, the social policies in Estonia, Latvia, and Lithuania, for instance, will be likely better than what a Russian government would have had in store, and Croatians will prosper more under home-rule than if they had remained under Serbian control. Secession, then, will not eliminate cultural differences and rank orders; and indeed, it may well accentuate them. And yet, precisely in laying bare the cultural differences and different ranks of socio-economic development of various people secession will in time provide the best stimulus for the cultural and economic advancement of all people, developed and undeveloped alike.

than its neighbors.[16] Ultimately, with as many territories as separate households, villages, or towns, the opportunities for economically motivated emigration is maximized and government power over a domestic economy minimized.

Specifically, the smaller the country, the greater will be the pressure to opt for free trade rather than protectionism. All government interference with foreign trade forcibly limits the range of mutually beneficial interterritorial exchanges and thus leads to relative impoverishment, at home as well as abroad.[17] But the smaller a territory and its internal markets, the more dramatic this effect will be. A country the size of the U.S., for instance, might attain comparatively high standards of living even if it renounced all foreign trade, provided it possessed an unrestricted internal capital and consumer goods market. In contrast, if predominantly Serbian cities or counties seceded from surrounding Croatia, and if they pursued the same protectionism, this would likely spell disaster. Consider a single household as the conceivably smallest secessionist unit. By engaging in unrestricted free trade, even the smallest territory can be fully integrated into the world market and partake of every advantage of the division of labor, and its owners may become the wealthiest people on earth. The existence of a single wealthy individual

---

[16]An excellent example of the reform pressure caused by emigration is provided by the case of former East Germany. Having fallen under the control of the Soviet Union and turned socialist in the wake of World War II, East Germany suffered from its very inception from a massive outflow of people leaving for the more liberal and hence prosperous interventionist (social-democratic) West Germany. By the early 1960s, the number of emigrants had swollen to about 1,000 per day. In reaction, on August 13, 1961, the East German government felt compelled to erect a border system, with walls, barbed wire, electrified fences, mine fields, automatic shooting devices, and watchtowers almost nine-hundred miles long, for the sole purpose of preventing East Germans from running away from socialism. From 1961 until the spring of 1989 the problem could thus be contained. However, when allied socialist Hungary then began to relax its border controls *vis-à-vis* Austria, persuaded, as it now turns out, by members of the Paneuropean Union led by Otto von Habsburg, the wave of East German emigration immediately resumed. In fact, within just a few days the number of East Germans escaping to the West via Hungary rose to more than 2,000 per day. It was these events, above all else, that led first to the overthrow of the Honecker regime in East Germany, then, on the forever memorable November 9, 1989, to the dismantling of the Berlin Wall, and finally, in the following year, to the reunification of Germany. See on this Hans-Hermann Hoppe, "De-Socialization in a United Germany," *Review of Austrian Economics* 5, no. 2 (1991).

[17]See on this Mises, *Liberalism*, pp. 130ff.; Rothbard, *Power and Market*, pp. 47ff.; idem, *The Dangerous Nonsense of Protectionism* (Auburn, Ala.: Ludwig von Mises Institute, 1988).

anywhere is living proof of this. On the other hand, if the same household owners decided to forego all interterritorial trade, abject poverty or death would result. Accordingly, the smaller a territory and its internal markets, the more likely it is that it will opt for free trade.

Moreover, secession also promotes *monetary* integration. The process of centralization has also resulted in monetary disintegration: the destruction of the former international commodity (gold) money standard and its replacement with a dollar-dominated system of freely fluctuating government paper monies, i.e., a global, U.S.-led government counterfeiting cartel. However, a system of freely fluctuating paper currencies—the Friedmanite–monetarist ideal—is strictly speaking no monetary system at all.[18] It is a system of partial *barter*—dysfunctional of the very purpose of money of facilitating rather than complicating exchange. This becomes obvious once it is recognized that from the point of view of economic theory, there is no special significance attached to the way national borders are drawn. Yet if one then imagines a proliferation of ever smaller national territories, ultimately to the point where each household forms its own country, Friedman's proposal is revealed for what it is—an outright absurdity. For if every household were to issue its own paper currency, the world would be right back at barter. No one would accept anyone else's paper, economic calculation would be impossible, and trade would come to a virtual standstill.[19] It is only due

---

[18]See also Murray N. Rothbard, *The Case for a 100 Percent Gold Dollar* (Auburn, Ala.: Ludwig von Mises Institute, 1991); idem, "Gold vs. Fluctuating Fiat Exchange Rates," in idem, *The Logic of Action One* (Cheltenham, U.K.: Edward Elgar, 1997); idem, *The Case Against the Fed* (Auburn, Ala.: Ludwig von Mises Institute, 1995); Hans-Hermann Hoppe, "How is Fiat Money Possible?— or, The Devolution of Money and Credit," *Review of Austrian Economics* 7, no.2 (1994).

[19]See on this in particular Rothbard, *The Case for a 100 Percent Gold Dollar*. "One problem," explains Rothbard,

> that every monetary statist and nationalist has failed to face is the geographical boundary of each money. If there should be national fluctuating fiat money, what should be the boundaries of the "nation"? Surely political frontiers have little or no economic meaning. . . . Logically, the ultimate in freely fluctuating fiat moneys is a different money issued by each and every individual. . . . I think it would be instructive if some economist devoted himself to an intensive analysis of what such a world would look like. I think it safe to say that the world would be back to an enormously complex and chaotic form of barter. . . . For there would no longer be any sort of monetary medium for exchanges. Each separate exchange would require a different "money." In fact, since money *means* a general medium of exchanges, it is doubtful if the very concept of *money* would any longer apply. . . . In short, fluctuating fiat moneys are disintegrative of the very function of money itself. . . . They contradict the essence of the monetary function. (pp. 55–61)

to centuries of political centralization and the fact that only a relatively small number of countries and national currencies remain, and hence that the disintegrative consequences and calculational difficulties are far less severe, that this could have been overlooked. From this theoretical insight it follows that secession, provided it proceeds far enough, will actually promote monetary integration. In a world of hundreds of thousands of independent political units, each country would have to abandon the current fiat money system which has been responsible for the greatest worldwide inflation in all of human history and once again adopt an international commodity money system such as the gold standard.

Secessionism, and the growth of separatist and regionalist movements throughout the world represent not an anachronism, but potentially the most progressive historical forces, especially in light of the fact that with the fall of the Soviet Union we have moved closer than ever to the establishment of a "new world order." Secession increases ethnic, linguistic, religious, and cultural diversity, while centuries of centralization have stamped out hundreds of distinct cultures.[20] Secession will end the forced integration brought about by centralization, and rather than stimulating social strife and cultural leveling, it will promote the peaceful, cooperative competition of different, territorially separate cultures. In particular, it eliminates the immigration problem increasingly plaguing the countries of Western Europe as well as the U.S. Presently, whenever the central government permits immigration, it allows foreigners to proceed—literally on government-owned roads—to any of its residents' doorsteps, regardless of whether or not these residents desire such proximity to foreigners. Thus, to a large extent "free immigration" is forced integration. Secession solves this problem by letting smaller territories each have their own admission standards and determine

---

Hence, Rothbard concludes:

The more general the money, the greater the scope for division of labor and for the interregional exchange of goods and services that stem from the market economy A monetary medium is therefore critical to the free market, and the wider the use of this money, the more extensive the market and the better it can function. In short, true freedom of trade does require an international commodity money . . . gold and silver. Any breakup of such an international medium by statist fiat paper inevitably cripples and disintegrates the free market, and robs the world of the fruits of that market. (pp. 58–61)

[20]See on this theme also Adolf Gasser, *Gemeindefreiheit als Rettung Europas* (Basel: Verlag Bücherfreunde, 1943).

independently with whom they will associate on their own territory and with whom they prefer to cooperate from a distance.[21]

Lastly, secession promotes economic integration and development. The process of centralization has resulted in the formation of an international, U.S.-dominated government cartel of managed migration, trade, and fiat money, ever more invasive and burdensome governments, globalized welfare–warfare statism and economic stagnation or even declining standards of living. Secession, if it is extensive enough, could change all this. The world would consist of tens of thousands of distinct countries, regions and cantons, and of hundreds of thousands of independent free cities such as the present-day "oddities" of Monaco, Andorra, San Marino, Liechtenstein, Hong Kong, and Singapore. Greatly increased opportunities for economically motivated migration would result, and the world would be one of small liberal governments economically integrated through free trade and an international commodity money such as gold. It would be a world of unheard of prosperity, economic growth, and cultural advancement.[22]

---

[21]See on this also Murray N. Rothbard, "Nations by Consent: Decomposing the Nation State"; Peter Brimelow, *Alien Nation* (New York: Random House, 1995); *Immigration and the American Identity*, Thomas Fleming, ed. (Rockford, Ill.: Rockford Institute, 1995); also chaps. 7, 9, and 10 below.

[22]With respect to the cultural advancement which can be expected from this development, it is appropriate to conclude with some pertinent observations by the greatest German writer and poet, Johann Wolfgang von Goethe (1749–1832). On October 23, 1828, when Germany was still splintered into thirty-nine independent states, Goethe explained in a conversation with Johann Peter Eckermann (*Gespräche mit Goethe in den letzten Jahren seines Lebens*) on the desirability of German political unity, that

I do not fear that Germany will not be united; . . . she is united, because the German Taler and Groschen have the same value throughout the entire Empire, and because my suitcase can pass through all thirty-six states without being opened. . . . Germany is united in the areas of weights and measures, trade and migration, and a hundred similar things. . . . One is mistaken, however, if one thinks that Germany's unity should be expressed in the form of one large capital city, and that this great city might benefit the masses in the same way that it might benefit the development of a few outstanding individuals. . . . A thoughtful Frenchman, I believe Daupin, has drawn up a map regarding the state of culture in France, indicating the higher or lower level of enlightenment of its various "Departments by lighter or darker colors. There we find, especially in the southern provinces, far away from the capital, some "Departments painted entirely in black, indicating a complete cultural darkness. Would this be the case if the beautiful France had *ten* centers, instead of just *one*, from which light and life radiated? . . . What makes Germany great is her admirable popular culture,

---

which has penetrated all parts of the Empire evenly. And is it not the many different princely residences from whence this culture springs and which are its bearers and curators? Just assume that for centuries only the two capitals of Vienna and Berlin had existed in Germany, or even only a single one. Then, I am wondering, what would have happened to the German culture and the widespread prosperity that goes hand in hand with culture. . . . Germany has twenty universities strewn out across the entire Empire, more than one hundred public libraries, and a similar number of art collections and natural museums; for every prince wanted to attract such beauty and good. Gymnasia, and technical and industrial schools exist in abundance; indeed, there is hardly a German village without its own school. How is it in this regard in France! . . . Furthermore, look at the number of German theaters, which exceeds seventy. . . . The appreciation of music and song and their performance is nowhere as prevalent as in Germany, . . . Then think about cities such as Dresden, Munich, Stuttgart, Kassel, Braunschweig, Hannover, and similar ones; think about the energy that these cities represent; think about about the effects they have on neighboring provinces, and ask yourself, if all of this would exist, if such cities had not been the residences of princes for a long time. . . . Frankfurt, Bremen, Hamburg, Lübeck are large and brilliant, and their impact on the prosperity of Germany is incalculable. Yet, would they remain what they are if they were to lose their independence and be incorporated as provincial cities into one great German Empire? I have reason to doubt this.

6
On Socialism and Desocialization

Wealth can be brought into existence or increased in three and only three ways: by perceiving certain nature-given things as scarce and actively bringing them into one's possession before anyone else has done so (homesteading); by producing goods with the help of one's labor and such previously appropriated resources; or by acquiring a good through voluntary, contractual transfer from a previous appropriator or producer. Acts of original appropriation turn something which no one had previously perceived as scarce into an income-providing asset; acts of production are by their very nature aimed at the transformation of a less valuable asset into a more valuable one; and every contractual exchange concerns the exchange and redirection of specific assets from the hands of those who value their possession less to those who value them more.[1]

---

[1]It should be noted that each of these activities fulfills the requirements of a so-called Pareto-superior move, i.e., of enhancing the welfare of at least one individual without diminishing that of another. Hence, even in the absence of the possibility of interpersonal comparison of utility, every one of these activities can be said to increase *social* welfare. On Vilfredo Pareto's strictures regarding the meaningful use of the term *social welfare* see his *Manual of Political Economy* (New York: Augustus M. Kelley, 1971), where he writes:

> Consider any position, and assume that we move away from it by a very small amount, consistent with the restrictions [of achieving the greatest possible welfare of the individuals of a collectivity]. If in so doing the welfare of all individuals of the collectivity is increased, it is obvious that the new position is more advantageous to each one of them; and vice versa, it is less so if the welfare of all the individuals is decreased. Moreover, the welfare of some of them can remain the same, without changing these conclusions. But on the other hand, if this small movement increases the welfare of certain individuals and decreases that of others, we can no longer state positively that it is advantageous to the entire collectivity to carry out this movement. (p. 451)

Now, if a man uses his body ("labor") in order to appropriate, i.e., bring under his control, some other nature-given things (unowned "land"), this action demonstrates

From this it follows that socialism can only lead to impoverishment.

First of all, under socialism, ownership of productive assets is assigned to a collective of individuals regardless of each member's prior action or inaction relative to the owned assets. In effect, socialist ownership favors the nonhomesteader, the nonproducer, and the noncontractor and disadvantages homesteaders, producers, and contractors. Accordingly, there will be less original appropriation of natural resources whose scarcity is realized, there will be less production of new and less upkeep of old factors of production, and there will be less contracting, for all of these activities involve costs. Under a regime of collective ownership the cost of performing them is raised, and that of not performing them is lowered.[2]

Second, since means of production cannot be sold under socialism, no market prices for factors of production exist. Without such prices, cost-accounting is impossible. Inputs cannot be compared with outputs, and it is impossible to decide if their usage for a given purpose is worthwhile or leads to the squandering of scarce resources in the pursuit of projects with relatively little or no importance for consumers. Because he is not permitted to take offers from private individuals who might see an alternative way of using a given means of production, the socialist caretaker of capital goods does not know what his foregone

---

that he values these things. Hence, he must have gained utility in appropriating them. At the same time, his action does not make anyone else worse off, for in appropriating previously unowned resources nothing is taken away from others. Others could have appropriated these resources, too, if they had considered them valuable. Yet, they demonstrably did not do so. Indeed, their failure to appropriate them demonstrates their preference for *not* appropriating them. Thus, they cannot possibly be said to have lost any utility as a result of another's appropriation. Proceeding from the basis of acts of original appropriation, any further act, whether of production or consumption is equally Pareto-superior on demonstrated preference grounds, provided that it does not affect the physical integrity of the resources appropriated or produced with appropriated means by others. The producer–consumer is better off, while everyone else is left in control of the same quantity of goods as before. As a result, no one can be said to be worse off. Finally, every voluntary exchange of goods proceeding from this basis is a Pareto-superior change as well, because it can only take place if both exchange parties expect to benefit from it, while the supply of goods controlled in action (owned) by others remains unchanged. See further on this Murray N. Rothbard, "Toward a Reconstruction of Utility and Welfare," in idem *The Logic of Action One* (Cheltenham, U.K.: Edward Elgar, 1997); Jeffrey Herbener, "The Pareto Rule and Welfare Economics," *Review of Austrian Economics* 10, no. 1 (1997).

[2]See Hans-Hermann Hoppe, *A Theory of Socialism and Capitalism: Economics, Politics, and Ethics* (Boston: Kluwer, 1989).

opportunities are. Hence, permanent misallocations of production factors must ensue.[3]

Third, even *given* some initial allocation, since input factors and the output produced are owned collectively, every single producer's incentive to increase the quantity and/or quality of his individual output is systematically diminished, and his incentive to use input factors so as to avoid their over- or underutilization is reduced. Instead, with gains and losses in the socialist firm's capital and sales account socialized instead of attributed to specific, individual producers, everyone's inclination toward laziness and negligence is systematically encouraged. Hence, an inferior quality and/or quantity of goods will be produced and permanent capital consumption will ensue.[4]

Fourth, under a regime of private property, the person who owns a resource can determine independently of others what to do with it. If he wants to increase his wealth and/or rise in social status, he can only do so by better serving the most urgent wants of voluntary consumers through the use he makes of his property. With collectively owned factors of production, collective decisionmaking mechanisms are required. Every decision as to what, how, and for whom to produce, how much to pay or charge, and whom to promote or demote, is a political affair. Any disagreement must be settled by superimposing one person's will on another's view, and this invariably creates winners and losers. Hence, if one wants to climb the ladder under socialism, one must resort to one's political talents. It is not the ability to initiate, to work, and to respond to the needs of consumers that assures success. Rather, it is by means of persuasion, demagoguery, and intrigue, through promises, bribes, and threats that one rises to the top. Needless to say, this politicalization of

---

[3]See Ludwig von Mises, *Economic Calculation in the Socialist Commonwealth* (Auburn, Ala.: Ludwig von Mises Institute, 1980); idem, *Socialism: An Economic and Sociological Analysis* (Indianapolis, Ind.: Liberty Fund, 1981); idem, *Human Action: A Treatise on Economics*, Scholar's Edition (Auburn, Ala.: Ludwig von Mises Institute, 1998); Murray N. Rothbard, *Man, Economy, and State*, 2 vols. (Auburn Ala.: Ludwig von Mises Institute, 1993), esp. pp. 544–50, 585–86; idem, "Ludwig von Mises and Economic Calculation under Socialism," and "The End of Socialism and the Calculation Debate Revisited," in idem, *The Logic of Action One*; Joseph Salerno, "Ludwig von Mises as Social Rationalist," *Review of Austrian Economics* 4 (1990).

[4]See further on this Hans-Hermann Hoppe, "Desocialization in a United Germany," *Review of Austrian Economics* 5, no. 2 (1991); Murray N. Rothbard, *Power and Market* (Kansas City: Sheed Andrews and McMeel, 1977) esp. pp. 172–89; Ludwig von Mises, *Bureaucracy* (New Rochelle, N.Y.: Arlington House, 1969), esp. chap. 3.

society, implied by any system of collective ownership, contributes even more to impoverishment.[5]

II

The manifest bankruptcy of socialism all across Eastern Europe since the late 1980s, after some seventy years of "social experimentation," provides a sad illustration of the validity of economic theory. What does the theory that long ago predicted this result as inevitable[6] now imply regarding how Eastern Europe can rise most quickly from the ruins of socialism? Since the ultimate cause of its economic misery is the collective ownership of factors of production, the solution and key to a prosperous future is privatization. Yet how should socialized property be privatized?[7]

---

[5]See further on this Friedrich A. Hayek, *The Road to Serfdom* (Chicago: University of Chicago Press, 1944), esp. chap. 10; also *The Politicization of Society*, Kenneth S. Templeton, ed. (Indianapolis, Ind.: Liberty Fund, 1979). It should be emphasized here in particular that, contrary to widespread belief, the lack of democracy has essentially nothing to do with socialism's inefficiency. It is not the rules according to which politicians are selected for their office that constitutes the problem. It is politics and political decisionmaking as such. Instead of each producer deciding independently what to do with particular resources, as under a regime of private property and contractualism, with socialized factors of production each decision requires a collective's permission. It is irrelevant to the producer how those giving permission are chosen. What matters to him is that permission must be sought at all. As long as this is the case, the incentive for producers to produce is reduced and impoverishment will continue. Private property is as incompatible with democracy, then, as with any other form of political rule. Rather, with the institution of private property an "anarchy of production" is established, in which no one rules anyone, and all producers' relations are voluntary and thus mutually beneficial.

[6]See in particular Mises, *Socialism*; also *Collectivist Economic Planning*, Friedrich A. Hayek, ed. (London: Routledge and Sons, 1935); Trygve J.B. Hoff, *Economic Calculation in a Socialist Society* (Indianapolis, Ind.: Liberty Fund, 1981).

[7]While a vast body of literature dealing with the socialization of private property exists, little has been written on how to desocialize. The reason for this neglect, one would suspect, is to be found in most Western intellectuals' persistent explicit or implicit socialist predilections. Given these, any treatment of the problem of desocialization must appear simply irrelevant; for why should anyone ever want to go back from an allegedly "higher stage of social evolution," i.e., socialism, to a lower one, i.e., capitalism? Even within the Mises School at best only implicit advice on this most pressing problem confronting the people of Eastern Europe can be found. For one of the few exceptions see Murray N. Rothbard, "How To Desocialize?" and "A Radical Prescription for the Socialist Bloc," in *The Economics of Liberty*, Llewellyn H. Rockwell, Jr., ed. (Auburn, Ala.: Ludwig von Mises Institute, 1990); idem, "How and How Not To Desocialize," *Review of Austrian Economics* 6, no.1 (1992); Jeffrey Herbener, "The Role of Entrepreneurship in Desocialization," *Review of Austrian Economics* 6, no. 1 (1992).

An elementary yet fundamental moral observation must precede the answer to this question.[8] Since socialism cannot arise without the expropriation of assets originally "created" and owned by individual homesteaders, producers, and/or contractors, all socialist property, ill-begotten from the very start, should be forfeited. No government, even if freely elected, can be considered the owner of any socialist property, for a criminal's heir, even if himself innocent, does not become the legitimate owner of illegitimately acquired assets. Because of his personal innocence he remains exempt from prosecution, but all of his "inherited" gains must immediately revert to the original victims, and their repossession of socialist property must take place without their being required to pay anything. In fact, to charge a victimized population a price for the reacquisition of what was originally its own would itself be a crime and would forever take away any innocence that a government previously might have had.[9]

More specifically, all original property titles should be recognized immediately, regardless of who presently owns them. Insofar as the claims of original private owners or their heirs clash with those of the current assets' users, the former should override the latter. Only if a current user can prove that an original owner–heir's claim is illegitimate—that the title to the property in question had initially been acquired by coercive or fraudulent means—should a user's claim prevail and should he be recognized as the legitimate owner.[10]

---

[8]On the ethical theory underlying the following considerations see in particular Murray N. Rothbard, *The Ethics of Liberty* (New York: New York University Press, 1998); Hans-Hermann Hoppe, *The Economics and Ethics of Private Property* (Boston: Kluwer, 1993).

[9]Empirically, this is what post-communist governments have by and large done, of course. Particularly noteworthy in this regard is the case of Germany. After the reunification of Germany in 1991, the (conservative) German government, backed by its supreme court, refused to return any of the property that had been expropriated from 1946 to 1949, under Soviet–Russian direction, in former East Germany (more than 50 percent of all agriculturally used land!) to its original owners. Instead, the government sold this land to its own favored "clients," which in many cases included the former communist expropriators-turned-capitalists. By contrast, to this day the original owners or their heirs have not received a penny in compensation.

[10]In those cases in which current users actually bought expropriated assets from the government, they should seek compensation from those responsible for this sale, and the government officials accountable for it should be compelled to repay the purchase price. On the question of criminal possession, restitution, burden of proof, and other related issues see Rothbard, *The Ethics of Liberty*, esp. chaps. 9–11;

Regarding socialist property that is not reclaimed in this way, syndicalist ideas should be implemented; that is, the ownership of assets should immediately be transferred to those who use them—the farmland to the farmers, the factories to the workers, the streets to the street workers or the residents, the schools to the teachers, the bureaus to the bureaucrats, and so on.[11] To break up the mostly over-sized socialist production conglomerates, the syndicalist principle should be applied to those production units in which a given individual's work is actually performed, i.e., to individual office buildings, schools, streets or blocks of streets, factories and farms. Unlike syndicalism, yet of the utmost importance, the property shares thus acquired should be freely tradeable and a stock market established so as to allow a separation of the functions of owner–capitalists and non-owning employees, and the smooth and continuous transfer of assets from less into more value-productive hands.[12]

Hans-Hermann Hoppe, *Eigentum, Anarchie und Staat* (Opladen: Westdeutscher Verlag, 1987), esp. chap. 4.

[11]The reference to "syndicalist ideas" here is not to be interpreted as an endorsement of the program of syndicalism. See also the following note 12. Quite to the contrary, the syndicalist slogan "the railways to the railway men, the mines to the miners, the factories to the factory hands" was originally meant to be a program of the *expropriation* of the private owners of capitalist enterprises. "Syndicalism like Socialism," writes Mises,

> aims at the abolition of the separation of workers from the means of production, only it proceeds by another method. Not all workers will become the owners of all the means of production; those in a particular industry or undertaking or the workers engaged in a complete branch of production will obtain the means of production employed in it. (*Socialism*, p. 240)

The use of syndicalist ideas here is proposed to the very opposite effect, i.e., as a means of *privatizing* previously socialized factors of production *in such cases where no identifiable original (expropriated) private owner of these factors exists.* Furthermore, the ethical rationale for the application of the syndicalist slogan in those—and *only* those—cases lies in the fact that such a privatization scheme approximates most closely the method described by John Locke of the first (original) just appropriation of previously unowned resources. The railwaymen have in fact "mixed their labor" with the railroads, and the miners with the mines. Hence, their claim to these resources must be deemed better founded than anyone else's.

[12]According to the original syndicalist program which aims to abolish permanently the separation of the worker from the means of production [see note 11 above], any trade or sale of his "property-share" by the worker must be precluded. "If syndicalist reform is to mean more than the mere redistribution of productive goods," explains Mises,

> then it cannot allow the property arrangements of Capitalism to persist in regard to the means of production. It must withdraw productive goods

Two problems are connected with this privatization strategy. First, what is to be done in the case of newly erected structures—which according to the proposed scheme would be owned by their current productive users—built on land that is to revert to a different original owner? While it may appear straightforward enough to award each current producer with an equal property share,[13] how many shares

from the market. Individual citizens must not dispose of the shares in the means of production allotted to them; for under Syndicalism these are bound up with the person of the owner in a much closer way than is the case in the liberal society. (*Socialism*, p. 242)

In effect, under syndicalism the worker is not "owner" in the normal sense of the word; for ownership, as Mises notes, "is always where the power to dispose resides. . . . Private property exists only where the individual can deal with his private ownership in the means of production in the way he considers most advantageous." (pp. 244–45) In fact, if workers were permitted to dispose of their shares, conditions would quickly return to the capitalist *status quo ante* with a clear separation of owner-capitalists (property) on the one hand and workers (labor) on the other. However, if this is not permitted, explains Mises, then insurmountable difficulties arise, unless it is unrealistically assumed

that no changes occur in the methods of production, in the relations of supply and demand, in technique, or in population. . . . If changes in the direction and extent of demand or in the technique of production cause changes in the organization of the industry, which require the transfer of workers from one concern to another or from one branch of production to another, the question immediately arises what is to be done with the shares of these workers in the means of production. Should the workers and their heirs keep the shares in those industries to which they happened to belong at the actual time of syndicalization and enter the new industries as simple workers earning wages, without being allowed to draw any part of the property income? Or should they lose their share on leaving an industry and in return receive a share per head equal to that possessed by the workers already occupied in the new industry? Either solution would quickly violate the principle of Syndicalism. . . . if the worker on his departure from an industry loses his share and on entering another industry acquires a share in that, those workers who stood to lose by the change would, naturally, oppose energetically every change in production. The introduction of a process making for greater productivity of labor would be resisted if it displaced workers or might displace them. On the other hand the workers in an undertaking or branch of industry would oppose any development by the introduction of new workers if it threatened to reduce their income from property. In short, Syndicalism would make every change in production practically impossible. Where it existed there could be no question of economic progress. (pp. 242–44)

See further on syndicalism Mises, *Human Action*, chap. 23; idem, *Money, Method, and the Market Process* (Boston: Kluwer, 1990), chap. 18.

[13]Instead of awarding equal property shares to all current producers, for justice to prevail it would actually be preferable to award unequal shares in accordance

should go to the land owner? Structures and land cannot be physically separated. In terms of economic theory, they are absolutely specific complementary production factors whose relative contribution to their joint value product cannot be disentangled. In this case there is no alternative but to bargain.[14] This—contrary to the first impression that it might lead to permanent, unresolvable conflict—should hardly cause many headaches, for invariably there are only two parties and strictly limited resources involved in any such dispute. Moreover, to find a quick, mutually agreeable compromise is in both parties' interest, and if either party possesses a weaker bargaining position it is clearly the landowner (because he cannot sell the land without the structure owners' consent while they could dismantle the structure without needing the landowner's permission).

Second, the syndicalist privatization strategy implies that producers in capital intensive industries would have a relative advantage as compared to those in labor intensive industries. The value of the property shares received by the former would exceed the wealth awarded to the latter, and this unequal distribution of wealth would require justification, or so it seems. In fact, such justification is readily available. Contrary to widespread "liberal" (i.e., social democratic) beliefs, there is nothing ethically wrong with inequality.[15] Indeed, the problem of privatizing formerly socialized property is almost perfectly analogous to that of establishing private property in a "state of nature," i.e., when resources are previously unowned. In this situation, according to the central Lockean idea of natural rights which coincides with most people's natural sense of justice, private property is established through acts of homesteading: by mixing one's labor with nature-given resources before anyone else has done so.[16] Insofar as any differences between the quality of

---

with the time that a worker has served within a given production unit. This would also permit the inclusion of currently retired workers in the proposed privatization scheme and thus solve the so-called pension problem.

[14]On the economic theory of bargaining see Rothbard, *Man, Economy, and State*, pp. 308–12; also Mises, *Human Action*, p. 336.

[15]See Murray N. Rothbard, *Egalitarianism As a Revolt Against Nature and Other Essays* (Washington, D.C.: Libertarian Review Press, 1974); also: Robert Nozick, *Anarchy, State, and Utopia* (New York: Basic Books, 1974), chap. 8; Helmut Schoeck, *Envy: A Theory of Social Behavior* (New York: Harcourt, Brace and World, 1970); idem, *Das Recht auf Ungleichheit* (Munich: Herbig, 1979); idem, *Ist Leistung Unanständig?* (Osnabrueck: Fromm, 1978); Erik von Kuehnelt-Leddihn, *Liberty or Equality* (Front Royal, Va.: Christendom Press, 1993).

[16]See John Locke, *Two Treatises of Government*, book 2, sect. 27, where he writes:

nature-given resources exist, as will surely be the case, the outcome generated by the homesteading ethic will be inequality rather than equality. The syndicalist privatization approach is merely the application of this homesteading principle to slightly changed circumstances. The socialized factors of production are already homesteaded by particular individuals. Only their property right regarding particular production factors has been ignored so far, and all that would occur under the proposed scheme is that this unjustifiable situation would finally be rectified. If such rectification results in inequalities, this is no more unfair

---

Though the earth and all inferior creatures be common to all men, yet every man has a "property" in his own "person." This nobody has any right to but himself. The "labor" of his body and the "work" of his hands, we may say, are properly his. Whatsoever, then, he removes out of the state that Nature hath provided and left it in, he hath mixed his labour with it, and joined to it something that is his own, and thereby makes it his property. It being by him removed from the common state Nature placed it in, it hath by this labor something annexed to it that excludes the common right of other men. For this "labor" being the unquestionable property of the laborer, no man but he can have a right to what that is once joined to, at least where there is enough, and as good left in common for others.

See also note 11 above. In order to forestall any misunderstanding, the endorsement of Locke here refers exclusively to his central "homesteading" idea. It does not include an endorsement of the first statement of the just quoted passage or of the infamous "proviso" which concludes the passage. To the contrary, the first statement regarding the "common" ownership of nature requires unnecessary as well as unsubstantiable theological presuppositions. Prior to an act of original appropriation, nature is and must be regarded as simply unowned. Thus, the proviso is plainly inconsistent with Locke's main idea and must be abandoned. See on this also Richard A. Epstein, *Takings* (Cambridge, Mass.: Harvard University Press, 1985), pp. 10–12. From the rejection of Locke's initial premise it follows that criticisms of Locke's theory of original appropriation such as Herbert Spencer's in *Social Statics*, chaps. 9–10, must be rejected as invalid, too. Spencer shares Locke's initial premise, but based on this he concludes that this prohibits any private ownership in ground land whatsoever. Land, according to Spencer, can only be leased from "society" by paying a "ground rent" for its use. For a criticism of this proposal and similar ones made by Henry George and his followers see Rothbard, *Power and Market*, pp. 122–35.

For proponents of modern variants of the Lockean proviso and/or Spencer's land-egalitarianism, see Nozick, *Anarchy, State, and Utopia*, pp. 178ff., and Hillel Steiner, "The Natural Right to the Means of Production," *Philosophical Quarterly*, 27 (1977); for a refutation of these theoretical variants as self-contradictory see Jeffrey Paul, "Historical Entitlement and the Right to Natural Resources," in *Man, Economy and Liberty. Essays in Honor of Murray N. Rothbard*, Walter Block and Llewellyn H. Rockwell, Jr., eds. (Auburn, Ala.: Ludwig von Mises Institute, 1988), and Fred D. Miller, "The Natural Right to Private Property," in *The Libertarian Reader*, Tibor R. Machan, ed. (Totowa, N.J.: Rowman and Littlefield, 1982).

than the inequalities that would emerge under a regime of original, unadulterated homesteading.[17]

Moreover, our syndicalist proposal is economically more efficient than the only conceivable privatization alternative in line with the basic requirement of justice (the recognition that the government does not legitimately own the socialized economy; hence, selling or auctioning it off should be out of the question). According to the latter alternative, the entire population would receive equal shares in all of the country's assets not reclaimed by an original, expropriated owner. Aside from the questionable moral quality of this policy,[18] it would be extremely inefficient. For one thing, in order for such countrywide distributed shares to become tradeable property titles, they must specify to which particular resource they refer. Therefore, to implement this proposal, first a complete inventory of all of the country's assets would be required, or at least an inventory of all its distinctively separable production units. Second, even if such an inventory were finally assembled, the owners would consist by and large of individuals who knew next to nothing about the assets they owned. In contrast, under the nonegalitarian syndicalist–privatization scheme no inventory is necessary. Furthermore, initial ownership comes to rest exclusively with individuals who, because of their productive involvement with the assets owned by them, are by and large best informed to make a first realistic appraisal of such assets.

In conjunction with the privatization of all assets according to the principles outlined, the government should adopt a private property constitution and declare it to be the immutable basic law for the entire country. This constitution should be extremely brief and lay down the following principles in terms as unambiguous as possible: Every person, apart from being the sole owner of his physical body, has the right to

---

[17]For the most consistent and complete Lockean property rights theory see Rothbard, *The Ethics of Liberty*; idem, "Law, Property Rights, and Air Pollution," in, idem, *The Logic of Action Two* (Cheltenham, U.K.: Edward Elgar, 1997); for the theoretical justification of the homesteading principle in particular, as the indisputable axiomatic foundation of ethics see Hoppe, *Eigentum, Anarchie und Staat*, chap. 4; idem, *A Theory of Socialism and Capitalism*, chaps. 2 and 7; idem, *The Economics and Ethics of Private Property*, chaps. 8–11, and Appendix.

[18]How can one justify that ownership of productive assets be assigned without considering a given individual's actions or inactions in relation to the owned asset? More specifically, how can it be justified that someone who has contributed literally nothing to the existence or maintenance of a particular asset—and who might not even know that such an asset exists—own it in the same way as someone else who actively and objectifiably contributed to its existence or maintenance?

employ his private property in any way he sees fit so long as in so doing he does not uninvitedly change the physical integrity of another person's body or property. All interpersonal exchanges and all exchanges of property titles between private owners are to be voluntary (contractual). These rights of a person are absolute. Any person's infringement on them is subject to lawful prosecution by the victim of this infringement or his agent, and is actionable in accordance with the principles of the proportionality of punishment and of strict liability.[19]

As implied by this constitution, then, all existing wage and price controls, all property regulations and licensing requirements, and all import and export restrictions should be immediately abolished and complete freedom of contract, occupation, trade and migration introduced. Subsequently, the government, now propertyless, should declare its own continued existence unconstitutional—insofar as it depends on noncontractual property acquisitions, that is, taxation—and abdicate.[20]

III

The result of this complete abolition of socialism and the establishment of a pure private property society—an anarchy of private property owners, regulated exclusively by private property law—would be the quickest way to economic recovery for Eastern Europe. From the outset, by and large the population would be amazingly rich, for although the economies of Eastern Europe are in shambles, the countries are not destroyed. Real estate values are high, and despite all of the capital consumption of the past there are still massive amounts of capital goods in existence. With no government sector left and the entire national wealth in private hands, the people of Eastern Europe could soon become objects of envy among their West European counterparts.

---

[19]On the proportionality principle of punishment see Rothbard, *The Ethics of Liberty*, chap. 13; Hoppe, *Eigentum, Anarchie und Staat*, pp. 106–28; Stephan Kinsella, Punishment and Proportionality: The Estoppel Approach," *Journal of Libertarian Studies* 12, no. 1 (1996); idem, "Inalienability and Punishment," *Journal of Libertarian Studies* 14, no. 1 (1999); on the principle of strict liability also, Richard A. Epstein, "A Theory of Strict Liability," *Journal of Legal Studies* 2 (January 1973); also idem, *Medical Malpractice: The Case for Contract* (Burlingame, Calif.: Center for Libertarian Studies, Occasional Paper Series No. 9, 1979); Judith J. Thomson, *Rights, Restitution, and Risk* (Cambridge, Mass.: Harvard University Press, 1986), esp. chaps. 12 and 13.

[20]On the ethics and economics of stateless societies see Murray N. Rothbard, "Society Without a State," in *Anarchism (Nomos XIX)*; Roland Pennock and John W. Chapman, eds. (New York: New York University Press, 1978); idem, *For A New Liberty* (New York: Collier, 1978); Bruce Benson, *The Enterprise of Law: Justice Without the State* (San Francisco: Pacific Institute, 1991).

Moreover, releasing factors of production from political control and handing them over to private individuals who are allowed to use them as they see fit as long as they do not physically damage the resources owned by others provides the ultimate stimulus for future production. With an unrestricted market for capital goods, rational cost-accounting becomes possible. With profits as well as losses individualized, and reflected in an owner's capital- and sales-account, every single producer's incentive to increase the quantity and/or quality of his output and to avoid any over or under-utilization of his capital is maximized. In particular, the constitutional provision that only the physical integrity of property (not property values) be protected guarantees that every owner will undertake the greatest value-productive efforts—efforts to promote favorable changes in property values and to prevent and counter any unfavorable ones (as might result from another person's actions regarding his property).

Specifically, the abolishment of all price controls eliminate almost instantaneously all present shortages, and output would begin to increase immediately, both quantitatively as well as qualitatively. Unemployment would drastically increase temporarily, yet with flexible wage rates, without collective bargaining, and without unemployment subsidies it would quickly disappear. Initially, average wage rates would remain substantially below Western rates, but this, too, would soon change. Lured by comparatively low wages, by the fact that East Europeans will expectedly show a great need for cashing in (liquidating) their newly acquired capital assets so as to finance their current consumption, and above all by the fact that East Europe would be a no-tax, free-trade haven, large numbers of investors and huge amounts of capital would begin to flow in immediately.

The production of security—of police protection and of a judicial system—which is usually assumed to lie outside the province of free markets and be the proper function of government, would most likely be taken over by major Western insurance companies.[21] Providing insurance for personal property, police-action—the prevention and detection of crime as well as the exaction of compensation—is in fact part of

---

[21]On the economics of competitive, private security production see Gustave de Molinari, *The Production of Security* (New York: Center for Libertarian Studies, 1977); Rothbard, *Power and Market*, chap. 1; idem, *For A New Liberty*, chap. 12; Morris and Linda Tannehill, *The Market For Liberty* (New York: Laissez Faire Books, 1984); Hans-Hermann Hoppe, *The Private Production of Defense* (Auburn, Ala.: Ludwig von Mises Institute, 1998); see also Benson, *The Enterprise of Law*.

this industry's "natural" business (if it were not for governments preventing insurers from doing so and arrogating this task to itself, with all the usual and familiar inefficiencies resulting from such a monopolization). Likewise, being already in the business of arbitrating conflicts between claimants of competing insurers, insurance companies would naturally assume the function of a judicial system.

Yet more important than the entrance of big business, such as insurance companies into the field of security production, would be the influx of large numbers of small entrepreneurs, in particular from Western Europe. Facing a heavy tax burden in the welfare states of Western Europe as well as being stifled there by countless regulations (licensing requirements, labor protection laws, mandated working and shop-opening hours), an unregulated private property economy in Eastern Europe would be an almost irresistible attraction. Soon the large-scale influx of entrepreneurial talent and capital would begin to raise real wage rates, stimulate internal savings, and lead to a rapidly accelerating process of capital accumulation. Rather than leaving the East, migration would quickly take place in the opposite direction, with increasing numbers of Western Europeans abandoning welfare socialism for the unlimited opportunities offered in the East. Finally, faced with increasing losses of productive individuals, which would put even more pressure on their welfare budgets, the power elites of Western Europe would be forced to begin desocializing Western Europe as well.[22]

---

[22]It hardly needs to be mentioned that the actual course of desocialization in Eastern Europe since 1989 has proceeded along rather different lines from those proposed here (see also note 9 above). Nor should this come as a surprise.

Notwithstanding the dramatic convulsions that have occurred since 1989, the size of Eastern European governments in terms of personnel and resource ownership is still overwhelming, even by the already high Western standards. Furthermore, government personnel at local, provincial, and federal levels still consists largely of the same individuals as before 1989, and many of the post-communist political leaders of Eastern Europe were already prominent, and had risen to eminent positions, under communist rule. To most of them, classical-liberal and libertarian ideas were simply unheard of, but they were all too familiar with welfare-statist notions. Moreover, if the liberal-libertarian prescriptions of instant and complete privatization of all collective property outlined above had been put into effect, all government jobs would have disappeared immediately. Government employees would have been left to the vagaries of the market and forced to find new, productive occupations. Alternatively, if the familiar Western European welfare-state model were accepted as exemplary, and if the Eastern bureaucracies took charge of the irreversible trend toward desocialization, and thereby controlled and regulated the privatization of "nonvital" parts of their massive resource holdings (down to—but not below—Western levels), most bureaucratic

IV
POSTSCRIPT:
ON PRIVATIZATION IN WELFARE STATES

While it should be clear from the foregoing considerations why from a moral as well as an economic point of view the Western welfare states

---

jobs not only could be secured, but government revenue and the salaries of bureaucrats could actually increase. In addition, because of Western governments' interests in an "orderly" transition from socialism to welfare statism, Eastern bureaucracies and leaders adopting such a reform course could expect that at least part of the risks associated with it would be assumed, or financed, by their Western counterparts. Furthermore, during the communist era, cooperation between East and West was extremely limited. As a result of the inefficiencies of socialist production, Eastern Europe was incapable of selling anything to the West except raw materials and basic consumer goods, and Western transactions with the East bloc typically accounted for less than five percent of foreign trade. Foreign ownership in Eastern Europe was essentially outlawed. Not a single Eastern currency was freely convertible to Western currencies, and even political contacts were comparatively rare. However, with the collapse of communism, the Eastern European governments had something to offer. To be sure, West–East trade is still low, and in the immediate wake of the revolutionary upheavals across Eastern Europe it has even fallen. But without the dogma that "social" means the collective ownership of factors of production, some of the nationalized wealth of Eastern Europe has suddenly come up for grabs; and with the Eastern governments in control of the denationalization process, Western political leaders—and government-connected bankers and big businessmen—have immediately increased the contacts with their Eastern counterparts. In exchange for Western aid during the transition phase, Eastern governments now had real assets to sell. In addition, the East could assure eager Western buyers that from the outset the tax-and-regulation structure of the newly emerging economies of Eastern Europe would be harmonized with European Community standards. Most importantly, Eastern governments could sell the assurance that Eastern Europe's new banking system would be set up along familiar Western lines, with a governmentally controlled central bank, a fractional-reserve banking cartel of privately-owned commercial banks, and a convertible fiat money backed by reserves of Western fiat currencies, thereby allowing the Western banking system to initiate an internationally coordinated credit expansion, and thus, to establish monetary and financial hegemony over the newly emerging Eastern European economies.

Thus today, a decade after the collapse of socialism, the countries of Eastern Europe are well on the way toward Western welfare-statism ("social democracy"). Because of the partial privatization and the elimination of most (although by no means all) price controls, Eastern Europe's economic performance has certainly improved beyond its former desperate showing. This improvement has in turn brought its Western payoff in the form of increased economic integration: a widening of markets, an extensification and intensification of the division of labor, and an expanding volume of mutually beneficial international trade. However, due to the limited extent of privatization and the gradualist reform strategy, the Eastern recovery process has been painfully slow, causing seemingly permanent mass

require as thorough a reform as the former socialist countries of Eastern Europe, it is important to note that the *method* of privatization must be different in both cases. The syndicalist privatization strategy proposed for formerly socialist countries applied, as will be recalled, only in such cases where no identifiable previously expropriated private owner or heir of socialized factors of production existed. If such an owner–heir could be identified, then *he* should be again installed as private owner. If and only if no such owner–heir existed could it be considered just to install the current and/or past users of socialized production factors as their private owners, because they and only they have then an objectifiable, i.e., intersubjectively ascertainable, tie to these resources. Only they, of all people, have *de facto* homesteaded the factors of production in question. Thus, only their ownership claim can be said to have any "real" (objective) foundation.

By the same token, it would be *without* any "real" foundation whatsoever—and thus utterly *in*defensible from a moral point of view—if private ownership in the "publicly" owned production factors of the mixed (welfare state) economies of the Western world were assigned to public sector employees, i.e., the so-called civil servants, along the line of the syndicalist slogan "the public schools to the teachers, the universities to the professors, the post offices to the postal workers, the public land to the bureaucrats of the Bureau of Land Management, the court houses and police stations to the judges and policemen, etc." Indeed, to do so would constitute nothing less than a moral outrage, even in the rather typical case where the "public" property in question is *not* the result of a prior expropriation of some formerly private owner of this property by means of the government's power of "eminent domain" (in which case the property should be simply returned to the original owner–heir). Even in this case all "public" property is still the result of some form of expropriation, and although the proper identification of the victims of this expropriation is more difficult than in the clear-cut case of "eminent domain," it is by no means impossible. In any case, it is obvious that civil servants are typically not among the victims. Hence, they of all people have the least well-founded claim to private ownership of this property.

---

unemployment and rapid monetary inflation and currency crises. Moreover, because the average size of government in the countries of Eastern Europe is still significantly larger than in the semi-socialist countries of Western Europe, economic progress in Eastern Europe and the stimulus thereby given to the Western economies will only be temporary, and economic recovery and expansionism will likely soon be replaced by stagnation in the West and—on a permanently lower level—East alike.

Publicly owned buildings and structures were all financed by taxes, and as far as undeveloped public land is concerned, it is the result of a public, i.e., tax-funded and enforced, policy prohibiting the private appropriation and development of nature and natural resources. Hence, it would appear that it is taxpayers, in accordance with their amount of taxes paid, who should be given title to public buildings and structures, while undeveloped public land simply should be opened up to private homesteading. Keep in mind that civil servants are *not* tax*payers* (even though, in public discourse, they frequently fancy themselves to be so). Rather, their net income is typically paid out of taxes paid by other individuals working in the private sector of the economy. Civil servants are tax-*consumers* (just as public "welfare-recipients" are tax-consumers rather than tax-payers)[23]; hence, civil servants as well as welfare-recipients should be excluded from private ownership in formerly public buildings and structures. Both civil servants and welfare-recipients live off other people's tax payments, and it would add insult to injury if they, instead of those who had paid their salaries and handouts as well as the public buildings and structures that they occupy and control, should be awarded ownership of these buildings and structures.[24] As regards undeveloped public land available for private homesteading activities, every public land manager, ranger, etc., should be excluded for a similar reason from homesteading land currently occupied and formerly guarded by him against potential private developers. He may be permitted to homestead *other* public land that is presently occupied and formerly guarded against private development by *other* government agents. But to allow him to homestead land he currently occupies would give him an advantage over other potential homesteaders that would be manifestly unfair in light of the fact that it was he, paid in this by taxpayers, who had previously kept these taxpayers off and away from this land.

---

[23]See on this also chap. 4, esp. note 15.

[24]To be sure, a number of complications would arise in this privatization scheme. In order to determine the ownership shares granted to various individuals in buildings and structures currently "owned" by local, state, and federal governments, these individuals would have to provide documentation of their past payments of local, state, and federal taxes respectively, and in each case past welfare payments received must be deducted from taxes paid in order to arrive at a figure for the amount of *net* taxes paid. In a fully privatized market society, the task of finding a detailed solution to this problem would be typically assumed by private accountants, lawyers, and arbitration agencies, financed directly or indirectly—against a contingency free—by the individual claimants.

7

On Free Immigration and Forced Integration

I

The classical argument in favor of free immigration runs as follows: Other things being equal, businesses go to low-wage areas, and labor moves to high-wage areas, thus affecting a tendency toward the equalization of wage rates (for the same kind of labor) as well as the optimal localization of capital. An influx of migrants into a given-sized high-wage area will lower *nominal* wage rates. However, it will not lower *real* wage rates *if* the population is below its optimum size. To the contrary, if this is the case, the produced output will increase over-proportionally, and real incomes will actually rise. Thus, restrictions on immigration will harm the protected domestic workers *qua* consumers *more* than they gain *qua* producers. Moreover, immigration restrictions will increase the "flight" of capital abroad (the export of capital which otherwise might have stayed), still causing an equalization of wage rates (although somewhat more slowly), but leading to a less than optimal allocation of capital, thereby harming world living standards all-around.[1]

---

[1]"The law of migration and location," explains Ludwig von Mises,

makes it possible for us to form an exact concept of relative overpopulation. The world, or an isolated country from which emigration is impossible, is to be regarded as overpopulated in the absolute sense when the optimum of population—that point beyond which an increase in the number of people would mean not an increase but a decrease in welfare—is exceeded. A country is relatively overpopulated where, because of the large size of the population, work must go on under less favorable conditions of production than in other countries, so that, *ceteris paribus*, the same application of capital and labor yields a smaller output there. With complete mobility of persons and goods, relatively overpopulated territories would give up their population surplus to other territories until this disproportion had disappeared. *(Nation, State, and Economy* [New York: New York University Press, 1983], p. 58)

See also idem, *Human Action: A Treatise on Economics,* Scholar's Edition (Auburn, Ala.: Ludwig von Mises Institute, 1998), pp. 620–24; Murray N. Rothbard, *Power and Market: Government and the Economy* (Kansas City: Sheed Andrews and McMeel, 1977), pp. 52–55.

In addition, traditionally labor unions, and nowadays environmentalists, are opposed to free immigration, and this should *prima facie* count as another argument *in favor* of a policy of free immigration.[2]

II

As it is stated, the above argument in favor of free immigration is irrefutable. It would be foolish to attack it, just as it would be foolish to deny that free trade leads to higher living standards than does protectionism.[3]

It would also be wrong to attack the above case for free immigration by pointing out that because of the existence of a welfare state, immigration has become to a significant extent the immigration of welfare-bums, who do not increase but rather decrease average living standards even if the United States, for instance, is below her optimal population point. For this is not an argument against immigration but against the welfare state. To be sure, the welfare state should be destroyed in its entirety. However, the problems of immigration and welfare are analytically distinct problems and must be treated accordingly.

The problem with the above argument is that it suffers from two interrelated shortcomings which invalidate its unconditional pro-immigration conclusion and/or which render the argument applicable only to a highly unrealistic—long bygone—situation in human history.

The first shortcoming will only be touched upon. To libertarians of the Austrian School, it should be clear that what constitutes "wealth" and "well-being" is *subjective*. Material wealth is not the only thing that has value. Thus, even if real incomes rise due to immigration, it does not follow that immigration must be considered "good," for one might prefer lower living standards and a greater distance to other people over higher living standards and a smaller distance to others.[4]

---

[2]On the counterproductive effects of labor unions see William H. Hutt, *A Theory of Collective Bargaining* (Washington, D.C.: Cato Institute, 1980); idem, "Trade Unions: The Private Use of Coercive Power," *Review of Austrian Economics* 3 (1989); Morgan O. Reynolds, *Making America Poorer: The Cost of Labor Law* (Washington, D.C.: Cato Institute, 1987); on the environmentalist movement see Llewellyn H. Rockwell, Jr., *The Anti-Environmentalist Manifesto* (Burlingame, Calif.: Center for Libertarian Studies, 1993); Larry Abraham, *The Greening: The Environmentalists' Drive for Global Power* (Phoenix, Ariz.: Double A Publications, 1993).

[3]See on this chap. 8 below.

[4]See on this in particular Mises, *Human Action*, pp. 241–44; Murray N. Rothbard, *Man, Economy, and State*, 2 vols. (Auburn, Ala.: Ludwig von Mises Institute, 1993), pp. 183–200.

Instead, a second, related shortcoming will be the focus here. With regard to a given territory into which people immigrate, it is left unanalyzed who, if anyone, *owns* (controls) this territory. In fact, in order to render the above argument applicable, it is implicitly assumed that the territory in question is *un*owned, and that the immigrants enter virgin territory (open frontier). Obviously, today this can no longer be assumed. If this assumption is dropped, however, the problem of immigration takes on an entirely new meaning and requires fundamental rethinking.

III

For the purpose of illustration, let us first assume an anarcho-capitalist society. Though convinced that such a society is the only social order that can be defended as just, I do not want to explain here why this is the case.[5] Instead, I will employ it as a conceptual benchmark, because this will help explain the fundamental misconception of most contemporary free immigration advocates.

All land is privately owned, including all streets, rivers, airports, harbors, and so on. With respect to some pieces of land, the property title may be unrestricted; that is, the owner is permitted to do with his property whatever he pleases as long as he does not physically damage the property owned by others. With respect to other territories, the property title may be more or less severely restricted. As is currently the case in some housing developments, the owner may be bound by contractual limitations on what he can do with his property (voluntary zoning), which might include residential versus commercial use, no buildings more than four stories high, no sale or rent to Jews, Germans, Catholics, homosexuals, Haitians, families with or without children, or smokers, for example.

Clearly, under this scenario no such thing as freedom of immigration exists. Rather, many independent private property owners have the freedom to admit or exclude others from their own property in accordance with their own unrestricted or restricted property titles. Admission to some territories might be easy, while it might be nearly impossible to others. In any case, however, admission to the property of the admitting person does not imply a "freedom to move around," unless other property owners consent to such movement. There will be as much immigration

---

[5]See on this Murray N. Rothbard, *The Ethics of Liberty* (New York: New York University Press, 1998); Hans-Hermann Hoppe, *The Economics and Ethics of Private Property* (Boston: Kluwer, 1993); also chap. 9, note 16.

or nonimmigration, inclusivity or exclusivity, desegregation or segregation, nondiscrimination or discrimination based on racial, ethnic, linguistic, religious, cultural or whatever other grounds as individual owners or associations of individual owners allow.

Note that none of this, not even the most exclusive form of segregationism, has anything to do with a rejection of free trade and the adoption of protectionism. From the fact that one does not want to associate with or live in the neighborhood of Blacks, Turks, Catholics or Hindus, etc., it does not follow that one does not want to trade with them from a distance.[6] To the contrary, it is precisely the absolute voluntariness of human association *and* separation—the absence of any form of forced integration—that makes peaceful relationships—free trade—between culturally, racially, ethnically, or religiously distinct people possible.[7]

---

[6]As Ludwig von Mises reminds us,

even if such a thing as a natural and inborn hatred between various races existed, it would not render social cooperation futile ... Social cooperation has nothing to do with personal love or with a general commandment to love one another. People do not cooperate under the division of labor because they they love or should love one another. They cooperate because this best serves their own interests. Neither love nor charity nor any other sympathetic sentiments but rightly understood selfishness is what originally impelled man to adjust himself to the requirements of society, to respect the right and freedoms of his fellow men and to substitute peaceful collaboration for enmity and conflict. (*Human Action*, p. 168)

[7]Contrary to the currently fashionable multiculturalism, it might be pointed out here that no multicultural society—and especially no democratic one—has ever worked peacefully for very long. Peter Brimelow, *Alien Nation: Common Sense About America's Immigration Disaster* (New York: Random House, 1995), pp. 124–27, has provided some recent evidence to this effect. Working back from the present, look at the record: *Eritrea*, ruled by Ethiopia since 1952, splits off in 1993; *Czechoslovakia*, founded in 1918, splits into Czech and Slovak ethnic components in 1993; *Soviet Union*, splits into multiple ethnic components in 1991, and many of these components are threatened with further ethnic fragmentation; *Yugoslavia*, founded in 1918, splits into several ethnic components in 1991, and further breakup is still under way; *Lebanon*, founded 1920, effective partition of Christians and Muslims (under Syrian domination) since 1975; *Cyprus*, independent since 1960, effective partition of Greek and Turkish territories in 1974; *Pakistan*, independent since 1947, ethnically distinct Bangladesh splits off in 1971; *Malaysia*, independent since 1963, Chinese-dominated Singapore is expelled in 1965. The list goes on with cases, which have not yet been resolved: *India*, and the Sikhs and Kashmiris; *Sri Lanka*, and the Tamils; *Turkey, Iraq, Iran*, and the Kurds; *Sudan, Chad*, and the Arabs versus Blacks; *Nigeria*, and the Ibos; *Ulster*, and the Catholics versus the Protestants; *Belgium*, and the Flemish versus the Walloons; *Italy*, and the German-speaking South Tyrolians; *Canada*, and the French versus the English.

IV

In an anarcho-capitalist society there is no government and, accordingly, no clear-cut distinction between "inlanders" (domestic citizens) and foreigners. This distinction only arises with the establishment of a government, i.e., an institution which possesses a territorial monopoly of aggression (taxation). The territory over which a government's taxing power extends becomes "inland," and everyone residing outside of this territory becomes a foreigner. State borders (and passports), are an "unnatural" (coercive) institution. Indeed, their existence (and that of a domestic government) implies a two-fold distortion with respect to peoples' natural inclination to associate with others. First, inlanders cannot exclude the government (the taxman) from their own property and are subject to what one might call "forced integration" by government agents. Second, in order to be able to intrude on its subjects' private property so as to tax them, a government must invariably have control of existing roads, and it will employ its tax revenue to produce even more roads to gain even better access to all private property *qua* potential tax source. This over-production of roads does not result merely in the innocent facilitation of interregional trade—a lowering of transaction costs —as starry-eyed economists would have us believe but leads to forced domestic integration (artificial desegregation of separate localities).[8]

But is not Switzerland, with an assembly of Germans, French, Italians, and Romansh, an exception? Put briefly, the answer is no. All essential powers in Switzerland, in particular that of determining cultural and educational matters (schools), are concentrated in the hands of the *cantons* rather than those of the central government. And almost all of the 26 cantons and "half-cantons" are ethnically homogeneous. Seventeen cantons are almost exclusively German; 4 cantons are almost exclusively French; and 1 canton is predominantly Italian. Only 3 cantons are bilingual, the Swiss ethnic balance has been essentially stable, and there is only a limited amount of intercantonal migration. Even given these favorable circumstances, Switzerland *did* experience an unsuccessful, violently suppressed war of secession—the *Sonderbundskrieg* of 1847. Furthermore, the creation of the new, breakaway French-speaking canton of Jura from the predominantly German canton of Berne in 1979 was preceded by years of terrorist activity.

On the most likely genetic base of the human tendency to associate with "likes," and dissociate from "unlikes," see J. Philippe Rushton, "Gene-culture, Coevolution, and Genetic Similarity Theory: Implications for Ideology, Ethnic Nepotism, and Geopolitics," *Politics and the Life Sciences* 4 (1986); idem, *Race, Evolution, and Behavior* (New Brunswick, N.J.: Transaction Publishers, 1995).

[8]In fact, as noted by Max Weber, *Soziologie, Weltgeschichtliche Analysen, Politik* (Stuttgart: Kroener, 1964), p. 4, the famed roadways of ancient Rome were typically regarded as a *plague* rather than an *advantage*, because they were essentially military rather than trade routes.

Moreover, with the establishment of a government and state borders, immigration takes on an entirely new meaning. Immigration becomes immigration by foreigners across state borders, and the decision as to whether or not a person should be admitted no longer rests with private property owners or associations of such owners but with the *government* as the ultimate sovereign of all domestic residents and the ultimate super-owner of all their properties. Now, if the government excludes a person while even one domestic resident wants to admit this very person onto his property, the result is *forced exclusion* (a phenomenon that does not exist under private property anarchism). Furthermore, if the government admits a person while there is not a single domestic resident who wants to have this person on his property, the result is *forced integration* (also nonexistent under private property anarchism).

V

It is time to enrich the analysis through the introduction of a few "realistic" empirical assumptions. Let us assume that the government is privately owned. The ruler owns the entire country within state borders. He owns part of the territory outright (his property title is unrestricted), and he is partial owner of the rest (as landlord or residual claimant of all of his citizen–tenants real estate holdings, albeit restricted by some pre-existing rental contracts). He can sell and bequeath his property, and he can calculate and capture the monetary value of his capital (his country).

Traditional monarchies—and kings—are the closest historical examples of this form of government.[9]

What will a *king's* typical immigration and emigration policy be? Because he owns the entire country's capital value, he will tend to choose migration policies that preserve or enhance rather than diminish the value of his kingdom, assuming no more than his self-interest.

As far as *emigration* is concerned, a king would want to prevent the emigration of productive subjects, in particular of his best and most productive subjects, because losing them would lower the value of the kingdom. Thus, for example, from 1782 until 1824 a law prohibited the emigration of skilled workmen from Britain.[10] On the other hand, a king would want to expel his nonproductive and destructive subjects (criminals, bums, beggars, gypsies, vagabonds, etc.), for their removal from his

---

[9]See on this also chaps. 1–3.

[10]See A.M. Carr-Saunders, *World Population: Past Growth and Present Trends* (Oxford: Clarendon Press, 1936), p. 182.

territory would increase the value of his realm. For this reason Britain expelled tens of thousands of common criminals to North America and Australia.[11]

On the other hand, as far as *immigration* policy is concerned, a king would want to keep the mob, as well as all people of inferior productive capabilities, out. People of the latter category would only be admitted temporarily as seasonal workers without citizenship, and they would be barred from permanent property ownership. Thus, for example, after 1880 large numbers of Poles were hired as seasonal workers in Germany.[12] A king would only permit the permanent immigration of superior or at least above-average people; i.e., those, whose residence in his kingdom would increase his own property value. Thus, for example, after 1685 (with the revocation of the Edict of Nantes) tens of thousands of Huguenots were permitted to settle in Prussia; and similarly Peter the Great, Frederick the Great, and Maria Theresa later promoted the immigration and settlement of large numbers of Germans in Russia, Prussia, and the eastern provinces of Austria–Hungary.[13]

---

[11]Ibid., p. 47, estimates the number of criminals thus transported to North America from 1717 to 1776 at 50,000.

[12]See ibid., pp. 57, 145.

[13]See ibid., pp. 56–57. The settlement of Germans in Eastern Europe actually began in the eleventh century and was generally encouraged by various regional Slavic kings and princes who thereby hoped to promote the economic development of their realms. See Brimelow, *Alien Nation*, p. 131. A highly illuminating account of the social effects and repercussions of these migration policies in the multicultural Habsburg Empire is provided by Mises, *Nation, State, and Economy*, pp. 112–13.

> As a result of centuries-long colonization, the urban bourgeoisie and the urban intelligentsia were German everywhere in Austria and Hungary, large landownership was in great part Germanized, and everywhere, even in the middle of foreign-language territory, there were German peasant settlements. All of Austria outwardly bore a German stamp; everywhere German education and German literature were to be found. Everywhere in the Empire the Germans were also represented among the petty bourgeoisie, among the workers, and among the peasants, even though in many districts, especially in Galicia, in many parts of Hungary, and in the coastal territories, the German minority among the members of the lower strata of the population was quite small. But in the entire Empire (upper Italy excepted) the percentage of Germans among the educated and among the members of the higher strata was quite considerable, and all those educated persons and prosperous bourgeois who were not themselves German and did not want to acknowledge belonging to the German nation were German by their education, spoke German, read German, and appeared at least outwardly to be German. . . . Thus Austria no doubt was not German, but politically it

In brief, while through his immigration policies a king might not entirely avoid all cases of forced exclusion or forced integration, such policies would by and large do the same as what private property owners would do, if *they* could decide whom to admit and whom to exclude. That is, the king would be highly selective and very much concerned about *improving* the quality of the resident human capital so as to drive property values up rather than down.

VI

Migration policies become predictably different once the government is publicly owned. The ruler no longer owns the country's capital value but only has current use of it. He cannot sell or bequeath his position as ruler; he is merely a temporary caretaker. Moreover, "free entry" into the position of a caretaker government exists. In principle, anyone can become the ruler of the country.

As they came into existence on a worldwide scale after World War I, democracies offer historical examples of public government.[14]

What are a *democracy's* migration policies? Once again assuming no more than self-interest (maximizing monetary and psychic income: money and power), democratic rulers tend to maximize *current* income, which they can appropriate privately, at the expense of capital values, which they can *not* appropriate privately. Hence, in accordance with democracy's inherent egalitarianism of one-man-one-vote, they tend to pursue a distinctly egalitarian—nondiscriminatory—emigration and immigration policy.

As far as emigration policy is concerned, this implies that for a democratic ruler it makes little, if any, difference whether productive or unproductive people, geniuses or bums leave the country. They all have one equal vote. In fact, democratic rulers might well be more concerned

---

wore a German face. Every Austrian who wanted to take any interest at all in public affairs had to master the German language. For the members of the Czech and of the Slovene peoples, however, education and social ascent could be achieved only through Germanness. They still had no literature of their own that would have made it possible for them to do without the treasures of German culture. Whoever rose became German because precisely the members of the higher strata were German. The Germans saw that and believed that it had to be so. They were far from wanting to Germanize all non-Germans compulsorily, but they thought that this would take place on its own. They believed that every Czech and South Slav would try, even in his own interest, to adopt German culture.

[14]See on this also chaps. 1–3.

about the loss of a bum than that of a productive genius. While the loss of the latter would obviously lower the capital value of the country and loss of the former might actually increase it, a democratic ruler does not *own* the country. In the short run, which is of the most interest to a democratic ruler, the bum, voting most likely *in favor* of egalitarian measures, might be more valuable than the productive genius who, as egalitarianism's prime victim, will more likely vote *against* the democratic ruler.[15] For the same reason, quite unlike a king a democratic ruler undertakes little to actively *expel* those people whose presence within the country constitutes a negative externality (human trash which drives individual property values down). In fact, such negative externalities—unproductive parasites, bums, and criminals—are likely to be his most reliable supporters.

As far as immigration policies are concerned, the incentives and disincentives are likewise distorted, and the results are equally perverse. For a democratic ruler, it also matters little whether bums or geniuses, below or above-average civilized and productive people immigrate into the country. Nor is he much concerned about the distinction between temporary workers (owners of work permits) and permanent, property owning immigrants (naturalized citizens).[16] In fact, bums and unproductive people may well be preferred as residents and citizens, because they create more so-called "social" problems," and democratic rulers thrive on the existence of such problems. Moreover, bums and inferior people will likely support his egalitarian policies, whereas geniuses and superior people will not. The result of this policy of non-discrimination is forced integration: the forcing of masses of inferior immigrants onto domestic property owners who, if the decision were left to them, would have sharply discriminated and chosen very *different*

---

[15]To avoid any misunderstanding, it should be emphasized here that the difference between monarchical and democratic–republican government with respect to emigration policy is *not* one of restrictive versus unrestricted emigration. In fact, the most severe restrictions on emigration were imposed in the twentieth century, by the so-called socialist peoples' republics of Eastern Europe. Rather, the difference is one concerning the *type* of restrictions, respectively the *motivation* underlying such restrictions. Thus, whereas monarchical emigration restrictions were typically motivated by economic concerns, democratic–republican restrictions are typically motivated by power concerns, with the most frequent restriction being that one may not emigrate until one has fulfilled one's compulsory military service. See on this Carr-Saunders, *World Population*, p. 148.

[16]Of all major European countries it has been France, the country with the longest democratic–republican tradition, which has boasted the most "liberal," i.e., least restrictive, immigration and naturalization policy. See on this ibid., pp. 57, 145, 154.

neighbors for themselves. Thus, as the best available example of democracy at work, the United States immigration laws of 1965 eliminated all previous "quality" concerns and the explicit preference for *European* immigrants, replacing them with a policy of almost complete nondiscrimination (multiculturalism).[17]

---

[17]See Lawrence Auster, *The Path to National Suicide: An Essay on Immigration and Multiculturalism* (Monterey, Calif.: AICEF, 1990); *Immigration and the American Identity*, Thomas Fleming, ed. (Rockford, Ill.: Rockford Institute, 1995); George J. Borjas, *Friends or Strangers: The Impact of Immigrants on the U.S. Economy* (New York: Basic Books, 1990); idem, *Heaven's Door: Immigration Policy and the American Economy* (Princeton, N.J.: Princeton University Press, 1999); Brimelow, *Alien Nation*.

To put matters into perspective, Brimelow documents that from 1820 until 1967, when the new immigration laws went into effect, almost 90 percent of all immigrants were of European descent. In contrast, from 1967 until 1993, some 85 percent of the close to 17 million legal immigrants arriving in the U.S. came from the Third World, mostly Latin America and Asia (pp. 77, 281–85). Rather than selection by skill and job qualification as before 1967, the primary selection criteria currently are "family reunification," "asylum," and "diversity lottery" (pp. 78–84). Consequently, the average level of education and the average wage rate of immigrants has continually fallen as compared to their native American counterparts. Moreover, the welfare participation rate of immigrant households significantly exceeds—and increasingly so—that of the native population (which includes Blacks and Puerto Ricans with an already extremely high welfare participation rate). For instance, the welfare participation rate of Cambodian and Laotian immigrants is almost 50 percent; that of Vietnamese immigrants is above 25 percent; Dominican Republic 28 percent; Cuba 16 percent; former Soviet Union 16 percent; China 10 percent. As well, immigrants remain on the dole for increasingly longer periods (pp. 141–53, 287–88). Last but not least, Brimelow estimates that if the current trends of legal as well as illegal immigraton continue, the population of European descent, which has traditionally made up close to 90 percent of the U.S. population, will be on the verge of becoming a minority by the year 2050 (p. 63). But won't all of the immigrants be assimilated and become Americans? Not likely, because in order to be successfully assimilated, the influx of immigrants needs to be small in comparison to the host population. However, the current influx of about one million legal immigrants (and two to three-hundred-thousand illegal immigrants) per year is concentrated in just a few regions: California, Texas, Illinois, Florida, New York, and New Jersey—and most immigrants actually move to just six metropolitan areas: Los Angeles, Anaheim, Chicago, Miami, New York, and Washington, D.C. (p. 36). In these regions, the number of immigrants is proportionally so large that any assimilation is essentially out of the question. Rather than gradually being Americanized, then, in these areas immigrants have established foreign Third World "countries" on formerly American soil.

George Borjas notes further that

> almost a quarter of immigrant households received some type of assistance, compared to 15 percent of native households. . . . What's more, the use of public assistance by immigrants increases over time. It seems that assimilation involves learning not only about labor market

Indeed, the immigration policy of a democracy is the mirror image of its policy toward *internal* population movements: toward the voluntary association and dissociation, segregation and desegregation, and the physical distancing and approximating of various private property owners. Like a king, a democratic ruler promotes spatial over-integration by over-producing the "public good" of roads. However, for a democratic ruler, *un*like a king, it will not be sufficient that everyone can move next door to anyone else on government roads. Concerned about his *current* income and power rather than capital values and constrained by egalitarian sentiments, a democratic ruler will tend to go even further. Through nondiscrimination laws—one cannot discriminate against Germans, Jews, Blacks, Catholics, Hindus, homosexuals, etc.—the government will want to increase the physical access and entrance to everyone's property to everyone else. Thus, it is hardly surprising that the so-called "civil rights" legislation in the United States, which outlawed domestic discrimination on the basis of color, race, national origin, religion, gender, age, sexual orientation, disability, etc., and which thereby actually mandated forced integration,[18] coincided with the adoption of a nondiscriminatory immigration policy; i.e., mandated *inter*national desegregation (forced integration).

---

opportunities but also about the opportunities provided by the welfare state. . . . A study by the National Academy of Sciences concluded that immigration in fact raised the taxes of the typical native household in California by about $1,200 per year. . . . [As for refugees in particular,] the evidence indicates that . . . after 10 years in the United States, 16 percent of Vietnamese refugees, 24 percent of Cambodian refugees and 34 percent of Laotian refugees were still receiving public assistance. ("Heaven's Door: Immigration Policy and the American Economy," *Milken Institute Review* 1, no. 3 [1999]: 64–65, 79)

Moreover, Borjas emphasizes, "ethnicity matters in economic life, and it matters for a very long time" (p. 66). That is, the (increasingly high) skill differential between the native and the immigrant population does not quickly disappear as the result of cultural assimilation. Instead, immigrants typically move to "ethnic ghettos" which "incubate ethnic differences," and thus "ethnic skill differentials may persist for three generations" (p. 66).

[18]On the law and economics of "affirmative action" and discrimination see Richard A. Epstein, *Forbidden Grounds* (Chicago: University of Chicago Press, 1992); Walter Block and Michael Walker, eds., *Discrimination, Affirmative Action, and Equal Opportunity* (Vancouver: Frazer Institute, 1982); Hugh Murray, "White Male Privilege? A Social Construct for Political Oppression," *Journal of Libertarian Studies* 14, no. 1 (1999).

VII

The current situation in the United States and in Western Europe has nothing whatsoever to do with "free" immigration. It is forced integration, plain and simple, and forced integration is the predictable outcome of democratic one-man-one-vote rule. Abolishing forced integration requires the de-democratization of society and ultimately the abolition of democracy. More specifically, the power to admit or exclude should be stripped from the hands of the central government[19] and reassigned to the states, provinces, cities, towns, villages, residential districts, and ultimately to private property owners and their voluntary associations. The means to achieve this goal are decentralization and secession (both inherently undemocratic, and antimajoritarian).[20] One would be well on the way toward a restoration of the freedom of association and exclusion as is implied in the idea and institution of private property, and much of the social strife currently caused by forced integration would disappear, if only towns and villages could and would do what they did as a matter of course until well into the nineteenth century in Europe and the United States: to post signs regarding entrance requirements to the town, and once in town for entering specific pieces of property (no beggars, bums, or homeless, but also no Moslems, Hindus, Jews, Catholics, etc.); to expel as trespassers those who do not fulfill these requirements; and to solve the "naturalization" question somewhat along the Swiss model, where local assemblies, not the central government, determine who can and who cannot become a Swiss citizen.

What should one advocate as the relatively correct immigration policy, however, as long as the democratic central state is still in place and successfully arrogates the power to determine a uniform *national* immigration policy? The best one may hope for, even if it goes against the "nature" of a democracy and thus is not very likely to happen, is that the democratic rulers act *as if* they were the personal owners of the country and *as if* they had to decide who to include and who to exclude from their own personal property (into their very own houses). This means following a policy of the strictest discrimination *in favor of the human qualities of skill, character, and cultural compatibility*.

More specifically, it means distinguishing strictly between "citizens" (naturalized immigrants) and "resident aliens" and excluding the

---

[19]Until a U.S. Supreme Court ruling in 1875, the regulation of immigration into the United States was considered a state, rather than a federal, matter.

[20]See further on this chap. 5.

latter from all welfare entitlements. It means requiring, for resident alien status as well as for citizenship, the personal sponsorship by a resident citizen and his assumption of liability for all property damage caused by the immigrant. It implies requiring an existing employment contract with a resident citizen; moreover, for both categories but especially that of citizenship, it implies that all immigrants must demonstrate through tests not only English language proficiency, but all-around superior (above-average) intellectual performance and character structure as well as a compatible system of values—with the predictable result of a systematic pro-European immigration bias.[21]

---

[21]Currently, about one-half of the U.S. foreign-born citizens, after more than five years of presence in the U.S., still speak virtually no English. Of the largest immigrant group, Hispanics, well above two-thirds speak practically no English. See Brimelow, *Alien Nation*, pp. 88–89. Their level of intellectual performance is significantly below the U.S. average (ibid., p. 56); and growing evidence indicates that the crime rate of the immigrant population systematically exceeds that of the native-born population (pp. 182–86).

8

On Free Trade and
Restricted Immigration

I

It is frequently maintained that "free trade" is connected with "free immigration" as is "protectionism" with "restricted immigration." That is, the claim is made that while it is not impossible that someone might combine protectionism with free immigration or free trade with restricted immigration, these positions are intellectually inconsistent and thus erroneous. Hence, insofar as people seek to avoid errors, they should be the exception rather than the rule. The facts, insofar as they have a bearing on the issue, appear to be consistent with this claim. As the last Republican presidential primaries indicated, for instance, most professed free traders are advocates of relatively free and nondiscriminatory immigration policies, while most protectionists are proponents of highly restrictive and selective immigration policies.

Appearances to the contrary notwithstanding, I will argue that this thesis and its implicit claim are fundamentally wrong. In particular, I will demonstrate that free trade and restricted immigration are not only perfectly consistent but even mutually reinforcing policies. That is, it is not the advocates of free trade and restricted immigration who are wrong, but rather the proponents of free trade and free immigration. In taking the "intellectual guilt" out of the free-trade-and-restricted-immigration position and putting it where it actually belongs, I hope to promote a change in current public opinion and facilitate substantial political realignments.

II

Since the days of Ricardo, the case for free trade has been logically unassailable. For the sake of argumentative thoroughness it would be useful to summarize it briefly. The restatement will be in the form of a *reductio ad absurdum* of the protectionist thesis as proposed most recently by Patrick Buchanan.[1]

---

[1]David Ricardo's discussion can be found in his *Principles of Political Economy and Taxation* (New York: E.P. Dutton, 1948), chap. 7; the most brilliant nineteenth century

The central argument advanced in favor of protectionism is one of domestic job protection. How can American producers paying their workers $10 per hour possibly compete with Mexican producers paying $1 or less per hour? They cannot, and American jobs will be lost unless import tariffs are imposed to insulate American wages from Mexican competition. Free trade is only possible between countries that have equal wage rates and thus compete "on a level playing field." As long as this is not the case, as with the U.S. and Mexico, the playing field must be made level by means of tariffs. As for the consequences of such a policy of domestic job protection, Buchanan and his fellow protectionists claim that it will lead to domestic strength and prosperity, and in support of this claim, examples are cited of free-trade countries that lost their once preeminent international economic position, such as nineteenth-century England, and of protectionist countries which gained such preeminence, such as nineteenth-century America.

This or any other alleged "empirical proof" of the protectionist thesis must be rejected out of hand as containing a *post hoc, ergo propter hoc* fallacy. The inference drawn from historical data is no more convincing than if one were to conclude from the observation that rich people consume more than poor people that it must be consumption that makes a person rich. Indeed, protectionists such as Buchanan characteristically

---

defense of free trade and intellectual demolition of all forms of protectionist policies can be found in Frédéric Bastiat, *Economic Sophisms* (Irvington-on-Hudson, N.Y.: Foundation for Economic Education, 1975); and idem, *Selected Essays on Political Economy* (Irvington-on-Hudson, N.Y.: Foundation for Economic Education, 1975); for a modern, abstract and theoretically rigorous treatment of the subject of free trade see Ludwig von Mises, *Human Action: A Treatise on Economics,* Scholar's Edition (Auburn, Ala.: Ludwig von Mises Institute, 1998), chap. 8, esp. pp. 158ff.; Patrick J. Buchanan's contrary antifree trade pronouncements are presented in his *The Great Betrayal: How American Sovereignty and Social Justice are Sacrificed to the Gods of the Global Economy* (Boston: Little, Brown, 1998). Lest it be thought that protectionist views are restricted to journalistic or political circles see David S. Landes, *The Wealth and Poverty of Nations* (New York: Norton, 1998), esp. pp. 265ff., 452ff., 521ff., who displays views quite similar to Buchanan's. The free-trade doctrine, according to Landes, is a "religion" (p. 452) and its proponents such as William Stanley Jevons are "true believers" (p. 523). Landes quotes Jevons as stating (in 1883) that

> Freedom of trade may be regarded as a fundamental axiom of political economy. . . . We may welcome *bona fide* investigations into the state of trade, and the causes of our present depression, but we can no more expect to have our opinions on free trade altered by such an investigation, than the Mathematical Society would expect to have axioms of Euclid disproved during the investigation of a complex problem. (p. 453)

While he obviously disapproves of Jevons's contention, Landes (like Buchanan) does not attempt to provide anything resembling a refutation of it.

fail to understand what is actually involved in defending their thesis. Any argument in favor of international protectionism rather than free trade is simultaneously an argument in favor of interregional and interlocal protectionism. Just as different wage rates exist between the United States and Mexico, Haiti, or China, for instance, such differences also exist between New York and Alabama, or between Manhattan, the Bronx and Harlem. Thus, if it were true that international protectionism could make an entire nation prosperous and strong, it must also be true that interregional and interlocal protectionism could make regions and localities prosperous and strong. In fact, one may even go one step further. If the protectionist argument were right, it would amount to an indictment of all trade and a defense of the thesis that everyone would be the most prosperous and strongest if he never traded with anyone else and remained in self-sufficient isolation. Certainly, in this case no one would ever lose his job, and unemployment due to "unfair" competition would be reduced to zero. In thus deducing the ultimate implication of the protectionist argument, its complete absurdity is revealed, for such a "full-employment society" would not be prosperous and strong; it would be composed of people who, despite working from dawn to dusk, would be condemned to poverty and destitution or death from starvation.[2]

International protectionism, while obviously less destructive than a policy of interpersonal or interregional protectionism, would have precisely the same effect and be a recipe for America's further economic decline. To be sure, some American jobs and industries would be saved, but such "savings" would come at a price. The standard of living and the

---

[2]Murray N. Rothbard, *Power and Market* (Kansas City: Sheed Andrews and McMeel, 1977), p. 48 has offered this *reductio ad absurdum* of the protectionist thesis:

> Suppose that Jones has a farm, "Jones' Acres," and Smith works for him. Having become steeped in pro-tariff ideas, Jones exhorts Smith to "buy Jones . "Keep the money in Jones' Acres," "don't be exploited by the flood of products from the cheap labor of foreigners outside of Jones' Acres," and similar maxims become the watchword of the two men. To make sure that their aim is accomplished, Jones levies a 1000 percent tariff on the imports of all goods and services from "abroad," i.e., from outside the farm. As a result, Jones and Smith see their leisure, or "problem of unemployment," disappear as they work from dawn to dusk trying to eke out the production of all the goods they desire. Many they cannot raise at all; others they can, given centuries of effort. It is true that they reap the promise of the protectionists: "self-sufficiency," although the "sufficiency" is bare subsistence instead of a comfortable standard of living. Money is "kept at home," and they can pay each other very high *nominal* wages and prices, but the men find that the real value of their wages, in terms of goods, plummets drastically.

real income of the American consumers of foreign products would be forcibly reduced. The cost to all United States producers who use the protected industry's products as their own input factors would be raised, and they would be rendered less competitive internationally. Moreover, what could foreigners do with the money they earned from their U.S. imports? They could either buy American goods, or they could leave it in the U.S. and invest it, and if their imports were stopped or reduced, they would buy fewer American goods or invest smaller amounts. Hence, as a result of saving a few inefficient American jobs, a far greater number of efficient American jobs would be destroyed or never come into existence.[3]

---

[3]See further on this Murray N. Rothbard, *The Dangerous Nonsense of Protectionism* (Auburn, Ala.: Ludwig von Mises Institute, 1988). What the proponents of "fair" trade typically leave unanswered, Rothbard here points out, is *why* U.S. wage rates are higher than in Mexico or Taiwan in the first place.

> [I]f the American wage is twice that of the Taiwanese, it is because the American laborer is more heavily capitalized, is equipped with more and better tools, and is therefore, on the average, twice as productive. In a sense, I suppose, it is not "fair" for the American worker to make more than the Taiwanese, not because of his personal qualities, but because savers and investors have supplied him with more tools. But a wage rate is determined not just by personal quality but also by relative scarcity, and in the United States the worker is far scarcer compared to capital than he is in Taiwan. . . . Putting it another way, the fact that American wage rates are on the average twice that of the Taiwanese, does not make the cost of labor in the U.S. twice that of Taiwan. Since the U.S. labor is twice as productive, this means that the double wage rate in the U.S. is offset by the double productivity, so that the cost of labor per unit product in the U.S. and Taiwan tends, on the average, to be the same. One of the major protectionist fallacies is to confuse the price of labor (wage rates) with its cost, which also depends on its relative productivity. . . . Thus, the problem faced by American employers is not really with the "cheap labor" in Taiwan, because "expensive labor" in the U.S. is precisely the result of the bidding for scarce labor by U.S. employers. The problem faced by less efficient U.S. textile or auto firms is not so much cheap labor in Taiwan or Japan, but the fact that other U.S. industries are efficient enough to afford it, because they bid wages that high in the first place. . . . So, by imposing protective tariffs and quotas to save, bail out, and keep in place less efficient U.S. textile or auto or microchip firms, the protectionists are not only injuring the American consumer. They are also harming efficient U.S. firms and industries, which are prevented from employing resources now locked into incompetent firms, and who would otherwise be able to expand and sell their efficient products at home and abroad. (pp. 6–7)

See also Henry Hazlitt, *Economics in One Lesson* (New Rochelle, N.Y.: Arlington House, 1979), chap. 11 .

Thus, it is nonsense to claim that England lost its former preeminence because of its free trade policies. It lost its position *despite* its free trade policy, and *because* of the socialist policies which took hold in England during the last third of the nineteenth century.[4] Likewise, it is nonsense to claim that the rise of the United States to economic preeminence in the course of the nineteenth century was due to its protectionist policies. The United States attained this position *despite* its protectionism, and *because* of its unrivaled internal laissez-faire policies. Indeed, America's current economic decline, which Buchanan would want to halt and reverse, is not the result of her alleged free trade policies, but of the circumstance that America, in the course of the twentieth century, gradually adopted the same socialist policies that had ruined England earlier.[5]

III

Given the case for free trade, we will now develop the case for immigration restrictions to be combined with free trade policies. More specifically, we will build a successively stronger case for immigration restrictions: from the initial weak claim that free trade and immigration restrictions can be combined and do not exclude each other to the final strong claim that the principle underlying free trade actually requires such restrictions.

From the outset, it must be emphasized that not even the most restrictive immigration policy or the most exclusive form of segregationism has anything to do with a rejection of free trade and the adoption of protectionism. From the fact that one does not want to associate with or live in a neighborhood of Germans, Haitians, Chinese, Koreans, Mexicans, Moslems, Hindus, Catholics, etc., it does not follow that one does not want to trade with them from a distance. Moreover, even if it were the case that one's real income would rise as a result of immigration, it

---

[4]See on this William H. Greenleaf, *The British Political Tradition*, 3 vols. (London: Methuen, 1983–87), esp. vol. 1: *The Rise of Collectivism*; also Albert V. Dicey, *Lectures on the Relation Between Law and Public Opinion During the Nineteenth Century* (London: Macmillan, 1914).

[5]See on this Murray N. Rothbard, "Origins of the Welfare State in America," *Journal of Libertarian Studies* 12, no. 2 (1996); Robert Higgs, *Crisis and Leviathan* (New York: Oxford University Press, 1987); *A New History of Leviathan*, Ronald Radosh and Murray N. Rothbard, eds. (New York: E.P. Dutton, 1972); James Weinstein, *The Corporate Ideal in the Liberal State* (Boston: Beacon Press, 1968); Arthur A. Ekirch, *The Decline of American Liberalism* (New York: Atheneum, 1967); Gabriel Kolko, *Railroads and Regulation* (Princeton, N.J.: Princeton University Press, 1965); idem, *The Triumph of Conservatism* (New York: Free Press, 1963).

does not follow that immigration must be considered "good," for material wealth is not the only thing that matters. Rather, what constitutes "welfare" and "wealth" is *subjective*, and one might prefer lower material living standards and a greater distance from certain other people over higher material living standards and a smaller distance. It is precisely the absolute voluntariness of human association *and* separation—the absence of any form of forced integration—which makes peaceful relationships—free trade—between racially, ethnically, linguistically, religiously, or culturally distinct people possible.

The relationship between trade and migration is one of elastic substitutibility (rather than rigid exclusivity): the more (less) you have of one, the less (more) you need of the other. Other things being equal, businesses move to low-wage areas, and labor moves to high-wage areas, thus effecting a tendency toward the equalization of wage rates (for the same kind of labor) as well as the optimal localization of capital. With political borders separating high from low-wage areas, and with national (nation-wide) trade and immigration policies in effect, these normal tendencies—of immigration and capital export—are weakened with free trade and strengthened with protectionism. As long as Mexican products—the products of a low-wage area—can freely enter a high-wage area such as the United States, the incentive for Mexican people to move to the United States is reduced. In contrast, if Mexican products are prevented from entering the American market, the attraction for Mexican workers to move to the United States is increased. Similarly, when United States producers are free to buy from and sell to Mexican producers and consumers, capital exports from the United States to Mexico will be reduced; however, when United States producers are prevented from doing so, the attraction of moving production from the United States to Mexico is increased.[6]

Similarly, as the *foreign* trade policy of the United States affects immigration, so does its *domestic* trade policy. Domestic free trade is what is typically referred to as laissez-faire capitalism. In other words, the national government follows a policy of noninterference with the voluntary transactions between domestic parties (citizens) regarding their private property. The government's policy is one of helping to protect its citizens and their private property from domestic aggression, damage, or fraud (exactly as in the case of foreign trade and aggression). If the United States followed strict domestic free trade policies, immigration

---

[6]See further on this Ludwig von Mises, *Nation, State, and Economy* (New York: New York University Press, 1983), esp. pp. 56ff.; Rothbard, *Power and Market*, pp. 52ff.

from low-wage regions such as Mexico would be reduced, while when it pursues "social welfare" policies, immigration from low-wage areas is more attractive.

IV

To the extent that a high-wage area such as the United States engages in unrestricted free trade, internationally as well as domestically, the immigration pressure from low-wage countries will be kept low or reduced, and hence, the question as to what to do about immigration will be less urgent. On the other hand, insofar as the United States engages in protectionist policies against the products of low-wage areas products and in welfare policies at home, immigration pressure will be kept high or even raised, and the immigration question will assume great importance in public debate.

Obviously, the world's major high-wage regions—North America and Western Europe—are presently in this latter situation, in which immigration has become an increasingly urgent public concern.[7] In light of

---

[7]In order to put matters into proper perspective, it might be useful to supply some brief comments on these regions' free-trade and domestic-welfare records. These remarks concern in particular the situation in the U.S., but they apply by and large to the situation in Western Europe, too. Free trade means to impose neither import tariffs or quotas, nor to subsidize the exportation of goods or engage in any other export promotion schemes. In particular, free trade does not require any bilateral or multilateral agreements or treaties. Instead, free trade policies can be implemented instantaneously and unilaterally, and intergovernmental trade agreements, regardless of what they are called, must invariably be regarded as indicators of international trade *restrictions* rather than free trade. In light of this, the free trade record of the U.S. must be considered dismal. (See on this, for instance, James Gwartney, Robert Lawson and Walter Block, *Economic Freedom of the World 1975–1995* (Vancouver: Frazer Institute, 1996), pp. 35f, 299, 302.) A labyrinthine system of tariffs and regulation restricts the free importation of literally thousands of foreign goods, from raw materials to agricultural products, machine tools and high-technology products. At the same time, the U.S. government engages in a wide variety of export promotion schemes, ranging from simple export subsidies and foreign aid requiring the purchase of certain U.S. goods to massive financial bailouts of U.S. investors in foreign countries and open or concealed military pressure and threat. Moreover, with the so-called North American Free Trade Agreement (NAFTA), a document of about 2,400 pages (when free trade prescriptions can be summarized in two sentences!) the U.S. government, in collaboration with the governments of Canada and Mexico, has recently adopted another maze of international trade restrictions and regulations. In effect, NAFTA involves the upward-harmonization of the tax and regulation structure across North America (very much like the so-called European Union (EU) does for most of Western Europe). Similar strictures apply to the new creation, as the result of GATT's (General Agreement on Tariffs and Trade) recent

steadily mounting immigration pressure from the world's low-wage regions, three general strategies of dealing with immigration have been proposed: unconditional free immigration, conditional free immigration, and restrictive immigration. While our main concern will be with the latter two alternatives, a few observations regarding the unconditional free immigration position are appropriate, if only to illustrate the extent of its intellectual bankruptcy and irresponsibility.

According to proponents of unconditional free immigration, the United States *qua* high-wage area would invariably benefit from free immigration; hence, it should enact a policy of open borders, regardless of present conditions, i.e., even if the United States were entangled in protectionism and domestic welfare.[8] Surely, such a proposal must

---

"Uruguay Round," of the World Trade Organization. See on this *The Nafta Reader: Free-Market Critiques of the North American "Free Trade" Agreement* (Auburn, Ala.: Ludwig von Mises Institute, 1993), and *The WTO Reader: Free Market Critiques of the World Trade Organization* (Auburn, Ala.: Ludwig von Mises Institute, 1994). Clearly even more striking is the domestic welfare record of the U.S. (and similarly of Western Europe). The record in this regard is not uniform across the U.S. Public welfare assistance is higher in California than in Alabama, for example, which explains significant welfare-migration within the U.S. Suffice it to say, however, that U.S. welfare assistance, including cash grants as well as numerous in kind benefits such as food stamps, housing allowances, medicaid, aid to dependent children, and public education, etc., can easily reach a household net-income of $ 20,000 per year and rise as high as $ 40,000 per year.

[8]Such a position has been advocated repeatedly, for instance, by the editorial-page editors of the highly influential *Wall Street Journal* led by the neoconservative Robert Bartley. See, for example, *Wall Street Journal*, July 3, 1990, where a constitutional amendment is proposed: "There shall be no borders." Likewise, open border policies have been proposed by Stephen Moore of the Cato Institute, Donald Boudreaux of the Foundation for Economic Education, and Jacob Hornberger of the Future of Freedom Foundation. While these individuals and institutions typically refer to Julian L. Simon as their patron saint in this regard, Simon in fact does *not* advocate an open border policy. See his *The Economic Consequences of Immigration* (Cambridge, Mass.: Blackwell, 1987), p. 309. Far more modestly, Simon recommends instead "to increase immigration quotas in a series of increments of significant size—perhaps half a percent, or one percent of total population at each step—to check on any unexpected negative consequences" (ibid., p. 348, also p. 310). More importantly, Simon suggests weeding out those potential immigrants who will become a "welfare burden" (p. 319). He recommends discrimination in favor of "educated" immigrants and those who demonstrate proficiency in English (p. 327), he suggests giving "preference to applicants with financial assets" capable of making a "direct investment" in the host country (p. 328), and he is particularly fond of the idea of "selling the right of immigration into the U.S. to the highest bidders" (p. 329, 335). In his last published article, Simon moves still further away from advocating an open-door policy. See Julian L. Simon, "Are there Grounds for Limiting Immigration?" *Journal of Libertarian Studies* 13, no. 2 (1998).

strike a reasonable person as fantastic. Assume that the United States, or better still Switzerland, declared that there would no longer be any border controls, that anyone who could pay the fare might enter the country, and, as a resident, would then be entitled to every "normal" domestic welfare provision. Is there any doubt about the disastrous outcome of such an experiment in the present world? The United States, and even faster Switzerland, already weakened by protectionism and welfare, would be overrun by millions of third-world immigrants.[9] Welfare costs would quickly skyrocket, and the strangled economy would disintegrate and collapse, as the subsistence fund—the stock of capital accumulated in and inherited from the past (fathers and forefathers)—was plundered. Civilization would vanish from the United States and Switzerland, just as it once did from Greece and Rome.[10]

---

[9]Two useful figures may indicate the magnitude of the potential problem. For one, according to surveys conducted during the early 1990s in the former Soviet Union, more than 30 percent of the population, i.e., close to 100 million people, expressed the desire to emigrate. Second, during the 1990s the U.S. held an annual "diversity" lottery, offering visas to persons originating in "countries with low rates of immigration to the United States." The 1997 lottery attracted some 3.4 million applicants for 50,000 available visas.

[10]A truly remarkable position is staked out by Walter Block, "A Libertarian Case for Free Immigration," *Journal of Libertarian Studies* 13, no. 2 (1998). Block does not deny the above predicted consequences of an "open border policy." To the contrary, he writes,

> suppose unlimited immigration is made the order of the day while minimum wages, unions, welfare, and a law code soft on criminals are still in place in the host country. Then, it might well be maintained, the host country would be subjected to increased crime, welfarism, and unemployment. An open-door policy would imply not economic freedom, but forced integration with all the dregs of the world with enough money to reach our shores. (p. 179)

Nonetheless, Block then goes on to advocate an open-door policy, *regardless* of these predictable consequences, and he claims that such a stand is required by the principles of libertarian political philosophy. Given Block's undeniable credentials as a leading contemporary theoretician of libertarianism, it is worthwhile explaining where his argument goes astray and why libertarianism requires *no* such thing as an open-door policy. Block's pro-immigration stand is based on an analogy. "Take the case of the bum in the library," he states.

> What, if anything, should be done about him? If this is a private library, . . . the law should *allow* the owner of the library to forcibly evict such a person, if need be, at his own discretion. . . . But what if it is a public library? . . . As such, [libraries] are akin to an unowned good. Any occupant has as much right to them as any other. If we are in a revolutionary state of war, then the first homesteader may seize control. But if not, as at present, then, given "just war" considerations, any reasonable

Since unconditional free immigration must be regarded as a prescription for societal suicide, the typical position among free traders is the alternative of conditional free immigration. According to this view, the United States and Switzerland would have to first return to unrestricted free trade and abolish all tax-funded welfare programs, and only then could they open their borders to everyone who wanted to come. In the meantime, while the welfare state is still in place, immigration would be permitted subject to the condition that immigrants are excluded from domestic welfare entitlements.

While the error involved in this view is less obvious and the consequences less dramatic than those associated with the unconditional free immigration position, the view is nonetheless erroneous and harmful. To be sure, the immigration pressure on the United States and Switzerland would be reduced if this proposal were followed, but it would not disappear. Indeed, with foreign and domestic free trade policies, wage rates within the United States and Switzerland might further increase relative to those at other locations (with less enlightened economic policies). Hence, the attraction of both countries might even increase. In any case, some immigration pressure would remain, so some form of immigration policy would have to exist. Do the principles underlying free trade imply that this policy must be one of conditional "free immigration?" No, they do not. There is no analogy between free trade and free immigration, and restricted trade and restricted immigration. The phenomena of trade and immigration are different in one fundamental respect, and the meaning of "free" and "restricted" in conjunction with both terms is categorically different. People can move and migrate; goods and services of themselves cannot.

> interference with public property would be legitimate. . . . One could "stink up" the library with unwashed body odor, or leave litter around in it, or "liberate" some books, but one could not plant land mines on the premises to blow up innocent library users. (pp. 180–81)

The fundamental error in this argument, according to which everyone, foreign immigrants no less than domestic bums, has an equal right to domestic public property, is Block's claim that public property "is akin to an unowned good." In fact, there exists a fundamental difference between unowned goods and public property. The latter is *de facto* owned by the taxpaying members of the domestic public. They have financed this property; hence, they, in accordance with the amount of taxes paid by individual members, must be regarded as its legitimate owners. Neither the bum, who has presumably paid no taxes, nor any foreigner, who has most definitely not paid any domestic taxes, can thus be assumed to have any rights regarding public property whatsoever. See more on this in chap. 6 above, esp. the *Postscript*.

Put differently, while someone can migrate from one place to another without anyone else wanting him to do so, goods and services cannot be shipped from place to place unless both sender and receiver agree. Trivial as this distinction may appear, it has momentous consequences, for *free* in conjunction with trade means trade by invitation of private households and firms only; and *restricted* trade does not mean protection of households and firms from uninvited goods or services, but invasion and abrogation of the right of private households and firms to extend or deny invitations to their own property. In contrast, *free* in conjunction with immigration does not mean immigration by invitation of individual households and firms, but unwanted invasion or forced integration; and *restricted* immigration actually means, or at least can mean, the protection of private households and firms from unwanted invasion and forced integration. Hence, in advocating free trade and restricted immigration, one follows the same principle: of requiring an invitation for people as for goods and services.

The free trade and free market proponent who adopts the conditional free immigration position is involved in intellectual inconsistency. Free trade and markets mean that private property owners may receive or send goods from and to other owners without government interference. The government stays inactive *vis-à-vis* the process of foreign and domestic trade, because a paying recipient exists for every good or service sent; hence, every locational change, as the outcome of an agreement between sender and receiver, must be deemed mutually beneficial. The government's sole function is that of maintaining the very trading-process by protecting citizen and domestic property. However, with respect to the movement of people, the same government will have to do more to fulfill its protective function than merely permit events to take their own course because people, unlike products, possess a will and can migrate. Accordingly, population movements, unlike product shipments, are not *per se* mutually beneficial events, because they are not always—necessarily and invariably—the result of an agreement between a specific receiver and sender. There can be shipments (immigrants) without willing domestic recipients. In this case, immigrants are foreign invaders and immigration represents an act of invasion. Surely, a government's basic protective function would include the prevention of foreign invasions and the expulsion of foreign invaders. Just as surely then, in order to do so and subject immigrants to the same requirement as imports (of having to be invited by domestic residents), a government cannot rightfully allow the kind of free immigration advocated by most free traders. Just imagine again that the United States and

Switzerland threw their borders open to whoever wanted to come, provided only that immigrants be excluded from all welfare entitlements (which would be reserved for United States and Swiss citizens respectively). Apart from the sociological problem of thereby creating two distinct classes of domestic residents and thus causing severe social tensions, there is little doubt about the outcome of this experiment in the present world.[11] The result would be less drastic and less immediate than under the scenario of unconditional free immigration, but it would also amount to a massive foreign invasion and ultimately lead to the destruction of American and Swiss civilization. Even if no welfare-handouts were available to immigrants, this does not mean that they would actually have to work, since even life on and off the public streets and parks in the United States and Switzerland is comfortable as compared to "real" life in many other areas of the world. Thus, in order to fulfill its primary function as the protector of its citizens and their domestic property, a high-wage area government cannot follow an immigration policy of *laissez-passer*, but must engage in restrictive measures.[12]

V

From the recognition that proponents of free trade and markets cannot advocate free immigration without being inconsistent and contradicting themselves, and that therefore immigration must logically be restricted, it is but a small step to the further recognition of *how* it must be restricted. In fact, all high-wage area governments presently restrict immigration in one way or another. Nowhere is immigration "free," unconditionally or conditionally. However, the restrictions imposed on immigration by the United States and by Switzerland, for instance, are quite different. Which restrictions *should* exist? More precisely, which immigration restrictions is a free trader and free marketeer logically compelled to uphold and promote?

The guiding principle of a high-wage area country's immigration policy follows from the insight that to be free in the same sense as trade is free, immigration must be *invited*. The details follow from the further

---

[11]Note, that even if immigrants were excluded from all tax-funded welfare entitlements as well as the democratic "right" to vote, they would still be "protected" and covered by all currently existing antidiscrimination affirmative action laws, which would prevent domestic residents from "arbitrarily" excluding them from employment, housing, and any other form of "public" accommodation.

[12]For a brilliant literary treatment of the subject of "free" immigration see Jean Raspail, *The Camp of the Saints* (New York: Charles Scribner's Sons, 1975).

elucidation and exemplification of the concepts of invitation versus invasion and forced integration.

To this end, it is necessary to presuppose, as a conceptual benchmark, the existence of what political philosophers have described as a private property anarchy, anarcho-capitalism, or ordered anarchy.[13] All land is privately owned, including all streets, rivers, airports, and harbors. With respect to some pieces of land, the property title may be unrestricted; that is, the owner is permitted to do whatever he pleases with his property as long as he does not physically damage the property of others. With respect to other territories, the property title may be more or less restricted. As is currently the case in some housing developments, the owner may be bound by contractual limitations on what he can do with his property (restrictive covenants, voluntary zoning), which might include residential rather than commercial use, no buildings more than four stories high, no sale or rent to unmarried couples, smokers, or Germans, for instance.

Clearly, in this kind of society there is no such thing as freedom of immigration or an immigrant's right-of-way. Rather, there exists the freedom of many independent private property owners to admit or exclude others from their own property in accordance with their own restricted or unrestricted property titles. Admission to some territories might be easy, while to others it might be nearly impossible. Moreover, admission to the property of one party does not imply the "freedom to move around," unless other property owners have agreed to such movements. There will be as much immigration or nonimmigration, inclusivity or exclusivity, desegregation or segregation, nondiscrimination or discrimination as individual owners or associations of individual owners desire.[14]

---

[13]On the theory of anarcho-capitalism see Murray N. Rothbard, *The Ethics of Liberty* (New York: New York University Press, 1988); idem, *For A New Liberty* (New York: Collier, 1978); Hans-Hermann Hoppe, *The Economics and Ethics of Private Property* (Boston: Kluwer, 1993); David Friedman, *The Machinery of Freedom: Guide to Radical Capitalism* (La Salle, Ill.: Open Court, 1989); Morris and Linda Tannehill, *The Market for Liberty* (New York: Laissez Faire Books, 1984); Anthony de Jasay, *Against Politics: On Government, Anarchy, and Order* (London: Routledge, 1997).

[14]"If every piece of land in a country were owned by some person, group, or corporation," elaborates Murray N. Rothbard,

> this would mean that no immigrant could enter there unless invited to enter and allowed to rent, or purchase property. A totally privatized country would be as closed as the particular inhabitants and property owners desire. It seems clear, then, that the regime of open borders that

The reason for citing the model of an anarcho-capitalist society is that no such thing as forced integration (uninvited migration) is possible (permitted) within its framework. Under this scenario no difference between the physical movement of goods and the migration of people exists. Just as every product movement reflects an underlying agreement between sender and receiver, so are all movements of immigrants into and within an anarcho-capitalist society the result of an agreement between the immigrant and one or a series of receiving domestic property owners. Hence, even if the anarcho-capitalist model is ultimately rejected—and if for "realism's" sake the existence of a government and of "public" (in addition to private) goods and property is assumed—it brings into clear focus what a government's immigration policy would have to be *if and insofar* as this government derived its legitimacy from the sovereignty of the "people" and was viewed as the outgrowth of an agreement or "social contract" (as is presumably the case with all modern—post-monarchical—governments, of course). Surely, such a "popular" government, which assumed as its primary task the protection of its citizens and their property (the production of domestic security), would want to preserve rather than abolish this no-forced-integration feature of anarcho-capitalism.

In order to clarify what this implies, it is necessary to explain how an anarcho-capitalist society is altered by the introduction of a government, and how this affects the immigration problem. Since there is no government in

---

exists *de facto* in the U.S. really amounts to a compulsory opening by the central state, the state in charge of all streets and public land areas, and does not genuinely reflect the wishes of the proprietors. . . . Under total privatization, many local conflicts and externality problems—not merely the immigration problem—would be neatly settled. With every locale and neighborhood owned by private firms, corporations, or contractual communities, a true diversity would reign, according to the preferences of each community. Some neighborhoods would be ethnically or economically diverse, while others would be ethnically or economically homogeneous. Some localities would permit pornography or prostitution or drugs or abortions, while others would prohibit any or all of them. The prohibitions would not be state imposed, but would simply be requirements for residence or for use of some person's or community's land area. While statists, who have the itch to impose their values on everyone else, would be disappointed, every group or interest would at least have the satisfaction of living in neighborhoods of people who share its values and preferences. While neighborhood ownership would not provide Utopia or a panacea for all conflicts, it would at least provide a "second-best" solution that most people might be willing to live with. ("Nations by Consent: Decomposing the Nation–State," *Journal of Libertarian Studies* 11, no. 1 [1994]: 7)

an anarcho-capitalist society, there is no clear-cut distinction between inlanders (domestic citizens) and foreigners. This distinction appears only with the establishment of a government. The territory over which a government's power extends then becomes inland, and everyone residing outside of this territory becomes a foreigner. State borders (and passports), as distinct from private property borders (and titles to property), come into existence, and immigration takes on a new meaning. Immigration becomes immigration by foreigners across state borders, and the decision as to whether or not a person should be admitted no longer rests exclusively with private property owners or associations of such owners but ultimately with the government *qua* domestic security-producer monopolist. Now if the government excludes a person while a domestic resident exists who wants to admit this very person onto his property, the result is forced exclusion; and if the government admits a person while no domestic resident exists who wants to have this person on his property, the result is forced integration.

Moreover, hand-in-hand with the institution of a government comes the institution of public property and goods; that is, of property and goods owned collectively by all domestic residents and controlled and administered by the government. The larger or smaller the amount of public government ownership, the greater or smaller will be the potential problem of forced integration. Consider a socialist society like the former Soviet Union or East Germany, for example. All factors of production (capital goods), including all land and natural resources, are publicly owned. Accordingly, if the government admits an uninvited immigrant, it admits him to any place within the country; for without private land ownership there are no limitations on his internal migrations other than those decreed by government. Under socialism, therefore, forced integration can be spread everywhere and thereby immensely intensified. (In fact, in the Soviet Union and East Germany, for instance, the government could quarter a stranger in someone else's private house or apartment. This measure and the resulting high-powered forced integration was justified on grounds of the "fact" that all private houses rested on public land.[15])

Socialist countries are not high-wage areas, of course. Or if they are, they will not remain so for long. Their problem is not immigration but emigration pressure. The Soviet Union and East Germany prohibited

---

[15]By the same token, under socialism every form of internal migration was subject to government control. See on this Victor Zaslavsky and Yuri Lury, "The Passport System in the USSR and Changes in the Soviet Union," *Soviet Union* 8, no. 2 (1979).

emigration and killed people for trying to leave the country.[16] However, the problem of the extension and intensification of forced integration persists outside of socialism. To be sure, in nonsocialist countries such as the United States, Switzerland, and the Federal Republic of Germany, which *are* favorite immigration destinations, a government-admitted immigrant could not move just anywhere. His freedom of movement would be severely restricted by the extent of private property and private land ownership in particular. Yet by proceeding on public roads or with public means of transportation and by staying on public land and in public parks and buildings, an immigrant can cross every domestic resident's path, and move into virtually any neighborhood. The smaller the quantity of public property, the less likely this will occur, but as long as *any* public property exists it cannot be entirely avoided.

VI

A popular government that wants to safeguard its citizens and their domestic property from forced integration and foreign invaders has two methods of doing so: a corrective and a preventive one. The corrective method is designed to ameliorate the effects of forced integration once the event has taken place and the invaders are there. As indicated, to achieve this goal the government must reduce the quantity of public property and expand that of private property as much as possible, and whatever the ratio of private to public property may be, the government should help rather than hinder the enforcement of a private property owner's right to admit *and* exclude others from his property. If virtually all property is owned privately and the government assists in enforcing private ownership rights, the uninvited immigrants, even if they successfully crossed the border and entered the country, would not likely get much further.

The more completely this corrective measure is carried out (the higher the degree of private ownership), the smaller will be the need for protective measures, such as border defense. The cost of protection against foreign invaders along the United States–Mexico border, for instance, is comparatively high because for long stretches no private property exists on the U.S. side. However, even if the cost of border protection were lowered by means of privatization, it would not disappear as long

---

[16]See on this Hans-Hermann Hoppe, *A Theory of Socialism and Capitalism* (Boston: Kluwer, 1989), chap. 3; idem, "Desocialization in a United Germany," *Review of Austrian Economics* 5, no. 2 (1991); idem, "The Economic and Political Rationale for European Secessionism," in *Secession, State and Liberty*, David Gordon, ed. (New Brunswick, N.J.: Transaction Publishers, 1998).

as there are substantial income and wage differentials between high- and low-wage territories. Hence, in order to fulfill its basic protective function, a high-wage area government must also engage in preventive measures. At all ports of entry and along its borders, the government, as trustee of its citizens, must check all newly arriving persons for an entrance ticket; that is, a valid invitation by a domestic property owner; and anyone not in possession of such a ticket must be expelled at his own expense.

Valid invitations are contracts between one or more private domestic recipients, residential or commercial, and the arriving person. *Qua* contractual admission, the inviting party can only dispose of his own private property. Hence, similar to the scenario of conditional free immigration the admission implies that the immigrant will be excluded from all publicly funded welfare. On the other hand, it implies that the receiving party must assume legal responsibility for the actions of his invitee for the duration of his stay. The invitor is held liable to the full extent of his property for any crimes by the invitee committed against the person or property of any third party (as parents are held accountable for crimes committed by their offspring as long as these are members of the parental household). This obligation, which implies that invitors will have to carry liability insurance for all of their guests, ends once the invitee has left the country, or once another domestic property owner has assumed liability for the person in question by admitting him onto his property.

The invitation may be private (personal) or commercial, temporary or permanent, concerning only housing (accommodation, residency) or housing and employment, but there cannot be a valid contract involving only employment and no housing.[17] In any case, however, as a contractual relationship, every invitation may be revoked or terminated by the

---

[17] In the current legal environment wherein domestic property owners are essentially barred from engaging in any form of discriminatory action, the presence of foreign guestworkers would inevitably lead to widespread forced integration. Once admitted, based on an existing employment contract, these workers would then be able to use the courts in order to gain entrance also to housing, schooling, and any other form of "public" establishment or accommodation. Hence, in order to overcome this problem employers must be required to offer their guestworkers not just employment but housing and other things such as shopping, medical, training or entertainment facilities, i.e., the amenities of an entire self-contained factory town. For a discussion of the much maligned institution of factory towns see James B. Allen, *The Company Town in the American West* (Norman: Oklahoma University Press, 1966).

host; and upon termination, the invitee—whether tourist, visiting businessman, or resident alien—will be required to leave the country (unless another resident citizen enters into an invitation-contract with him).

The invitee, who is at all times subject to the potential risk of immediate expulsion, may lose his legal status as a nonresident or resident alien only upon acquiring citizenship. In accordance with the objective of making all immigration (like trade) invited-contractual, the fundamental requirement for citizenship is the acquisition of property ownership, or more precisely the ownership of real estate and residential property. In contrast, it would be inconsistent with the very idea of invited migration to award citizenship according to the territorial principle, as in the U.S., whereby a child born to a nonresident or resident alien in a host country automatically acquires U.S. citizenship. In fact, as most other high-wage area governments recognize, such a child should acquire the citizenship of his parents. Granting this child citizenship involves the nonfulfillment of a host country government's basic protective function and actually amounts to an invasive act perpetrated by the government against its own citizenry. Becoming a citizen means acquiring the right to stay in a country permanently, and a permanent invitation cannot be secured by any means other than purchasing residential property from a citizen resident. Only by selling real estate to a foreigner does a citizen indicate that he agrees to a guest's permanent stay, and only if the immigrant has purchased and paid for real estate and residential housing in the host country will he assume a permanent interest in his new country's well-being and prosperity. Moreover, finding a citizen who is willing to sell residential property and who is prepared and able to pay for it, although a necessary requirement for the acquisition of citizenship, may not also be sufficient. If and insofar as the domestic property in question is subject to restrictive covenants, the hurdles to be taken by a prospective citizen may be significantly higher.[18] In Switzerland, for instance, citizenship may require that the sale of residential property to foreigners be ratified by a majority of or even all of the directly affected local property owners.

VII

Judged by the immigration policy entailed by the objective of protecting one's own citizens from foreign invasion and forced integration and of rendering all international population movements invited and

---

[18]See on this also chap. 10, sect. 6, and Spencer H. MacCallum, *The Art of Community* (Menlo Park, Calif.: Institute for Humane Studies, 1970).

contractual migrations, the Swiss government does a significantly better job than the United States. It is relatively more difficult to enter Switzerland as an uninvited person, and it is more difficult to stay on as an uninvited alien. In particular it is far more difficult for a foreigner to acquire citizenship, and the legal distinction between resident citizens and resident aliens is more clearly preserved. These differences notwithstanding, the governments of both Switzerland and the U.S. are pursuing immigration policies that must be deemed far too permissive.

Moreover, the excessive permissiveness of their immigration policies and the resulting exposure of the Swiss and American population to forced integration by foreigners is further aggravated by the fact that the extent of public property in both countries (and other high-wage areas) is substantial; that tax-funded welfare provisions are high and growing and foreigners are not excluded; and that contrary to official pronouncements even the adherence to free trade policies is anything but perfect. Accordingly, in Switzerland, the U.S. and most other high-wage areas, popular protests against immigration policies have grown increasingly louder. It has been the purpose of this chapter not only to make the case for the privatization of public property, domestic laissez-faire, and international free trade, but in particular for the adoption of a restrictive immigration policy. By demonstrating that free trade is inconsistent with both unconditionally or conditionally free immigration and requires instead that migration be subject to the condition of being invited and contractual, it is our hope to contribute to more enlightened future policies in this area.

9

On Cooperation, Tribe, City, and State

I

Ludwig von Mises has explained the evolution of society—of human cooperation under the division of labor—as the combined result of two factors. These are first, the fact of differences among men (labor) and/or the inequalities of the geographical distribution of the nature-given factors of production (land); and second, the recognition of the fact that work performed under the division of labor is more productive than work performed in self-sufficient isolation. He writes:

> If and as far as labor under the division of labor is more productive than isolated labor, and if and as far as man is able to realize this fact, human action itself tends toward cooperation and association; man becomes a social being not in sacrificing his own concerns for the sake of a mythical Moloch, society, but in aiming at an improvement in his own welfare. Experience teaches that this condition—higher productivity achieved under division of labor—is present because its cause—the inborn inequality of men and the inequality in the geographical distribution of the natural factors of production—is real. Thus we are in a position to comprehend the course of social evolution.[1]

Several points are worth emphasizing here in order to reach a proper understanding of this fundamental insight of Mises's into the nature of society—points which will also help us realize some first, preliminary conclusions regarding the role of sex and race in social evolution. First, it is important to recognize that inequalities with respect to labor and/or land are a necessary but by no means a sufficient condition for the emergence of human cooperation. If all humans were identical and everyone were equipped with identical natural resources, everyone would produce the same qualities and quantities of goods, and the idea of exchange and cooperation would never enter anyone's mind. However, the existence of inequalities is not enough to bring about cooperation. There are also differences in the animal kingdom—most notably the

---

[1]Ludwig von Mises, *Human Action: A Treatise on Economics*, Scholar's Edition (Auburn, Ala.: Ludwig von Mises Institute, 1998), p. 160.

difference of sex (gender) among members of the same animal species as well as the difference between the various species and subspecies (races), yet there is no such thing as cooperation among animals. To be sure, there are bees and ants who are referred to as "animal societies." But they form societies only in a metaphorical sense.[2] The cooperation between bees and ants is assured purely by biological factors—by innate instincts. They cannot *not* cooperate as they do, and without some fundamental changes in their biological makeup, the division of labor among them is not in danger of breaking down. In distinct contrast, the cooperation between humans is the outcome of purposeful individual actions, of the conscious aiming at the attainment of individual ends. As a result, the division of labor among men is constantly threatened by the possibility of disintegration.

Within the animal kingdom, then, the difference between the sexes can only be said to be a factor of attraction—of reproduction and proliferation; whereas the differences of the species and subspecies can be referred to as a factor of repulsion—of separation or even of fatal antagonism, of evasion, of struggle, and annihilation. Moreover, within the animal kingdom it makes no sense to describe the behavior resulting from sexual attraction as either consensual (love) or nonconsensual (rape); nor does it make any sense to speak of the relationship between the members of different species or subspecies as one of hostility and hatred or of criminal and victim. In the animal kingdom there only exists interaction, which is neither cooperative (social) behavior nor criminal (antisocial) behavior. As Mises writes:

> There is interaction—reciprocal influence—between all parts of the universe: between the wolf and the sheep that he devours; between the germ and the man it kills; between the falling stone and the thing upon which it falls. Society, on the other hand, always involves men acting in cooperation with other men in order to let all participants attain their own ends.[3]

In addition to an inequality of labor and/or land, a second requirement must be fulfilled if human cooperation is to evolve. Men—at least two of them—must be capable of recognizing the higher productivity of a division of labor based on the mutual recognition of private property (of the exclusive control of every man over his own body and over his physical appropriations and possessions) as compared to either self-sufficient

---

[2]See on this Jonathan Bennett, *Rationality: An Essay Toward an Analysis* (London: Routledge and Kegan Paul, 1964).

[3]Mises, *Human Action*, p. 169.

isolation or aggression, depredation, and domination. That is, there must be a minimum of intelligence or rationality; and men—at least two of them—must have the sufficient moral strength to act on this insight and be willing to forego immediate gratification for even greater future satisfaction. But for intelligence and conscious will, writes Mises,

> men would have forever remained deadly foes of one another, irreconcilable rivals in their endeavors to secure a portion of the scarce supply of means of sustenance provided by nature. Each man would have been forced to view all other men as his enemies; his craving for the satisfaction of his own appetites would have brought him into an implacable conflict with all his neighbors. No sympathy could possibly develop under such a state of affairs.[4]

A member of the human race who is completely incapable of understanding the higher productivity of labor performed under a division of labor based on private property is not properly speaking a person (a *persona*), but falls instead in the same moral category as an animal—of either the harmless sort (to be domesticated and employed as a producer or consumer good, or to be enjoyed as a "free good") or the wild and dangerous one (to be fought as a pest). On the other hand, there are members of the human species who are capable of understanding the insight but who lack the moral strength to act accordingly. Such persons are either harmless brutes living outside of and separated from human society, or they are more or less dangerous criminals. They are persons who knowingly act wrongly and who besides having to be tamed or even physically defeated must also be punished in proportion to the severity of their crime to make them understand the nature of their wrongdoings and hopefully to teach them a lesson for the future. Human cooperation (society) can only prevail and advance as long as man is capable of subduing, taming, appropriating, and cultivating his physical and animalistic surroundings, and as long as he succeeds in suppressing crime, reducing it to a rarity by means of self-defense, property protection, and punishment.[5]

---

[4]Ibid, p. 144.

[5]Rarely has the importance of cognition and rationality for the emergence and maintenance of society been more strongly emphasized than by Mises. He explains that one

> may admit that in primitive man the propensity for killing and destroying and the disposition for cruelty were innate. We may also assume that under the conditions of earlier ages the inclination for aggression and murder was favorable to the preservation of life. Man was once a brutal beast. . . . But one must not forget that he was physically a weak animal;

II

As soon as these requirements are fulfilled, however, and as long as man, motivated by the knowledge of the higher physical productivity of a division of labor based on private property, is engaged in mutually beneficial exchanges, the "natural" forces of attraction arising from the differences in the sexes and the "natural" forces of repulsion or enmity arising from the differences between and even within the races, can be transformed into genuinely "social" relations. Sexual attraction can be transformed from copulation to consensual relations, mutual bonds, households, families, love, and affection.[6] (It testifies to the enormous

---

he would not have been a match for the big beasts of prey if he had not been equipped with a peculiar weapon, reason. The fact that man is a reasonable being, that he therefore does not yield without inhibitions to every impulse, but arranges his conduct according to reasonable delib- eration, must not be called unnatural from a zoological point of view. Rational conduct means that man, in face of the fact that he cannot satisfy all his impulses, desires, and appetites, foregoes the satisfaction of those which he considers less urgent. In order not to endanger the working of social cooperation, man is forced to abstain from satisfying those desires whose satisfaction would hinder establishment of societal institutions. There is no doubt that such a renunciation is painful. However, man has made his choice. He has renounced the satisfac- tion of some desires incompatible with social life and has given priority to the satisfaction of those desires which can be realized only or in a more plentiful way under a system of the division of labor.... This decision is not irrevocable and final. The choice of the fathers does not impair the sons' freedom to choose. They can reverse the resolution. Every day they can proceed to the transvaluation of values and prefer barbarism to civilization, or, as some authors say, the soul to the intellect, myths to reason, and violence to peace. But they must choose. It is impossible to have things incompatible with one another. (*Human Ac- tion*, pp. 171–72)

See on this also Joseph T. Salerno, "Ludwig von Mises as Social Rationalist," *Review of Austrian Economics* 4 (1990).

[6]"Within the frame of social cooperation," writes Mises,

there can emerge between members of society feelings of sympathy and friendship and a sense of belonging together. These feelings are the source of man's most delightful and most sublime experiences. They are the most precious adornment of life; they lift the animal species man to the heights of a really human existence. However, they are not, as some have asserted, the agents that have brought about social relationships. They are the fruits of social cooperation, they thrive only within its frame; they did not precede the establishment of social relations and are not the seeds from which they spring. (Ibid., p. 144)

"The mutual sexual attraction of male and female," Mises explains further,

productivity of the family-household that no other institution has proven more durable or capable of producing such emotions!) And inter- and intraracial repulsion can be transformed from feelings of enmity or hostility to a preference for cooperating (trading) with one another only indirectly—from afar and physically separated and spatially segregated—rather than directly, as neighbors and associates.[7]

Human cooperation—division of labor—based on the one hand on integrated family-households and on the other one on separated households, villages, tribes, nations, races, etc., wherein man's natural biological attractions and repulsions for and against one another are transformed into a mutually recognized system of spatial (geographical) allocation (of physical approximation and integration or of separation and segregation, and of direct or of indirect contact, exchange and trade), leads to improved standards of living, a growing population, further extensification and intensification of the division of labor, and increasing diversity and differentiation.[8]

As a result of this development and an ever more rapid increase of goods and desires which can be acquired and satisfied only indirectly, professional traders, merchants, and trading centers will emerge. Merchants

---

is inherent in man's animal nature and independent of any thinking and theorizing. It is permissible to call it original, vegetative, instinctive, or mysterious; . . . However, neither cohabitation, nor what precedes it and follows, generates social cooperation and societal modes of life. The animals too join together in mating, but they have not developed social relations. Family life is not merely a product of sexual intercourse. It is by no means natural and necessary that parents and children live together in the way in which they do in the family. The mating relation need not result in a family organization. The human family is an outcome of thinking, planning, and acting. It is this fact which distinguishes it radically from those animal groups which we call *per analogiam* animal families. (Ibid., p. 167)

[7]On the significance of race and ethnicity, and especially on "genetic similarity and dissimilarity" as a source of mutual attraction and repulsion see J. Philippe Rushton, *Race, Evolution, and Behavior* (New Brunswick, N.J.: Transaction Publishers, 1995); idem, "Gene Culture, Co-Evolution and Genetic Similarity Theory: Implications for Ideology, Ethnic Nepotism, and Geopolitics," *Politics and the Life Sciences* 4 (1986); idem, "Genetic Similarity, Human Altruism, and Group Selection," *Behavioral and Brain Sciences* 12 (1989); idem, "Genetic Similarity in Male Friendships," *Ethology and Sociobiology* 10 (1989); also Michael Levin, *Why Race Matters* (Westport, Conn.: Praeger, 1997); idem, "Why Race Matters: A Preview," *Journal of Libertarian Studies* 12, no. 2 (1996).

[8]See Murray N. Rothbard, "Freedom, Inequality, Primitivism, and the Division of Labor," in idem, *Egalitarianism as a Revolt Against Nature and Other Essays* (Auburn, Ala.: Ludwig von Mises Institute, 2000).

and cities function as the mediators of the indirect exchanges between territorially separated households and communal associations and thus become the sociological and geographical locus and focus of intertribal or interracial association. It will be within the class of merchants in which racially, ethnically, or tribally mixed marriages are relatively most common; and since most people, of both reference groups, typically disapprove of such alliances, it will be the wealthier members of the merchant class who can afford such extravagances. However, even the members of the wealthiest merchant families will be highly circumspect in such endeavors. In order not to endanger their own position as a merchant, great care must be taken that every mixed marriage is, or at least appears to the relevant ethnicities to be a marriage between "equals." Consequently, the racial mixture brought on by the merchant class will more likely than not contribute to genetic "luxuration" (rather than genetic "pauperization").[9] Accordingly, it will be in the big cities as the centers of international trade and commerce, where mixed couples and their offspring typically reside, where members of different ethnicities, tribes, races, even if they do not intermarry, still come into regular direct personal contact with each other (in fact, that *they* do so is required by the fact that their respective tribesmen back home do *not* have to deal directly with more or less distasteful strangers), and where the most elaborate and highly developed system of physical and functional integration and segregation will arise.[10] It will also be in the big cities where,

---

[9]See Wilhelm Mühlmann, *Rassen, Ethnien, Kulturen. Moderne Ethnologie* (Neuwied: Luchterhand, 1964), pp. 93–97. In general, apart from the upper strata of the class of merchants, peaceful racial or ethnic mixing is typically restricted to members of the social upper-class, i.e., to nobles and aristocrats. Thus, the racially or ethnically least pure families are characteristically the leading royal dynasties.

[10]For instance, Fernand Braudel has given the following description of the complex pattern of spatial separation and functional integration and the corresponding multiplicity of separate and competing jurisdictions developed in the great trading centers such as Antioch during the heyday of the Islamic civilization from the eighth to the twelfth century: At the city center

was the Great Mosque for the weekly sermon. . . . Nearby was the bazaar, i.e., the merchants' quarter with its streets and shops (the souk) and its caravanserais or warehouses, as well as the public baths . . . Artisans were grouped concentrically, starting from the Great Mosque: first, the makers and sellers of perfumes and incense, then the shops selling fabrics and rugs, the jewelers and food stores, and finally the humblest trades . . . curriers, cobblers, blacksmiths, potters, saddlers, dyers. Their shops marked the edges of the town. . . . In principle, each of these trades had its location fixed for all time. Similarly, the *maghzen* or Prince's quarter was in principle located on the outskirts of the city, well away

as the subjective reflection of this complex system of spatio-functional allocation, citizens will develop the most highly refined forms of personal and professional conduct, etiquette, and style. It is the city that breeds civilization and civilized life.

To maintain law and order within a big city, with its intricate pattern of physical and functional integration and separation, a great variety of jurisdictions, judges, arbitrators and enforcement agencies in addition to self-defense and private protection will come into existence. There will be what one might call *governance* in the city, but there will be no government (state).[11] For a government to arise it is necessary that one of these judges, arbitrators, or enforcement agencies succeed in establishing himself as a monopolist. That is, he must be able to insist that no citizen can choose anyone but him as the judge or arbitrator of last resort, and he must successfully suppress any other judge or arbitrator from trying to assume the same role (thereby competing against him). More interesting than the question of what a government is, however, are the following: How is it possible that one judge can acquire a judiciary monopoly, given that other judges will naturally oppose any such attempt; and what specifically makes it possible, and what does it imply, to establish a monopoly of law and order in a big city, i.e., over a territory with ethnically, tribally, and/or racially mixed populations?

---

from riots or popular revolts. Next to it, and under its protection, was the *mellah* or Jewish quarter. The mosaic was completed by a very great variety of residential districts, divided by race and religion: there were forty-five in Antioch alone. "The town was a cluster of different quarters, all living in fear of massacre." So Western colonists nowhere began racial segregation—although they nowhere suppressed it. (Braudel, *A History of Civilizations* [New York: Penguin Books, 1995], p. 66)

[11]See Otto Brunner, *Sozialgeschichte Europas im Mittelalter* (Göttingen: Vandenhoeck and Ruprecht, 1984), chap. 8; Henri Pirenne, *Medieval Cities* (Princeton, N.J.: Princeton University Press, 1969); Charles Tilly and Wim P. Blockmans, eds., *Cities and the Rise of States in Europe, 1000–1800* (Boulder, Colo.: Westview Press, 1994); Boudewijn Bouckaert, "Between the Market and the State: The World of Medieval Cities," in *Values and the Social Order*, Vol. 3, *Voluntary versus Coercive Orders*, Gerard Radnitzky, ed. (Aldershot, U.K.: Avebury, 1997). Incidentally, the much maligned Jewish *Ghettoes*, which were characteristic of European cities throughout the Middle Ages, were *not* indicative of an inferior legal status accorded to Jews or of anti-Jewish discrimination. To the contrary, the *Ghetto* was a place where Jews enjoyed complete self-government and where rabbinical law applied. See on this Guido Kisch, *The Jews in Medieval Germany* (Chicago: University of Chicago Press, 1942); also Erik von Kuehnelt-Leddihn, "Hebrews and Christians," *Rothbard–Rockwell Report* 9, no. 4 (April 1998).

First, almost by definition it follows that with the establishment of a city government interracial, tribal, ethnic, and clannish-familial tensions will increase because the monopolist, whoever he is, must be of one ethnic background rather than another; hence, his being the monopolist will be considered by the citizens of other ethnic backgrounds as an insulting setback, i.e., as an act of arbitrary discrimination against the people of another race, tribe, or clan. The delicate balance of peaceful interracial, interethnic, and interfamilial cooperation, achieved through an intricate system of spatial and functional integration (association) and separation (segregation), will be upset. Second, this insight leads directly to the answer as to how a single judge can possibly outmaneuver all others. In brief, to overcome the resistance by competing judges, an aspiring monopolist must shore up added support in public opinion. In an ethnically mixed milieu this typically means playing the "race card." The prospective monopolist must raise the racial, tribal, or clanish consciousness among citizens of his own race, tribe, clan, etc., and promise, in return for their support, to be *more* than an impartial judge in matters relating to one's own race, tribe, or clan (that is, exactly what citizens of other ethnic backgrounds are afraid of, i.e., of being treated with *less* than impartiality).[12]

At this stage in this sociological reconstruction let us, without further explanation, briefly introduce a few additional steps required to arrive at a realistic contemporary scenario regarding race, sex, society, and state. Naturally, a monopolist will try to maintain his position and possibly even turn it into an hereditary title (i.e., become a king). However, accomplishing this within an ethnically or tribally mixed city is a far more difficult task than within a homogeneous rural community. Instead, in big cities governments are far more likely to take on the form of a democratic republic—with "open entry" into the position of supreme ruler, competing political parties, and popular elections.[13] In the

---

[12]For a sociological treatment of the first (predemocratic) stage in the development of city states, characterized by aristocratic–patrician government founded on and riven by families (clans) and family conflicts, see Max Weber, *The City* (New York: Free Press, 1958), chap. 3. See also note 16 below.

[13]This statement regarding the characteristically democratic–republican —rather than monarchical—form of government in large commercial cities should not be misinterpreted as a simple empirical–historical proposition. Indeed, historically the formation of governments predates the development of large commercial centers. Most governments had been monarchical or princely governments, and when large commercial cities first arose the power of kings and princes typically also extended initially to these newly developing urban areas. Instead, the above

course of the political centralization process[14]—the territorial expansion of one government at the expense of another—this big city model of government, then, will become essentially its only form: that of a democratic state exercising a judicial monopoly over a territory with racially and/or ethnically widely diverse populations.

III

While the judicial monopoly of governments extends nowadays typically far beyond a single city and in some cases over almost an entire continent, the consequences for the relations between the races and sexes and spatial approximation and segregation of government (monopoly) can still be best observed in the great cities and their decline from centers of civilization to centers of degeneration and decay.

With a central government extending over cities and the countryside, countries, inlanders, and foreigners are created. This has no immediate effect on the countryside, where there are no foreigners (members of different ethnicities, races, etc.). But in the great trading centers, where there are mixed populations, the legal distinction between inlander and foreigner (rather than ethnically or racially distinct private property owners) will almost invariably lead to some form of forced exclusion and a reduced level of interethnic cooperation. Moreover, with a central state in place, the physical segregation and separation of city and countryside will be systematically reduced. In order to exercise its judicial monopoly, the central government must be able to access every inlander's private property, and to do so it must take control of all existing roads and even expand the existing system of roadways. Different households and villages are thus brought into closer contact than they might have preferred, and the physical distance and separation of city

---

statement should be interpreted as a *sociological* proposition concerning the unlikeliness of the *endogenous* origin of royal or princely rule over large commercial centers with ethnically mixed populations, i.e., as an answer to an essentially hypothetical and counterfactual question. See on this Max Weber, *Soziologie, Weltgeschichtliche Analysen, Politik* (Stuttgart: Kroener, 1964), pp. 41–42, who notes that kings and nobles, even if they resided in cities, were nonetheless decidedly *not city*-kings and *city*-nobles. The centers of their power rested outside of cities, in the countryside, and the grip that they held on the great commercial centers was only tenuous. Hence, the first experiments with democratic–republican forms of government occurred characteristically in cities which broke off and gained independence from their predominantly monarchical and rural surroundings.

[14]On the eliminative competition and inherent tendency of states toward centralization and territorial expansion—ultimately to the point of the establishment of a world government—see chaps. 5, 11, and 12.

and countryside will be significantly diminished. Thus, internally, forced integration will be promoted.

Naturally, this tendency toward forced integration due to the monopolization of roads and streets will be most pronounced in the cities. This tendency will be further stimulated if, as is typical, the government takes its seat in a city. A popularly elected government cannot help using its judicial monopoly to engage in redistributive policies in favor of its ethnic or racial constituency, which will invariably attract even more of its own tribe's members, and with changes in the government more members of even more and different tribes will be drawn from the countryside to the capital city to receive either government jobs or handouts. As a result, not only will the capital become relatively "oversized" (as other cities shrink). At the same time, due to the monopolization of "public" streets—whereon everyone may proceed wherever he wants—all forms of ethnic, tribal, or racial tensions and animosities will be stimulated.

Moreover, while interracial, tribal, and ethnic marriages were formerly rare and restricted to the upper strata of the merchant class, with the arrival of bureaucrats and bums from various racial, tribal, and ethnic backgrounds in the capital city, the frequency of interethnic marriage will increase, and the focus of interethnic sex—even without marriage—will increasingly shift from the upper class of merchants to the lower classes—even to the lowest class of welfare recipients. Rather than genetic luxuration, the consequence is increased genetic pauperization, a tendency furthered by the fact that government welfare support will naturally lead to an increase in the birthrate of welfare recipients relative to the birthrate of other members, in particular of members of the upper class of their tribe or race. As a result of this overproportional growth of low and even underclass people and an increasing number of ethnically, tribally, racially mixed offspring especially in the lower and lowest social strata, the character of democratic (popular) government will gradually change as well. Rather than the "race card" being essentially the only instrument of politics, politics becomes increasingly "class politics." The government rulers can and will no longer rely exclusively on their ethnic, tribal, or racial appeal and support, but increasingly they must try to find support across tribal or racial lines by appealing to the universal (not tribe or race specific) feeling of envy and egalitarianism, i.e., to social class (the untouchables or the slaves versus the masters, the workers versus the capitalists, the poor versus the rich, etc.).[15,16]

---

[15]See on this Helmut Schoeck, *Envy: A Theory of Social Behavior* (New York: Harcourt, Brace and World, 1970); Rothbard, *Egalitarianism as a Revolt Against Nature and*

The increasing admixture of egalitarian class politics to the preexisting tribal policies leads to even more—racial and social—tension and hostility and to an even greater proliferation of the low and under-class population. In addition to certain ethnic or tribal groups being driven out of the cities as a result of tribal policies, increasingly also members of the upper classes of all ethnic or tribal groups will leave the city for the suburbs (only to be followed—by means of public (government) transportation

---

Other Essays; and esp. "Freedom, Inequality, Primitivism, and the Division of Labor," in ibid.

[16]For a sociological treatment of this second—democratic or "plebeian"—stage in the development of city government, based on and riven by classes and "class conflicts" (rather than clans and family conflicts, as during the preceding development stage of patrician government), see Max Weber, *The City*, chap. 4. In contrast to patrician city government, plebeian government, Weber observes importantly, is characterized by

> a changed concept of the nature of law. . . . The beginning of legislation paralleled the abolition of patrician rule. Legislation initially took the form of charismatic statutes by the *aesymnetes* [governors possessing supreme power for a limited time]. But soon the new creation of permanent laws was accepted. In fact new legislation by the ecclesia became so usual as to produce a state of continuous flux. Soon a purely secular administration of justice applied to the laws or, in Rome, to the instructions of the magistrate. The creation of laws reached such a fluid state that eventually in Athens the question was directed yearly to the people whether existing laws should be maintained or amended. Thus it became an accepted premise that the law is artificially created and that it should be based upon the approval of those to whom it will apply. (pp. 170–71)

Likewise, in the medieval city states of Europe the "establishment of rule by the *popolo* had similar consequences. . . . It, too, ground out enormous editions of city laws and codified the common law and court rules (trial law) producing a surplus of statutes of all kinds and an excess of officials" (p. 172). Hand in hand with the changed concept of law goes a different political conduct.

> The political justice of the *popolo* system with its system of official espionage, its preference for anonymous accusations, accelerated inquisitorial procedures against magnates, and simplified proof (by "notoriety") was the democratic counterpart of the Venetian trials of the [aristocratic–patrician] Council of Ten. Objectively the *popolo* system was identified by: the exclusion of all members of families with a knightly style of life from office; obligating the notables by pledges of good conduct; placing the notables' family under bail for all members; the establishment of a special criminal law for the political offenses of the *magnates*, especially insulting the honor of a member of the populace; the prohibition of a noble's acquiring property bordering on that of a member of the populace without the latter's agreement. . . . Since noble families could be expressly accepted as part of the populace, [however,] even the offices of the *popolo* were nearly always occupied by noblemen. (pp. 160–61)

—by those very people whose behaviors they had tried to escape).[17] With the upper class and the merchants leaving in larger numbers, however, one of the last remaining civilizing forces will be weakened, and what is left behind in the cities will represent an increasingly negative selection of the population: of government bureaucrats who work but no longer live there, and of the lowlifes and the social outcasts of all tribes and races who live there yet who increasingly do not work but survive on welfare. (Just think of Washington, D.C.)

When one would think that matters could not possibly become worse, they do. After the race and the class card have been played and done their devastating work, the government turns to the sex and gender card, and "racial justice" and "social justice" are complemented by "gender justice."[18] The establishment of a government—a judicial monopoly—not only implies that formerly separated jurisdictions (as within ethnically or racially segregated districts, for instance) are forcibly integrated; it implies at the same time that formerly fully integrated jurisdictions (as within households and families) will be forcibly broken down or even dissolved. Rather than regarding intra-family or household matters (including subjects such as abortion, for instance) as no one else's business to be judged and arbitrated within the family by the head of the household or family members,[19] once a judicial monopoly has been established, its agents—the government—also become and will naturally strive to expand their role as judge and arbitrator of last resort in all family matters. To gain popular support for its role the government (besides playing one tribe, race, or social class against another) will likewise promote divisiveness within the family: between the sexes—husbands and wives—and the generations—parents and children.[20] Once again, this will be particularly noticeable in the big cities.

Every form of government welfare—the compulsory wealth or income transfer from "haves" to "havenots"lowers the value of a person's

---

[17]See on this tendency Edward Banfield, *The Unheavenly City Revisited* (Boston: Little, Brown, 1974).

[18]See on this Murray N. Rothbard, "The Great Women's Lib Issue: Setting it Straight," in *Egalitarianism as a Revolt Against Nature and Other Essays;* Michael Levin, *Feminism and Liberty* (New Brunswick, N.J.: Transaction Publishers, 1987).

[19]See Robert Nisbet, *Prejudices: A Philosophical Dictionary* (Cambridge, Mass.: Harvard University Press, 1982), pp. 1–8, 110–17.

[20]See on this Murray N. Rothbard, "Kid Lib," in *Egalitarianism as a Revolt Against Nature and Other Essays.*

membership in an extended family-household system as a social system of mutual cooperation and help and assistance. Marriage loses value. For parents the value and importance of a "good" upbringing (education) of their own children is reduced. Correspondingly, for children less value will be attached and less respect paid to their own parents. Owing to the high concentration of welfare recipients, in the big cities family disintegration is already well advanced. In appealing to gender and generation (age) as a source of political support and promoting and enacting sex (gender) and family legislation, invariably the authority of heads of families and households and the "natural" intergenerational hierarchy within families is weakened and the value of a multi-generational family as the basic unit of human society diminished. Indeed, as should be clear, as soon as the government's law and legislation supersedes family law and legislation (including inter-family arrangements in conjunction with marriages, joint-family offspring, inheritance, etc.), the value and importance of the institution of a family can only be systematically eroded. For what is a family if it cannot even find and provide for its own internal law and order! At the same time, as should be clear as well but has not been sufficiently noted, from the point of view of the government's rulers, their ability to interfere in internal family matters must be regarded as the ultimate prize and the pinnacle of their own power. To exploit tribal or racial resentments or class envy to one's personal advantage is one thing. It is quite another accomplishment to use the quarrels arising within families to break up the entire—generally harmonious—system of autonomous families: to uproot individuals from their families to isolate and atomize them, thereby increasing the state's power over them. Accordingly, as the government's family policy is implemented, divorce, singledom, single parenting, and illegitimacy, incidents of parent, spouse, and child-neglect or abuse, and the variety and frequency of "nontraditional" lifestyles (homosexuality, lesbianism, communism, and occultism) increase as well.[21]

Parallel to this development will be a gradual but steady surge in crime and criminal behavior. Under monopolistic auspices, law will invariably be transformed into legislation. As a result of an unending process of income and wealth redistribution in the name of racial, social, and/or gender justice, the very idea of justice as universal and immutable

---

[21]See on this Allan C. Carlson, "What Has Government Done to Our Families?" *Essays in Political Economy* (Auburn, Ala.: Ludwig von Mises Institute, 1991); Bryce J. Christensen, "The Family vs. the State," *Essays in Political Economy* (Auburn, Ala.: Ludwig von Mises Institute, 1992).

principles of conduct and cooperation will be eroded and ultimately destroyed. Rather than being conceived of as something preexisting (and to be discovered), law is increasingly considered as government made law (legislation). Accordingly, not only will legal uncertainty increase, but in reaction the social rate of time preference will rise (i.e., people in general will become more present-oriented and have an increasingly shorter planning horizon). Moral relativism will also be promoted. For if there is no such thing as an ultimate right, then there is also no such thing as an absolute wrong. Indeed, what is right today may be wrong tomorrow, and *vice versa*. Rising time preferences combined with moral relativism, then, provides the perfect breeding ground for criminals and crimes—a tendency especially evident in the big cities. It is here that the dissolution of families is most advanced, that the greatest concentration of welfare recipients exists, that the process of genetic pauperization has progressed furthest, and that tribal and racial tensions as the outcome of forced integration are most virulent. Rather than centers of civilization, cities have become centers of social disintegration and cesspools of physical and moral decay, corruption, brutishness, and crime.[22]

IV

What follows from all of this? Clearly, Western civilization has been on a course of self-destruction for quite some time. Can this course be stopped, and if so, how? I wish I could be optimistic, but I am not so sure that there is sufficient reason for optimism. To be sure, history is ultimately determined by ideas, and ideas can, at least in principle, change almost instantly. But in order for ideas to change it is not sufficient for people to see that something is wrong. At least a significant number must also be intelligent enough to recognize what it is that is wrong. That is, they must understand the basic principles upon which society—human cooperation—rests—the very principles explained here. And they must have sufficient will power to act according to this insight. But it is precisely this which one must increasingly doubt. Civilization and culture do have a genetic (biological) basis. However, as the result of statism—of forced integration, egalitarianism, welfare policies, and family

---

[22]See on this Edward C. Banfield, "Present-Orientedness and Crime," in *Assessing the Criminal*, Randy E. Barnett and John Hagel, eds. (Cambridge, Mass.: Ballinger, 1977); David Walters, "Crime in the Welfare State," in *Criminal Justice?: The Legal System vs. Individual Responsibility*, Robert J. Bidinotto, ed. (Irvington-on-Hudson, N.Y.: Foundation for Economic Education, 1994); also James Q. Wilson, *Thinking About Crime* (New York: Vintage Books, 1985).

destruction—the genetic quality of the population has most certainly declined.[23] Indeed, how could it not when success is systematically punished and failure rewarded? Whether intended or not, the welfare state promotes the proliferation of intellectually and morally inferior people and the results would be even worse were it not for the fact that crime rates are particularly high among these people, and that they tend to eliminate each other more frequently.

However, even if all of this does not give much hope for the future, all is not lost. There still remain some pockets of civilization and culture. Not in the cities and metropolitan areas, but in the heartland (countryside). In order to preserve these, several requirements must be fulfilled: The state—a judicial—monopoly must be recognized as the source of decivilization: states do not create law and order, they destroy it. Families and households must be recognized as the source of civilization. It is essential that the heads of families and households reassert their ultimate authority as judge in all internal family affairs. (Households must be declared extraterritorial territory, like foreign embassies.) Voluntary spatial segregation, and discrimination, must be recognized as not bad but good things that facilitate peaceful cooperation between different ethnic and racial groups. Welfare must be recognized as a matter exclusively of families and voluntary charity, and state welfare as nothing but the subsidization of irresponsibility.

---

[23]See on this Seymour W. Itzkoff, *The Decline of Intelligence in America* (Westport, Conn.: Praeger, 1994); idem, *The Road to Equality: Evolution and Social Reality* (Westport, Conn.: Praeger, 1992).

10
On Conservatism and Libertarianism

Let me begin by discussing two possible meanings of the term conservative. The first meaning is to refer to someone as conservative who generally supports the *status quo*; that is, a person who wants to conserve whatever laws, rules, regulations, moral and behavioral codes happen to exist at any given point in time.

Because different laws, rules, and political institutions are in place at different times and/or different locations, what a conservative supports depends on and changes with place and time. To be a conservative means nothing specific at all except to like the existing order, whatever that may be.

The first meaning can be discarded, then.[1] The term conservative must have a different meaning. What it means, and possibly only can mean, is this: Conservative refers to someone who believes in the existence of a natural order, a natural state of affairs which corresponds to the nature of things: of nature and man. This natural order is and can be disturbed by accidents and anomalies: by earthquakes and hurricanes, diseases, pests, monsters and beasts, by two-headed horses or four-legged humans, cripples and idiots, and by war, conquest and tyranny. But it is not difficult to distinguish the normal from the anomaly, the essential from the accidental. A little bit of abstraction removes all the

---

[1]To state this is not to claim that no one has ever adopted this meaning of conservatism. In fact, a prominent example of a conservative who comes very close to accepting the definition rejected here as useless is Michael Oakeshott, "On Being Conservative," in idem, *Rationalism in Politics and other Essays* (Indianapolis, Ind.: Liberty Fund, 1991). For Oakeshott, conservatism is

> not a creed or a doctrine, but a disposition. . . . [It is] a propensity to use and to enjoy what is available rather than to wish for or to look for something else; to delight in what is present rather than what was or what may be. . . . [It is] to prefer the tried to the untried, fact to mystery, the actual to the possible, the limited to the unbounded, the near to the distant, the sufficient to the superabundant, the convenient to the perfect, present laughter to utopian bliss. (pp. 407–08)

clutter and enables nearly everyone to "see" what is and what is not natural and in accordance with the nature of things. Moreover, the natural is at the same time the most enduring state of affairs. The natural order is ancient and forever the same (only anomalies and accidents undergo change), hence, it can be recognized by us everywhere and at all times.

Conservative refers to someone who recognizes the old and natural through the "noise" of anomalies and accidents and who defends, supports, and helps to preserve it against the temporary and anomalous. Within the realm of the humanities, including the social sciences, a conservative recognizes families (fathers, mothers, children, grandchildren) and households based on private property and in cooperation with a community of other households as the most fundamental, natural, essential, ancient, and indispensable social units. Moreover, the family household also represents the model of the social order at large. Just as a hierarchical order exists in a family, so is there a hierarchical order within a community of families—of apprentices, servants, and masters, vassals, knights, lords, overlords, and even kings—tied together by an elaborate and intricate system of kinship relations; and of children, parents, priests, bishops, cardinals, patriarchs or popes, and finally the transcendent God. Of the two layers of authority, the earthly physical power of parents, lords, and kings is naturally subordinate and subject to control by the ultimate spiritual-intellectual authority of fathers, priests, bishops, and ultimately God.

Conservatives (or more specifically, Western Greco-Christian conservatives), if they stand for anything, stand for and want to preserve the family and the social hierarchies and layers of material as well as spiritual-intellectual authority based on and growing out of family bonds and kinship relations.[2]

---

[2]See Robert Nisbet, "Conservatism," in *A History of Sociological Analysis*, Tom Bottomore and Robert Nisbet, eds. (New York: Basic Books, 1978); Robert Nisbet, *Conservatism: Dream and Reality* (Minneapolis: University of Minnesota Press, 1986). "Naturally," writes Nisbet, "the conservatives, in their appeal to tradition, were not endorsing each and every idea or thing handed down from the past. The philosophy of traditionalism is, like all such philosophies, selective. A salutary tradition must come from the past but it must also be desirable in itself" (ibid., p. 26). "The two central concepts in conservative philosophy," Nisbet goes on to explain, are "property" and (voluntarily acknowledged) "authority," which in turn imply both "liberty" and "order" (pp. 34–35). "Property," in conservative philosophy, "is more than external appendage to man, mere inanimate servant of human need. It is, above anything else in civilization, the very condition of man's humanness, his superiority over the entire natural world" (p. 56).

II

Let me now come to an evaluation of contemporary conservatism, and then go on to explain why conservatives today must be antistatist libertarians and, equally important, why libertarians must be conservatives.

Modern conservatism, in the United States and Europe, is confused and distorted. This confusion is largely due to democracy. Under the influence of representative democracy and with the transformation of the U.S. and Europe into mass democracies from World War I, conservatism

---

> Much of the conservative veneration for the family lies in its historic affinity between family and property. It is usually the rule for any family to seek as much advantage for its children and other members as is possible.... There is no issue over which conservative has fought liberal and socialist as strenuously as on threats through law to loosen property from family grasp, by taxation or by any other form of redistribution. (p. 52)
>
> Almost everything about the medieval law of family and marriage, including the stringent emphasis upon chastity of the female, the terrible penalty that could be exerted against adultery by the wife, springs from a nearly absolute reverence for property, for legitimate heritability of property. (p. 57)

Similarly, the conservative emphasis on authority and social rank orders, and the affinity to medieval—pre-Reformation—Europe as a model of social organization, is rooted in the primacy of family and property. "There is," explains Nisbet,

> no principle more basic to the conservative philosophy than that of the inherent and absolute incompatibility between liberty and equality. Such incompatibility springs from the contrary objectives of the two values. The abiding purpose of liberty is its protection of individual and family property—a word used in its widest sense to include the immaterial as well as the material in life. The inherent objective of equality, on the other hand, is that of some kind of redistribution or leveling of the unequally shared material and immaterial values of a community. Moreover, individual strengths of mind and body being different from birth, all efforts to compensate through law and government for this diversity of strengths can only cripple the liberties of those involved; especially the liberties of the strongest and the most brilliant. (p. 47)

For the conservative, then, the preservation of property and liberty requires the existence of a natural elite or aristocracy, and he is accordingly strictly opposed to democracy. Indeed, notes Nisbet, "for most conservatives socialism appeared as an almost necessary emergent of democracy and totalitarianism an almost equally necessary product of social democracy" (p. 92). On the incompatibility of liberty and equality (and democracy) see also Erik von Kuehnelt-Leddihn, *Liberty or Equality?* (Front Royal, Va.: Christendom Press, 1993); on the conservative emphasis on a *nobilitas naturalis* as a sociological prerequisite of liberty see also Wilhelm Röpke, *Jenseits von Angebot und Nachfrage* (Bern: Paul Haupt, 1979), chap. 3.3.

was transformed from an antiegalitarian, aristocratic, antistatist ideological force into a movement of culturally conservative statists: the
right wing of the socialists and social democrats. Most self-proclaimed
contemporary conservatives are concerned, as they should be, about the
decay of families, divorce, illegitimacy, loss of authority, multiculturalism, alternative lifestyles, social disintegration, sex, and crime. All of
these phenomena represent anomalies and scandalous deviations from
the natural order. A conservative must indeed be opposed to all of these
developments and try to restore normalcy. However, most contemporary conservatives (at least most of the spokesmen of the conservative
establishment) either do not recognize that their goal of restoring normalcy requires the most drastic, even revolutionary, antistatist social
changes, or (if they know about this) they are members of the "fifth
column" engaged in destroying conservatism from inside (and hence,
must be regarded as evil).

That this is largely true for the so-called neoconservatives does not
require further explanation here. Indeed, as far as their leaders are concerned, one suspects that most of them are of the latter (evil) kind. They are
not truly concerned about cultural matters but recognize that they must
play the cultural-conservatism card so as not to lose power and promote
their entirely different goal of global social democracy.[3] However, it is

---

[3]On contemporary American conservatism see in particular Paul Gottfried, *The
Conservative Movement*, rev. ed. (New York: Twayne Publishers, 1993); George H.
Nash, *The Conservative Intellectual Movement in America* (New York: Basic Books,
1976); Justin Raimondo, *Reclaiming the American Right: The Lost Legacy of the Conservative Movement* (Burlingame, Calif.: Center for Libertarian Studies, 1993); see further also chap. 11. The fundamentally statist character of American neoconservatism is
best summarized by a statement of one of its leading intellectual champions, the
former Trotskyite Irving Kristol: "[T]he basic principle behind a conservative welfare state ought to be a simple one: wherever possible, people should be allowed to
keep their own money—rather than having it transferred (via taxes to the state)—*on
the condition that they put it to certain defined uses.*" *Two Cheers for Capitalism* (New
York: Basic Books, 1978), p. 119 (emphasis added). This view is essentially identical
to that held by modern—post-Marxist—European Social-Democrats. Thus, Germany's Social Democratic Party (SPD), for instance, in its *Godesberg Program* of 1959,
adopted as its core motto the slogan "as much market as possible, as much state as
necessary."

A second, somewhat older but nowadays almost indistinguishable branch of
contemporary American conservatism is represented by the *new* (post World War II)
conservatism launched and promoted, with the assistance of the CIA, by William Buckley and his *National Review*. Whereas the old (pre-World War II) American conservatism
had been characterized by decidedly anti-interventionist (isolationist) foreign policy
views, the trademark of Buckley's new conservatism has been its rabid militarism and interventionist foreign policy. In an article, "A Young Republican's

also true of many conservatives who are genuinely concerned about family disintegration or dysfunction and cultural rot. I am thinking here in particular of the conservatism represented by Patrick Buchanan and his movement.[4] Buchanan's conservatism is by no means as different from that of the conservative Republican party establishment as he and his followers fancy themselves. In one decisive respect their brand of conservatism is in full agreement with that of the conservative establishment: both are statists. They differ over what exactly needs to be done to restore normalcy to the U.S., but they agree that it must be done by the state. There is not a trace of principled antistatism in either.

View," published three years before the launching of his *National Review* in *Commonweal*, on January 25, 1952, Buckley thus summarized what would become the new conservative credo: In light of the threat posed by the Soviet Union, "we [new conservatives] have to accept Big Government for the duration —for neither an offensive nor a defensive war can be waged . . . except through the instrument of a totalitarian bureaucracy within our shores." Conservatives, Buckley wrote, were duty-bound to promote "the extensive and productive tax laws that are needed to support a vigorous anti-Communist foreign policy," as well as the "large armies and air forces, atomic energy, central intelligence, war production boards and the attendant centralization of power in Washington." Not surprisingly, since the collapse of the Soviet Union in the late 1980s, essentially nothing in this philosophy has changed. Today, the continuation and preservation of the American welfare–warfare state is simply excused and promoted by new and neo-conservatives alike with reference to other foreign enemies and dangers: China, Islamic fundamentalism, Saddam Hussein, "rogue states," and/or the threat of "global terrorism." Regarding this new Buckleyite conservatism, Robert Nisbet has noted that of

> all the *mis*ascription of the word "conservative". . . the most amusing, in an historical light, is surely the application of 'conservative' to the last-named [i.e., the budget-expanding enthusiasts for great increases in military expenditures]. For in America throughout the twentieth century, and including four substantial wars abroad, conservatives had been steadfastly the voices of non-inflationary military budgets, and an emphasis on trade in the world instead of American nationalism. In the two World Wars, in Korea, and in Viet Nam, the leaders of American entry into the war were such renowned liberal-progressives as Woodrow Wilson, Franklin Roosevelt, Harry Truman and John F. Kennedy. In all four episodes conservatives, both in the national government and in the rank and file, were largely hostile to intervention; were isolationists indeed. (*Conservatism*, p. 103)

And on Ronald Reagan in particular, during whose administration the new and neoconservative movement were fused and amalgamated, Nisbet has noted that Reagan's "passion for crusades, moral and military, is scarcely American-conservative," (ibid, p. 104).

[4]See Patrick J. Buchanan, *Right from the Beginning* (Washington, D.C.: Regnery Gateway, 1990); idem, *The Great Betrayal: How American Sovereignty and Social Justice are Sacrificed to the Gods of the Global Economy* (New York: Little, Brown, 1998).

Let me illustrate by quoting Samuel Francis, one of the leading theo-reticians and strategists of the Buchananite movement. After deploring "anti-white" and "anti-Western" propaganda, "militant secularism, ac-quisitive egoism, economic and political globalism, demographic inun-dation, and unchecked state centralism," he expounds on a new spirit of "America First," which "implies not only putting national interests over those of other nations and abstractions like 'world leadership,' 'global harmony,' and the 'New World Order,' but also giving priority to the nation over the gratification of individual and subnational interests." So far so good. But how does he propose to fix the problem of moral degen-eration and cultural rot? Those parts of the federal Leviathan responsi-ble for the proliferation of moral and cultural pollution such as the Department of Education, the National Endowment of the Arts, the Equal Employment Opportunity Commission, and the federal judiciary should be closed or cut down to size. But there is no opposition against the state's involvement in educational matters. There is no recognition that the natural order in education means that the state has nothing to do with it. Education is entirely a family matter.[5]

Moreover, there is no recognition that moral degeneracy and cul-tural rot have deeper causes and cannot simply be cured by state-im-posed curriculum changes or exhortations and declamations. To the contrary, Francis proposes that the cultural turn-around—the restora-tion of normalcy—can be achieved *without* a fundamental change in the structure of the modern welfare state. Indeed, Buchanan and his ide-ologues explicitly defend the three core institutions of the welfare state:

---

[5]Buchanan and his intellectual allies want to abolish the federal government's control over educational matters and return such control to the level of states or, better still, local government. However, neoconservatives and most of the leaders of the so-called Christian Right and the "moral majority" simply desire (far worse from a genuinely conservative point of view) the replacement of the current, left-lib-eral elite in charge of national education by another one, i.e., themselves. "From Burke on," Robert Nisbet has criticized this posture, "it has been a conservative precept and a sociological principle since Auguste Comte that the surest way of weakening the family, or any vital social group, is for the government to assume, and then monopolize, the family's historic functions." In contrast, much of the con-temporary American Right "is less interested in Burkean immunities from govern-ment power than it is in putting a maximum of governmental power in the hands of those who can be trusted. It is control of power, not diminution of power, that ranks high."

From the traditional conservative's point of view it is fatuous to use the family—as evangelical crusaders regularly do—as the justification for their tireless crusades to ban abortion categorically, to bring the Department of Justice in on every Baby Doe, to mandate by constitution the imposition of social security, medicare, and unemployment subsidies. They even want to expand the "social" responsibilities of the state by assigning to it the task of "protecting," by means of national import and export restrictions, American jobs, especially in industries of national concern, and "insulate the wages of U.S. workers from foreign laborers who must work for $1 an hour or less."

In fact, Buchananites freely admit that they are statists. They detest and ridicule capitalism, laissez-faire, free markets and trade, wealth, elites, and nobility; and they advocate a new populist—indeed proletarian—conservatism which amalgamates social and cultural conservatism and social or socialist economics. Thus, continues Francis,

> while the left could win Middle Americans through its economic measures, it lost them through its social and cultural radicalism, and while the right could attract Middle Americans through appeals to law and order and defense of sexual normality, conventional morals and religion, traditional social institutions and invocations of nationalism and patriotism, it lost Middle Americans when it rehearsed its old bourgeois economic formulas.[6]

Hence, it is necessary to combine the economic policies of the left and the nationalism and cultural conservatism of the right, to create "a new identity synthesizing both the economic interests and cultural–national loyalties of the proletarianized middle class in a separate and unified political movement."[7] For obvious reasons this doctrine is not so named, but there is a term for this type of conservatism: It is called social nationalism or national socialism.

I will not concern myself here with the question whether or not Buchanan's conservatism has mass appeal and whether or not its diagnosis of American politics is sociologically correct. I doubt that this is the case, and certainly Buchanan's fate during the 1995 and 2000 Republican presidential primaries does not indicate otherwise. Rather, I want to address the more fundamental questions: Assuming that it does have such appeal; that is, assuming that cultural conservatism and social-socialist

---

"voluntary" prayers in the public schools, and so on. (Nisbet, *Conservatism*, pp. 104–05)

[6]Samuel T. Francis, "From Household to Nation: The Middle American populism of Pat Buchanan," *Chronicles* (March 1996): 12–16; see also idem, *Beautiful Losers: Essays on the Failure of American Conservatism* (Columbia: University of Missouri Press, 1993); idem, *Revolution from the Middle* (Raleigh, N.C.: Middle American Press, 1997).

[7]Francis, "From Household to Nation, pp. 12–16.

economics can be *psychologically* combined (that is, that people can hold both of these views simultaneously without cognitive dissonance), can they also be effectively and practically (economically and praxeologically) combined? Is it possible to maintain the current level of economic socialism (social security, etc.) and reach the goal of restoring cultural normalcy (natural families and normal rules of conduct)?

Buchanan and his theoreticians do not feel the need to raise this question, because they believe politics to be solely a matter of will and power. They do not believe in such things as economic laws. If only people want something, and they are given the power to implement their will, everything can be achieved. The "dead Austrian economist" Ludwig von Mises, to whom Buchanan referred contemptuously during his campaign, characterized this belief as "historicism," the intellectual posture of the German *Kathedersozialisten*, the academic Socialists of the Chair, who justified any and all statist measures.

But historicist contempt and ignorance of economics does not alter the fact that inexorable economic laws exist. You cannot have your cake and eat it too, for instance. Or what you consume now cannot be consumed again in the future. Or producing more of one good requires producing less of another. No wishful thinking can make such laws go away. To believe otherwise can only result in practical failure. "In fact," noted Mises, "economic history is a long record of government policies that failed because they were designed with a bold disregard for the laws of economics."[8] In light of elementary and immutable economic laws, the Buchananite program of social nationalism is just another bold but impossible dream. No wishful thinking can alter the fact that maintaining the core institutions of the present welfare state and wanting to return to traditional families, norms, conduct, and culture are incompatible goals. You can have one—socialism (welfare)—or the other—traditional morals—but you cannot have both, for social nationalist economics, the

---

[8]Ludwig von Mises, *Human Action: A Treatise on Economics*, Scholar's Edition (Auburn, Ala.: Ludwig von Mises Institute, 1998), p. 67. "Princes and democratic majorities," writes Mises leading directly up to this verdict,

> are drunk with power. They must reluctantly admit that they are subject to the laws of nature. But they reject the very notion of economic law. Are they not the supreme legislators? Don't they have the power to crush every opponent? No war lord is prone to acknowledge any limits other than those imposed on him by a superior armed force. Servile scribblers are always ready to foster such complacency by expounding the appropriate doctrines. They call their garbled presumptions "historical economics."

pillar of the current welfare state system Buchanan wants to leave untouched, is the very cause of cultural and social anomalies.

In order to clarify this, it is only necessary to recall one of the most fundamental laws of economics which says that all compulsory wealth or income redistribution, regardless of the criteria on which it is based, involves taking from some—the havers of something—and giving it to others—the non-havers of something. Accordingly, the incentive to be a haver is reduced, and the incentive to be a non-haver increased. What the haver has is characteristically something considered "good," and what the non-haver does not have is something "bad" or a deficiency. Indeed, this is the very idea underlying any redistribution: some have too much good stuff and others not enough. The result of every redistribution is that one will thereby produce less good and increasingly more bad, less perfection and more deficiencies. By subsidizing with tax funds (with funds taken from others) people who are poor (bad), more poverty will be created. By subsidizing people because they are unemployed (bad), more unemployment will be created. By subsidizing unwed mothers (bad), there will be more unwed mothers and more illegitimate births, etc.[9]

Obviously, this basic insight applies to the entire system of so-called social security that has been implemented in Western Europe (from the 1880s onward) and the U.S. (since the 1930s): of compulsory government "insurance" against old age, illness, occupational injury, unemployment, indigence, etc. In conjunction with the even older compulsory system of public education, these institutions and practices amount to a massive attack on the institution of the family and personal responsibility. By relieving individuals of the obligation to provide for their own income, health, safety, old age, and children's education, the range and temporal horizon of private provision is reduced, and the value of marriage, family, children, and kinship relations is lowered. Irresponsibility, shortsightedness, negligence, illness and even destructionism (bads) are promoted, and responsibility, farsightedness, diligence, health and conservatism (goods) are punished. The compulsory old age insurance system in particular, by which retirees (the old) are subsidized from taxes imposed on current income earners (the young), has systematically weakened the natural intergenerational bond between parents, grandparents, and children. The old need no

---

[9]On the counterproductive nature of all interventionist policies see Ludwig von Mises, *A Critique of Interventionism* (New Rochelle, N.Y.: Arlington House, 1977); idem, *Interventionism: An Economic Analysis* (Irvington-on-Hudson, N.Y.: Foundation for Economic Education, 1998).

longer rely on the assistance of their children if they have made no provision for their own old age; and the young (with typically less accumulated wealth) must support the old (with typically more accumulated wealth) rather than the other way around, as is typical within families. Consequently, not only do people want to have fewer children—and indeed, birthrates have fallen in half since the onset of modern social security (welfare) policies—but also the respect which the young traditionally accorded to their elders is diminished, and all indicators of family disintegration and malfunctioning, such as rates of divorce, illegitimacy, child abuse, parent abuse, spouse abuse, single parenting, singledom, alternative lifestyles, and abortion, have increased.[10]

Moreover, with the socialization of the health care system through institutions such as Medicaid and Medicare and the regulation of the insurance industry (by restricting an insurer's right of refusal: to exclude any individual risk as uninsurable, and discriminate freely, according to actuarial methods, between different group risks) a monstrous machinery of wealth and income redistribution at the expense of responsible individuals and low-risk groups in favor of irresponsible actors and high-risk groups has been put in motion. Subsidies for the ill, unhealthy and disabled breed illness, disease, and disability and weaken the desire to work for a living and to lead healthy lives. One can do no better than quote the "dead Austrian economist" Ludwig von Mises once more:

> being ill is not a phenomenon independent of conscious will. . . . A man's efficiency is not merely a result of his physical condition; it depends largely on his mind and will. . . . The destructionist aspect of accident and health insurance lies above all in the fact that such institutions promote accident and illness, hinder recovery, and very often create, or at any rate intensify and lengthen, the functional disorders which follow illness or accident. . . . To feel healthy is quite different from being healthy in the medical sense. . . . By weakening or completely destroying the will to be well and able to work, social insurance creates illness and inability to work; it produces the habit of complaining—which is in itself a neurosis—and neuroses of other kinds. . . . As a social institution it makes a people sick bodily and mentally or at least helps to multiply, lengthen, and intensify disease. . . . Social insurance has thus made the neurosis of the insured a dangerous public disease.

---

[10]See Allan C. Carlson, *Family Questions: Reflections on the American Social Crisis* (New Brunswick, N.J.: Transaction Publishers, 1988); idem, *The Swedish Experiment in Family Politics* (New Brunswick, N.J.: Transaction Publishers, 1990); idem, *From Cottage to Work Station: The Family's Search for Social Harmony in the Industrial Age* (San Francisco: Ignatius Press, 1993); Charles Murray, *Losing Ground: American Social Policy 1950–1980* (New York: Basic Books, 1984).

Should the institution be extended and developed the disease will spread. No reform can be of any assistance. We cannot weaken or destroy the will to health without producing illness.[11]

I do not wish to explain here the economic nonsense of Buchanan's and his theoreticians' even further-reaching idea of protectionist policies (of protecting American wages). If they were right, their argument in favor of economic protection would amount to an indictment of all trade and a defense of the thesis that everyone (each family) would be better off if he (it) never traded with anyone else. Certainly, in this case no one could ever lose his job, and unemployment due to "unfair" competition would be reduced to zero. Yet such a full-employment society would not be prosperous and strong; it would be composed of people (families) who, despite working from dawn to dusk, would be condemned to poverty and starvation. Buchanan's international protectionism, while less destructive than a policy of interpersonal or interregional protectionism, would result in precisely the same effect. This is not conservatism (conservatives want families to be prosperous and strong). This is economic destructionism.[12]

In any case, what should be clear by now is that most if not all of the moral degeneration and cultural rot—the signs of decivilization—all around us are the inescapable and unavoidable results of the welfare state and its core institutions. Classical, old-style conservatives knew this, and they vigorously opposed public education and social security. They knew that states everywhere were intent upon breaking down and ultimately destroying families and the institutions and layers and hierarchies of authority that are the natural outgrowth of family based communities in order to increase and strengthen their own power.[13] They

---

[11]Ludwig von Mises, *Socialism: An Economic and Sociological Analysis* (Indianapolis, Ind.: Liberty Fund, 1981), pp. 431–32.

[12]See Murray N. Rothbard, *The Dangerous Nonsense of Protectionism* (Auburn, Ala.: Ludwig von Mises Institute, 1988); also chap. 8 above.

[13]"From the conservative point of view," writes Robert Nisbet, "the abolition or sharp curtailment of intermediate associations in the social order spelled the creation of the atomized masses on the one hand and, on the other, increasingly centralized forms of political power" ("Conservatism," p. 100). During the Middle Ages, Nisbet explains elsewhere (quoting Pollard's study of Wolsey), power

was dilute, not because it was distributed in many hands, but because it was derived from many independent sources. There were the liberties of the church, based on law superior to that of the King; there was the law of nature, graven in the hearts of men and not to be erased by royal writs; and there was the prescription of immemorial local and feudal custom

knew that in order to do so states would have to take advantage of the natural rebellion of the adolescent (juvenile) against parental authority. And they knew that socialized education and socialized responsibility were the means of bringing about this goal. Social education and social security provide an opening for the rebellious youth to escape parental authority (to get away with continuous misbehavior). Old conservatives knew that these policies would emancipate the individual from the discipline imposed by family and community life only to subject it instead to the direct and immediate control of the state.[14] Furthermore, they knew, or at least had a hunch, that this would lead to a systematic infantilization of society—a regression, emotionally and mentally, from adulthood to adolescence or childhood.

In contrast, Buchanan's populist-proletarian conservatism—social nationalism—shows complete ignorance of all of this. Combining cultural conservatism and welfare-statism is impossible, and hence, economic nonsense. Welfare-statism—social security in any way, shape or form—breeds moral and cultural rot and degeneration. Thus, if one is indeed concerned about America's moral decay and wants to restore normalcy to society and culture, one must oppose all aspects of the modern social-welfare state. A return to normalcy requires no less than the complete elimination of the present social security system: of unemployment insurance, social security, medicare, medicaid, public education, etc.

---

stereotyping a variety of jurisdictions and impeding the operation of a single will. (*Community and Power* [New York: Oxford University Press, 1962], p. 110)

In distinct contrast,

[t]he modern State is monistic; its authority extends directly to *all* individuals within its boundaries. So-called diplomatic immunities are but the last manifestation of a larger complex of immunities which once involved a large number of internal religious, economic, and kinship authorities. For administrative purposes the State may deploy into provinces, departments, districts, or "states," just as the army divides into regiments and battalions. But like the army, the modern State is based upon a residual unity of power.... Th[is] extraordinary unity of relationship in the contemporary State, together with its massive accumulation of effective functions, makes the control of the State the greatest single goal, or prize, in modern struggles for power. Increasingly the objectives of economic and other interest associations become not so much the preservation of favored *immunities* from the State as the capturing or directing of the political power itself. (Ibid, p. 103)

[14]On the role of public education in this see in particular Murray N. Rothbard, *Education, Free and Compulsory: The Individual's Education* (Wichita, Kans.: Center for Independent Education, 1972).

—and thus the near complete dissolution and deconstruction of the current state apparatus and government power. If one is ever to restore normalcy, government funds and power must dwindle to or even fall below their nineteenth century levels. Hence, true conservatives must be hard-line libertarians (antistatists). Buchanan's conservatism is false: it wants a return to traditional morality but at the same time advocates keeping the very institutions in place that are responsible for the perversion and destruction of traditional morals.

III

Most contemporary conservatives, then, especially among the media darlings, are not conservatives but socialists—either of the internationalist sort (the new and neoconservative warfare–welfare statists and global social democrats) or of the nationalist variety (the Buchananite populists). Genuine conservatives must be opposed to both. In order to restore social and cultural normalcy, true conservatives can only be radical libertarians, and they must demand the demolition—as a moral and economic perversion—of the entire structure of social security. If conservatives must be libertarians, why must libertarians be conservatives? If conservatives must learn from libertarians, must libertarians also learn from conservatives?

First, a few terminological clarifications are in order. The term libertarianism, as employed here, is a twentieth-century phenomenon, or more accurately, a post-World War II phenomenon, with intellectual roots in both classical (eighteenth and nineteenth) century—liberalism and even older natural law philosophy. It is a product of modern (enlightenment) rationalism.[15] Culminating in the work of Murray N. Rothbard, the fountainhead of the modern libertarian movement, and in particular his *Ethics of Liberty*, libertarianism is a rational system of ethics (law).[16] Working within the tradition of classical political philosophy

---

[15]On the history of the libertarian movement see Nash, *The Conservative Intellectual Movement in America*; Gottfried, *The Conservative Movement*; Raimondo, *Reclaiming the American Right*; for an interesting insider account of the early stages in the movement's development see Jerome Tuccille, *It Usually Begins with Ayn Rand* (San Francisco: Fox and Wilkes, [1972] 1997).

[16]See Murray N. Rothbard, *The Ethics of Liberty* (New York: New York University Press, [1982] 1997); idem, *For A New Liberty: The Libertarian Manifesto* (New York: Collier, [1973] 1978); idem, *Power and Market: Government and the Economy* (Kansas City: Sheed Andrews and McMeel, [1970] 1977); idem, *Man, Economy, and State* (Auburn, Ala.: Ludwig von Mises Institute, [1962] 1993); idem, *Economic Thought Before Adam Smith* (Cheltenham, U.K.: Edward Elgar, 1995); idem, *Classical Economics* (Cheltenham, U.K.: Edward Elgar, 1995).

—of Hobbes, Grotius, Pufendorf, Locke, and Spencer—and employing the same ancient analytical (conceptual) tools and logical apparatus as they do, libertarianism (Rothbardianism) is a systematic law code, derived by means of logical deduction from a single principle, the validity of which (and this is what makes it an ultimate principle, i.e., an ethical *axiom*, and the libertarian law code an axiomatic–deductive theory of justice) cannot be disputed without falling prey to logical-practical (praxeological) or performative contradictions (that is, without implicitly affirming what one explicitly denies). This axiom is the ancient principle of original appropriation: Ownership of scarce resources—the right of an exclusive control over scarce resources (private property)—is acquired through an act of original appropriation (by which resources are taken out of a state of nature and put into a state of civilization). If this were not so, no one could ever begin to act (do or propose anything); hence, any other principle is praxeologically impossible (and argumentatively indefensible). From the principle of original appropriation—the first-use-first-own principle—rules concerning the transformation and the transfer (exchange) of originally appropriated resources are derived, and all of ethics (law), including the principles of punishment, is then reconstructed in terms of a theory of property rights: all human rights are property rights, and all human rights violations are property rights violations. The upshot of this libertarian theory of justice is well-known in these circles: the state, according to the most influential strand of libertarian theory, the Rothbardian one, is an outlaw organization, and the only social order that is just is a system of private property anarchy.

I do not want to further analyze or defend the libertarian theory of justice at this point. Let me only confess that I believe the theory to be true, indeed to be irrefutably true.[17] Rather, I want to turn to the question

---

[17]See Rothbard, *The Ethics of Liberty*; Hans-Hermann Hoppe, *The Economics and Ethics of Private Property* (Boston: Kluwer, 1993). Briefly, two central arguments have been advanced in defense of this claim. The first, initially outlined by Rothbard, proceeds via an *argumentum a contrario*. If, contrary to the principle of first or original appropriation, a person A were *not* considered the owner of his visibly (demonstrably, and intersubjectively ascertainably) appropriated body and the standing room and places originally (prior to everyone else) appropriated through him by means of his body, then only two alternative arrangements exist. Either *another* later-coming person B must be recognized as the owner of A's body and the places originally appropriated by A, or both A *and* B must be considered equal co-owners of all bodies and places. (The third conceivable alternative, that *no one* should own *any* body and originally appropriated place, can be ruled out as an impossibility. Acting *requires* a body and standing room and we cannot *not* act; hence, to adopt this alternative would imply the instant death of all of mankind.) In the first case, A would be

of the relationship between libertarianism and conservatism (the belief in a natural social order based and centered on families). Some superficial commentators, mostly from the conservative side, such as Russell

---

reduced to the rank of B's slave and subject of exploitation. B is the owner of the body and places originally appropriated by A, but A in turn is not the owner of the body and places so appropriated by B. Under this ruling, two categorically distinct classes of persons are constituted: slaves or *Untermenschen* such as A and masters or *Übermenschen* such as B, to whom different "laws" apply. Hence, while such a ruling is certainly *possible*, it must be discarded from the outset as a human ethic, equally and universally applicable for everyone *qua* human being (rational animal). For a rule to aspire to the rank of a law—a *just* rule—it is necessary that it apply equally and universally to everyone. The rule under consideration manifestly does not fulfill this universalization requirement. Alternatively, in the second case of universal and equal co-ownership the universalization requirement is apparently fulfilled. However, this alternative suffers from another, even more severe deficiency, because if it were adopted all of mankind would perish immediately, for every action of a person requires the use of scarce means (at least his body and its standing room). However, if all goods were co-owned by everyone, then no one at any time or place would be allowed to do anything unless he had previously secured everyone else's consent to do so. Yet how could anyone grant such consent if he were not the exclusive owner of his own body (including its vocal chords) by means of which this consent would be expressed? Indeed, he would first need others' consent in order to be allowed to express his own, but these others could not give their consent without first having his, etc. Thus, only the first alternative—the principle of original appropriation—is left. It fulfills the universalization requirement and it is praxeologically possible.

The second argument, first advanced by this author and yielding essentially the same conclusion, has the form of an impossibility theorem. The theorem proceeds from a logical reconstruction of the necessary conditions—*Bedingungen der Möglichkeit*—of *ethical* problems and an exact definition and delineation of the purpose of ethics. First, for ethical problems to arise *conflict* between separate and independent agents must exist (or must at least be possible); and a conflict can only emerge in turn with respect to *scarce means* or "economic" goods. A conflict is possible neither with respect to superabundant or "free" goods such as, under normal circumstances, the air that we breathe, nor with respect to scarce but non-appropriable goods such as the sun or the clouds, i.e., the "*conditions*," rather than the "*means*," of human action). Conflict is possible only with respect to controllable ("appropriable") means such as a specific piece of land, tree or cave situated in a specific and unique spatio-temporal relation *vis-à-vis* the sun and/or the rain clouds. Hence, the task of ethics is to propose rules regarding the "proper" versus the "improper" *use of scarce means*. That is, ethics concerns the assignment of rights of exclusive control over scarce goods, i.e., *property rights*, in order to rule out conflict. Conflict, however, is not a sufficient prerequisite for ethical problems, for one can come into conflict also with a gorilla or a mosquito, for instance, yet such conflicts do not give rise to *ethical* problems. Gorillas and mosquitoes pose merely a *technical* problem. We must learn how to successfully manage and control the movements of gorillas and mosquitoes just as we must learn to manage and control the inanimate objects of our environment. Only if both parties to a conflict are capable of propositional exchange, i.e., argumentation, can one speak of an ethical problem; that is,

Kirk, have characterized libertarianism and conservatism as incompatible, hostile, or even antagonistic ideologies.[18] In fact, this view is entirely mistaken. The relationship between libertarianism and conservatism is one of praxeological compatibility, sociological complementarity, and reciprocal reinforcement.

In order to explain this, let me first point out that most, though not all, leading libertarian thinkers were, as a matter of empirical fact, social-cultural conservatives: defenders of traditional, bourgeois morals and manners. Most notably, Murray Rothbard, the single most important and influential libertarian thinker, was an outspoken cultural conservative. So was Rothbard's most important teacher, Ludwig von Mises. (Ayn Rand, another major influence on contemporary libertarianism, is a different matter, of course.)[19] While this does not prove much (it does

---

only if the gorilla and/or the mosquito could, in principle, pause in their conflictuous activity and express "yes" or "no," i.e., present an argument, would one owe them an answer. The impossibility theorem proceeds from this proposition in clarifying, first, its *axiomatic* status. No one can deny, without falling into performative contradictions, that the common rationality as displayed by the ability to engage in propositional exchange constitutes a necessary condition for ethical problems because this denial would itself have to be presented in the form of a proposition. Even an ethical relativist who admits the existence of ethical questions, but denies that there are any valid answers, cannot deny the validity of this proposition (which accordingly has been referred to also as the "*a priori* of argumentation"). Second, it is pointed out that everything that must be presupposed by argumentation cannot in turn be argumentatively disputed without getting entangled in a performative contradiction, and that among such presuppositions there exist not only *logical* ones, such as the laws of propositional logic (e.g., the law of identity), but also *praxeological* ones. Argumentation is not just free-floating propositions but always involves also at least two distinct *arguers*, a proponent and an opponent, i.e., *argumentation* is a subcategory of human *action*. Third, it is then shown that the mutual recognition of the principle of original appropriation, by both proponent *and* opponent, constitutes the praxeological presupposition of argumentation. No one can propose anything and expect his opponent to convince himself of the validity of this proposition or else deny it and propose something else unless his and his opponent's right to exclusive control over their "own" originally appropriated body (brain, vocal chords, etc.) and its respective standing room were already presupposed and assumed as valid. Finally, if the recognition of the principle of original appropriation forms the praxeological presupposition of argumentation, then it is impossible to provide a propositional justification for any other ethical principle without running thereby into performative contradictions.

[18]See Russell Kirk, *The Conservative Mind* (Chicago: Regnery, 1953); idem, *A Program for Conservatives* (Chicago: Regnery, 1955).

[19]On Rothbard see the contributions to *Murray N. Rothbard: In Memoriam*, Llewellyn H. Rockwell, Jr., ed. (Auburn, Ala.: Ludwig von Mises Institute, 1995), especially the contribution by Joseph T. Salerno; on Mises see Murray N. Rothbard,

prove only that libertarianism and conservatism can be *psychologically* reconciled), it is indicative of a *substantive* affinity between the two doctrines. It is not difficult to recognize that the conservative and the libertarian views of society are perfectly compatible (congruent). To be sure, their methods are distinctly different. One is (or appears to be) empiristic, sociological, and descriptive, and the other rationalistic, philosophical, logical, and constructivist. This difference notwithstanding, both agree in one fundamental respect, however. Conservatives are convinced that the "natural" and "normal" is old and widespread (and thus can be discerned always and everywhere). Similarly, libertarians are convinced that the principles of justice are eternally and universally valid (and hence, must have been essentially known to mankind since its very beginnings). That is, the libertarian ethic is not new and revolutionary, but old and conservative. Even primitives and children are capable of grasping the validity of the principle of original appropriation, and most people usually recognize it as an unquestionable matter of fact.

Moreover, as far as the object on which conservatives and libertarians focus is concerned—on the one hand families, kinship relations, communities, authority and social hierarchy, and on the other hand property and its appropriation, transformation and transfer—it should be clear that while they do not refer to identical entities, they still speak about different aspects of one and the same object: human actors and social cooperation. Extensively, that is, their realm of inquiry (frame of reference) is identical. Families, authority, communities, and social ranks are the empirical-sociological concretization of the abstract philosophical-praxeological categories and concepts of property, production, exchange, and contract. Property and property relations do not exist apart from families and kinship relations. The latter shape and determine the specific form and configuration of property and property relations, while they are at the same time constrained by the universal and eternal laws of scarcity and property. In fact, as we have already seen, families considered normal by conservative standards are *household* families, and the family disintegration and moral and cultural decay which contemporary conservatives deplore is largely the result of the

Ludwig von Mises: Scholar, Creator, Hero (Auburn, Ala.: Ludwig von Mises Institute, 1988); Jeffrey A. Tucker and Llewellyn H. Rockwell, Jr., "The Cultural Thought of Ludwig von Mises," *Journal of Libertarian Studies* 10, no. 1 (1991); on Rand see Tuccille, *It Usually Begins with Ayn Rand*; Murray N. Rothbard, *The Sociology of the Ayn Rand Cult* (Burlingame, Calif.: Center for Libertarian Studies, [1972] 1990), and from the Randian side Barbara Branden, *The Passion of Ayn Rand* (Garden City, N.Y.: Doubleday, 1986).

erosion and destruction of households (estates) as the economic basis of families by the modern welfare state. Thus, the libertarian theory of justice can actually provide conservatism with a more precise definition and a more rigorous moral defense of its own end (the return to civilization in the form of moral and cultural normalcy) than conservatism itself could ever offer. In doing so it can further sharpen and strengthen conservatism's traditional antistatist outlook.[20]

IV

While the intellectual creators of modern libertarianism were cultural conservatives, and while the libertarian doctrine is fully compatible and congruent with the conservative worldview (and does not, as some conservative critics claim, entail an "atomistic individualism" and "acquisitive egoism"), corrupted by the modern welfare state the libertarian movement has undergone a significant transformation. To a large extent (and completely so in the eyes of the media and the public), it has become a movement that combines radical antistatism and market economics with cultural leftism, counter and multiculturalism, and personal hedonism; that is, it is the exact opposite of the Buchananite program of culturally conservative socialism: countercultural capitalism.

Earlier it was noted that the Buchananite program of social(ist) nationalism does not seem to have much mass appeal, at least not in the United States. This is true to an even larger extent for the libertarian attempt to synthesize market economics with counter- and multiculturalism. Yet as was the case with conservatism before, in this case, too, my central concern is not about mass appeal and whether or not certain ideas can be psychologically combined and integrated, but whether or not these ideas can be combined practically and effectively. It is my plan to show that they cannot, and that much of contemporary libertarianism is false, counterproductive libertarianism (much like Buchanan's conservatism is false and counterproductive).

That much of modern libertarianism is culturally leftist is not due to any such leanings among the major libertarian theoreticians. As noted, they were for the most part cultural conservatives. Rather, it was the

[20]On the relationship between (traditionalist) conservatism and (rationalist) libertarianism see Ralph Raico, "The Fusionists on Liberalism and Tradition," *New Individualist Review* 3, no. 3 (1964); M. Stanton Evans, "Raico on Liberalism and Religion," *New Individualist Review* 4, no. 2 (1966); Ralph Raico, "Reply to Mr. Evans," *ibidem*; also *Freedom and Virtue: The Conservative–Libertarian Debate*, George W. Carey, ed. (Lanham, Md.: University Press of America, 1984).

result of a superficial understanding of the libertarian doctrine by many of its fans and followers, and this ignorance has its explanation in a historical coincidence and the mentioned tendency, inherent in the social-democratic welfare state, of promoting a process of intellectual and emotional infantilization (decivilization of society).

The beginnings of the modern libertarian movement in the United States go back to the mid-1960s. In 1971 the Libertarian party was founded, and in 1972 the philosopher John Hospers was nominated as its first presidential candidate. It was the time of the Vietnam War. Simultaneously, promoted by the major "advances" in the growth of the welfare state from the early and mid-1960s onward in the United States and similarly in Western Europe (the so-called civil rights legislation and the war on poverty), a new mass-phenomenon emerged. A new "Lumpenproletariat" of intellectuals and intellectualized youths—the products of an ever expanding system of socialist (public) education—"alienated" from mainstream "bourgeois" morals and culture (while living far more comfortably than the Lumpenproletariat of old off the wealth created by this mainstream culture) arose. Multiculturalism and cultural relativism (live and let live) and egalitarian antiauthoritarianism (respect no authority) were elevated from temporary and transitory phases in mental development (adolescence) to permanent attitudes among grown-up intellectuals and their students.

The principled opposition of the libertarians to the Vietnam War coincided with the somewhat diffuse opposition to the war by the New Left. In addition, the anarchistic upshot of the libertarian doctrine appealed to the countercultural left.[21] For did not the illegitimacy of the

---

[21]While ultimately judged a failure by most of its former protagonists, the alliance between the fledgling libertarian movement and the New Left during the mid- and late-1960s can be understood as motivated by two considerations. On the one hand, by the mid-1960s American conservatism was almost completely dominated by William Buckley and his *National Review*. In contrast to the decidedly anti-interventionist (isolationist) conservatism of the Old Right, the "new conservatism" espoused by Buckley and the *National Review* and represented most visibly by the 1964 Republican presidential candidate, Barry Goldwater, was an ardently pro-war, pro-militaristic, and even imperialist movement. Based on this, any form of libertarian–conservative alliance had to be judged as simply out of the question. On the other hand, when the New Left began to emerge around 1965, it appeared far more libertarian on crucial issues than the conservatives for two reasons later summarized by Rothbard:

(1) [The New Left's] increasingly thoroughgoing opposition to the Vietnam War, U.S. imperialism, and the draft—the major political issues of that period, in contrast to conservative support for these policies. And (2) its forswearing of the old-fashioned statism and Social Democracy of the

state and the nonaggression axiom (that one shall not initiate or threaten to initiate physical force against others and their property) imply that everyone was at liberty to choose his very own nonaggressive lifestyle? Did this not imply that vulgarity, obscenity, profanity, drug use, promiscuity, pornography, prostitution, homosexuality, polygamy, pedophilia or any other conceivable perversity or abnormality, insofar as they were victimless crimes, were no offenses at all but perfectly normal and legitimate activities and lifestyles? Not surprisingly, then, from the outset the libertarian movement attracted an unusually high number of abnormal and perverse followers. Subsequently, the countercultural ambiance and multicultural-relativistic "tolerance" of the libertarian movement attracted even greater numbers of misfits, personal or professional failures, or plain losers. Murray Rothbard, in disgust, called them the "nihilo-libertarians" and identified them as the "modal" (typical and representative) libertarians. They fantasized of a society where everyone would be free to choose and cultivate whatever nonaggressive lifestyle, career, or character he wanted, and where, as a result of free-market economics, everyone could do so on an elevated level of general prosperity. Ironically, the movement that had set out to dismantle the state and restore private property and market economics was largely appropriated, and its appearance shaped, by the mental and emotional products of the welfare state: the new class of permanent adolescents.[22]

> Old Left led the New Left to semi-anarchistic positions, to what seemed to be thoroughgoing opposition to the existing Welfare–Warfare post-New Deal corporate state, and to the State-ridden bureaucratic university system.

Writing nearly a decade later, Rothbard acknowledged a two-fold strategic error in his erstwhile attempt to forge an alliance between libertarians and the New Left:

> (a) gravely overestimating the emotional stability, and the knowledge of economics, of these fledgling libertarians; and, as a corollary, (b) gravely underestimating the significance of the fact that these [libertarian] cadre were weak and isolated, that there was no libertarian *movement* to speak of, and therefore that hurling these youngsters into an alliance with a far more numerous and powerful group was bound to lead to a high incidence of defection . . . into real leftism of the left-wing-anarchist-Maoist-syndicalist variety. *(Toward a Strategy of Libertarian Social Change* [unpublished manuscript, 1977], pp. 159, 160–61)

[22]Murray N. Rothbard has given the following portrait of the "modal libertarian" (ML):

> ML is indeed a *he;* . . . The ML was in his twenties twenty years ago, and is now in his forties. That is neither as banal, or as benign as it sounds, because it means that the movement has not really grown in twenty

V

This intellectual combination could hardly end happily. Private property capitalism and egalitarian multiculturalism are as unlikely a combination as socialism and cultural conservatism. And in trying to

---

years; . . . The ML is fairly bright, and fairly well steeped in libertarian theory. But he knows nothing and cares less about history, culture, the context of reality or world affairs. His only reading or cultural knowledge is science fiction, . . . The ML does not, unfortunately hate the State because he sees it as the unique social instrument of organized aggression against person and property. Instead, the ML is an adolescent rebel against everyone around him: first, against his parents, second against his family, third against his neighbors, and finally against society itself. He is especially opposed to institutions of social and cultural authority: in particular against the bourgeoisie from whom he stemmed, against bourgeois norms and conventions, and against such institutions of social authority as churches. To the ML, then, the State is not a unique problem; it is only the most visible and odious of many hated bourgeois institutions: hence the zest with which the ML sports the button, "Question Authority." . . . And hence, too, the fanatical hostility of the ML toward Christianity. I used to think that this militant atheism was merely a function of the Randianism out of which most modern libertarians emerged two decades ago. But atheism is not the key, for let someone in a libertarian gathering announce that he or she is a witch or a worshiper of crystal-power or some other New Age hokum, and that person will be treated with great tolerance and respect. It is only Christians that are subject to abuse, and clearly the reason for the difference in treatment has nothing to do with atheism. But it has everything to do with rejecting and spurning bourgeois American culture; and any kind of kooky cultural cause will be encouraged in order to tweak the noses of the hated bourgeoisie. . . . In point of fact, the original attraction of the ML to Randianism was part and parcel of his adolescent rebellion: what better way to rationalize and systematize rejection of one's parents, family, and neighbors than to join a cult which denounces religion and which trumpets the absolute superiority of yourself and your cult leaders, as contrasted to the robotic "second-handers" who supposedly people the bourgeois world? A cult, furthermore, which calls upon you to spurn your parents, family, and bourgeois associates, and to cultivate the alleged greatness of your own individual ego (suitably guided, of course, by Randian leadership). . . . the ML, if he has a real world occupation, such as an accountant or lawyer, is generally a lawyer without a practice, and accountant without a job. The ML's modal occupation is computer programmer; . . . Computers appeal indeed to the ML's scientific and theoretical bent; but they also appeal to his aggravated nomadism, to his need not to have a regular payroll or regular abode. . . . The ML also has the thousand-mile stare of the fanatic. He is apt to buttonhole you at the first opportunity and go on at great length about his own particular "great discovery" about his mighty manuscript which is crying out for publication if only it

combine what cannot be combined, much of the modern libertarian movement actually contributed to the further erosion of private property rights (just as much of contemporary conservatism contributed to the erosion of families and traditional morals). What the countercultural libertarians failed to recognize, and what true libertarians cannot emphasize enough, is that the restoration of private property rights and laissez-faire economics implies a sharp and drastic increase in social "discrimination" and will swiftly eliminate most if not all of the multicultural-egalitarian life style experiments so close to the heart of left libertarians. In other words, libertarians must be radical and uncompromising conservatives.

Contrary to the left libertarians assembled around such institutions as the Cato Institute and the Institute for Justice, for instance, who seek the assistance of the central government in the enforcement of various policies of nondiscrimination and call for a nondiscriminatory or "free" immigration policy,[23] true libertarians must embrace discrimination, be

---

hadn't been suppressed by the Powers That Be.... But above all, the ML is a moocher, a bunco artist, and often an outright crook. His basic attitude toward other libertarians is "Your house is my house." ... in short, whether they articulate this "philosophy" or not, [MLs] are libertarian-communists: anyone with property is automatically expected to "share" it with the other members of his extended libertarian "family." ("Why Paleo?" *Rothbard–Rockwell Report* 1, no. 2 [May 1990]: 4–5; also idem, "Diversity, Death, and *Reason*," *Rothbard–Rockwell Report* 2, no. 5 [May 1991])

Also see Llewellyn H. Rockwell, Jr., *The Case for Paleolibertarianism and Realignment on the Right* (Burlingame, Calif.: Center for Libertarian Studies, 1990).

[23]More specifically, left-libertarians (LLs) employ and promote the employment of the federal government and its courts to squash discriminatory and presumably antilibertarian state and/or local laws and regulations; they thus contribute, regardless of their *intention*, to the antilibertarian end of strengthening the central state. Correspondingly, LLs typically look favorably upon Lincoln and the Union government because the Union victory over the secessionist Confederacy resulted in the abolition of slavery, but they fail to recognize that *this* way of achieving the libertarian goal of abolishing slavery must lead to a drastic increase in the power of the central (federal) government, and that the Union victory in the Southern War of Independence indeed marks one of the great leaps forward in the growth of the modern federal Leviathan and hence represents a profoundly antilibertarian episode in American history. Further, while LLs criticize the current practice of "affirmative action" as a quota system, they do not reject the so-called civil-rights legislation from which the present practice developed as entirely and fundamentally incompatible with the cornerstone of libertarian political philosophy, i.e., private property rights. To the contrary, LLs are very much concerned about "civil rights," most prominently the "right" of gays and other alternative life-stylers not to

it internal (domestic) or external (foreign). Indeed, private property means discrimination. I, not you, own such and such. I am entitled to exclude you from my property. I may attach conditions to your using my

be discriminated against in employment and housing. Accordingly, they look favorably on the U.S. Supreme Court decision in *Brown vs. Board of Education* to outlaw segregation and the proto-socialist "civil rights" leader Martin Luther King. To be sure, LLs typically recognize the categorical difference between private and so-called public property, and at least in theory they admit that private property owners ought to have the right to discriminate regarding their own property as they please. But the LLs distinctly egalitarian concern for the lofty yet elusive idea of the "progressive extension of *dignity*" (instead of *property rights*) to "women, to people of different religions and different races" [David Boaz, p. 16, reference below; my emphasis], misleads them to accept the very *principle* of "nondiscrimination," even if it is only applied and restricted to public property and the public sector of the economy. (Hence the LLs advocacy of a nondiscriminatory or "free" immigration policy.) Theoretically, LLs thereby commit the error of regarding public property as if it were either unowned "land" open to unrestricted universal homesteading (while in fact all public property has been financed by domestic taxpayers), or as if it were "communal" property open to every domestic citizen on an equal basis (while in fact some citizens have paid more taxes than others, and some, i.e., those whose salaries or subsidies were paid *out of* taxes, have paid no taxes at all). Worse, in accepting the principle of non-discrimination for the realm of public property, LLs in fact contribute to the further aggrandizement of state power and the diminution of private property rights, for in today's state-ridden world, the dividing line between private and public has become increasingly fuzzy. All private property borders on and is surrounded by public streets; virtually every business sells some of its products to some government agency or across state borders; and countless private firms and organizations (such as private universities, for instance) regularly receive government funding. Hence, as seen from the perspective of the agents of the state, there is practically nothing left that is genuinely "private" and thus does not fall under government purview. Based on this all-pervasive entanglement of the state and public property with private business and private property, and given the government's unique—coercive—bargaining power, it can be safely predicted that the policy of "non-discrimination" will not remain a principle merely of *public* policy for long, but will instead increasingly become a general and ultimately universal principle, extending to and encompassing everyone and everything, public *and* private. (Characteristically, LLs are typically also proponents of Milton Friedman's school voucher proposal and are thus, it would seem, totally unaware that the implementation of the voucher plan would invariably lead to the expansion of government control from public schools to one including private schools and the destruction of whatever autonomous decisionmaking rights the latter schools presently still possess.)

For representative examples of left-libertarian thought see, for instance, Clint Bolick, *Grassroots Tyranny: The Limits of Federalism* (Washington, D.C.: Cato Institute, 1993); idem, *The Affirmative Action Fraud: Can We Restore the American Civil Rights Vision?* (Washington, D.C.: Cato Institute, 1996); and David Boaz, *Libertarianism: A Primer* (New York: Free Press, 1997); for a rebuttal of the left-libertarian views of Bolick and Boaz from the right or "paleo-libertarian" perspective see Murray N. Rothbard, "The Big Government Libertarians: The Anti-Left-Libertarian Manifesto,"

property, and I may expel you from my property. Moreover, You and I, private property owners, may enter and put our property into a restrictive (or protective) covenant. We and others may, if we both deem it beneficial, impose limitations on the future use that each of us is permitted to make with our property.

The modern welfare state has largely stripped private property owners of the right to exclusion implied in the concept of private property. Discrimination is outlawed. Employers cannot hire whom they want. Landlords cannot rent to whom they want. Sellers cannot sell to whomever they wish; buyers cannot buy from whomever they wish to buy. And groups of private property owners are not permitted to enter in whatever restrictive covenant they believe to be mutually beneficial. The state has thus robbed the people of much of their personal and physical protection. Not to be able to exclude others means not to be able to protect oneself. The result of this erosion of private property rights under the democratic welfare state is forced integration. Forced integration is ubiquitous. Americans must accept immigrants they do not want. Teachers cannot get rid of lousy or ill-behaved students, employers are stuck with poor or destructive employees, landlords are forced to live with bad renters, banks and insurance companies are not allowed to avoid bad risks, restaurants and bars must accommodate unwelcome customers, and private clubs and covenants are compelled to accept members and actions in violation of their very own rules and restrictions. Moreover, on public, i.e., government property in particular, forced integration has taken on a dangerous form: of norm and lawlessness.[24]

Rothbard–Rockwell Report 4, no. 12 (December 1993); idem, "Big Government Libertarians," *Rothbard–Rockwell Report* 5, no. 11 (November 1994); and Jeffrey A. Tucker's review of Boaz' book in the *Journal of Libertarian Studies* 13, no. 1 (1997).

[24]"Every property owner," Murray N. Rothbard elaborated,

> should have the absolute right to sell, hire, or lease his money or other property to anyone whom he chooses, which means he has the absolute right to "discriminate" all he damn pleases. If I have a plant and want to hire only six-foot albinos, and I can find willing employees, I should have the right to do so, even though I might well lose my shirt doing so. . . . If I own an apartment complex and want to rent only to Swedes without children, I should have the right to do so. Etc. Outlawing such discrimination, and restrictive covenants upholding it, was the original sin from which all other problems followed. Once admit that principle, and everything else follows as the night the day. . . . For if it is right and proper to outlaw my discriminating against blacks, then it is just as right and proper for the government to figure out if I am discriminating or not, and in that case, it is perfectly legitimate for them to employ quotas to test the proposition. . . . So what is the remedy for all

To exclude other people from one's own property is the very means by which an owner can avoid "bads" from happening: events that will lower the value of one's property. In not being permitted to freely exclude, the incidence of bads—ill-behaved, lazy, unreliable, rotten students, employees, customers—will increase and property values will fall. In fact, forced integration (the result of all nondiscrimination policies) breeds ill behavior and bad character. In civilized society, the ultimate price for ill behavior is expulsion, and all-around ill-behaved or rotten characters (even if they commit no criminal offense) will find themselves quickly expelled from everywhere and by everyone and become outcasts, physically removed from civilization. This is a stiff price to pay; hence, the frequency of such behavior is reduced. By contrast, if one is prevented from expelling others from one's property whenever their presence is deemed undesirable, ill behavior, misconduct, and outright rotten characters are encouraged (rendered less costly). Rather than being isolated and ultimately entirely removed from society, the "bums"—in every conceivable area of incompetency (bumhood)—are permitted to perpetrate their unpleasantries everywhere, so bum-like behavior and bums will proliferate. The results of forced integration are only too visible. All social relations—whether in private or business life—have become increasingly egalitarian (everyone is on a first name basis with everyone else) and uncivilized.

In distinct contrast, a society in which the right to exclusion is fully restored to owners of private property would be profoundly unegalitarian, intolerant, and discriminatory. There would be little or no "tolerance" and "open-mindedness" so dear to left-libertarians. Instead, one would be on the right path toward restoring the freedom of association and exclusion implied in the institution of private property, if only towns and villages could and would do what they did as a matter of course until well into the nineteenth century in Europe and the United States. There would be signs regarding entrance requirements to the town, and, once in town, requirements for entering specific pieces of property (for example, no beggars, bums, or homeless, but also no homosexuals, drug users, Jews, Moslems, Germans, or Zulus), and those who did not meet these entrance requirements would be kicked out as trespassers. Almost instantly, cultural and moral normalcy would reassert itself.

---

this? . . . What has to be done is to repudiate "civil rights" and antidiscrimination laws totally, and in the meanwhile, on a separate but parallel track, try to privatize as much and as fully as we can. ("Marshall, Civil Rights, and the Court," *Rothbard–Rockwell Report* 2, no. 8 [August 1991]: 4 and 6)

Left-libertarians and multi- or countercultural lifestyle experimentalists, even if they were not engaged in any crime, would once again have to pay a price for their behavior. If they continued with their behavior or lifestyle, they would be barred from civilized society and live physically separate from it, in ghettos or on the fringes of society, and many positions or professions would be unattainable to them. In contrast, if they wished to live and advance within society, they would have to adjust and assimilate to the moral and cultural norms of the society they wanted to enter. To thus assimilate would not necessarily imply that one would have to give up one's substandard or abnormal behavior or lifestyle altogether. It would imply, however, that one could no longer "come out" and exhibit one's alternative behavior or lifestyle in public. Such behavior would have to stay in the closet, hidden from the public eye, and physically restricted to the total privacy of one's own four walls. Advertising or displaying it in public would lead to expulsion.[25]

---

[25]To avoid any misunderstanding, it might be useful to point out that the predicted rise in discrimination in a purely libertarian world does *not* imply that the form and extent of discrimination will be the same or similar everywhere. To the contrary, a libertarian world could and likely would be one with a great variety of locally separated communities engaging in distinctly different and far-reaching discrimination. Explains Murray N. Rothbard:

> In a country, or a world, of totally private property, including streets, and of private contractual neighborhoods consisting of property-owners, these owners can make any sort of neighborhood-contracts they wish. In practice, then, the country would be a truly "gorgeous mosaic,". . . ranging from rowdy Greenwich Village-type contractual neighborhoods, to socially conservative homogeneous WASP neighborhoods. Remember that all deeds and covenants would once again be totally legal and enforceable, with no meddling government restrictions upon them. So that considering the drug question, if a proprietary neighborhood contracted that no one would use drugs, and Jones violated the contract and used them, his fellow community-contractors could simply enforce the contract and kick him out. Or, since no advance contract can allow for all conceivable circumstances, suppose that Smith became so personally obnoxious that his fellow neighborhood-owners wanted him ejected. They would then have to buy him out—probably on terms set contractually in advance in accordance with some "obnoxious" clause. ("The 'New Fusionism': A Movement For Our Time," *Rothbard–Rockwell Report* 2, no. 1 [January 1991]: 9–10)

Notwithstanding the variety of discriminatory policies pursued by different proprietary communities, however, and as will be further argued in the following above, for the sake of self-preservation each of these communities will have to recognize and enforce some strict and rather inflexible limitations with respect to its internal tolerance; that is, *no* proprietary community can be as "tolerant" and "nondiscriminatory" as left-libertarians wish *every* place to be.

Moreover, true conservative libertarians—in contrast to left-libertarians—must not only recognize and emphasize the *fact* that there *will be* a sharp increase in discrimination (exclusion, expulsion) in a libertarian society wherein private property rights are fully restored to the owners of private households and estates; more importantly, they will have to recognize—and conservatives and conservative insights can be helpful in achieving this—that this *ought* to be so: that is, that there *should* be strict discrimination *if* one wants to reach the goal of a private property anarchy (or a pure private law society). Without continued and relentless discrimination, a libertarian society would quickly erode and degenerate into welfare state socialism. Every social order, including a libertarian or conservative one, requires a self-enforcement mechanism. More precisely, social orders (unlike mechanical or biological systems) are not maintained automatically; they require conscious effort and purposeful action on the part of the members of society to prevent them from disintegrating.[26]

VI

The standard libertarian model of a community is one of individuals who, instead of living physically separated and isolated from one another, associate with each other as neighbors living on adjacent but separately owned pieces of land. However, this model is too simplistic. Presumably, the reason for choosing neighbors over isolation is the fact that for individuals participating in and partaking of the benefits of the division of labor, a neighborhood offers the added advantage of lower transaction costs; that is, a neighborhood facilitates exchange. As a consequence, the value of an individually owned piece of land will be enhanced by the existence of neighboring pieces of land owned by others. However, while this may indeed be true and constitute a valid reason for choosing a neighborhood over physical isolation, it is by no means always true. A neighborhood also involves risks and may lead to falling rather than increasing property values, for even if one assumes, in accordance with the model under consideration, that the *initial* establishment of neighboring property was mutually beneficial, and even if it is further assumed that all members of a community refrain from criminal activity, it might still happen that a formerly "good" neighbor turns obnoxious, that he does not take care of his property or changes it so as to negatively affect the property values of other community members, or that he simply refuses to participate in any cooperative effort directed at

---

[26]See on this in particular Mises, *Human Action*, esp. chap. 9; Joseph T. Salerno, "Ludwig von Mises as Social Rationalist," *Review of Austrian Economics* 4 (1990).

improving the value of the community as a whole.[27] Hence, in order to overcome the difficulties inherent in community development when the land is held in divided ownership, the formation of neighborhoods and communities has in fact proceeded along different lines from those suggested in the above mentioned model.

Rather than being composed of adjacent pieces of land owned in severalty, then, neighborhoods have typically been proprietary or covenantal communities, founded and owned by a single proprietor who would "lease" separate parts of the land under specified conditions to selected individuals.[28] Originally, such covenants were based on kinship relations, with the role of the proprietor performed by the head of a family or clan. In other words, just as the actions of the immediate family members are coordinated by the head and owner of the household within a single family household, so was the function of directing and

---

[27]See on this Spencer H. MacCallum, *The Art of Community* (Menlo Park, Calif.: Institute for Humane Studies, 1970). "So long as individuals have ownership in parts less than the whole," notes MacCallum,

> their interests will collide with the interests of others and with the common interest in any proposal that would affect land values unevenly. Yet, to avoid such measures would be to throw out planning and coordination of land uses completely, and with it ultimately all land value.... Aggravating the situation further is the absence of effective leadership to arbitrate the conflicts or to salvage the best of the bad situation. Lacking is someone who, while not identified with any special interest in the community, is at the same time strongly concerned for the success of the community as a whole. (p. 57)

> [P]roperty in land cannot be moved to an environment more favorable for its use. Its value as an economic good is a function of its surroundings. Its higher use therefore depends upon rearranging the environment to conform to it. . . . Since the possible uses of a site depend on surrounding land uses (ultimately, all human action is land use of one kind or another), it is essential for its most productive use that the uses of accessible surrounding land be coordinated. Seldom can this be done effectively under a multiplicity of separate authorities. If surrounding sites are owned in severalty, the several owners may or may not be able to accommodate their various uses to a comprehensive plan, depending on many, often fortuitous, factors affecting the ability and wishes of each. They are neighbors of circumstance, not of convenience. (p. 78)

[28]To avoid any misunderstanding, the term "lease" is used here to include the sale of anything less than the full title to this thing. Thus, for example, the proprietor may sell all the rights to a house and a piece of land, *except* for the right to build a house over a certain height or of other than a certain design or to use the land for any other than residential purposes, etc., which rights are retained by the proprietary seller. See on this Rothbard, *The Ethics of Liberty*, p. 146.

coordinating the land uses of groups of neighboring households traditionally fulfilled by the head of an extended kinship group.[29] In modern
times, characterized by massive population growth and a significant
loss in the importance of kinship relations, this original libertarian
model of a proprietary community has been replaced by new and familiar developments such as shopping malls and "gated communities."
Both shopping centers and gated residential communities are owned by
a single entity, either an individual or a private corporation, and the
relationship between the community proprietor and his renters and
residents is purely contractual. The proprietor is an entrepreneur seeking profits from developing and managing residential and/or business
communities which attract people as places where they want to reside
and/or carry on their business. "The proprietor," elaborates Spencer
MacCallum,

> builds value in the inventory of community land chiefly by satisfying
> three functional requirements of a community which he alone as an
> owner can adequately fulfill: *selection of members, land planning,* and
> *leadership.* . . . The first two functions, membership selection and land
> planning, are accomplished by him automatically in the course of de-
> termining to whom, and for what purpose, to let the use of land. The
> third function, leadership, is his natural responsibility and also his
> special opportunity, since his interest alone is the success of the whole
> community rather than that of any special interest within it. Assigning
> land automatically establishes the kinds of tenants and their spatial
> juxtaposition to one another and, hence, the economic structure of the
> community. . . . Leadership also includes arbitration of differences
> among tenants, as well as guidance and participation in joint efforts. . . .
> [Indeed], in a fundamental sense the security of the community is a
> part of the owner's real estate function. Under land planning, he

---

[29]"[T]he proprietary community is not unique to our time and culture," explains
MacCallum.

> Its roots are deep in human history. . . . Within households, in the
> primitive world, land is commonly administered by an elder male in the
> line of property succession. For groups of households, it may be admin-
> istered by a clan or lineage or other group head who is commonly an
> elder male of the kin group of widest span. And similarly at the village
> level. This is "the familiar pattern," in anthropologist Melville
> Herskovits' words, "of village land ownership held in trust and adminis-
> tered by the village head in behalf of its members, native or adopted, and
> family ownership, for which the head of the family is trustee." The
> system is sometimes called *seignorialism* since the distributive authority
> is exercised by a senior member of the kin group at the span or level of
> organization in question. (*The Art of Community,* p. 69)

supervises the design of all construction from the standpoint of safety. He also chooses tenants with a view to their compatibility and complementarity with other members of the community and learns to anticipate in the leases and to provide in other ways against disputes developing among tenants. By his informal peacemaking and arbitrating, he resolves differences that might otherwise become serious. In these many ways he ensures "quiet possession," as it was so admirably phrased in the language of the Common Law, for his tenants.[30]

Clearly then, the task of maintaining the covenant entailed in a libertarian (proprietary) community is first and foremost that of the proprietor. Yet he is but one man, and it is impossible for him to succeed in this task unless he is supported in his endeavor by a majority of the members of the community in question. In particular, the proprietor needs the support of the the community elite, i.e., the heads of households and firms most heavily invested in the community. In order to protect and possibly enhance the value of their property and investments, both proprietor and the community elite must be willing and prepared to take two forms of protective measures. First, they must be willing to defend themselves by means of physical force and punishment against external invaders and domestic criminals. But second and equally important, they must also be willing to defend themselves, by means of ostracism, exclusion and ultimately expulsion, against those community members who advocate, advertise or propagandize actions incompatible with the very purpose of the covenant: to protect property and family.[31]

---

[30]MacCallum, *The Art of Community*, pp. 63, 66, 67. Moreover,

> [o]nce the ownerships are organized as participation in a single property, it becomes the common interest of the owners to redevelop and manage the whole as a unit in the most productive way, even to replanning the formerly fixed pattern of streets and common areas. It becomes their single interest to provide not only optimum physical environment, but optimum social environment as well—through an effective manager who can serve inconspicuously as expediter, peacemaker, and active catalyst to promote the freest possible conditions for the occupants to pursue their respective interests. (p. 59)

[31]"On all levels of society, both primitive and modern" notes MacCallum on the importance of exclusion for the maintenance of social order, "exile is the natural and automatic remedy for default and fraud."

> [B]y dispossession he [the village head] exiles individuals who have made themselves intolerable (exactly as a shopping center manager fails to renew the lease of an incompatible tenant). However infrequent in the village, as compared with modern proprietary communities, membership control is still a functional requisite of community life for which there must be regular provision. (p. 70)

In this regard a community always faces the double and related threat of egalitarianism and cultural relativism. Egalitarianism, in every form and shape, is incompatible with the idea of private property. Private property implies exclusivity, inequality, and difference. And cultural relativism is incompatible with the fundamental—indeed foundational—fact of families and intergenerational kinship relations. Families and kinship relations imply cultural absolutism. As a matter of socio-psychological fact, both egalitarian and relativistic sentiments find steady support among ever new generations of adolescents. Owing to their still incomplete mental development, juveniles, especially of the male variety, are always susceptible to both ideas. Adolescence is marked by regular (and for this stage normal) outbreaks of rebellion by the young against the discipline imposed on them by family life and parental authority.[32] Cultural relativism and multiculturalism provide the ideological instrument of emancipating oneself from these constraints. And egalitarianism—based on the infantile view that property is "given" (and thus distributed arbitrarily) rather than individually appropriated and produced (and hence, distributed justly, i.e., in accordance with personal productivity)—provides the intellectual means by which the rebellious youths can lay claim to the economic resources necessary for a life free of and outside the disciplinary framework of families.[33]

The enforcement of a covenant is largely a matter of prudence, of course. How and when to react, and what protective measures to take, requires judgment on the part of the members of the community and especially the proprietor and the community elite. Thus, for instance, so long as the threat of moral relativism and egalitarianism is restricted to a small proportion of juveniles and young adults for only a brief period in life (until they settle back into family-constrained adulthood), it may

---

And in a footnote to this, he adds:

> Anthropologist Raymond Firth records an expression of exile from the Pacific island society of Tikopia that evokes in its simplicity the pathos of the Anglo-Saxon poem, "The Wanderer." Inasmuch as all land was owned by the chiefs, an exiled person had no recourse but to canoe out to sea—to suicide or to life as a stranger on other islands. The expression for a person who is exiled translates that such a person "has no place on which to stand." (*The Art of Community*, p. 77)

[32]See on this Konrad Lorenz, *Civilized Man's Eight Deadly Sins* (New York: Harcourt Brace Jovanovich, 1974), chap. 7; also Sigmund Freud, *Civilization and its Discontents* (New York: W.W. Norton, 1989).

[33]See also Helmut Schelsky, *Die Arbeit tun die anderen. Klassenkampf und Priesterherrschaft der Intellektuellen* (Munich: Deutscher Taschenbuch Verlag, 1977).

well be sufficient to do nothing at all. The proponents of cultural relativism and egalitarianism would represent little more than temporary embarassments or irritations, and punishment in the form of ostracism can be quite mild and lenient. A small dose of ridicule and contempt may be all that is needed to contain the relativistic and egalitarian threat. The situation is very different, however, and rather more drastic measures might be required, once the spirit of moral relativism and egalitarianism has taken hold among adult members of society: among mothers, fathers, and heads of households and firms.

As soon as mature members of society habitually express acceptance or even advocate egalitarian sentiments, whether in the form of democracy (majority rule) or of communism, it becomes essential that other members, and in particular the natural social elites, be prepared to act decisively and, in the case of continued nonconformity, exclude and ultimately expel these members from society. In a covenant concluded among proprietor and community tenants for the purpose of protecting their private property, no such thing as a right to free (unlimited) speech exists, not even to unlimited speech on one's own tenant-property. One may say innumerable things and promote almost any idea under the sun, but naturally no one is permitted to advocate ideas contrary to the very purpose of the covenant of preserving and protecting private property, such as democracy and communism. There can be no tolerance toward democrats and communists in a libertarian social order. They will have to be physically separated and expelled from society. Likewise, in a covenant founded for the purpose of protecting family and kin, there can be no tolerance toward those habitually promoting lifestyles incompatible with this goal. They—the advocates of alternative, non-family and kin-centered lifestyles such as, for instance, individual hedonism, parasitism, nature-environment worship, homosexuality, or communism—will have to be physically removed from society, too, if one is to maintain a libertarian order.

VII

It should be obvious then that and why libertarians must be moral and cultural conservatives of the most uncompromising kind. The current state of moral degeneration, social disintegration and cultural rot is precisely the result of too much—and above all erroneous and misconceived—tolerance. Rather than having all habitual democrats, communists, and alternative lifestylists quickly isolated, excluded and expelled from civilization in accordance with the principles of the covenant, they were tolerated by society. Yet this toleration only encouraged and promoted even more egalitarian and relativistic sentiments and attitudes, until at last the point was reached where the authority of excluding anyone for anything had effectively evaporated (while the power of the state, as manifested in state-sponsored forced integration policies, had correspondingly grown).

Libertarians, in their attempt to establish a free natural social order, must strive to regain from the state the right to exclusion inherent in private property. Yet even before they accomplish this and in order to render such an achievement even possible, libertarians cannot soon enough begin to reassert and exercise, to the extent that the situation still permits them to do so, their right to exclusion in everyday life. Libertarians must distinguish themselves from others by practicing (as well as advocating) the most extreme form of intolerance and discrimination against egalitarians, democrats, socialists, communists, multiculturalists, environmentalists, ill manners, misconduct, incompetence, rudeness, vulgarity, and obscenity. Like true conservatives, who will have to dissociate themselves from the false social(ist) conservatism of the Buchananites and the neoconservatives, true libertarians must visibly and ostentatiously dissociate themselves from the false multi-countercultural and anti-authoritarian egalitarian left-libertarian impostors.

11

On the Errors of Classical Liberalism and the Future of Liberty

I

Classical liberalism has been in decline for more than a century. Since the second half of the nineteenth century, in the U.S. as well as in Western Europe, public affairs have increasingly been shaped instead by socialist ideas. In fact, the twentieth century may well be described as the century *par excellence* of socialism: of communism, fascism, national socialism, and most enduringly of social democracy (modern American liberalism and neoconservatism).[1]

---

[1]The term liberalism here and in the following is used in its original or classical meaning as defined, for instance, by its foremost twentieth-century proponent, Ludwig von Mises, in his 1927 treatise *Liberalism: In the Classical Tradition* (Irvington-on-Hudson, N.Y.: Foundation for Economic Education, 1985), on p. 19:

> The program of liberalism . . . if condensed into a single word, would have to read: *property*, that is, private ownership of the means of production (for in regard to commodities ready for consumption, private ownership is a matter of course and is not disputed even by the socialists and communists). All the other demands of liberalism result from this fundamental demand.

By contrast, modern American "liberalism" has almost the opposite meaning, which can be traced back to John Stuart Mill and his 1859 book *On Liberty* as the fountainhead of modern moderate—social-democratic—socialism. Mill, notes Mises (ibid., p. 195),

> is the originator of the thoughtless confounding of liberal and socialist ideas that led to the decline of English liberalism and to the undermining of the living standards of the English people. . . . Without a thorough study of Mill it is impossible to understand the events of the last two generations [1927!]. For Mill is the great advocate of socialism. All the arguments that could be advanced in favor of socialism are elaborated by him with loving care. In comparison with Mill all other socialist writers—even Marx, Engels, and Lassalle—are scarcely of any importance.

For a detailed and devastating critique of John Stuart Mill from a liberal-libertarian perspective see Murray N. Rothbard, *Classical Economics: An Austrian Perspective on the History of Economic Thought* (Cheltenham, U.K.: Edward Elgar, 1995), vol. 2, chap. 8.

To be sure, this decline has not been a continuous one. Matters did not always become worse from a liberal viewpoint. There were also some reprieves. As a result of World War II, for instance, West Germany and Italy experienced significant liberalization in comparison to the *status quo ante* under national socialism and fascism. Similarly, the collapse of the communist Soviet Empire in the late 1980s has led to a remarkable liberalization across Eastern Europe. However, as much as liberals welcomed these events, they were not indicative of a renaissance of liberalism. Rather, the liberalization of Germany and Italy in the aftermath of World War II and the current post-communist liberalization of Eastern Europe were the outcome of external and accidental events: of military defeat and/or outright economic bankruptcy. It was in each case liberalization by default of the old system, and the default option adopted subsequently was simply a variant of socialism: social democracy as exemplified by the U.S. as the only surviving—not yet militarily defeated or economically bankrupt—superpower.

Thus, even if liberals have enjoyed a few periods of reprieve, ultimately the displacement of liberalism by socialism has been complete. Indeed, so complete has been the socialist victory that today, at the beginning of the twentieth-first century, some neoconservatives have waxed triumphantly about the "End of History" and the arrival of the "Last Man," i.e., of the last millenium of global, U.S.-supervised social democracy and a new *homo socio-democraticus*.[2]

---

[2]See Francis Fukuyama, "The End of History?" *The National Interest* 16 (Summer 1989); idem, *The End of History and the Last Man* (New York: Avon Books, 1993). Summing up his own thesis, Fukuyama there writes that

> I argued that a remarkable consensus concerning the legitimacy of liberal [i.e., social-democratic] democracy as a system of government had emerged throughout the world over the past few years, as it conquered rival ideologies like hereditary monarchy, fascism, and most recently communism. More than that, however, I argued that liberal democracy may constitute the "end point of mankind's ideological evolution" and the "final form of human government," and as such constituted "the end of history." That is, while earlier forms of government were characterized by grave defects and irrationalities that led to their eventual collapse, liberal democracy was arguably free from such fundamental internal contradictions. . . . This did not mean that the natural cycle of birth, life, and death would end, that important events would no longer happen, or that newspapers reporting them would cease to be published. It meant, rather, that there would be no further progress in the development of underlying principles and institutions, because all of the really big questions had been settled. (pp. xi–xii)

II

Even if one regards the Hegelian aspirations of this interpretation as preposterous, according to which liberalism marks only a transitory stage in the evolution of the fully-developed social democratic man,[3] liberals still must be pained at the mere *appearance* of truth of neoconservative

---

The neoconservative movement to which Fukuyama belongs emerged in the late 1960s and early 1970s, when the American left became increasingly involved with Black Power politics, affirmative action, pro-Arabism, and the "counterculture." In opposition to these tendencies, many traditional left-wing (frequently former Trotskyite) intellectuals and cold war "liberals," led by Irving Kristol and Norman Podhoretz, broke ranks with their old allies, frequently crossing over from the long-time haven of left-wing politics, the Democratic party, to the Republicans. Since then the neoconservatives, while insignificant in sheer numbers, have gained unrivaled influence in American politics, promoting typically a "moderate" welfare state ("democratic capitalism"), "cultural conservatism" and "family values," and an interventionist ("activist") and in particular Zionist ("pro-Israel") foreign policy. Represented by figures such as Irving Kristol and his wife Gertrude Himmelfarb, and son William Kristol; Norman Podhoretz and his wife, Midge Decter, son John Podhoretz, and sons-in-law Steven Munson and Elliott Abrams; by Daniel Bell, Peter Berger, Nathan Glazer, Seymour Martin Lipset, Michael Novak, Aaron Wildavsky, James Q. Wilson; and journalist–commentators such as David Frum, Paul Gigot, Morton Kondracke, Charles Krauthammer, Michael Lind, Joshua Muravchik, Emmett Tyrrell, and Ben Wattenberg, the neoconservatives now exercise controlling interest in such publications as *National Interest*, *Public Interest*, *Commentary*, the *New Republic*, the *American Spectator*, the *Weekly Standard*, the *Washington Post*, and the *Wall Street Journal*, and they have close ties to several major foundations such as Bradley, Olin, Pew, Scaife, and Smith-Richardson. See on this Paul Gottfried, *The Conservative Movement*, rev. ed. (New York: Twayne Publishers, 1993); also George H. Nash, *The Conservative Intellectual Movement in America* (New York: Basic Books, 1976).

[3]Thus, writes Fukuyama,

> for a very large part of the world, there is now no ideology with pretensions to universality that is in a position to challenge liberal democracy, and no universal principle of legitimacy other than the sovereignty of the people. . . . we have trouble imagining a world that is radically better than our own, or a future that is not essentially democratic and capitalist. . . . we cannot picture to ourselves a world that is *essentially* different from the present one, and at the same time better. . . . it is precisely if we look not just at the past fifteen years, but at the *whole scope of history*, that liberal democracy begins to occupy a special kind of place. . . . there is a fundamental process at work that dictates a common evolutionary pattern for *all* human societies - in short, something like a Universal History of mankind in the direction of liberal democracy. . . . if we are now at a point where we cannot imagine a world substantially different from our own, in which there is is no apparent or obvious way in which the future will represent a fundamental improvement over our current order, then we must also take into consideration the possibility that History itself might be at an end. (*The End of History*, pp. 45–51)

philosophizing. Nor can they console themselves with the knowledge that social democracy also is bound to collapse economically. They knew that communism had to collapse, yet when it did, this did not inaugurate a liberal renaissance. There is no *a priori* reason to assume that the future breakdown of social democracy will bear any more favorable results.

Assuming that the course of human history is determined by ideas (rather than "blind forces") and historical changes are the result of ideological shifts in public opinion, it follows that the socialist transformation of the last hundred years must be understood as the result of liberalism's intellectual—philosophical and theoretical—defeat, i.e., the increasing rejection in public opinion of the liberal doctrine as faulty.[4] In this situation, liberals can react in two ways. On the one hand, they may still want to maintain that liberalism is a sound doctrine and that the public rejects it in spite of its truth. In this case, one must explain why people cling to false beliefs, even if they are aware of correct liberal ideas.[5] Does the truth not always hold its own attraction and rewards? Furthermore, one must explain why the liberal truth is *increasingly* rejected in favor of socialist falsehoods. Did the population become more indolent or degenerate? If so, how can this be explained?[6] On the other hand, one may consider the rejection as indicative of an error in one's doctrine. In this case, one must reconsider its theoretical foundations and identify the error which can account not only for the doctrine's rejection as false but more importantly for the actual course of events. In other words, the socialist transformation must be explained as an intelligible and systematically predictable progressive deconstruction and degeneration of liberal political theory originating in and logically arising from this error as the ultimate source of all subsequent socialist confusion.

III

Liberalism's central and momentous error lies in its theory of government.[7]

---

[4]See on this Ludwig von Mises, *Theory and History: An Interpretation of Social and Economic Evolution* (Auburn, Ala.: Ludwig von Mises Institute, 1985), esp. part 4.

[5]For an attempt in this direction see Ludwig von Mises, *The Anti-Capitalistic Mentality* (South Holland, Ill.: Libertarian Press, 1972).

[6]For an attempt in this direction see Seymour Itzkoff, *The Decline of Intelligence in America* (Westport, Conn.: Praeger, 1994). Itzkoff here undertakes to explain the social degeneration observable in particular in the U.S. as the outcome of dysgenic effects promoted by public welfare policies.

[7]See on the following in particular Murray N. Rothbard, *The Ethics of Liberty* (New York: New York University Press, 1998); Hans-Hermann Hoppe, *The Economics and Ethics of Private Property* (Boston: Kluwer, 1993).

Classical-liberal political philosophy—as personified by Locke and most prominently displayed in Jefferson's *Declaration of Independence*—was first and foremost a moral doctrine. Drawing on the philosophy of the Stoics and the late Scholastics, it centered around the notions of self-ownership, original appropriation of nature-given (unowned) resources, property, and contract as universal human rights implied in the nature of man *qua* rational animal.[8] In the environment of princely and royal rulers, this emphasis on the universality of human rights placed the liberal philosophy naturally in radical opposition to every established government.[9] For a liberal, every man, whether king or peasant, was subject to the same universal and eternal principles of justice, and a government either could derive its justification from a contract between private property owners or it could not be justified at all.[10] But could *any* government be so justified?

The affirmative liberal answer is well-known. It set out from the undeniably true proposition that, mankind being what it is, murderers, robbers, thieves, thugs, and con artists will always exist, and life in society will be impossible if they are not threatened with physical punishment.

---

[8]See also Ernst Cassirer, *The Myth of the State* (New Haven, Conn.: Yale University Press, 1946), esp. chaps. 8 and 13; Richard Tuck, *Natural Rights: Their Origin and Development* (Cambridge: Cambridge University Press, 1979); Murray N. Rothbard, *Economic Thought Before Adam Smith: An Austrian Perspective on the History of Economic Thought* (Cheltenham, U.K.: Edward Elgar, 1995), vol. 1, esp. chap. 4: Hans-Hermann Hoppe, "The Western State as a Paradigm: Learning from History," *Politics and Regimes. Religion and Public Life* 30 (1997).

[9]Thus Ludwig von Mises, *Nation, State, and Economy* (New York: New York University Press, 1983) characterizes liberalism as "hostile to princes" (p. 33). In order to avoid any misunderstanding it should be noted, however, that this sweeping verdict applies, and is indeed applied by Mises only to the "absolute" rulers of seventeenth- and eighteenth-century Europe. It does *not* apply also to earlier, medieval kings and princes, who were typically just *primus inter pares*, i.e., voluntarily acknowledged authorities held to be subject to the same universal natural law as everyone else. See on this Fritz Kern, *Kingship and Law in the Middle Ages* (Oxford: Blackwell, 1948).

[10]Thus Cassirer writes:

> The doctrine of the state-contract becomes in the seventeenth century a self-evident axiom of political thought. . . . this fact marks a great and decisive step. For if we adopt this view, if we reduce the legal and social order to free individual acts, to a voluntary contractual submission of the governed, all mystery is gone. There is nothing less mysterious than a contract. A contract must be made in full awareness of its meaning and consequences; it presupposes the free consent of all parties concerned. If we can trace the state to such an origin, it becomes a perfectly clear and understandable fact. (*The Myth of the State*, pp. 172–73)

In order to maintain a liberal social order, liberals insisted, it is necessary that its members be in the position to pressure (by threatening or applying violence) anyone who does not respect the life and property of others to acquiesce to the rules of society. From this correct premise, liberals concluded that this indispensable task of maintaining of law and order is the unique function of government.[11]

Whether this conclusion is correct or not hinges on the definition of government. It is correct if government simply means any individual or firm that provides protection and security services to a voluntary paying clientele of private property owners. However, this was not the definition of government adopted by liberals. For a liberal, government is not simply a specialized firm. Rather, government possesses two unique characteristics. Unlike a normal firm, it possesses a compulsory territorial monopoly of jurisdiction (ultimate decisionmaking) and the right to tax. However, if one assumes *this* definition of government, then the liberal conclusion is false. It does *not* follow from the right and need for the protection of person and property that protection rightfully should or effectively can be provided by a monopolist of jurisdiction and taxation. To the contrary, it can be demonstrated that any such institution is incompatible with the rightful and effective protection of property.

According to liberal doctrine, private property rights logically and temporally precede any government. They are the result of acts of original appropriation, production, and/or exchange from prior to later owner and concern the owner's right to exclusive jurisdiction over definite physical resources. In fact, it is the very purpose of private property to establish physically separate domains of exclusive jurisdiction in order to avoid possible conflicts concerning the use of scarce resources.[12] No private property owner can possibly surrender his right to ultimate jurisdiction over and physical protection of his property to someone else

---

[11]See Mises, *Liberalism*, p. 37.

[12]The liberal position was summed up nicely by the eighteenth century French physiocrat Mercier de la Rivière, at one time *intendant* of Martinique and for a brief period advisor to Catherine the Great of Russia, in his *L'Ordre Naturel*. By virtue of his reason, he explained, man was capable of recognizing the laws leading to his greatest happiness, and all social ills follow from the disregard of these laws of human nature. In human nature, the right of self-preservation implies the right to property, and any individual property in man's products from the soil requires property in the land itself. But the right to property would be meaningless without the freedom of using it, so liberty is derived from the right to property. People flourish as social animals, and through trade and exchange of property they maximize the happiness of all. See Rothbard, *Economic Thought Before Adam Smith*, p. 370.

unless he sells or otherwise transfers his property (in which case someone else gains exclusive jurisdiction over it). Every property owner may partake of the advantages of the division of labor, however, and seek more or better protection of his property through cooperation with other owners and their property. Every property owner may buy from, sell to, or otherwise contract with anyone else concerning more or better property protection, and every property owner may at any time unilaterally discontinue any such cooperation with others or change his respective affiliations. Thus, in order to meet the demand for protection, it would be rightfully possible and is economically likely that specialized individuals or agencies would arise which would provide protection, insurance, and arbitration services to voluntary clients for a fee.[13]

While it is easy to conceive of the contractual origin of a system of competitive security suppliers, it is inconceivable how private property owners could possibly enter a contract which entitled another agent to compel anyone within a given territory to come to it exclusively for protection and judicial decisionmaking, barring any other agent from offering protection services. Such a monopoly-contract would imply that every private property owner had surrendered his right to ultimate decisionmaking and the protection of his person and property permanently to someone else. In effect, in transferring this right onto someone else, a person would submit himself into permanent slavery. According to liberal doctrine, any such submission-contract is from the outset impermissible (hence null and void), because it contradicts the praxeological foundation of all contracts, i.e., private property and individual self-ownership.[14] No one rightfully can or likely will agree to render his

---

[13]See on this Murray N. Rothbard, *Power and Market: Government and the Economy* (Kansas City: Sheed Andrews and McMeel, 1977), chap. 1.

[14]The contract theory of the state here criticized originated with Thomas Hobbes and his works *De Cive* (chaps. 5–7) and *Leviathan* (chaps. 17–19). Hobbes there claimed that the legal bond between the ruler and the subjects, once it has been tied, is indissoluble. However, notes Cassirer,

> most influential writers on politics in the seventeenth century rejected the conclusions drawn by Hobbes. They charged the great logician with a contradiction in terms. If a man could give up his personality [i.e., his right to self-ownership] he would cease being a moral being. He would become a lifeless thing—and how could such a thing obligate itself—how could it make a promise or enter into a social contract? This fundamental right, the right to personality, includes in a sense all the others. To maintain and to develop his personality is a universal right. It is not subject to the freaks and fancies of single individuals and cannot, therefore, be transferred from one individual to another. The contract of

person and property permanently defenseless against the actions of someone else. Similarly inconceivable is the notion that anyone would endow his monopolistic protector with the permanent right to tax. No one can or will enter a contract that allowed a protector to determine unilaterally, without consent of the protected, the sum that the protected must pay for his protection.

Since Locke, liberals have tried to solve this internal contradiction through the makeshift of "tacit," "implicit" or "conceptual" agreements, contracts, or constitutions. Yet all of these characteristically tortuous and confused attempts have only contributed to one and the same unavoidable conclusion: That it is impossible to derive a justification for government from explicit contracts between private property owners.[15]

> rulership which is the legal basis of all civil powers has, therefore, its inherent limits. There is no *pactum subjectionis*, no act of submission by which man can give up the state of a free agent and enslave himself. For by such an act of renunciation he would give up that very character which constitutes his nature and essence: he would lose his humanity. (*The Myth of the State*, p. 195)

[15]On John Locke's views on "consent" see his *Two Treatises on Government*, Book II, sec. 119–22. Recognizing that government is not based on "express" consent, he writes there,

> the difficulty is, what ought to be looked upon as a tacit consent, and how far it binds—i.e., how far any one shall be looked on to have consented, and thereby submitted to any government, where he has made no expression of it at all. And to this I say, that every man that hath any possession or enjoyment of any part of the dominions of any government doth hereby give his tacit consent, and is as far forth obliged to obedience to the laws of that government, during such enjoyment, as any one under it, whether this his possession be of land to him and his heirs for ever, or a lodging only for a week; or whether it be barely traveling freely on the highway; and, in effect, it reaches as far as the very being of any one within the territories of that government. (sec. 119)

In effect, according to Locke, once a government has come into existence, regardless of whether one has expressly agreed to its rule in the first place or not and no matter what this government does in the following, one has "tacitly" consented to it and whatever it does as long as one continues to live in "its" territory. That is, every government always has the unanimous consent of everyone residing under its jurisdiction, and only emigration—"exit"—counts as a "no" vote and the withdrawal of consent according to Locke (sec. 121).

For a modern, even less convincing (or rather more absurd) attempt along the same lines see James M. Buchanan and Gordon Tullock, *The Calculus of Consent* (Ann Arbor: University of Michigan Press, 1962), and James M. Buchanan, *The Limits of Liberty: Between Anarchy and Leviathan* (Chicago: University of Chicago Press, 1975). As Locke before them, Buchanan and Tullock recognize that no government, anywhere, is based on express consent or explicit contracts. But not to worry, they assure

IV

Liberalism's erroneous acceptance of the institution of government as consistent with the basic liberal principles of self-ownership, original appropriation, property, and contract, consequently led to its own destruction.

First and foremost, it follows from the initial error concerning the moral status of government that the liberal solution to the eternal human problem of security—a constitutionally limited government—is a contradictory, praxeologically impossible ideal. Contrary to the original liberal intent of safeguarding liberty and property, every minimal government has the inherent tendency to become a maximal government.

---

us, for this does not mean that governments do not nonetheless rest on unanimous consent. Even if actual disagreements and real nay-sayers exist, this fact might merely obscure some underlying and more profound agreement and unanimously shared consensus on the level of "constitutional choice" and decisionmaking. However, this underlying deeper agreement on the "rules of the game," we are then told by Buchanan and Tullock, is also not an actual agreement—in fact, no constitution has ever been expressly agreed upon by everyone concerned. Rather, it is what they refer to as a "conceptual" agreement and "conceptual" unanimity. In so twisting a real "no" into a conceptual "yes," Buchanan and Tullock then first come to diagnose the state as a voluntary institution on a par with private business firms:

> The market and the State are both devices through which cooperation is organized and made possible. Men cooperate through exchange of goods and services in organized markets, and such cooperation implies mutual gain. The individual enters into an exchange relation in which he furthers his own interest by providing some product or service that is of direct benefit of the individual on the other side of the transaction. At base, political and collective action under the individualistic view of the State is much the same. Two or more individuals find it mutually advantageous to join forces to accomplish certain common purposes. In a real sense, they "exchange" inputs in the securing of the commonly shared output. (*The Calculus of Consent*, p. 19)

Moreover, by the same token, Buchanan claims to have discovered a justification for the *status quo*, whatever it happens to be. "The institutions of the status quo" always embody and describe an "existing and ongoing implicit social contract." Even

> when an original contract may never have been made, when current members of the community sense no moral or ethical obligation to adhere to the terms that are defined in the status quo, and ... when such a contract ... may have been violated many times over. ... The *status quo* defines that which exists. Hence, regardless of its history, it must be evaluated as if it were legitimate contractually. (Buchanan, *The Limits of Liberty*, pp. 96, 84–85)

Once the principle of government—judicial monopoly and the power to tax—is incorrectly accepted as just, any notion of restraining government power and safeguarding individual liberty and property is illusory. Predictably, under monopolistic auspices the price of justice and protection will continually rise and the quality of justice and protection fall. A tax-funded protection agency is a contradiction in terms, for it is an expropriating property protector that will inevitably lead to more taxes and less protection. Even if, as liberals have proposed, a government limited its activities exclusively to the protection of preexisting private property rights, the further question of *how much* security to produce would arise. Motivated (as everyone is) by self-interest and the disutility of labor but equipped with the unique power to tax, a government agent's goal will invariably be to *maximize expenditures* on protection (and almost all of a nation's wealth can conceivably be consumed by the cost of protection) and at the same time to *minimize the production* of protection. The more money one can spend and the less one must work to produce, the better off one will be.[16]

Moreover, a judicial monopoly will inevitably lead to a steady deterioration in the quality of protection. If no one can appeal for justice except to government, justice will be perverted in favor of the government, constitutions, and supreme courts notwithstanding. Constitutions and supreme courts are government constitutions and agencies, and whatever limitations on government action they might contain or

---

[16]Explains Murray N. Rothbard, *For A New Liberty* (New York: Collier, 1978), pp. 215–16:

> [T]here is a common fallacy, held even by most advocates of laissez-faire, that the government must supply "police protection," as if police protection were a single, absolute entity, a fixed quantity of something which the government supplies to all. . . . In actual fact, there are almost infinite degrees of all sorts of protection. For any given person or business, the police can provide everything from a policeman on the beat who patrols once a night, to two policemen patrolling constantly on each block, to cruising patrol cars, to one or even several round-the-clock personal bodyguards. Furthermore, there are many other decisions the police must make, the complexity of which becomes evident as soon as we look beneath the veil of the myth of absolute "protection." How shall the police allocate their funds which are, of course, always limited as are the funds of all other individuals, organizations, and agencies? How much shall the police invest in electronic equipment? fingerprinting equipment? detectives as against uniformed police? patrol cars as against foot police, etc? . . . The point is that the government has no rational way to make these allocations. The government only knows that it has a limited budget.

find is invariably decided by agents of the very institution under consideration. Predictably, the definition of property and protection will continually be altered and the range of jurisdiction expanded to the government's advantage.[17]

Second, it follows likewise from the error regarding the moral status of government that the traditional liberal preference for and attachment to local (decentralized and territorially small) government is inconsistent and contradictory.[18] Contrary to the original liberal intent, every government, including local government, has an inherent tendency toward centralizing and ultimately becoming a world government.

Once it is incorrectly accepted that in order to protect and enforce peaceful cooperation between two individuals A and B, it is justified and necessary to have a judicial monopolist X, a twofold conclusion follows. If more than one territorial monopolist exists, X, Y, and Z, then, just as there can presumably be no peace among A and B without X, so can there be no peace between the monopolists X, Y, and Z as long as they remain in a "state of anarchy" with each other. Hence, in order to fulfill the liberal *desideratum* of universal and eternal peace, all political centralization and unification, and ultimately the establishment of a single world government, is justified and necessary.[19]

---

[17]Explains Murray N. Rothbard, *For A New Liberty*, p. 48:

> [N]o constitution can interpret or enforce itself; it must be interpreted by *men*. And if the ultimate power to interpret a constitution is given to the government's own Supreme Court, then the inevitable tendency is for the Court to continue to place its imprimatur on ever-broader powers for its own government. Furthermore, the highly touted "checks and balances" and "separations of powers" in the American government are flimsy indeed, since in the final analysis all of these divisions are part of the same government and are governed by the same set of rulers.

[18]On the characteristic liberal preference for decentralized government see Wilhelm Röpke, *Jenseits von Angebot und Nachfrage* (Berne: Paul Haupt, 1979), chap. 5.

[19]Interestingly, while socialists of all stripes—traditional Marxists, social democrats, American "liberals" and neoconservatives—have typically shown little difficulty in accepting the idea of world government and have thus at least been consistent, classical liberals have rarely if ever acknowledged the fact that by the logic of their own doctrine they too are forced to be advocates of a single, unified world government and clung instead, inconsistently, to the idea of decentralized government. Now theoretical consistency is not necessarily a good thing; and if a theory is consistent but false, one might well admit that it may be preferable to be inconsistent. However, an inconsistent theory can never be true, and in not facing up to the inconsistency of their theoretical position liberals have typically neglected to pay attention to and account for two important, and from their own viewpoint "anomalous" phenomena. On the one hand, if law and order requires a single,

Last, it follows from the error of accepting government as just that the ancient idea of the universality of human rights and the unity of law is confused and, under the heading "equality before the law," transformed into a vehicle of egalitarianism. As opposed to the antiegalitarian or even aristocratic sentiment of old liberals,[20] once the idea of universal human rights is combined with government, the result will be egalitarianism and the destruction of human rights.

Once a government has been incorrectly assumed as just and hereditary princes and kings ruled out as incompatible with the idea of universal human rights, the question of how to square government with the idea of the universality and equality of human rights arises. The liberal answer is to open participation and entry into government on equal terms to everyone *via* democracy. Everyone—not just the hereditary class of nobles—is permitted to become a government official and exercise every government function. However, this democratic equality before the law is something entirely different from and incompatible with the idea of *one* universal law, equally applicable to everyone, everywhere, and at all times. In fact, the former objectionable schism and inequality of the higher law of kings versus the subordinate law of ordinary subjects is fully preserved under democracy in the separation of public versus private law and the supremacy of the former over the latter.[21] Under democracy,

---

monopolistic judge and enforcer (government), as they claim, why does the relationship between, say, German and American businessmen appear to be just as peaceful as that between, say, New York and California businessmen, despite the fact that the former live in a "state of anarchy" *vis-à-vis* each other? Isn't this positive proof that it is *not* necessary to have government in order to have peace?! On the other hand, while the relationship between the citizens and firms of different countries is neither more nor less peaceful than that between citizens and firms of one and the same country, it appears to be equally obvious that the relationship of any one *government*, say the U.S., *vis-à-vis* both its own citizens as well as other (foreign) governments and their citizens is anything but peaceful. Indeed, in his well-known book *Death by Government* (New Brunswick, N.J.: Transaction Publishers, 1995), Rudolph Rummel has estimated that in the course of the twentieth century alone, governments have been responsible for the deaths of approximately 170 million people. Isn't this positive proof, then, that the liberal view concerning the "state of anarchy" as conflict-ridden and of "statism" as the *sine qua non* of security and peace is just about the reverse of the truth?

[20]On the aristocratic roots of liberalism see Bertrand de Jouvenel, *On Power: The Natural History of its Growth* (New York: Viking, 1949), chap. 17; Erik von Kuehnelt-Leddihn, *Liberty or Equality* (Front Royal, Va.: Christendom Press, 1993).

[21]On the distinction between private and public law see Bruno Leoni, *Freedom and the Law* (Indianapolis, Ind.: Liberty Fund, 1991); Friedrich A. Hayek, *Law, Legislation, and Liberty* (Chicago: University of Chicago Press, 1973), vol. 1, esp. chap. 6.

everyone is equal insofar as entry into government is open to all on equal terms. In a democracy no *personal* privileges or privileged persons exist. However, *functional* privileges and privileged functions exist. As long as they act in official capacity, public officials are governed and protected by public law and occupy thereby a privileged position *vis-à-vis* persons acting under the mere authority of private law (most fundamentally in being permitted to support their own activities by taxes imposed on private law subjects).[22] Privilege and legal discrimination will not disappear. To the contrary. Rather than being restricted to princes and nobles, privilege, protectionism, and legal discrimination will be available to all and can be exercised by everyone.

Predictably, under democratic conditions the tendency of every monopoly to increase prices and decrease quality will only be stronger and more pronounced. As hereditary monopolist, a king or prince regarded the territory and people under his jurisdiction as his personal property and engaged in the monopolistic exploitation of his "property." Under democracy, monopoly, and monopolistic exploitation do not disappear. Even if everyone is permitted to enter government, this does eliminate the distinction between the rulers and the ruled. Government and the governed are not one and the same person. Instead of a prince who regards the country as his private property, a temporary and interchangeable caretaker is put in monopolistic charge of the country. The caretaker does not own the country, but as long as he is in office he is permitted to use it to his and his protégés' advantage. He owns its current use—*usufruct*

---

[22]The incompatibility of private and public law has been succinctly summarized by Randy E. Barnett, "Fuller, Law, and Anarchism," *The Libertarian Forum* (February 1976), p. 7:

> For example, the State says that citizens may not take from another by force and against his will that which belongs to another. And yet the State through its power to tax "legitimately" does just that. . . . More essentially, the State says that a person may use force upon another only in self-defense, i.e., only as a defense against another who initiated the use of force. To go beyond one's right of self-defense would be to aggress on the rights of others, a violation of one's legal duty. And yet the State by its claimed monopoly forcibly imposes its jurisdiction on persons who may have done nothing wrong. By doing so it aggresses against the rights of its citizens, something which its rules say citizens may not do.

To this one might want to add only two more pertinent observations: The State says to its citizens "do not kidnap or enslave another man." And yet the State itself does precisely this in conscripting its citizens into its army. And the State says to its citizens "do not kill or murder your fellow men." And yet the State does precisely this once it has declared a "state of war" to exist. See also Rothbard, *The Ethics of Liberty*, chaps. 22, and 23.

—but not its capital stock. This will not eliminate exploitation. To the contrary, it will make exploitation less calculating and more likely to be carried out with little or no regard to the capital stock. In other words, exploitation will be shortsighted.[23] Moreover, with free entry into and public participation in government, the perversion of justice will proceed even faster. Instead of protecting preexisting private property rights, democratic government will become a machine for the continual redistribution of preexisting property rights in the name of illusory "social security," until the idea of universal and immutable human rights disappears and is replaced by that of law as positive government-made legislation.

V

In light of this, an answer to the question of the future of liberalism can be sought.

Because of its own fundamental error regarding the moral status of government, liberalism actually contributed to the destruction of everything it had originally set out to preserve and protect: liberty and property. Once the principle of government had been incorrectly accepted, it was only a matter of time until the ultimate triumph of socialism over liberalism. The present neoconservative "End of History" of global U.S. enforced social democracy is the result of two centuries of liberal confusion. Thus, liberalism in its present form has no future. Rather, its future is social democracy, and the future has already arrived (and we know that it does not work).

Once the premise of government is accepted, liberals are left without argument when socialists pursue this premise to its logical end. If monopoly is just, then centralization is just. If taxation is just, then more taxation is also just. And if democratic equality is just, then the expropriation of private property owners is just, too (while private property is not). Indeed, what can a liberal say in favor of *less* taxation and redistribution?

---

[23] As Rothbard notes in this connection, it

is curious that almost all writers parrot the notion that private owners, possessing time preference, must take the "short view," while only government officials can take the "long view" and allocate property to advance the "general welfare." The truth is exactly the reverse. The private individual, secure in his property and in his capital resource, can take the long view, for he wants to maintain the capital value of his resource. It is the government official who must take and run, who must plunder the property while he is still in command. (*Power and Market*, p. 189)

If it is admitted that taxation and monopoly are just, then the liberal has no principle moral case to make.[24] To lower taxes is not a *moral* imperative. Rather, the liberal case is exclusively an economic one. For instance, lower taxes will produce certain long-run economic benefits. However, at least in the short-run and for some people (the current tax recipients) lower taxes also imply economic costs. Without moral argument at his disposal, a liberal is left only with the tool of cost-benefit analysis, but any such analysis must involve an interpersonal comparison of utility, and such a comparison is impossible (scientifically impermissible).[25] Hence, the outcome of cost-benefit analyses is arbitrary, and every proposal justified with reference to them is mere opinion. In this situation, democratic socialists only appear more upfront, consistent, and consequent, while liberals come across as starry-eyed, confused, and unprincipled or even opportunistic. They accept the basic premise of the current order—of democratic government—but then constantly lament its antiliberal outcome.

If liberalism is to have any future, it must repair its fundamental error. Liberals will have to recognize that no government can be contractually justified, that every government is destructive of what they want

---

[24]Thus, writes Murray N. Rothbard,

if it is legitimate for a government to tax, why not tax its subjects to provide other goods and services that may be useful to consumers: why shouldn't the government, for example, build steel plants, provide shoes, dams, postal service, etc.? For each of these goods and services is useful to consumers. If the laissez-fairists object that the government should not build steel plants or shoe factories and provide them to consumers (either free or for sale) because tax-coercion has been employed in constructing these plants, well then the same objection can of course be made to governmental police or judicial service. The government should be acting no more immorally, from a laissez-faire point of view, when providing housing or steel than when providing police protection. Government limited to protection, then, cannot be sustained *even within* the laissez-faire ideal itself, much less from any other consideration. It is true that the laissez-faire ideal could still be employed to prevent such "second degree" coercive activities of government (i.e., coercion *beyond* the initial coercion of taxation) as price control or outlawry of pornography; but the "limits" have now become flimsy indeed, and may be stretched to virtually complete collectivism, in which the government only supplies goods and services, yet supplies all of them. (*The Ethics of Liberty*, p. 182)

[25]See Lionel Robbins, *The Nature and Significance of Economic Science* (New York: New York University Press, 1984); Murray N. Rothbard, "Toward a Reconstruction of Utility and Welfare Economics," in idem, *The Logic of Action One* (Cheltenham, U.K.: Edward Elgar, 1997).

to preserve, and that protection and the production of security can only be rightfully and effectively undertaken by a system of competitive security suppliers. That is, liberalism will have to be transformed into the theory of private property anarchism (or a private law society), as first outlined nearly one-hundred-fifty years ago by Gustave de Molinari and in our own time fully elaborated by Murray Rothbard.[26]

Such a theoretical transformation would have an immediate twofold effect. On the one hand, it would lead to a purification of the contemporary liberal movement. Social democrats in liberal clothes and many high-ranking liberal government functionaries would swiftly disassociate themselves from this new liberal movement. On the other hand, the transformation would lead to the systematic radicalization of the liberal movement. For those members of the movement who still hold on to the classic notion of universal human rights and the idea that self-ownership and private property rights precede all government and legislation, the transition from liberalism to private property anarchism is only a small intellectual step, especially in light of the obvious failure of democratic government to provide the only service that it was ever intended to provide (that of protection). Private property anarchism is simply consistent liberalism; liberalism thought through to its ultimate conclusion, or liberalism restored to its original intent.[27] However, this small theoretical step has momentous practical implications.

---

[26]On Gustave de Molinari see his *The Production of Security* (New York: Center for Libertarian Studies, 1977); David M. Hart, "Gustave de Molinari and the Anti-Statist Liberal Tradition," Parts I, II and III, *Journal of Libertarian Studies* 5, no. 3 (1981), 5, no. 4 (1981), and 6, no. 1 (1982); on Murray N. Rothbard see besides the works cited above also his *Man, Economy, and State*, 2 vols. (Auburn, Ala.: Ludwig von Mises Institute, 1993).

[27]An instructive example for the logical-theoretical affinity of classical liberalism and private property anarchism, i.e., radical libertarianism, is provided by Ludwig von Mises and his influence. Mises's best known students today are Friedrich A. Hayek and Murray N. Rothbard. The former became Mises's student in the 1920s, *before* Mises had fully worked out his own intellectual system, and would essentially become a moderate (right-wing) social democrat. (See on this assessment Hans-Hermann Hoppe, "F.A. Hayek on Government and Social Evolution: A Critique," *Review of Austrian Economics* 7, no. 1 [1994].) Rothbard on the other hand became Mises's student in the 1950s, *after* Mises had worked out his entire system in his *magnum opus Human Action: A Treatise on Economics*, and would become *the* theoretician of anarcho-capitalism. Unshaken, Mises would maintain his original theoretical position as a minimum-state liberal. Yet, while distancing himself equally from Hayek's left-wing and Rothbard's right-wing deviationism, it is clear from Mises's review of Rothbard's first *magnum opus, Man, Economy, and State,* in *The New Individualist Review* 2, no. 3 (Fall 1962) that it was Rothbard to whom he felt a greater theoretical affinity. More importantly, of the following generations of intellectuals

In taking this step, liberals would renounce their allegiance to the present system, denounce democratic government as illegitimate, and reclaim their right to self-protection. Politically, with this step they would return to the very beginnings of liberalism as a revolutionary creed. In denying the validity of all hereditary privileges, classical liberals would be placed in fundamental opposition to all established governments. Characteristically, liberalism's greatest political triumph —the American Revolution—was the outcome of a secessionist war.[28] And in the *Declaration of Independence*, in justifying the actions of the American colonists, Jefferson affirmed that "governments are instituted among men, deriving their just powers from the consent of the governed," to secure the right to "life, liberty, and the pursuit of happiness"; and

> that whenever any form of government becomes destructive of these ends, it is the right of the people to alter or abolish it, and to institute new government, laying its foundation on such principles, and organizing its powers in such form, as to them shall seem most likely to effect their safety and happiness.

Private property anarchists would only reaffirm the classic liberal right "to throw off such government, and to provide new guards for their future security."

Of course, by itself the renewed radicalism of the liberal movement would be of little consequence (although as the American Revolution teaches, radicalism may well be popular). Instead, it is the inspiring vision of a fundamental alternative to the present system which flows from this new radicalism that will finally break the social democratic machine. Rather than supranational political integration, world-government, constitutions, courts, banks, and money, global social democracy, and universal and ubiquitous multiculturalism, anarchist-liberals propose the decomposition of the nation state into its constituent heterogeneous parts. As their classic forebearers, new liberals do not seek to takeover any government. They ignore government. They only want to

---

up to the present, few of those who fully absorbed the work of Mises *and* Hayek *and* Rothbard have remained true to the "original" Mises, and fewer still have become Hayekians, while the overwhelming majority has come to adopt Rothbard's revisions of the Misesian system as the logically consequent fulfillment of Mises's own original theoretical intent. See also note 30 below.

[28]On the radical liberal-libertarian ideological sources of the American revolution see Bernard Bailyn, *The Ideological Origins of the American Revolution* (Cambridge, Mass.: Harvard University Press, 1967); Murray N. Rothbard, *Conceived in Liberty*, 4 vols. (New Rochelle, N.Y.: Arlington House, 1975–79).

be left alone by government, and secede from its jurisdiction to organize their own protection. Unlike their predecessors who merely sought to replace a larger government with a smaller one, however, new liberals pursue the logic of secession to its end. They propose unlimited secession, i.e., the unrestricted proliferation of independent free territories, until the state's range of jurisdiction finally withers away.[29] To this end—and in complete contrast to the statist projects of "European Integration" and a "New World Order"—they promote the vision of a world of tens of thousands of free countries, regions, and cantons, of hundreds of thousands of independent free cities—such as the present-day oddities of Monaco, Andorra, San Marino, Liechtenstein, (formerly) Hong Kong, and Singapore—and even more numerous free districts and neighborhoods, economically integrated through free trade (the smaller the territory, the greater the economic pressure of opting for free trade!) and an international gold-commodity money standard.

If and when this alternative liberal vision gains prominence in public opinion, the end of the social democratic "End of History" will give rise to a liberal renaissance.

---

[29]Interestingly, just as Jefferson and the American *Declaration of Independence* consider secession from a government's jurisdiction a basic human right, so Ludwig von Mises, the twentieth-century's foremost champion of liberalism, has been an outspoken proponent of the right to secede as implied in the most fundamental human right to self-determination. Thus he writes:

> The right of self-determination in regard to the question of membership in a state thus means: whenever the inhabitants of a particular territory, whether it be a single village, a whole district, or a series of adjacent districts, make it known, by a freely conducted plebiscite, that they no longer wish to remain united to a state . . . their wishes are to be respected and complied with. This is the only feasible and effective way of preventing revolutions and civil and international wars. . . . If it were in any way possible to grant this right of self-determination to every individual, it would have to be done. (Mises, *Liberalism*, pp. 109–10)

Essentially, with this statement Mises has already crossed the line separating classical liberalism and Rothbard's private property anarchism; for a government allowing unlimited secession is of course no longer a compulsory monopolist of law and order but a voluntary association. Thus notes Rothbard with regard to Mises' pronouncement, "[o]nce admit *any* right of secession whatever, and there is no logical stopping-point short of the right of *individual* secession, which logically entails anarchism, since then individuals may secede and patronize their own defense agencies, and the State has crumbled" (*The Ethics of Liberty*, p. 182); see also idem, *Power and Market*, pp. 4–5, and idem, "The Laissez-Faire Radical: A Quest for the Historical Mises," *Journal of Libertarian Studies* 5, no. 3 (1981).

12

On Government and the Private Production of Defense

It is the right of the people to alter or abolish it, and to institute new government, laying its foundation on such principles, and organizing its powers in such form, as to them shall seem most likely to effect their safety and happiness.
(Declaration of Independence)

I

Among the most popular and consequential beliefs of our age is the belief in collective security. Nothing less significant than the legitimacy of the modern state rests on this belief.

I will demonstrate that the idea of collective security is a myth that provides no justification for the modern state, and that all security is and must be private. First off, I will present a two-step reconstruction of the myth of collective security, and at each step raise a few theoretical concerns.

The myth of collective security can also be called the Hobbesian myth. Thomas Hobbes, and countless political philosophers and economists after him, argued that in the state of nature, men would constantly be at each others' throats. *Homo homini lupus est.* Put in modern jargon, in the state of nature a permanent 'underproduction' of security would prevail. Each individual, left to his own devices and provisions, would spend "too little" on his own defense, resulting in permanent interpersonal warfare. The solution to this presumably intolerable situation, according to Hobbes and his followers, is the establishment of a state. In order to institute peaceful cooperation among themselves, two individuals, A and B, require a third independent party, S, as ultimate judge and peacemaker. However, this third party, S, is not just another individual, and the good provided by S, that of of security, is not just another "private" good. Rather, S is a *sovereign* and has as such two unique powers. On the one hand, S can insist that his *subjects*, A and B, not seek protection from anyone but him; that is, S is a compulsory territorial monopolist of protection. On the other hand, S can determine unilaterally how much A and B must spend on their own security; that is, S has the power to impose taxes in order to provide security "collectively."

There is little use in quarreling over whether man is as bad and wolf-like as Hobbes supposes or not, except to note that Hobbes's thesis obviously cannot mean that man is driven only and exclusively by aggressive instincts. If this were the case, mankind would have died out long ago. The fact that he did not demonstrates that man also possesses reason and is capable of constraining his natural impulses. The quarrel is only with the Hobbesian solution. *Given* man's nature as a *rational* animal, is the proposed solution to the problem of insecurity an *improvement*? Can the institution of a state reduce aggressive behavior and promote peaceful cooperation, and thus provide for better private security and protection? The difficulties with Hobbes's argument are obvious. For one, regardless of how bad men are, S—whether king, dictator, or elected president—is still one of them. Man's nature is not transformed upon becoming S. Yet how can there be better protection for A and B, if S must *tax* them in order to provide it? Is there not a contradiction within the very construction of S as an expropriating property protector? In fact, is this not exactly what is also—and more appropriately—referred to as a *protection racket*? To be sure, S will make peace between A and B but only so that he himself can rob both of them more profitably. Surely S is better protected, but the more he is protected, the less A and B are protected from attacks by S. Collective security, it would seem, is not better private security. Rather, it is the private security of the state, S, achieved through the expropriation, i.e., the economic disarmament, of its subjects. Further, statists from Thomas Hobbes to James Buchanan have argued that a protective state S would come about as the result of some sort of "constitutional" contract.[1] Yet who in his right mind would agree to a contract that allowed one's protector to determine unilaterally—and irrevocably—the sum that the protected must pay for his protection? The *fact* is no one ever has![2]

---

[1]James M. Buchanan and Gordon Tullock, *The Calculus of Consent* (Ann Arbor: University of Michigan Press, 1962); James M. Buchanan, *The Limits of Liberty* (Chicago: University of Chicago Press, 1975); for a critique see Murray N. Rothbard, "Buchanan and Tullock's *Calculus of Consent*," in idem, *The Logic of Action Two* (Cheltenham, U.K.: Edward Elgar, 1995); idem, "The Myth of Neutral Taxation," ibid.; Hans-Hermann Hoppe, *The Economics and Ethics of Private Property* (Boston: Kluwer, 1993), chap. 1.

[2]See on this in particular Lysander Spooner, *No Treason: The Constitution of No Authority* (Larkspur, Colo.: Pine Tree Press, 1966).

Let me interrupt my discussion and return to the reconstruction of the Hobbesian myth. Once it is assumed that in order to institute peaceful cooperation between A and B it is necessary to have a state S, a two-fold conclusion follows. If more than one state exists, S1, S2, S3, then, just as there can presumably be no peace among A and B without S, so can there be no peace between the states S1, S2, and S3 as long as they remain in a state of nature (i.e., a state of anarchy) with regard to each other. Consequently, in order to achieve *universal* peace, political centralization, unification, and ultimately the establishment of a single world government, are necessary.

It is useful to indicate what can be taken as noncontroversial. To begin with, the argument is correct, as far as it goes. If the premise is correct, then the consequence spelled out does follow. As well, the empirical assumptions involved in the Hobbesian account appear at first glance to be borne out by the facts. It is true that states are constantly at war with each other, and a historical tendency toward political centralization and global rule does indeed appear to be occurring. Quarrels arise only with the explanation of this fact and tendency, and the classification of a single unified world state as an improvement in the provision of private security and protection. There appears to be an empirical anomaly for which the Hobbesian argument cannot account. The reason for the warring among different states S1, S2, and S3, according to Hobbes, is that they are in a state of anarchy *vis-à-vis* each other. However, before the arrival of a single world state not only are S1, S2, and S3 in a state of anarchy relative to each other but in fact every subject of one state is in a state of anarchy *vis-à-vis* every subject of any other state. Accordingly, just as much war and aggression should exist between the private citizens of various states as between different states. Empirically, however, this is not so. The private dealings between foreigners appear to be significantly less war-like than the dealings between different governments. Nor does this seem to be surprising. After all, a state agent S, in contrast to everyone of its subjects, can rely on domestic taxation in the conduct of his "foreign affairs." Given his natural human aggressiveness, is it not obvious that S will be more brazen and aggressive in his conduct toward foreigners if he can externalize the cost of such behavior onto others? Surely, I would be willing to take greater risks and engage in more provocation and aggression if I could make others pay for it. And surely there would be a tendency of one state—one protection racket—to want to expand its territorial protection monopoly at the expense of other states and thus bring about world government as the ultimate result of interstate competition.[3] But how is this an improvement in the provision of private security and protection? The opposite seems to be the case. The world state is the winner of all wars and the last surviving protection racket. Doesn't this make it particularly dangerous? Will not the physical power of any single world government be overwhelming as compared to that of any one of its individual subjects?

II

Let me pause in my abstract theoretical considerations to take a brief look at the empirical evidence bearing on the issue at hand. As noted at the outset, the myth of collective security is as widespread as it is consequential. I am not aware of any survey on this matter, but I would venture to predict that the Hobbesian myth is accepted more or less unquestioningly by well over 90 percent of the adult population; that a state is indispensable for protection and defense. However, to believe something does not make it true. Rather, if what one believes is false, one's actions will lead to failure. What about the evidence? Does it support Hobbes and his followers, or does it confirm the opposite anarchist fears and contentions?

The U.S. was explicitly founded as a "protective" state *à la* Hobbes. Let me quote to this effect from Jefferson's *Declaration of Independence*:

> We hold these truths to be self-evident: that all men are created equal; that they are endowed by their Creator with inalienable rights; that among these are life, liberty, and the pursuit of happiness: that to secure these rights, governments are instituted among men, deriving their just powers from the consent of the governed.

Here we have it: The U.S. government was instituted to fulfill one and only one task: the protection of life and property. Thus, it should provide the perfect example for judging the validity of the Hobbesian claim as to the status of states as protectors. After more than two centuries of protective statism, what is the status of our protection and peaceful human cooperation? Was the American experiment in protective statism a success?

According to the pronouncements of our state rulers and their intellectual bodyguards (of whom there are more than ever before), we are better protected and more secure than ever. We are supposedly protected from global warming and cooling, from the extinction of animals and plants, from the abuses of husbands and wives, parents and

---

[3]See Hans-Hermann Hoppe, "The Trouble with Classical Liberalism," *Rothbard–Rockwell Report* 9, no. 4 (1998).

employers, from poverty, disease, disaster, ignorance, prejudice, racism, sexism, homophobia, and countless other public enemies and dangers. In fact, however, matters are strikingly different. In order to provide us with all this 'protection,' the state managers expropriate more than 40 percent of the incomes of private producers year in and year out. Government debt and liabilities have increased uninterruptedly, thus increasing the need for future expropriations. Owing to the substitution of government paper money for gold, financial insecurity has increased sharply, and we are continually robbed through currency depreciation. Every detail of private life, property, trade, and contract is regulated by ever higher mountains of laws (legislation), thereby creating permanent legal uncertainty and moral hazard. In particular, we have been gradually stripped of the right to exclusion implied in the very concept of private property. As sellers we cannot sell to and as buyers we cannot buy from whomever we wish. And as members of associations we are not permitted to enter into whatever restrictive covenant we believe to be mutually beneficial. As Americans, we must accept immigrants we do not want as our neighbors. As teachers, we cannot get rid of ill-behaved students. As employers, we are stuck with incompetent or destructive employees. As landlords, we are forced to cope with bad tenants. As bankers and insurers, we are not allowed to avoid bad risks. As restaurant or bar owners, we must accommodate unwelcome customers. And as members of private associations, we are compelled to accept individuals and actions in violation of our own rules and restrictions. In short, the more the state has increased its expenditures on 'social' security and 'public' safety, the more our private property rights have been eroded, the more our property has been expropriated, confiscated, destroyed, or depreciated, and the more we have been deprived of the very foundation of all protection: economic independence, financial strength, and personal wealth.[4] The path of every president and practically every member of Congress is littered with hundreds of thousands of nameless victims of personal economic ruin, financial bankruptcy, emergency, impoverishment, despair, hardship, and frustration.

The picture appears even bleaker when we consider foreign affairs. Seldom during its entire history has the continental U.S. been territorially attacked by any foreign army. (Pearl Harbor was the result of a preceding U.S. provocation.) Yet the U.S. has the distinction of having had a government that declared war against a large part of its own popu-

---

[4]See Hans-Hermann Hoppe, "Where the Right Goes Wrong," *Rothbard–Rockwell Report* 8, no. 4 (1997).

lation and engaged in the wanton murder of hundreds of thousands of its own citizens. Moreover, while the relations between American citizens and foreigners do not appear to be unusually contentious, almost from its very beginnings the U.S. government relentlessly pursued aggressive expansionism. Beginning with the Spanish–American war, reaching a peak in World War I and World War II, and continuing to the present, the U.S. government has become entangled in hundreds of foreign conflicts and risen to the rank of the world's dominant imperialist power. Thus, nearly every president since the turn of this century has also been responsible for the murder, killing, or starvation of countless innocent foreigners all over the world. In short, while we have become more helpless, impoverished, threatened and insecure, the U.S. government has become ever more brazen and aggressive. In the name of "national" security, it "defends" us, equipped with enormous stockpiles of weapons of aggression and mass destruction, by bullying ever new "Hitlers," big or small, and all suspected Hitlerite sympathizers anywhere and everywhere outside of the territory of the U.S.[5]

The empirical evidence thus seems clear. The belief in a protective state appears to be a patent error, and the American experiment in protective statism a complete failure. The U.S. government does not protect us. To the contrary, there exists no greater danger to our life, property, and prosperity than the U.S. government, and the U.S. president in particular is the world's single most threatening and armed danger, capable of ruining everyone who opposes him and destroying the entire globe.

III

Statists react much like socialists when faced with the dismal economic performance of the Soviet Union and its satellites. They do not necessarily deny the disappointing facts, but they try to argue them away by claiming that these facts are the result of a systematic discrepancy (deviancy) between "real" and "ideal" or "true" statism (respectively

---

[5]See *The Costs of War: America's Pyrrhic Victories*, John V. Denson, ed. (New Brunswick, N.J.: Transaction Publishers, 1997); idem, "A Century of War: Studies in Classical Liberalism" (Auburn, Ala.: Ludwig von Mises Institute, 1999). Since the end of World War II, for instance, the United States government has intervened militarily in China (1945–46), Korea (1950–53), China (1950–53), Iran (1953), Guatemala (1954), Indonesia (1958), Cuba (1959-60), Guatemala (1960), Congo (1964), Peru (1965), Laos (1964–73), Vietnam (1961–73), Cambodia (1969–70), Guatemala (1967–69), Grenada (1983), Lebanon (1983), Libya (1986), El Salvador (1980s), Nicaragua (1980s) Panama (1989), Iraq (1991–99), Bosnia (1995), Sudan (1998), Afghanistan (1998), and Yugoslavia (1999). Moreover, the United States government has troops stationed in nearly one-hundred-fifty countries around the world.

socialism). To this day, socialists claim that "true" socialism has not been refuted by the empirical evidence, and that everything would have turned out well and unparalleled prosperity would have resulted if only Trotsky's, or Bukharin's, or better still their very own brand of socialism, rather than Stalin's, had been implemented. Similarly, statists interpret all seemingly contradictory evidence as only accidental. If only some other president had come to power at this or that turn in history or if only this or that constitutional change or amendment had been adopted, everything would have turned out beautifully, and unparalleled security and peace would have resulted. Indeed, this may still happen in the future, if their own policies are employed.

We have learned from Ludwig von Mises how to respond to the socialists' evasion (immunization) strategy.[6] As long as the defining characteristic—the essence—of socialism, i.e., the absence of the private ownership of factors of production, remains in place, no reform will be of any help. The idea of a socialist *economy* is a *contradiction in terms*, and the claim that socialism represents a 'higher,' more efficient mode of social production is absurd. In order to reach one's own ends efficiently and without waste within the framework of an exchange economy based on division of labor, it is necessary that one engage in monetary calculation (cost-accounting). Everywhere outside the system of a primitive self-sufficient single household economy, monetary calculation is the sole tool of rational and efficient action. Only by comparing inputs and outputs arithmetically in terms of a common medium of exchange (money) can a person determine whether his actions are successful or not. In distinct contrast, socialism means to have *no* economy, no economizing, at all, because under these conditions monetary calculation and cost-accounting is impossible by definition. If no private property in factors of production exists, then no prices for any production factor exists, hence, it is impossible to determine whether or not they are employed economically. Accordingly, socialism is not a higher mode of production but rather economic chaos and regression to primitivism.

How to respond to the statists' evasion strategy has been explained by Murray N. Rothbard.[7] But Rothbard's lesson, while equally simple and clear and of even more momentous implications, has remained to

---

[6]Ludwig von Mises, *Socialism: An Economic and Sociological Analysis* (Indianapolis, Ind.: Liberty Classics, 1981); Hans-Hermann Hoppe, *A Theory of Socialism and Capitalism* (Boston: Kluwer, 1989), chap. 6.

[7]Murray N. Rothbard, *The Ethics of Liberty* (New York: New York University Press, 1998), esp. chaps. 22 and 23.

this day far less known and appreciated. So long as the defining characteristic—the essence—of a state remains in place, he explained, no reform, whether of personnel or constitutional, will be to any avail. *Given the principle of government—judicial monopoly and the power to tax—any notion of limiting its power and safeguarding individual life and property is illusory.* Under monopolistic auspices the price of justice and protection must rise and its quality must fall. A tax-funded protection agency is a contradiction in terms and will lead to ever more taxes and less protection. Even if a government limited its activities exclusively to the protection of preexisting property rights (as every "protective" state is supposed to do), the further question of *how much* security to provide would arise. Motivated (like everyone else) by self-interest and the disutility of labor but with the unique power to tax, a government's answer will invariably be the same: to *maximize expenditures* on protection—and almost all of a nations' wealth can conceivably be consumed by the cost of protection—and at the same time to *minimize* the *production* of protection. Furthermore, a judicial monopoly must lead to a deterioration in the quality of justice and protection. If one can only appeal to government for justice and protection, justice and protection will be perverted in favor of government, constitutions and supreme courts notwithstanding. After all, constitutions and supreme courts are *state* constitutions and courts, and whatever limitations to government action they might contain is determined by agents of the very institution under consideration. Accordingly, the definition of property and protection will continually be altered and the range of jurisdiction expanded to the government's advantage.

Hence, Rothbard pointed out, it follows that just as socialism cannot be reformed but must be abolished in order to achieve prosperity, so can the institution of the state not be reformed but must be abolished in order to achieve justice and protection. "Defense in the free society (including such defense services to person and property as police protection and judicial findings)," Rothbard concluded,

> would therefore have to be supplied by people or firms who (a) gained their revenue voluntarily rather than by coercion and (b) did not—as the State does—arrogate to themselves a compulsory monopoly of police or judicial protection. . . . defense firms would have to be as freely competitive and as noncoercive against noninvaders as are all other suppliers of goods and services on the free market. Defense services, like all other services, would be marketable and marketable only.[8]

---

[8]Murray N. Rothbard, *Power and Market* (Kansas City: Sheed Andrews and McMeel, 1977), p. 2.

That is, every private property owner would be able to partake of the advantages of the division of labor and seek better protection of his property than that afforded through self-defense by cooperation with other owners and their property. Anyone could buy from, sell to, or otherwise contract with anyone else concerning protective and judicial services, and one could at any time unilaterally discontinue any such cooperation with others and fall back on self-reliant defense or change one's protective affiliations.

IV

Having reconstructed the myth of collective security—the myth of the state—and criticized it on theoretical and empirical grounds, I now must take on the task of constructing the positive case for private security and protection. In order to dispel the myth of collective security, it is not just sufficient to grasp the *error* involved in the idea of a protective state. It is just as important, if not more so, to gain a clear understanding of how the nonstatist security alternative would effectively work. Rothbard, building on the pathbreaking analysis of the French–Belgian economist Gustave de Molinari,[9] has given us a sketch of the workings of a free-market system of protection and defense.[10] As well, we are in debt to Morris and Linda Tannehill for their brilliant insights and analyses in this regard.[11] Following their lead, I will proceed with my analysis and provide a more comprehensive view of the alternative—nonstatist—system of security production and its ability to handle attacks, not just by individuals or gangs but in particular also by states.

Widespread agreement exists among liberal-libertarians such as Molinari, Rothbard, and the Tannehills as well as most other commentators on the matter that defense is a form of insurance, and defense expenditures represent a sort of insurance premium (price). Accordingly, as Rothbard and the Tannehills in particular would emphasize, within the framework of a complex modern economy based on worldwide division of labor, the most likely candidates to offer protection and defense services are insurance agencies. The better the protection of insured property, the lower are the damage claims and hence an insurer's costs. Thus, to provide efficient protection appears to be in every insurer's own

---

[9]Gustave de Molinari, *The Production of Security* (New York: Center for Libertarian Studies, 1977).

[10]Rothbard, *Power and Market*, chap. 1; idem, *For A New Liberty* (New York: Collier, 1978), chaps. 12 and 14.

[11]Morris Tannehill and Linda Tannehill, *The Market for Liberty* (New York: Laissez Faire Books, 1984), esp. part 2.

financial interest. Indeed, although restricted and hampered by the state, even now insurance agencies provide wideranging services of protection and indemnification (compensation) to injured private parties. Insurance companies fulfill a second essential requirement. Obviously, anyone offering protection services must appear able to deliver on his promises in order to find clients. That is, he must possess the economic means—the manpower as well as the physical resources—necessary to accomplish the task of dealing with the dangers, actual or imagined, of the real world. On this count insurance agencies appear to be perfect candidates, too. They operate on a nationwide and even international scale, and they own large property holdings dispersed over wide territories and beyond single state boundaries. Accordingly, they have a manifest self-interest in effective protection, and are 'big' and economically powerful. Furthermore, all insurance companies are connected through a network of contractual agreements of mutual assistance and arbitration as well as a system of international reinsurance agencies, representing a combined economic power which dwarfs that of most existing governments.

Let me further analyze and systematically clarify this suggestion: that protection and defense are 'insurance' and can be provided by insurance agencies. To reach this goal, two issues must be addressed. First off, it is not possible to insure oneself against every risk of life. I cannot insure myself against committing suicide, for instance, or against burning down my own house, becoming unemployed, not feeling like getting out of bed in the morning, or not suffering entrepreneurial losses, because in each case I have full or partial control over the likelihood of the respective outcome. Risks such as these must be assumed individually. No one but I can possibly deal with them. Hence, the first question must be what makes protection and defense an insurable rather than an uninsurable risk? After all, as we have just seen, this is not self-evident. In fact, does not everyone have considerable control over the likelihood of an attack on and invasion of his person and property? Do I not deliberately bring about an attack by assaulting or provoking someone else, for instance, and is not protection then an uninsurable risk, like suicide or unemployment, for which each person must assume sole responsibility?

The answer is a qualified yes and no. Yes, insofar as no one can possibly offer *un*conditional protection, i.e., insurance against any invasion whatsoever. That is, unconditional protection can only be provided, if at all, by each individual on his own and for himself. But the answer is no, insofar as *conditional* protection is concerned. Only attacks and invasions that are provoked by the victim cannot be insured. Unprovoked and thus 'accidental' attacks can be insured against, however.[12] That is, protection becomes an insurable good only if and insofar as an insurance agent contractually restricts the actions of the insured so as to exclude every possible 'provocation' on their part. Various insurance companies may differ with respect to the specific definition of provocation, but there can be no difference between insurers with regard to the principle that everyone must systematically exclude (prohibit) all provocative and aggressive action among its own clients.

As elementary as this first insight into the essentially defensive—nonaggressive and nonprovocative—nature of protection-insurance may seem, it is of fundamental importance. For one, it implies that any known aggressor and provocateur would be unable to find an insurer, and hence, would be economically isolated, weak and vulnerable. On the other hand, it implies that anyone wanting more protection than that afforded by self-reliant self-defense could do so only if and insofar as he submitted himself to specified norms of nonaggressive, civilized conduct. Further, the greater the number of insured people—and in a modern exchange economy most people want more than just self-defense for their protection—the greater would be the economic pressure on the remaining uninsured to adopt the same or similar standards of nonaggressive social conduct. Moreover, as the result of competition between insurers for voluntarily paying clients, a tendency toward falling prices per insured property values would come about.

At the same time, a system of competing insurers would have a twofold impact on the development of law and thus contribute further to reduce conflict. On the one hand, the system would allow for systematically *increased variability and flexibility of law*. Rather than imposing a uniform set of standards onto everyone (as under statist conditions), insurance agencies could and would compete against each other not just *via* price but in particular also through product differentiation and development. Insurers could and would differ and distinguish themselves

---

[12]On the "logic" of insurance see Ludwig von Mises, *Human Action: A Treatise on Economics* (Chicago: Regnery, 1966), chap. 6; Murray N. Rothbard, *Man, Economy, and State*, 2 vols. (Auburn, Ala.: Ludwig von Mises Institute, 1993), pp. 498ff.; Hans-Hermann Hoppe, "On Certainty and Uncertainty, Or: How Rational Can Our Expectations Be?" *Review of Austrian Economics* 10, no. 1 (1997); also Richard von Mises, *Probability, Statistics and Truth* (New York: Dover, 1957); Frank H. Knight, *Risk, Uncertainty, and Profit* (Chicago: University of Chicago Press, 1971).

with respect to the behavioral code imposed on and expected of their clients, with respect to rules of evidence and procedure, and/or with respect to the sort and assignment of awards and punishments. There could and would exist side by side, for instance, Catholic insurers applying Canon law, Jewish insurers applying Mosaic law, Muslims applying Islamic law, and Non-believers applying Secular law of one variant or another, all of them sustained by and vying for a voluntarily paying clientele. Consumers could and would choose, and sometimes change, the law applied to them and their property. That is, no one would be forced to live under "foreign" law; and hence, a prominent source of conflict would be eliminated.

On the other hand, a system of insurers offering competing law codes would promote a tendency toward the *unification of law*. The "domestic"—Catholic, Jewish, Roman, Germanic, etc.—law would apply and be binding only on the persons and properties of the insured, the insurer, and all others insured by the same insurer under the same law. Canon law, for instance, would apply only to professed Catholics and deal solely with intra-Catholic conflict and conflict resolution. Yet it would also be possible for a Catholic to interact, come into conflict with, and wish to be protected from the subscribers of other law codes, e.g., a Muslim. From this no difficulty would arise so long as Catholic and Islamic law reached the same or a similar conclusion regarding the case and contenders at hand. But if competing law codes arrive at distinctly different conclusions (as they would in at least *some* cases by virtue of the fact that they represent *different* law codes) a problem would arise. The insured would want to be protected against the contingency of intergroup conflict, too, but "domestic" (intragroup) law would be of no avail in this regard. In fact, at a minimum two distinct "domestic" law codes would be involved, and they would come to different conclusions. In such a situation it could not be expected that one insurer and the subscribers of his law code, say the Catholics, would simply subordinate their judgment to that of another insurer and his law, say that of the Muslims, or *vice versa*. Rather, each insurer—Catholic and Muslim alike—would have to contribute to the development of intergroup law, i.e., law applicable in cases of disagreement among competing insurers and law codes. And because the intergroup law provisions that an insurer offered to its clients could appear credible to them, and hence a *good*, only if and insofar as the same provisions were also accepted by other insurers (and the more of them, the better), competition would promote the development and refinement of a body of law that incorporated the widest—intergroup, cross-cultural, etc.—legal-moral consensus and agreement and thus represented the greatest common denominator among various competing law codes.[13]

More specifically, because competing insurers and law codes could and would disagree regarding the merit of at least *some* of the cases brought jointly before them, every insurer would be compelled to submit itself and its clients in these cases from the outset to arbitration by an independent third party. This third party would not just be independent of the two disagreeing parties, however. It would at the same time be the *unanimous choice* of both parties. And as objects of unanimous choice, arbitrators then would represent or even personify "consensus" and "agreeability." They would be agreed upon because of their commonly perceived ability of finding and formulating mutually agreeable, i.e., "fair," solutions in cases of intergroup disagreement. Moreover, if an arbitrator failed in this task and arrived at conclusions that were perceived as "unfair" or "biased" by either one of the insurers and/or their clients, this person would not likely be chosen again as an arbitrator in the future.

Consequently, protection and security *contracts* would come into existence as the first fundamental result of competition between insurers for a voluntarily paying clientele. Insurers (unlike states) would offer their clients contracts with well-specified property and product descriptions and clearly defined and delineated duties and obligations. Likewise, the relationship between insurers and arbitrators would be defined and governed by contract. Each party to a contract, for the duration or until fulfillment of the contract, would be bound by its terms and conditions; and every change in the terms or conditions of a contract would require the unanimous consent of all parties concerned. That is, under competition (unlike under statist conditions), no "legislation" would or could exist. No insurer could get away (as a state can) with "promising" its clients "protection" without letting them know how or at what price, and insisting that it could, if it so desired, unilaterally change the terms and conditions of the protector–client relationship. Insurance-clients would demand something significantly "better," and insurers would comply and supply *contracts* and constant *law*, instead of *promises* and shifting and changing *legislation*. Furthermore, as a result of the continual cooperation of various insurers and arbitrators a tendency toward the unification of property and contract law and the

---

[13]See on this Hans-Hermann Hoppe, *Eigentum, Anarchie und Staat* (Opladen: Westdeutscher Verlag, 1987), pp. 122–26.

harmonization of the rules of procedure, evidence and conflict resolution (including such questions as liability, tort, compensation, and punishment) would be set in motion. On account of buying protection-insurance, everyone would become tied into a global competitive enterprise of striving to reduce conflict and enhance security. Moreover, every single conflict and damage claim, regardless where and by or against whom, would fall into the jurisdiction of one or more specific insurance agencies and would be handled either by an individual insurer's "domestic" law or by the "international" law provisions and procedures agreed upon in advance by a group of insurers, thus assuring (*ex ante*) complete and perfect legal stability and certainty.

V

Now a second question must be addressed. Even if the status of defensive protection as an insurable good is granted, distinctly different forms of insurance exist. Let us consider just two characteristic examples: insurance against natural disasters, such as earthquakes, floods, hurricanes, and insurance against industrial accidents or disasters, such as malfunctions, explosions, and defective products. The former can serve as an example of group or mutual insurance. Some territories are more prone to natural disasters than others; accordingly, the demand for and price of insurance will be higher in some areas than others. However, every location *within* certain territorial borders is regarded by the insurer as homogeneous with respect to the risk concerned. The insurer presumably knows the frequency and extent of the event in question for the region as a whole, but he knows nothing about the particular risk of any specific location within the territory. In this case, every insured person will pay the same premium per insured value, and the premiums collected in one time period will presumably be sufficient to cover all damage claims during the same time period (otherwise the insurance industry will incur losses). Thus, the particular individual risks are pooled and insured mutually.

In contrast, industrial insurance can serve as an example of individual insurance. Unlike natural disasters, the insured risk is the outcome of human action, i.e., of production efforts. Every production process is under the control of an individual producer. No producer *intends* to fail or experience a disaster, and as we have seen only accidental—non-intended—disasters are insurable. Yet even if production is largely controlled and generally successful, every producer and production technology is subject to occasional mishaps and accidents beyond his control—a margin of error. However, since it is the outcome (intended or not) of individual production efforts and production techniques, this risk of industrial accidents is essentially different from one producer and production process to another. Accordingly, the risk of different producers and production technologies cannot be pooled, and every producer must be insured individually. In this case, the insurer will have to know the frequency of the questionable event over time, but he cannot know the likelihood of the event at any specific point in time, except that at all times the same producer and production technology are in operation. There is no presumption that the premiums collected during any given period will be sufficient to cover all damage claims arising during that period. Rather, the profit-making presumption is that all premiums collected over many time periods will be sufficient to cover all claims during the same multi-period time span. Consequently, in this case an insurer must hold capital reserves in order to fulfill its contractual obligation, and in calculating his premiums he must take the present value of these reserves into account.

The second question is what kind of insurance can protect against aggression and invasion by other actors? Can it be provided as group insurance, as for natural disasters, or must it be offered in the form of individual insurance, as in the case of industrial accidents?

Note that both forms of insurance represent only the two possible extremes of a continuum, and that the position of any particular risk on this continuum is not definitively fixed. Owing to scientific and technological advances in metereology, geology, or engineering, for instance, risks that were formerly regarded as homogeneous (allowing for mutual insurance) can become more and more dehomogenized. Noteworthy is this tendency in the field of medical and health insurance. With the advances of genetics and genetic engineering—genetic fingerprinting—medical and health risks previously regarded as homogeneous (unspecific) with respect to large numbers of people have become increasingly more specific and heterogeneous.

With this in mind, can anything specific be said about protection insurance in particular? I would think so. After all, while all insurance requires that the risk be accidental from the standpoint of the insurer and the insured, the accident of an aggressive invasion is distinctly different from that of natural or industrial disasters. Whereas natural disasters and industrial accidents are the outcome of natural forces and the operation of laws of nature, aggression is the outcome of human actions; and whereas nature is 'blind' and does not discriminate between individuals, whether at the same point in time or over time, an aggressor can discriminate and deliberately target specific victims and choose the timing of his attack.

VI

Let me first contrast defense-protection insurance with that against natural disasters. Frequently an analogy between the two is drawn, and it is instructive to examine if or to what extent it holds. The analogy is that just as every individual within certain geographical regions is threatened by the same risk of earthquakes, floods, or hurricanes, so does every inhabitant within the territory of the U.S. or Germany, for instance, face the same risk of being victimized by a foreign attack. Some superficial similarity—to which I shall come shortly—notwithstanding, it is easy to recognize two fundamental shortcomings in the analogy. For one, the borders of earthquake, flood, or hurricane regions are established according to objective physical criteria and hence can be referred to as 'natural.' In distinct contrast, political boundaries are 'artificial' boundaries. The borders of the U.S. changed throughout the entire nineteenth century, and Germany did not exist as such until 1871 and was composed of thirty-eight separate countries. Surely, no one would want to claim that this redrawing of the U.S. or German borders was the outcome of the discovery that the security risk of every American or German within the greater U.S. or Germany was, contrary to the previously held opposite belief, homogeneous (identical).

There is a second obvious shortcoming. Nature—earthquakes, floods, hurricanes—is blind in its destruction. It does not discriminate between more and less valuable locations and objects but 'attacks' indiscriminately. In distinct contrast, an aggressor–invader can and does discriminate. He does not attack or invade worthless locations and things, like the Sahara desert, but targets locations and things that are valuable. Other things being equal, the more valuable a location and an object, the more likely it will be the target of an invasion.

This raises the next crucial question. If political borders are arbitrary and attacks are never indiscriminate but directed specifically toward valuable places and things, are there any nonarbitrary borders separating different security-risk (attack) zones? The answer is yes. Such nonarbitrary borders are those of private property. Private property is the result of the appropriation and/or production of particular physical objects or effects by specific individuals at specific locations. Every appropriator–producer (owner) demonstrates with his actions that he regards the appropriated and produced things as valuable (goods), otherwise he would not have appropriated or produced them. The borders of everyone's property are objective and intersubjectively ascertainable. They are simply determined by the extension and dimension of the things appropriated and/or produced by any one particular individual. And the borders of all valuable places and things are coextensive with the borders of all property. At any given point in time, every valuable place and thing is owned by someone; only worthless places and things are owned by no one.

Surrounded by other men every appropriator and producer can also become the object of an attack or invasion. Every property—in contrast to things (matter)—is necessarily valuable; hence, every property owner becomes a possible target of other men's aggressive desires. Consequently every owner's choice of the location and form of his property will, among countless other considerations, also be influenced by security concerns. Other things equal, everyone will prefer safer locations and forms of property to locations and forms which are less safe. Yet regardless of where an owner and his property are located and whatever the property's physical form, every owner, by virtue of not abandoning his property even in view of potential aggression, demonstrates his personal willingness to protect and defend these possessions.

However, if the borders of private property are the only nonarbitrary borders standing in systematic relation to the risk of aggression, then it follows that as many different security zones as there are separately owned property holdings exist, and that these zones are no larger than the extension of these holdings. That is, even more so than in the case of industrial accidents, the insurance of property against aggression would seem to be an example of individual rather than group (mutual) protection

Whereas the accident-risk of an individual production process is typically independent of its location—such that if the process were replicated by the same producer at different locations his margin of error would remain the same—the risk of aggression against private property—the production plant—is different from one location to another. By its very nature as privately appropriated and produced goods, property is always separate and distinct. Every property is located at a different place and under the control of a different individual, and each location faces a unique security risk. It can make a difference for my security, for instance, if I reside in the countryside or the city, on a hill or in a valley, or near or far from a river, ocean, harbor, railroad, or street. In fact, even contiguous locations do not face the same risk. It can make a difference, for instance, if I reside higher or lower on the mountain than my neighbor, upstream or downstream, closer or more distant from the ocean, or simply north, south, west, or east of him. Moreover, every property, wherever it is located, can be shaped and transformed by its owner so as to increase its safety and reduce the likelihood of aggression. I may acquire a gun or safe-deposit box, for instance, or I may be able to shoot down an attacking plane from my backyard or own a laser gun that can kill an aggressor thousands of miles away. Thus, no location and no property are like any other. Every owner will have to be insured individually, and to do so every aggression-insurer must hold sufficient capital reserves.

VII

The analogy typically drawn between insurance against natural disasters and external aggression is fundamentally flawed. As aggression is never indiscriminate but selective and targeted, so is defense. Everyone has different locations and things to defend, and no one's security risk is the same as anyone else's, yet the analogy contains a kernel of truth. However, any similarity between natural disasters and external aggression is due *not* to the nature of aggression and defense but to the rather specific nature of *state*-aggression and defense (interstate warfare). As explained above, a state is an agency that exercises a compulsory territorial monopoly of protection and the power to tax, and any such agency will be comparatively more aggressive because it can externalize the costs of such behavior onto its subjects. However, the existence of a state does not just increase the frequency of aggression; it changes its entire character. The existence of states—and especially of democratic states—implies that aggression and defense—war—will tend to be transformed into total—undiscriminating—war.[14]

Consider for a moment a completely stateless world. While most property owners would be individually insured by large, often multinational insurance companies endowed with huge capital reserves, as bad risks most if not all aggressors would be without any insurance

---

[14]On the relationship between state and war, and on the historical transformation from limited (monarchical) to total (democratic) war, see Ekkehard Krippendorff, *Staat und Krieg* (Frankfurt/M.: Suhrkamp, 1985); Charles Tilly, "War Making and State Making as Organized Crime," in *Bringing the State Back In*, Peter B. Evans, Dietrich Rueschemeyer, Theda Skocpol, eds. (Cambridge: Cambridge University Press, 1985); John F. C. Fuller, *The Conduct of War* (New York: Da Capo Press, 1992); Michael Howard, *War in European History* (New York: Oxford University Press, 1976); Hans-Hermann Hoppe, "Time Preference, Government, and the Process of Decivilization," in *The Costs of War*, John V. Denson, ed. (New Brunswick, N.J.: Transaction Publishers, 1997); also this volume, pp. 1–44. Erik von Kuehnelt-Leddihn, *Leftism Revisited* (Washington, D.C.: Regnery, 1990).

whatever. In this situation, every aggressor or group of aggressors would want to limit their targets, preferably to uninsured property, and avoid all "collateral damage," as they would otherwise find themselves confronted with one or many economically powerful professional defense agencies. Likewise, all defensive violence would be highly selective and targeted. All aggressors would be specific individuals or groups, located at specific places and equipped with specific resources. In response to attacks on their clients, insurance agencies would specifically target these locations and resources for retaliation, and they would avoid any collateral damage as they would otherwise become entangled with and liable to other insurers.

All of this changes fundamentally in a statist world with interstate warfare. If one state, the U.S., attacks another, for instance Iraq, this is not just an attack by a limited number of people, equipped with limited resources and located at a clearly identifiable place. Rather, it is an attack by all Americans and with all of their resources. Every American supposedly pays taxes to the U.S. government and is thus *de facto*, whether he wishes to be or not, implicated in every government aggression. Hence, while it is obviously false to claim that every American faces an equal risk of being attacked by Iraq (low or nonexistent as such a risk is, it is certainly higher in New York City than in Wichita, Kansas, for instance) every American is rendered equal with respect to his own active, if not always voluntary, participation in each of his government's aggressions.

Second, just as the attacker is a state, so is the attacked, Iraq. As its U.S. counterpart, the Iraqi government has the power to tax its population or draft it into its armed forces. As taxpayer or draftee, every Iraqi is implicated in his government's defense just as every American is drawn into the U.S. government's attack. Thus, the war becomes a war of all Americans against all Iraqis, i.e., total war. The strategy of both the attacker and the defender state will be changed accordingly. While the attacker still must be selective regarding the targets of his attack, if for no other reason than that even taxing agencies (states) are ultimately constrained by scarcity, the aggressor has little or no incentive to avoid or minimize collateral damage. To the contrary, since the entire population and national wealth is involved in the defensive effort, collateral damage, whether of lives or property, is even desirable. No clear distinction between combatants and noncombatants exists. Everyone is an enemy, and all property provides support for the attacked government. Hence, everyone and everything becomes fair game. Likewise, the defender state will be little concerned about collateral damage resulting from its own retaliation against the attacker. Every citizen of the attacker state and all of their property is a foe and enemy property and thus becomes a possible target of retaliation. Moreover, every state, in accordance with this character of interstate war, will develop and employ more weapons of mass destruction, such as atomic bombs, rather than long range precision weapons, such as one might imagine, laser gun.

Thus, the similarity between war and natural catastrophes their seemingly indiscriminate destruction and devastation—is exclusively a feature of a statist world.

VIII

This brings on the last problem. We have seen that just as all property is private, so is and must all defense be insured individually by capitalized insurance agencies, very much like industrial accident insurance. We have also seen that both forms of insurance differ in one fundamental respect. In the case of defense insurance, the location of the insured property matters. The premium per insured value will be different at different locations. Furthermore, aggressors can move around, their arsenal of weapons may change, and the entire character of aggression can alter with the presence of states. Thus, even given an initial property location, the price per insured value can alter with changes in the social environment or surroundings of this location. How would a system of competitive insurance agencies respond to this challenge? In particular, how would it deal with the existence of states and state aggression?

In answering these questions it is essential to recall some elementary economic insights. Other things being equal, private property owners generally and business owners in particular prefer locations with low protection costs (insurance premiums) and rising property values to those with high protection costs and falling property values. Consequently, there is a tendency toward the migration of people and goods from high risk and falling property value areas into low risk and increasing property value areas. Furthermore, protection costs and property values are directly related. Other things being equal, higher protection costs (greater attack risks) imply lower or falling property values, and lower protection costs imply higher or increasing property values. These laws and tendencies shape the operation of a competitive system of insurance-protection agencies.

Whereas a tax-funded monopolist will manifest a tendency to raise the cost and price of protection, private profit-loss insurance agencies strive to reduce the cost of protection and thus bring about falling prices. At the same time insurance agencies are more interested than anyone else in rising property values because this implies not only that their own property holdings appreciate but that there will also be more of other people's property for them to insure. In contrast, if the risk of aggression increases and property values fall, there is less value to be insured while the cost of protection and price of insurance rises, implying poor business conditions for an insurer. Consequently, insurance companies would be under permanent economic pressure to promote the former favorable and avert the latter unfavorable condition.

This incentive structure has a fundamental impact on the operation of insurers. First, as for the seemingly easier case of the protection against common crime and criminals, a system of competitive insurers would lead to a dramatic change in current crime policy. To recognize the extent of this change, it is instructive to look first at the present and familiar statist crime policy. While it is in the interest of state agents to combat common private crime (if only so that there is more property left for them to tax), as tax-funded agents they have little or no interest in being particularly effective at the task of preventing it, or if it has occurred, at compensating its victims and apprehending and punishing the offenders. Moreover, under democratic conditions, insult will be added to injury, for if everyone—aggressors as well as nonaggressors and residents of high crime locations as well as those of low crime locations—can vote and be elected to government office, a systematic redistribution of property rights from nonaggressors to aggressors and the residents of low crime areas to those of high crime areas comes into effect and crime will actually be promoted. Accordingly, crime and the demand for private security services of all kinds are currently at an all-time high. Even more scandalously, instead of compensating the victims of crimes it did not prevent (as it should have), the government forces victims to pay again as taxpayers for the cost of the apprehension, imprisonment, rehabilitation and/or entertainment of their aggressors. And rather than requiring higher protection prices in high crime locations and lower ones in low crime locations, as insurers would, the government does the exact opposite. It taxes more in low crime and high property value areas than in high crime and low property value ones, or it even subsidizes the residents of the latter locations—the slums—at the expense of those of the former, eroding the social conditions unfavorable to crime while promoting those favorable to it.[15]

---

[15]On crime and punishment, past and present, see Terry Anderson and P.J. Hill, "The American Experiment in Anarcho-Capitalism: The *Not* So Wild, Wild West," *Journal of Libertarian Studies* 3, no. 1 (1979); Bruce L. Benson, "Guns for Protection, and Other Private Sector Responses to the Government's Failure to

The operation of competitive insurers would present a striking contrast. For one, if an insurer could not prevent a crime, it would have to indemnify the victim. Thus, above all insurers would want to be effective in crime prevention. If they still could not prevent it, they would want to be efficient in the detection, apprehension, and punishment of criminal offenders, because in finding and arresting an offender, the insurer could force the criminal—rather than the victim and its insurer—to pay for the damages and cost of indemnification.

More specifically, just as insurance companies currently maintain and continually update a detailed local inventory of property values, so would they maintain and continually update a detailed local inventory of crimes and criminals. Other things being equal, the risk of aggression against any private property location increases with the proximity and the number and resources of potential aggressors. Thus, insurers would be interested in gathering information on actual crimes and known criminals and their locations, and it would be in their mutual interest of minimizing property damage to share this information with each other (just as banks now share information on bad credit risks with each other). Furthermore, insurers would also be particularly interested in gathering information on potential (not yet committed and known) crimes and aggressors, and this would lead to a fundamental overhaul of and improvement in current—statist—crime statistics. In order to predict the future incidence of crime and thus calculate its current price (premium), insurers would correlate the frequency, description, and character of crimes and criminals with the social surroundings in which they occur and operate. And always under competitive pressure, they would develop and continually refine an elaborate system of demographic and sociological crime indicators.[16] That is, every neighborhood would be described, and its risk assessed, in terms of a multitude of crime indicators, such as the composition of its inhabitants' sexes, age groups, races,

---

Control Crime," *Journal of Libertarian Studies* 8, no. 1 (1986); Roger D. McGrath, *Gunfighters, Highwaymen and Vigilantes: Violence on the Frontier* (Berkeley: University of California Press, 1984); James Q. Wilson and Richard J. Herrnstein, *Crime and Human Nature* (New York: Simon and Schuster, 1985); Edward C. Banfield, *The Unheavenly City Revisited* (Boston: Little, Brown, 1974).

[16]For an overview of the extent to which official—statist—statistics, in particular on crime, deliberately ignores, misrepresents or distorts the known facts for reasons of so-called public policy (political correctness) see J. Philippe Rushton, *Race, Evolution, and Behavior* (New Brunswick, N.J.: Transaction Publishers, 1995); Michael Levin, *Why Race Matters* (Westport, Conn.: Praeger, 1997).

nationalities, ethnicities, religions, languages, professions, and incomes.

Consequently, and in distinct contrast to the present situation, all interlocal, regional, racial, national, ethnic, religious, and linguistic income and wealth redistribution would disappear, and a constant source of social conflict would be removed permanently. Instead, the emerging price (premium) structure would tend to accurately reflect the risk of each location and its particular social surrounding such that one would only be asked to pay for the insurance risk of himself and of that associated with his particular neighborhood. More importantly, based on its continually updated and refined system of statistics on crime and property values and further motivated by the noted migration tendency from high-risk-low-value (henceforth "bad") to low-risk-high-value (henceforth "good") locations, a system of competitive aggression insurers would promote a tendency toward civilizational progress (rather than decivilization).

Governments—and democratic governments in particular—erode "good" and promote "bad" neighborhoods through their tax and transfer policy. They do so also, and with possibly an even more damaging effect, through their policy of forced integration. This policy has two aspects. On the one hand, for the owners and residents in "good" locations and neighborhoods who are faced with an immigration problem, forced integration means that they must accept, without discrimination, every domestic immigrant, as transient or tourist on public roads, as customer, client, resident, or neighbor. They are prohibited by their government from excluding anyone, including anyone they consider an undesirable potential risk, from immigration. On the other hand, for the owners and residents in "bad" locations and neighborhoods (who experience emigration rather than immigration), forced integration means that they are prevented from effective self-protection. Rather than being allowed to rid themselves of crime through the expulsion of known criminals from their neighborhood, they are forced by their government to live in permanent association with their aggressors.[17]

The results of a system of private protection insurers would be in striking contrast to these only all too familiar decivilizing effects and tendencies of statist crime protection. To be sure, insurers would be unable to eliminate the differences between "good" and "bad" neighborhoods. In fact, these differences might even become more

---

[17]See Hans-Hermann Hoppe, "Free Immigration or Forced Integration?" *Chronicles* (July 1995).

pronounced.However,drivenbytheirinterestin rising property values and falling protection costs, insurers would promote a tendency to improve by uplifting and cultivating both "good" *and* "bad" neighborhoods. Thus, in "good" neighborhoods insurers would adopt a policy of selective immigration. Unlike states, they could and would not want to disregard the discriminating inclinations among the insured toward immigrants. To the contrary, even more so than any one of their clients, insurers would be interested in discrimination, i.e., in admitting only those immigrants whose presence adds to a lower crime risk and increased property values and in excluding those whose presence leads to a higher risk and lower property values. That is, rather than eliminating discrimination, insurers would rationalize and perfect its practice. Based on their statistics on crime and property values, and in order to reduce the cost of protection and raise property values, insurers would formulate and continually refine various restrictive (exclusionary) rules and procedures relating to immigration and immigrants and thus give quantitative precision—in the form of prices and price differences—to the value of discrimination (and the cost of nondiscrimination) between potential immigrants (as high or low risk and value-productive).

Similarly, in "bad" neighborhoods the interests of the insurers and the insured would coincide. Insurers would not want to suppress the expulsionist inclinations among the insured toward known criminals. They would rationalize such tendencies by offering selective price cuts (contingent on specific clean-up operations). Indeed, in cooperation with one another, insurers would want to expel known criminals not just from their immediate neighborhood but from civilization altogether, into the wilderness or open frontier of the Amazon jungle, the Sahara, or the polar regions.

IX

What about defense against a state? How would insurers protect us from state aggression?

First off, it is essential to remember that governments as compulsory, tax-funded monopolies are inherently wasteful and inefficient in whatever they do. This is also true for weapons technology and production, and military intelligence and strategy, especially in our age of high technology. Accordingly, states would not be able to compete within the same territory against voluntarily financed insurance agencies. Moreover, most important and general among the restrictive rules relating to immigration and designed by insurers to lower protection cost and increase property values would be a rule concerning government agents.

States are inherently aggressive and pose a permanent danger to every insurer and insured. Thus, insurers in particular would want to exclude or severely restrict—as a potential security risk—the immigration (territorial entry) of all known government agents, and they would induce the insured, either as a condition of insurance or of a lower premium, to exclude or strictly limit any direct contact with any known government agent, be it as visitor, customer, client, resident, or neighbor. That is, wherever insurance companies operated (in all free territories) state agents would be treated as undesirable outcasts, potentially more dangerous than any common criminal. Accordingly, states and their personnel would be able to operate and reside only in territorial separation from, and on the fringes of, free territories. Furthermore, owing to the comparatively lower economic productivity of statist territories, governments would be continually weakened by the emigration of their most value-productive residents.

Now, what if such a government should decide to attack or invade a free territory? This would be easier said than done. Who and what would it attack? There would be no state opponent. Only private property owners and their private insurance agencies would exist. No one, least of all the insurers, would have presumably engaged in aggression or even provocation. If there were any aggression or provocation against the state at all, this would be the action of a particular person, and in this case the interest of the state and insurance agencies would fully coincide. Both would want to see the attacker punished and held accountable for all damages. But without any aggressor–enemy, how could the state justify an attack not to mention an indiscriminate attack? And surely it would have to justify it, for the power of every government, even the most despotic one, ultimately rests on opinion and consent, as La Boétie, Hume, Mises, and Rothbard have explained.[18] Kings and presidents can issue an order to attack, of course, but there must be scores of men willing to execute their order to put it into effect. There must be generals receiving and following the order, soldiers willing to march, kill, and be killed, and domestic producers willing to continue producing to fund the war. If this consensual willingness were absent because the orders of the state rulers were considered illegitimate, even

---

[18]Etienne de la Boétie, *The Politics of Obedience: The Discourse of Voluntary Servitude* (New York: Free Life Editions, 1975); David Hume, "The First Principles of Government," in idem, *Essays. Moral, Political and Literary* (Oxford: Oxford University Press, 1971); Ludwig von Mises, *Liberalism: In the Classical Tradition* (San Francisco: Cobden Press, 1985); Murray N. Rothbard, *Egalitarianism as a Revolt Against Nature and Other Essays* (Auburn, Ala.: Ludwig von Mises Institute, [1974] 2000).

the seemingly most powerful government would be rendered ineffectual and collapse, as the recent examples of the Shah of Iran and the Soviet Union have illustrated. Hence, from the viewpoint of the leaders of the state an attack on free territories would be considered extremely risky. No propaganda effort, however elaborate, would make the public believe that its attack was anything but an aggression against innocent victims. In this situation, the rulers of the state would be happy to maintain monopolistic control over their present territory rather than run the risk of losing legitimacy and all of their power in an attempt at territorial expansion.

As unlikely as this may be, what if a state still attacked and/or invaded a neighboring free territory? In this case the aggressor would not encounter an unarmed population. Only in statist territories is the civilian population characteristically unarmed. States everywhere aim to disarm their own citizenry so as to be better able to tax and expropriate it. In contrast, insurers in free territories would not want to disarm the insured. Nor could they. For who would want to be protected by someone who required him as a first step to give up his ultimate means of self-defense? To the contrary, insurance agencies would encourage the ownership of weapons among their insured by means of selective price cuts.

In addition to the opposition of an armed private citizenry, the aggressor state would run into the resistance of not only one but in all likelihood several insurance and reinsurance agencies. In the case of a successful attack and invasion, these insurers would be faced with massive indemnification payments. Unlike the aggressing state, however, these insurers would be efficient and competitive firms. Other things being equal, the risk of an attack—and hence the price of defense insurance—would be higher in locations in close proximity to state territories than in places far away from any state. To justify this higher price, insurers would have to demonstrate defensive readiness *vis-à-vis* any possible state aggression to their clients in the form of intelligence services, the ownership of suitable weapons and materials, and military personnel and training. In other words, the insurers would be effectively equipped and trained for the contingency of a state attack and ready to respond with a two-fold defense strategy. On the one hand, insofar as their operations in free territories are concerned insurers would be ready to expel, capture, or kill every invader while trying to avoid or minimize all collateral damage. On the other hand, insofar as their operations on state territory are concerned insurers would be prepared to target the aggressor (the state) for retaliation. That is, insurers would be ready to counterattack and kill, whether with long-range precision weapons or assassination commandos, state agents from the top of the government hierarchy of king, president, or prime minister on downward while seeking to avoid or minimize all collateral damage to the property of innocent civilians (nonstate agents). They would thereby encourage internal resistance against the aggressor government, promote its delegitimization, and possibly incite the liberation and transformation of the state territory into a free country.

X

I have come full circle with my argument. First, I have shown that the idea of a protective state and state protection of private property is based on a fundamental theoretical error and that this error has had disastrous consequences: the destruction and insecurity of all private property and perpetual war. Second, I have shown that the correct answer to the question of who is to defend private property owners from aggression is the same as for the production of every other good or service: private property owners, cooperation based on the division of labor, and market competition. Third, I have explained how a system of private profit-loss insurers would effectively minimize aggression, whether by private criminals or states, and promote a tendency toward civilization and perpetual peace. The only task outstanding is to implement these insights: to withdraw one's consent and willing cooperation from the state and to promote its delegitimization in public opinion so as to persuade others to do the same. Without the erroneous public perception and judgment of the state as just and necessary and without the public's voluntary cooperation, even the seemingly most powerful government would implode and its powers evaporate. Thus liberated, we would regain our right to self-defense and be able to turn to freed and unregulated insurance agencies for efficient professional assistance in all matters of protection and conflict resolution.

13

On the Impossibility of Limited Government and the Prospect for Revolution

In a recent survey, people of different nationalities were asked how proud they were to be American, German, French, etc., and whether or not they believed that the world would be a better place if other countries were just like their own. The countries ranking highest in terms of national pride were the United States and Austria. As interesting as it would be to consider the case of Austria, here I shall concentrate on the U.S. and the question whether and to what extent the American claim can be justified.

In the following, I will identify three main sources of American national pride. I will argue that the first two are justified sources of pride, while the third actually represents a fateful error. Finally, I will go on to explain how this error might be repaired.

I

The first source of national pride is the memory of America's not-so-distant colonial past as a country of pioneers.

In fact, the English settlers coming to North America were the last example of the glorious achievements of what Adam Smith referred to as "a system of natural liberty": the ability of men to create a free and prosperous commonwealth from scratch. Contrary to the Hobbesian account of human nature—*homo homini lupus est*—the English settlers demonstrated not just the viability but also the vibrancy and attractiveness of a stateless, anarcho-capitalist social order. They demonstrated how, in accordance with the views of John Locke, private property originated naturally through a person's original appropriation—his purposeful use and transformation—of previously unused land (wilderness). Furthermore, they demonstrated that, based on the recognition of private property, division of labor, and contractual exchange, men were capable of protecting themselves effectively against antisocial aggressors: first and foremost by means of self-defense (less crime existed then than exists now), and as society grew increasingly prosperous and complex, by means of specialization, i.e., by institutions and agencies such as property registries, notaries, lawyers, judges, courts, juries, sheriffs, mutual defense associations, and popular militias.[1] Moreover, the American colonists demonstrated the fundamental sociological importance of the institution of covenants: of associations of linguistically, ethnically, religiously, and culturally homogeneous settlers led by and subject to the internal jurisdiction of a popular leader–founder to ensure peaceful human cooperation and maintain law and order.[2]

II

The second source of national pride is the American Revolution.

In Europe there had been no open frontiers for centuries and the intra-European colonization experience lay in the distant past. With the growth of the population, societies had assumed an increasingly hierarchical structure: of free men (freeholders) and servants, lords and vassals, overlords, and kings. While distinctly more stratified and aristocratic than colonial America, the so-called feudal societies of medieval Europe were also typically stateless social orders. A state, in accordance with

---

[1]On the influence of Locke and Lockean political philosophy on America see Edmund S. Morgan, *The Birth of the Republic: 1763–89* (Chicago: University of Chicago Press, 1992), pp. 73–74:

> When Locke described his state of nature, he could explain it most vividly by saying that "in the beginning all the World was America." And indeed many Americans had had the actual experience of applying labor to wild land and turning it into their own. Some had even participated in social compacts, setting up new governments in wilderness areas where none had previously existed. (p. 74)

On crime, protection, and defense in particular see Terry Anderson and P.J. Hill, "The American Experiment in Anarcho-Capitalism: The *Not* So Wild, Wild West," *Journal of Libertarian Studies* 3, no. 1 (1979); Roger D. McGrath, *Gunfighters, Highwaymen, and Vigilantes: Violence on the Frontier* (Berkeley: University of California Press, 1984).

[2]Contrary to currently popular multicultural myths, America was decidedly *not* a cultural "melting pot." Rather, the settlement of the North American continent confirmed the elementary sociological insight that all human societies are the outgrowth of families and kinship systems and hence, are characterized by a high degree of internal homogeneity, i.e., that 'likes' typically associate with 'likes' and distance and separate themselves from 'unlikes.' Thus, for instance, in accordance with this general tendency, Puritans preferably settled in New England, Dutch Calvinists in New York, Quakers in Pennsylvania and the southern parts of New Jersey, Catholics in Maryland, and Anglicans as well as French Huguenots in the Southern

generally accepted terminology, is defined as a compulsory territorial monopolist of law and order (an ultimate decisionmaker). Feudal lords and kings did not typically fulfill the requirements of a state: they could only "tax" with the consent of the taxed, and on his own land every free man was as much a sovereign (ultimate decisionmaker) as the feudal king was on his.[3] However, in the course of many centuries these originally stateless societies had gradually transformed into absolute—statist—monarchies. While they had initially been acknowledged voluntarily as protectors and judges, European kings had at long last succeeded in establishing themselves as hereditary heads of state. Resisted by the aristocracy but helped along by the "common people," they had become absolute monarchs with the power to tax without consent and to make ultimate decisions regarding the property of free men.

These European developments had a twofold effect on America. On the one hand, England was also ruled by an absolute king, at least until 1688, and when the English settlers arrived on the new continent, the

---

colonies. See further on this David Hackett Fisher, *Albion's Seed: Four British Folkways in America* (New York: Oxford University Press, 1989).

[3]See Fritz Kern, *Kingship and Law in the Middle Ages* (Oxford: Blackwell, 1948); Bertrand de Jouvenel, *Sovereignty: An Inquiry into the Political Good* (Chicago: University of Chicago Press, 1957), esp. chap. 10; idem, *On Power: The Natural History of its Growth* (New York: Viking, 1949); Robert Nisbet, *Community and Power* (New York: Oxford University Press, 1962).

"Feudalism," Nisbet sums up elsewhere (*Prejudices: A Philosophical Dictionary* [Cambridge, Mass.: Harvard University Press, 1982], pp. 125–31),

> has been a word of invective, of vehement abuse and vituperation, for the past two centuries. . . . [especially] by intellectuals in spiritual service to the modern, absolute state, whether monarchical, republican, or democratic. [In fact,] feudalism is an extension and adaptation of the kinship tie with a protective affiliation with the war band or knighthood. . . . Contrary to the modern political state with its principle of territorial sovereignty, for most of a thousand-year period in the West protection, rights, welfare, authority, and devotion inhered in a personal, not a territorial, tie. To be the "man" of another man, in turn the "man" of still another man, and so on up to the very top of the feudal pyramid, each owing the other either service or protection, is to be in a feudal relationship. The feudal bond has much in it of the relation between warrior and commander, but it has even more of the relation between son and father, kinsman and patriarch. . . . [That is, feudal ties are essentially] private, personal, and contractual relationships. . . . The subordination of king to law was one of the most important of principles under feudalism.

See also notes 8, 9, and 10 below.

king's rule was extended to America. Unlike the settlers' founding of private property and their private—voluntary and cooperative—production of security and administration of justice, however, the establishment of the royal colonies and administrations was not the result of original appropriation (homesteading) and contract—in fact, no English king had ever set foot on the American continent—but of usurpation (declaration) and imposition.

On the other hand, the settlers brought something else with them from Europe. There, the development from feudalism to royal absolutism had not only been resisted by the aristocracy but it was also opposed theoretically with recourse to the theory of natural rights as it originated within Scholastic philosophy. According to this doctrine, government was supposed to be contractual, and every government agent, including the king, was subject to the same universal rights and laws as everyone else. While this may have been the case in earlier times, it was certainly no longer true for modern absolute kings. Absolute kings were usurpers of human rights and thus illegitimate. Hence, insurrection was not only permitted but became a duty sanctioned by natural law.[4]

The American colonists were familiar with the doctrine of natural rights. In fact, in light of their own personal experience with the achievements and effects of natural liberty and as religious dissenters who had left their mother country in disagreement with the king and the Church of England, they were particularly receptive to this doctrine.[5]

Steeped in the doctrine of natural rights, encouraged by the distance of the English king, and stimulated further by the puritanical censure of royal idleness, luxury and pomp, the American colonists rose up to free themselves of British rule. As Thomas Jefferson wrote in the Declaration of Independence, government was instituted to protect life, liberty, and the pursuit of happiness. It drew its legitimacy from the consent of the governed. In contrast, the royal British government claimed that it could tax the colonists without their consent. If a government failed to do what it was designed to do, Jefferson declared, "it is the right of the people to alter or abolish it, and to institute new government, laying its foundation on

---

[4]See Lord Acton, "The History of Freedom in Christianity," in idem, *Essays in the History of Liberty* (Indianapolis, Ind.: Liberty Classics, 1985), esp. p. 36.

[5]On the liberal-libertarian ideological heritage of the American settlers see Murray N. Rothbard, *For A New Liberty* (New York: Collier, 1978), chap. 1; idem, *Conceived in Liberty*, 4 vols. (Auburn, Ala.: Ludwig von Mises Institute, 1999); Bernard Bailyn, *The Ideological Origins of the American Revolution* (Cambridge, Mass.: Harvard University Press, 1967).

such principles, and organizing its powers in such form, as to them shall seem most likely to effect their safety and happiness."

III

But what was the next step once independence from Britain had been won? This question leads to the third source of national pride—the American Constitution—and the explanation as to why this constitution, rather than being a legitimate source of pride, represents a fateful error.

Thanks to the great advances in economic and political theory since the late 1700s, in particular at the hands of Ludwig von Mises and Murray N. Rothbard, we are now able to give a precise answer to this question. According to Mises and Rothbard, once there is no longer free entry into the business of the production of protection and adjudication, the price of protection and justice will rise and their quality will fall. Rather than being a protector and judge, a compulsory monopolist will become a protection racketeer: the destroyer and invader of the people and property that he is supposed to protect, a warmonger, and an imperialist.[6] Indeed, the inflated price of protection and the perversion of the ancient law by the English king, both of which had led the American colonists to revolt, were the inevitable result of compulsory monopoly. Having successfully seceded and thrown out the British occupiers, it would only have been necessary for the American colonists to let the existing homegrown institutions of self-defense and private (voluntary and cooperative)

---

[6]This fundamental insight was first clearly stated by the French–Belgian economist Gustave de Molinari in an article published in 1849 (*The Production of Security* [New York: Center for Libertarian Studies, 1977]). De Molinari reasoned:

That in all cases, for all commodities that serve to provide for the tangible or intangible needs of the consumer, it is in the consumer's best interest that labor and trade remain free, because freedom of labor and trade have as their necessary and permanent result the maximum reduction of price.... Whence it follows: That no government should have the right to prevent another government from going into competition with it, or to require consumers of security to come exclusively to it for this commodity. (p. 3) If, on the contrary, the consumer is not free to buy security wherever he pleases, you forthwith see open up a large profession dedicated to arbitrariness and bad management. Justice becomes slow and costly, the police vexatious, individual liberty is no longer respected, the price of security is abusively inflated and inequitably apportioned, according to the power and influence of this or that class of consumers. (pp. 13–14)

protection and adjudication by specialized agents and agencies take care of law and order.

This did not happen, however. The Americans not only did not let the inherited royal institutions of colonies and colonial governments wither away into oblivion; they reconstituted them within the old political borders in the form of independent states, each equipped with its own coercive (unilateral) taxing and legislative powers.[7] While this would have been bad enough, the new Americans made matters worse by adopting the American Constitution and replacing a loose confederation of independent states with the central (federal) government of the United States.

This Constitution provided for the substitution of a popularly elected parliament and president for an unelected king, but it changed nothing regarding their power to tax and legislate. To the contrary, while the English king's power to tax without consent had only been assumed rather than explicitly granted and was thus in dispute,[8] the Constitution explicitly granted this very power to Congress. Furthermore, while kings, in theory even absolute kings, had not been considered the makers but only the interpreters and executors of preexisting and immutable law, i.e., as judges rather than legislators,[9] the Constitution explicitly

---

[7]Furthermore, in accordance with their original royal charter the newly independent states of Georgia, the Carolinas, Virginia, Connecticut, and Massachusetts, for instance, claimed the Pacific Ocean as their western boundary; and based on such obviously unfounded, usurped ownership claims, they—and subsequently as their 'legal heir' the Continental Congress and the United States—proceeded to sell western territories to private homesteaders and developers in order to pay off their debt and/or fund current government operations.

[8]See Bruno Leoni, *Freedom and the Law* (Indianapolis, Ind.: Liberty Classics, 1991), p. 118. Leoni here notes that several scholarly commentators on the Magna Carta, for instance, have pointed out that

> an early medieval version of the principle "no taxation without representation" was intended as "no taxation without the consent of the individual taxed," and we are told that in 1221, the Bishop of Winchester, "summoned to consent to a scutage tax, refused to pay, after the council had made the grant, on the ground that he dissented, and the Exchequer upheld his plea."

[9]See Kern, *Kingship and Law in the Middle Ages,* who writes that

> there is, in the Middle Ages, no such thing as the "first application of a legal rule." Law is old; new law is a contradiction in terms; for either new law is derived explicitly or implicitly from the old, or it conflicts with the old, in which case it is not lawful. The fundamental idea remains the same; the old law is the true law, and the true law is the old law. According to medieval ideas, therefore, the enactment of new law is not

vested Congress with the power of legislating, and the president and the Supreme Court with the power of executing and interpreting such legislated law.[10]

In effect, what the American Constitution did was only this: Instead of a king who regarded colonial America as his private property and the colonists as his tenants, the Constitution put temporary and interchangeable caretakers in charge of the country's monopoly of justice and protection. These caretakers did not own the country, but as long as they were in office, they could make use of it and its residents to their

---

possible at all; and all legislation and legal reform is conceived of as the restoration of the good old law which has been violated. (p. 151)

Similar views concerning the permanency of law and the impermissibility of legislation were still held by the eighteenth-century French physiocrats such as, for instance, Mercier de la Rivière, author of a book on *L'Ordre Naturel* and one time governor of Martinique. Called upon for advice on how to govern by the Russian Czarina Catherine the Great, de la Riviere is reported to have replied that law must be based

on one [thing] alone, Madame, the nature of things and man. . . . To give or make laws, Madame, is a task which God has left to no one. Ah! What is man, to think of himself capable of dictating laws to beings whom he knows not? The science of government is to study and recognize the laws which God has so evidently engraven in the very organization of man, when He gave him existence. To seek to go beyond this would be a great misfortune and a destructive undertaking. (Quoted in Murray N. Rothbard, *Economic Thought Before Adam Smith: An Austrian Perspective on the History of Economic Thought* [Cheltenham, U.K.: Edward Elgar, 1995], vol. 1, p. 371)

See also de Jouvenel, *Sovereignty*, pp. 172–73 and 189.

[10]The much cherished modern view, according to which the adoption of "constitutional government" represents a major civilizational advance from arbitrary government to the rule of law and which attributes to the United States a prominent or even preeminent role in this historical breakthrough, then, must be considered seriously flawed. This view is obviously contradicted by documents such as the Magna Carta (1215) or the Golden Bull (1356). More importantly, it misrepresents the nature of pre-modern governments. Such governments either entirely lacked the most arbitrary and tyrannical of all powers, i.e., the power to tax and legislate without consent; or even if they did possess these powers, governments were severely restricted in exercising them because such powers were widely regarded as illegitimate, i.e., as usurped rather than justly acquired. In distinct contrast, modern governments are defined by the fact that the powers to tax and legislate are recognized explicitly as legitimate; that is, all "constitutional" governments, whether in the U.S. or anywhere else, constitute *state*-governments. Robert Nisbet is thus correct in noting that a pre-modern

king may have ruled at times with a degree of irresponsibility that few modern governmental officials can enjoy, but it is doubtful whether, in terms of effective powers and services, any king of even the seventeenth-century "absolute monarchies" wielded the kind of authority that now

own and their protégés advantage. However, as elementary economic theory predicts, this institutional setup will not eliminate the self-inter-est-driven tendency of a monopolist of law and order towards increased exploitation. To the contrary, it only tends to make his exploitation less calculating, more shortsighted, and wasteful. As Rothbard explained:

> while a private owner, secure in his property and owning its capital value, plans the use of his resource over a long period of time, the government official must milk the property as quickly as he can, since he has no security of ownership. . . . government officials own the *use* of resources but not their capital value (except in the case of the "private property" of a hereditary monarch). When only the current use can be owned, but not the resource itself, there will quickly ensue uneconomic exhaustion of the resources, since it will be to no one's benefit to con-serve it over a period of time and to every owner's advantage to use it up as quickly as possible. . . . The private individual, secure in his property and in his capital resource, can take the long view, for he wants to maintain the capital value of his resource. It is the government official who must take and run, who must plunder the property while he is still in command.[11]

Moreover, because the Constitution provided explicitly for "open entry" into state-government—anyone could become a member of Con-gress, president, or a Supreme Court judge—resistance against state

---

inheres in the office of many high-ranking officials in the democracies. There were then too many social barriers between the claimed power of the monarch and the effective execution of this power over individuals. The very prestige and functional importance of church, family, gild, and local community as allegiances limited the absoluteness of the State's power. (*Community and Power*, pp. 103–04)

[11]Murray N. Rothbard, *Power and Market: Government and the Economy* (Kansas City: Sheed Andrews and McMeel, 1977), pp. 188–89. See further on this chaps. 1–3. In light of these considerations—and in contrast to common wisdom on the mat-ter—one reaches the same conclusion regarding the ultimate "success" of the American revolution as H.L. Mencken, *A Mencken Chrestomathy* (New York: Vintage Books, 1982):

> Political revolutions do not often accomplish anything of genuine value; their one undoubted effect is simply to throw out one gang of thieves and put in another. . . . Even the American colonies gained little by their revolt in 1776. For twenty-five years after the Revolution they were in far worse condition as free states than they would have been as colonies. Their government was more expensive, more inefficient, more dishonest, and more tyrannical. It was only the gradual material pro-gress of the country that saved them from starvation and collapse, and that material progress was due, not to the virtues of their new govern-ment, but to the lavishness of nature. Under the British hoof they would have got on as well, and probably a great deal better. (pp. 145–46)

property invasions declined; and as the result of "open political competition" the entire character structure of society became distorted, and more and more bad characters rose to the top.[12] For free entry and competition is not always good. Competition in the production of goods is good, but competition in the production of bads is not. Free competition in killing, stealing, counterfeiting, or swindling, for instance, is not good; it is worse than bad. Yet this is precisely what is instituted by open political competition, i.e., democracy.

In every society, people who covet another man's property exist, but in most cases people learn not to act on this desire or even feel ashamed for entertaining it.[13] In an anarcho-capitalist society in particular, anyone acting on such a desire is considered a criminal and is suppressed by physical violence. Under monarchical rule, by contrast, only one person—the king—can act on his desire for another man's property, and it is this that makes him a potential threat. However, because only he can expropriate while everyone else is forbidden to do likewise, a king's every action will be regarded with utmost suspicion.[14] Moreover, the selection of a king is by accident of his noble birth. His only characteristic qualification is his upbringing as a future king and preserver of the dynasty and its possessions. This does not assure that he will not be evil, of course. However, at the same time it does not preclude that a king might actually be a harmless dilettante or even a decent person.

In distinct contrast, by freeing up entry into government, the Constitution permitted anyone to openly express his desire for other men's property; indeed, owing to the constitutional guarantee of "freedom of speech," everyone is protected in so doing. Moreover, everyone is permitted to act on this desire, provided that he gains entry into government; hence, under the Constitution everyone becomes a potential threat.

To be sure, there are people who are unaffected by the desire to enrich themselves at the expense of others and to lord it over them; that is, there are people who wish only to work, produce, and enjoy the fruits of their labor. However, if politics—the acquisition of goods by political means (taxation and legislation)—is permitted, even these harmless people will be profoundly affected. In order to defend themselves against attacks on their liberty and property by those who have fewer moral scruples, even

---

[12]See on the following Hans-Hermann Hoppe, *Eigentum, Anarchie und Staat. Studien zur Theorie des Kapitalismus* (Opladen: Westdeutscher Verlag, 1987), pp. 182ff.

[13]See Helmut Schoeck, *Envy: A Theory of Social Behavior* (New York: Harcourt, Brace and World, 1970).

[14]See de Jouvenel, *On Power*, pp. 9–10.

these honest, hardworking people must become "political animals" and spend more and more time and energy developing their political skills. Given that the characteristics and talents required for political success—of good looks, sociability, oratorical power, charisma, etc.—are distributed unequally among men, then those *with* these particular characteristics and skills will have a sound advantage in the competition for scarce resources (economic success) as compared to those *without* them.

Worse still, given that in every society more "have-nots" of everything worth having exist than "haves," the politically talented who have little or no inhibition against taking property and lording it over others will have a clear advantage over those with such scruples. That is, open political competition favors aggressive (hence dangerous) rather than defensive (hence harmless) political talents and will thus lead to the cultivation and perfection of the peculiar skills of demagoguery, deception, lying, opportunism, corruption, and bribery. Therefore, entrance into and success within government will become increasingly impossible for anyone hampered by moral scruples against lying and stealing. Unlike kings then, congressmen, presidents, and Supreme Court judges do not and cannot acquire their positions accidentally. Rather, they reach their position because of their proficiency as morally uninhibited demagogues. Moreover, even outside the orbit of government, within civil society, individuals will increasingly rise to the top of economic and financial success *not* on account of their productive or entrepreneurial talents or even their superior defensive political talents, but rather because of their superior skills as unscrupulous political entrepreneurs and lobbyists. Thus, the Constitution virtually assures that exclusively dangerous men will rise to the pinnacle of government power and that moral behavior and ethical standards will tend to decline and deteriorate all-around.

Moreover, the constitutionally provided "separation of powers" makes no difference in this regard. Two or even three wrongs do not make a right. To the contrary, they lead to the proliferation, accumulation, reinforcement, and aggravation of error. Legislators cannot impose their will on their hapless subjects without the cooperation of the president as the head of the executive branch of government, and the president in turn will use his position and the resources at his disposal to influence legislators and legislation. And although the Supreme Court may disagree with particular acts of Congress or the president, Supreme Court judges are nominated by the president and confirmed by the Senate and remain dependent on them for funding. As an integral part of the institution of government, they have no interest in limiting but every interest in expanding the government's, and hence their own, power.[15]

---

[15]See on this the brilliant and indeed prophetic analysis by John C. Calhoun, *A Disquisition on Government* (New York: Liberal Arts Press, 1953), esp. pp. 25–27. There Calhoun notes that a

> written constitution certainly has many advantages, but it is a great mistake to suppose that the mere insertion of provisions to restrict and limit the powers of the government, without investing those for whose protection they are inserted with the means of enforcing their observance, will be sufficient to prevent the major and dominant party from abusing its powers. Being the party in possession of the government, they will . . . be in favor of the powers granted by the constitution and opposed to the restrictions intended to limit them. As the major and dominant parties, they will have no need of these restrictions for their protection. . . . The minor or weaker party, on the other contrary, would take the opposite direction and regard them as essential to their protection against the dominant party. . . . But where there are no means by which they could compel the major party to observe these restrictions, the only resort left them would be a strict construction of the constitution. . . . To which the major party would oppose a liberal construction—one which which would give to the words of the grant the broadest meaning of which they were susceptible. It would then be construction against construction—the one to contract and the other to enlarge the powers of the government to the utmost. But of what possible avail could the strict construction of the minor party be, against the liberal interpretation of the major, when the one would have all the powers of the government to carry its construction into effect and the other be deprived of all means of enforcing its construction? In a contest so unequal, the result would not be doubtful. The party in favor of restrictions would be overpowered. . . . The end of the contest would be the subversion of the constitution. . . . the restrictions would ultimately be annulled and the government be converted into one of unlimited powers. . . . Nor would the division of government into separate and, as it regards each other, independent departments prevent this result. . . . as each and all the departments—and, of course, the entire government—would be under the control of the numerical majority, it is too clear to require explanation that a mere distribution of its powers among its agents or representatives could do little or nothing to counteract its tendency to oppression and abuse of power.

In sum, then, Rothbard has commented on this analysis,

> the Constitution has proved to be an instrument for ratifying the expansion of State power rather than the opposite. As Calhoun saw, any written limits that leave it to government to interpret its own powers are bound to be interpreted as sanctions for expanding and not binding those powers. In a profound sense, the idea of binding down power with the chains of a written constitution has proved to be a noble experiment

IV

After more than two centuries of "constitutionally limited government," the results are clear and incontrovertible. At the outset of the
American "experiment," the tax burden imposed on Americans was
light, indeed almost negligible. Money consisted of fixed quantities of
gold and silver. The definition of private property was clear and seemingly immutable, and the right to self-defense was regarded as sacro-
sanct. No standing army existed, and, as expressed in Washington's
Farewell Address, a firm commitment to free trade and a noninterventionist foreign policy appeared to be in place. Two hundred years later, matters have changed dramatically.[16] Now, year in and year out the
American government expropriates more than 40 percent of the incomes of private producers, making even the economic burden imposed
on slaves and serfs seem moderate in comparison. Gold and silver have
been replaced by government-manufactured paper money, and Americans are being robbed continually through money inflation. The meaning of private property, once seemingly clear and fixed, has become

---

that failed. The idea of a strictly limited government has proved to be
utopian; some other, more radical means must be found to prevent the
growth of the aggressive State. (*For A New Liberty*, p. 67)

See also Anthony de Jasay, *Against Politics: On Government, Anarchy, and Order*
(London: Routledge, 1997), esp. chap. 2.

[16]Robert Higgs, *Crisis and Leviathan: Critical Episodes in the Growth of American
Government* (New York: Oxford University Press 1987), p. ix, contrasts the early
American experience to the present:

There was a time, long ago, when the average American could go about
his daily business hardly aware of the government—especially the federal government. As a farmer, merchant, or manufacturer, he could
decide what, how, when, and where to produce and sell his goods,
constrained by little more than market forces. Just think: no farm subsidies, price supports, or acreage controls; no Federal Trade Commission;
no antitrust laws; no Interstate Commerce Commission. As an employer,
employee, consumer, investor, lender, borrower, student, or teacher, he
could proceed largely according to his own lights. Just think: no National Labor Relations Board; no federal consumer "protection" laws; no
Security and Exchange Commission; no Equal Employment Opportunity Commission; no Department of Health and Human Services. Lack-
ing a central bank to issue national paper currency, people commonly
used gold coins to make purchases. There were no general sales taxes, no
Social Security taxes, no income taxes. Though governmental officials
were as corrupt then as now—maybe more so—they had vastly less to be
corrupt with. Private citizens spent about fifteen times more than all
governments combined.—Those days, alas, are long gone.

obscure, flexible, and fluid. In fact, every detail of private life, property, trade, and contract is regulated and reregulated by ever higher mountains of paper laws (legislation), and with increasing legislation, ever more legal uncertainty and moral hazards have been created, and lawlessness has replaced law and order. Last but not least, the commitment to free trade and noninterventionism has given way to a policy of protectionism, militarism, and imperialism. In fact, almost since its beginnings the U.S. government has engaged in relentless aggressive expansionism and, starting with the Spanish–American War and continuing past World War I and World War II to the present, the U.S. has become entangled in hundreds of foreign conflicts and risen to the rank of the world's foremost warmonger and imperialist power. In addition, while American citizens have become increasingly more defenseless, insecure, and impoverished, and foreigners all over the globe have become ever more threatened and bullied by U.S. military power, American presidents, members of Congress, and Supreme Court judges have become ever more arrogant, morally corrupt, and dangerous.[17]

What can possibly be done about this state of affairs? First, the American Constitution must be recognized for what it is—an error. As the Declaration of Independence noted, government is supposed to protect life, property, and the pursuit of happiness. Yet in granting government the power to tax and legislate without consent, the Constitution cannot possibly assure this goal but is instead the very instrument for invading and destroying the rights to life, liberty, and the pursuit of happiness. It is absurd to believe that an agency which may tax without consent can be a property protector. Likewise, it is absurd to believe that an agency with legislative powers can preserve law and order. Rather, it must be recognized that the Constitution is itself unconstitutional, i.e., incompatible with the very doctrine of natural human rights that inspired the American Revolution.[18] Indeed, no one in his right mind would agree to a contract that allowed one's alleged protector to determine unilaterally

---

[17]On the growth of U.S. government, and in particular the role of war in this development, see *The Costs of War: America's Pyrrhic Victories*, John V. Denson, ed. (New Brunswick, N.J.: Transaction Publishers, 1997); Higgs, *Crisis and Leviathan*; Ekkehart Krippendorff, *Staat und Krieg* (Frankfurt/M.: Suhrkamp, 1985), esp. pp. 90–116; *A New History of Leviathan*, Ronald Radosh and Murray N. Rothbard, eds. (New York: Dutton, 1972); Arthur A. Ekirch, *The Decline of American Liberalism* (New York: Atheneum, 1967).

[18]For the most forceful statement to this effect see Lysander Spooner, *No Treason: The Constitution of No Authority* (Colorado Springs, Colo.: Ralph Myles, 1973); also Murray N. Rothbard, *The Ethics of Liberty* (New York: New York University Press, 1998), esp. chaps. 22 and 23.

—without one's consent—and irrevocably—without the possibility of exit—how much to charge for protection; and no one in his right mind would agree to an irrevocable contract which granted one's alleged protector the right to ultimate decisionmaking regarding one's own person and property, i.e., of unilateral law*making*.[19]

Second, it is necessary to offer a positive and inspiring alternative to the present system.

While it is important that the memory of America's past as a land of pioneers and an effective *anarcho-capitalist* system based on self-defense and popular militias be kept alive, we cannot return to the feudal past or the time of the American Revolution. Yet the situation is not hopeless. Despite the relentless growth of statism over the course of the past two centuries, economic development has continued and our living standards have reached spectacular new heights. Under these circumstances a completely new option has become viable: the provision of law and order by freely competing private (profit and loss) insurance agencies.[20]

---

[19]In fact, any such protection-contract is not only empirically unlikely, but logically-praxeologically impossible. By "agreeing-to-be-taxed-and-legislated-in-order-to-be-protected" a person would in effect surrender (alienate) all of his property to the taxing authority and submit himself into permanent slavery to the legislative agency. Yet any such contract is from the outset impermissible, and hence null and void, because it contradicts the very nature of protection-contracts, namely the *self-ownership of someone to be protected* and the existence of *something owned by the protected* (rather than his protector), i.e., private—separate—property.

Interestingly, despite the fact that no known state-constitution has ever been agreed upon by everyone falling under its jurisdiction and despite the apparent impossibility that this fact could ever be different, political philosophy, from Hobbes over Locke on down to the present, abounds with attempts to provide a contractual justification for the state. The reason for these seemingly endless endeavors is obvious: either a state can be justified as the outcome of contracts, or it cannot be justified at all. Unsurprisingly, however, this search, much like that for a squared circle or a perpetual mobile, has come up empty and merely generated a long list of disingenuous, if not fraudulent, pseudo-justifications by means of *semantic fiat*: "no contract" *is really* an "implicit," or "tacit," or "conceptual" contract. In short, "no" *really means* "yes." For a prominent modern example of this Orwellian "newspeak" see James M. Buchanan and Gordon Tullock, *The Calculus of Consent* (Ann Arbor: University of Michigan Press, 1962); James M. Buchanan, *The Limits of Liberty* (Chicago: University of Chicago Press, 1975); idem, *Freedom in Constitutional Contract* (College Station: Texas A and M University Press, 1977). For a critique of Buchanan and the so-called Public Choice School see Murray N. Rothbard, *The Logic of Action Two* (Cheltenham, U.K.: Edward Elgar, 1997), chaps. 4 and 17; Hans-Hermann Hoppe, *The Economics and Ethics of Private Property* (Boston: Kluwer, 1993), chap. 1.

[20]See on the following also chap. 12; Morris and Linda Tannehill, *The Market for Liberty* (New York: Laissez Faire Books, 1984), esp. chap. 8.

While hampered by the state, even now insurance agencies protect private property owners upon payment of a premium against a multitude of natural and social disasters, from floods and hurricanes to theft and fraud. Thus, it would seem that the production of security and protection is the very purpose of insurance. Moreover, people would not turn to just anyone for a service as essential as that of protection. Rather, as de Molinari noted,

> before striking a bargain with (a) producer of security, . . . they will check if he is really strong enough to protect them. . . . (and) whether his character is such that they will not have to worry about his instigating the very aggressions he is supposed to suppress.[21]

In this regard insurance agencies also seem to fit the bill. They are "big" and in command of the resources— physical and human—necessary to accomplish the task of dealing with the dangers, actual or imagined, of the real world. Indeed, insurers operate on a national or even international scale, and they own substantial property holdings dispersed over wide territories and beyond the borders of single states and thus have a manifest self-interest in effective protection. Furthermore, all insurance companies are connected through a complex network of contractual agreements on mutual assistance and arbitration as well as a system of international reinsurance agencies representing a combined economic power which dwarfs most if not all contemporary governments, and they have acquired this position because of their reputation as effective, reliable, and honest businesses.

While this may suffice to establish insurance agencies as a possible alternative to the role currently performed by states as providers of law and order, a more detailed examination is needed to demonstrate the principal superiority of such an alternative to the *status quo*. In order to do this, it is only necessary to recognize that insurance agencies can neither tax nor legislate; that is, the relationship between the insurer and the insured is consensual. Both are free to cooperate or not to cooperate, and this fact has momentous implications. In this regard, insurance agencies are categorically different from states.

The advantages of having insurance agencies provide security and protection are as follows. First off, competition among insurers for paying clients will bring about a tendency toward a continuous fall in the price of protection (per insured value), thus rendering protection more

---

[21]De Molinari, *The Production of Security*, p. 12.

affordable. In contrast, a monopolistic protector who may tax the protected will charge ever higher prices for his services.[22]

Second, insurers will have to indemnify their clients in the case of actual damage; hence, they must operate efficiently. Regarding social disasters (crime) in particular, this means that the insurer must be concerned above all with effective prevention, for unless he can prevent a crime, he will have to pay up. Further, if a criminal act cannot be prevented, an insurer will still want to recover the loot, apprehend the offender, and bring him to justice, because in so doing the insurer can reduce his costs and force the criminal—rather than the victim and his insurer—to pay for the damages and cost of indemnification. In distinct contrast, because compulsory monopolists states do not indemnify victims and because they can resort to taxation as a source of funding, they have little or no incentive to prevent crime or to recover loot and capture criminals. If they do manage to apprehend a criminal, they typically force the victim to pay for the criminal's incarceration, thus adding insult to injury.[23]

----

[22]As Rothbard has explained, even

> if government is to be limited to "protection" of person and property, and taxation is to be "limited" to providing that service only, then *how* is the government to decide *how much* protection to provide and how much taxes to levy? For, contrary to the limited government theory, "protection" is no more a collective, one-lump "thing" than any other good or service in society. . . . Indeed, "protection" could conceivably imply anything from one policeman for an entire country, to supplying an armed bodyguard and a tank for every citizen—a proposition which would bankrupt the society posthaste. But who is to decide on how much protection, since it is undeniable that every person would be *better* protected from theft and assault if provided with an armed bodyguard than if he is not? On the free market, decisions on how much and what quality of any good or service should be supplied to each person are made by means of voluntary purchases by each individual; but what criterion can be applied when the decision is made by *government*? The answer is none at all, and such governmental decisions can only be purely arbitrary. (*The Ethics of Liberty*, pp. 180–81)

See also Murray N. Rothbard, *For A New Liberty* (New York: Collier, 1978), pp. 215ff.

[23]Comments Rothbard:

> The idea of primacy for restitution to the victim has great precedent in law; indeed, it is an ancient principle of law which has been allowed to wither away as the State has aggrandized and monopolized the institutions of justice. . . . In fact, in the Middle Ages generally, restitution to the victim was the dominant concept of punishment; only as the State grew

Third and most importantly, because the relationship between insurers and their clients is voluntary, insurers must accept private property as an ultimate "given" and private property rights as immutable law. That is, in order to attract or retain paying clients, insurers will have to offer contracts with specified property and property damage descriptions, rules of procedure, evidence, compensation, restitution, and punishment as well as intra- and interagency conflict resolution and arbitration procedures. Moreover, out of the steady cooperation between different insurers in mutual interagency arbitration proceedings, a tendency toward the unification of law—of a truly universal or "international" law—will emerge. Everyone, by virtue of being insured, would thus become tied into a global competitive effort to minimize conflict and aggression; and every single conflict and damage claim, regardless of where and by or against whom, would fall into the jurisdiction of exactly one or more specific and innumerable insurance agencies and their contractually agreed to arbitration procedures, thereby creating "perfect" legal certainty. In striking contrast, as tax-funded monopoly protectors states do not offer the consumers of protection anything even faintly resembling a service contract. Instead, they operate in a contractual void that allows them to make up and change the rules of the game as they go along. Most remarkably, whereas insurers must submit themselves to independent third party arbitrators and arbitration proceedings in order to attract voluntary paying clients, states, insofar as they allow for arbitration at all, assign this task to another state-funded and state-dependent judge.[24]

> more powerful . . . the emphasis shifted from restitution to the victim, . . . to punishment for alleged crimes committed "against the State." . . . What happens nowadays is the following absurdity: A steals $15,000 from B. The government tracks down, tries, and convicts A, all at the expense of B, as one of the numerous taxpayers victimized in this process. Then, the government, instead of forcing A to repay B or work at forced labor until that debt is paid, forces B, the victim, to pay taxes to support the criminal in prison for ten or twenty years' time. Where in the world is the justice here? (*The Ethics of Liberty*, pp. 86–87)

[24]Insurance agencies, insofar as they enter into a bilateral contract with each of their clients, fully satisfy the ancient and original *desideratum* of "representative" government of which Bruno Leoni has noted that "political representation was closely connected in its origin with the idea that the representatives act as agents of other people and according to the latter's will" (*Freedom and the Law*, pp. 118–19; see also note 8 above). In distinct contrast, modern democratic government involves the complete perversion—indeed, the nullification—of the original idea of representative government. Today, a person is deemed to be politically "represented" no matter what, i.e., regardless of his own will and actions or that of his representative.

Further implications of this fundamental contrast between insurers as contractual versus states as noncontractual providers of security deserve special attention.

Because they are not subject to and bound by contracts, states typically outlaw the ownership of weapons by their "clients," thus increasing their own security at the expense of rendering their alleged clients defenseless. In contrast, no voluntary buyer of protection insurance would agree to a contract that required him to surrender his right to self-defense and be unarmed or otherwise defenseless. To the contrary,

---

A person is considered represented if he votes, but also if he does not vote. He is considered represented if the candidate he has voted for is elected, but also if another candidate is elected. He is represented, whether the candidate he voted or did not vote for does or does not do what he wished him to do. And he is considered politically represented, whether "his" representative will find majority support among all elected representatives or not. "In truth," as Lysander Spooner has pointed out,

> voting is not to be taken as proof of consent. . . . On the contrary, it is to be considered that, without his consent having even been asked a man finds himself environed by a government that he cannot resist; a government that forces him to pay money, render service, and forego the exercise of many of his natural rights, under peril of weighty punishments. He sees, too, that other men practice this tyranny over him by use of the ballot. He sees further, that, if he will but use the ballot himself, he has some chance of relieving himself from this tyranny of others, by subjecting them to his own. In short, he finds himself, without his consent, so situated that, if he uses the ballot, he may become a master, if he does not use it, he must become a slave. And he has no other alternative than these two. In self-defense, he attempts the former. His case is analogous to that of a man who has been forced into battle, where he must either kill others, or be killed himself. Because, to save his own life in battle, a man attempts to take the lives of his opponents, it is not to be inferred that the battle is one of his own choosing. (p. 15) . . . [Consequently, the elected government officials] are neither our servants, agents, attorneys, nor representatives . . . [for] we do not make ourselves responsible for their acts. If a man is my servant, agent, or attorney, I necessarily make myself responsible for all his acts done within the limits of the power that I have entrusted to him. If I have entrusted him, as my agent, with either absolute power, or any power at all, over the persons or properties of other men than myself, I thereby necessarily make myself responsible to those other persons for any injuries he may do them, so long as he acts within the limits of the power I have granted him. But no individual who may be injured in his person or property, by acts of Congress, can come to the individual electors, and hold them responsible for these acts of their so-called agents or representatives. This fact proves that these pretended agents of the people, of everybody, are really the agents of nobody. (*No Treason*, p. 29)

insurance agencies would encourage the ownership of guns and other protective devices among their clients by means of selective price cuts, because the better the private protection of their clients, the lower the insurers' protection and indemnification costs will be.

Moreover, because they operate in a contractual void and are independent of voluntary payment, states arbitrarily define and redefine what is and what is not a punishable "aggression" and what does and does not require compensation. By imposing a proportional or progressive income tax and redistributing income from the rich to the poor, for instance, states in effect define the rich as aggressors and the poor as their victims. (Otherwise, if the rich were *not* aggressors and the poor *not* their victims, how could taking something from the former and giving it to the latter be justified?) Or by passing affirmative action laws, states effectively define whites and males as aggressors and blacks and women as their victims. For insurance agencies, any such business conduct would be impossible for two fundamental reasons.[25]

First, every insurance involves the pooling of particular risks into risk classes. It implies that to some of the insured more will be paid out than what they paid in, and to others less. However, and this is decisive, no one knows in advance who the "winners" and who the "losers" will be. Winners and losers—and any income redistribution among them—will be randomly distributed. Otherwise, if winners and losers could be systematically predicted, losers would not want to pool their risk with winners but only with other losers because this would lower their insurance premium.

Second, it is not possible to insure oneself against any conceivable "risk." Rather, it is only possible to insure oneself against "accidents," i.e., risks over whose outcome the insured has no control whatsoever and to which he contributes nothing. Thus, it is possible to insure oneself against the risk of death or fire, for instance, but it is not possible to insure oneself against the risk of committing suicide or setting one's own house on fire. Similarly, it is impossible to insure oneself against the risk of business failure, of unemployment, of not becoming rich, of not feeling like getting up and out of bed in the morning, or of disliking

---

[25]On the "logic" of insurance see Ludwig von Mises, *Human Action: A Treatise on Economics*, Scholar's Edition (Auburn, Ala.: Ludwig von Mises Institute, 1998), chap. 6; Murray N. Rothbard, *Man, Economy, and State*, 2 vols. (Auburn, Ala.: Ludwig von Mises Institute, 1993), pp. 498ff.; Hans-Hermann Hoppe, "On Certainty and Uncertainty, Or: How Rational Can Our Expectations Be?" *Review of Austrian Economics* 10, no. 1 (1997).

one's neighbors, fellows or superiors, because in each of these cases one has either full or partial control over the event in question. That is, an individual can affect the likelihood of the risk. By their very nature, the avoidance of risks such as these falls into the realm of individual responsibility, and any agency that undertook their insurance would be slated for immediate bankruptcy. Most significantly for the subject under discussion, the uninsurability of individual actions and sentiments (in contradistinction to accidents) implies that it is also impossible to insure oneself against the risk of damages which are the result of one's prior aggression or provocation. Rather, every insurer must restrict the actions of its clients so as to exclude all aggression and provocation on their part. That is, any insurance against social disasters such as crime must be contingent on the insured submitting themselves to specified norms of nonaggressive—civilized—conduct.

Accordingly, while states as monopolistic protectors can engage in redistributive policies benefiting one group of people at the expense of another, and while as tax-supported agencies they can even "insure" uninsurable risks and protect provocateurs and aggressors, voluntarily funded insurers would be systematically prevented from doing any such thing. Competition among insurers would preclude any form of income and wealth redistribution among various groups of insured, for a company engaging in such practices would lose clients to others refraining from them. Rather, every client would pay exclusively for his own risk, respectively that of people with the same (homogeneous) risk-exposure as he faces.[26] Nor would voluntarily funded insurers be able to "protect" any person from the consequences of his own erroneous, foolish, risky, or aggressive conduct or sentiment. Competition between insurers would instead systematically encourage individual responsibility, and any known provocateur and aggressor would be excluded as a bad

---

[26]In being compelled, on the one hand, to place individuals with the same or similar risk-exposure into the same risk group and to charge each of them the same price per insured value; and in being compelled, on the other hand, to distinguish accurately between various classes of individuals with objectively (factually) different group risks and to charge a different price per insured value for members of different risk groups (with the price differentials accurately reflecting the degree of heterogeneity between the members of such different groups), insurance companies would systematically promote the above-mentioned natural human tendency (see note 2 above) of "like people" to associate and to discriminate against and physically separate themselves from "unlikes." On the tendency of states to break up and destroy homogeneous groups and associations through a policy of forced integration see chaps. 7, 9, and 10.

insurance risk from any insurance coverage whatsoever and be rendered an economically isolated, weak, and vulnerable outcast.

Finally, with regard to foreign relations, because states can externalize the costs of their own actions onto hapless taxpayers, they are permanently prone to becoming aggressors and warmongers. Accordingly, they tend to fund and develop weapons of aggression and mass destruction. In distinct contrast, insurers will be prevented from engaging in any form of external aggression because any aggression is costly and requires higher insurance premiums, implying the loss of clients to other, nonaggressive competitors. Insurers will engage exclusively in defensive violence and instead of acquiring weapons of aggression and mass destruction, they will tend to invest in the development of weapons of defense and of targeted retaliation.[27]

V

Even though all of this is clear, how can we ever succeed in implementing such a fundamental constitutional reform? Insurance agencies are presently restricted by countless regulations which prevent them from doing what they could and naturally would do. How can they be freed from these regulations?

Essentially, the answer to this question is the same as that given by the American revolutionaries more than two-hundred years ago: through the creation of free territories and by means of secession.

In fact today under democratic conditions this answer is even truer than it was in the days of kings. For then, under monarchical conditions, the advocates of an antistatist liberal-libertarian social revolution still had an option that has since been lost. Liberal-libertarians in the old days could—and frequently did—believe in the possibility of simply converting the king to their view, thereby initiating a "revolution from the top." No mass support was necessary for this—just the insight of an enlightened prince.[28] However realistic this might have been then, today this top-down strategy of social revolution would be impossible. Not only are political leaders selected nowadays according to their demagogic talents and proven record as habitual immoralists, as has been explained above; consequently, the chance of converting them to liberal-libertarian views must be considered even lower than that of

---

[27]See also chap. 12; and Tannehill and Tannehill, *The Market for Liberty*, chaps. 11, 13, and 14.

[28]See on this Murray N. Rothbard, "Concepts of the Role of Intellectuals in Social Change Toward Laissez-Faire," *Journal of Libertarian Studies* 9, no. 2 (1990).

converting a king who simply inherited his position. Moreover, the state's protection monopoly is now considered public rather than private property, and government rule is no longer tied to a particular individual but to specified functions exercised by anonymous functionaries. Hence, the one-or-few-men-conversion strategy *can* no longer work. It does not matter if one converts a few top government officials—the president and some leading senators or judges, for instance—because within the rules of democratic government no single individual has the power to abdicate the government's monopoly of protection. Kings had this power, but presidents do not. The president can resign from his position, of course, only to have it taken over by someone else. He cannot dissolve the governmental protection monopoly because according to the rules of democracy, "the people," not their elected representatives, are considered the "owners" of government.

Thus, rather than by means of a top-down reform, under the current conditions one's strategy must be one of a bottom-up revolution. At first, the realization of this insight would seem to make the task of a liberal-libertarian social revolution impossible. For does this not imply that one would have to persuade a majority of the public to vote for the abolition of democracy and an end to all taxes and legislation? And is this not sheer fantasy, given that the masses are always dull and indolent, and even more so given that democracy, as explained above, promotes moral and intellectual degeneration? How in the world can anyone expect that a majority of an increasingly degenerate people accustomed to the "right" to vote should ever voluntarily renounce the opportunity of looting other people's property? Put this way, one must admit that the prospect of a social revolution must indeed be regarded as virtually nil. Rather, it is only on second thought, upon regarding secession as an integral part of any bottom-up strategy, that the task of a liberal-libertarian revolution appears less than impossible, even if it still remains a daunting one.

How does secession fit into a bottom-up strategy of social revolution? More importantly, how can a secessionist movement escape the Southern Confederacy's fate of being crushed by a tyrannical and dangerously armed central government?

In response to these questions it is first necessary to remember that neither the original American Revolution nor the American Constitution were the result of the will of the majority of the population. A third of the American colonists were actually Tories, and another third was occupied with daily routines and did not care either way. No more than a third of the colonists were actually committed to and supportive of the revolution, yet they carried the day. And as far as the Constitution is concerned, the overwhelming majority of the American public was opposed to its adoption, and its ratification represented more of a *coup 'd'etat* by a tiny minority than the general will. All revolutions, whether good or bad, are started by minorities; and the secessionist route toward social revolution, which necessarily involves the breaking-away of a smaller number of people from a larger one, takes explicit cognizance of this important fact.

Second, it is necessary to recognize that the ultimate power of every government—whether of kings or caretakers—rests solely on opinion and not on physical force. The agents of government are never more than a small proportion of the total population under their control. This implies that no government can possibly enforce its will upon the entire population unless it finds widespread support and voluntary cooperation within the nongovernmental public. It implies likewise that every government can be brought down by a mere change in public opinion, i.e., by the withdrawal of the public's consent and cooperation.[29] And while it is undeniably true that after more than two centuries of democracy the American public has become so degenerate, morally and intellectually, that any such withdrawal must be considered impossible on a nationwide scale, it would not seem insurmountably difficult to win a secessionist-minded majority in sufficiently small districts or regions of the country. In fact, given an energetic minority of intellectual elites inspired by the vision of a free society in which law and order is provided by competitive insurers, and given furthermore that—certainly in the U.S., which owes its very existence to a secessionist act—secession is still held to be legitimate and in accordance with the "original"

---

[29]On the fundamental importance of public opinion for government power see Etienne de la Boétie, *The Politics of Obedience: The Discourse of Voluntary Servitude* (New York: Free Life Editions, 1975), with an introduction by Murray N. Rothbard; David Hume, "On the First Principles of Government," in idem, *Essays: Moral, Political and Literary* (Oxford: Oxford University Press, 1971); Mises, *Human Action*, chap. 9, sect. 3. Mises there (p. 189) notes:

> He who wants to apply violence needs the voluntary cooperation of some people. . . . The tyrant must have a retinue of partisans who obey his orders of their own accord. Their spontaneous obedience provides him with the apparatus he needs for the conquest of other people. Whether or not he succeeds in making his sway last depends on the numerical relation of the groups, those who support him voluntarily and those whom he beats into submission. Though a tyrant may temporarily rule through a minority if this minority is armed and the majority is not, in the long run a minority cannot keep a majority in subservience.

democratic ideal of *self-determination* (rather than majority rule)[30] by a substantial number of people, there seems to be nothing unrealistic about assuming that such secessionist majorities exist or can be created at hundreds of locations all over the country. In fact, under the rather realistic assumption that the U.S. central government as well as the social-democratic states of the West in general are bound for economic bankruptcy (much like the socialist peoples' democracies of the East collapsed economically some ten years ago), present tendencies toward political disintegration will likely be strengthened in the future. Accordingly, the number of potential secessionist regions will continue to rise, even beyond its current level.

Finally, the insight into the widespread and growing secessionist potential also permits an answer to the last question regarding the dangers of a central government crackdown.

While it is important in this regard that the memory of the secessionist past of the U.S. be kept alive, it is even more important for the success of a liberal-libertarian revolution to avoid the mistakes of the second failed attempt at secession. Fortunately, the issue of slavery, which complicated and obscured the situation in 1861,[31] has been resolved. However, another important lesson must be learned by comparing the failed second American experiment with secession to the successful first one.

The first American secession was facilitated significantly by the fact that at the center of power in Britain, public opinion concerning the secessionists was hardly unified. In fact, many prominent British figures such as Edmund Burke and Adam Smith, for instance, openly sympa- °
thized with the secessionists. Apart from purely ideological reasons,

---

[30]See on this "old" liberal conception of democracy, for instance, Mises, *Liberalism: In the Classical Tradition* (Irvington-on-Hudson, N.Y.: Foundation for Economic Education, 1985). "The right to self-determination in regard to the question of membership in a state," writes Mises,

> thus means: whenever the inhabitants of a particular territory, whether it be a single village, a whole district, or a series of adjacent districts, make it known, by a freely conducted plebiscite, that they no longer wish to remain united to the state to which they belong at the time, but wish either to form an independent state or to attach themselves to some other state, their wishes are to be respected and complied with. This is the only feasible and effective way of preventing revolutions and civil and international wars. (p. 109)

[31]For a careful analysis of the issues involved in the War of Southern Independence see Thomas J. DiLorenzo, "The Great Centralizer. Abraham Lincoln and the War Between the States," *Independent Review* 3, no. 2 (1998).

which rarely affect more than a handful of philosophical minds, this lack of a unified opposition to the American secessionists in British public opinion can be attributed to two complementary factors. On the one hand, a multitude of regional and cultural-religious affiliations as well as of personal and family ties between Britain and the American colonists existed. On the other hand, the American events were considered far from home and the potential loss of the colonies as economically insignificant. In both regards, the situation in 1861 was distinctly different. To be sure, at the center of political power, which had shifted to the northern states of the U.S. by then, opposition to the secessionist Southern Confederacy was not unified, and the Confederate cause also had supporters in the North. However, fewer cultural bonds and kinship ties existed between the American North and South than had existed between Britain and the American colonists, and the secession of the Southern Confederacy involved about half the territory and a third of the entire population of the U.S. and thus struck Northerners as close to home and as a significant economic loss. Therefore, it was comparatively easier for the northern power elite to mold a unified front of "progressive" Yankee culture *versus* a culturally backward and "reactionary" Dixieland.

In light of these considerations, then, it appears strategically advisable not to attempt again what in 1861 failed so painfully: for contiguous states or even the entire South trying to break away from the tyranny of Washington, D.C. Rather, a modern liberal-libertarian strategy of secession should take its cues from the European Middle Ages when, from about the twelfth until well into the seventeenth century (with the emergence of the modern central state), Europe was characterized by the existence of hundreds of free and independent cities, interspersed into a predominantly feudal social structure.[32] By choosing this model and striving to create a U.S. punctuated by a large and increasing number of territorially disconnected free cities—a multitude of Hong Kongs, Singapores, Monacos, and Liechtensteins strewn out over the entire continent—two otherwise unattainable but central objectives can be accomplished. First, besides recognizing the fact that the liberal-libertarian potential is distributed highly unevenly across the country, such a strategy of piecemeal withdrawal renders secession less threatening

---

[32]On the importance of the free cities of medieval Europe on the subsequent development of the uniquely European tradition of (classical) liberalism see *Cities and The Rise of States in Europe, A.D. 1000 to 1800*, Charles Tilly and Wim P. Blockmans, eds. (Boulder, Colo.: Westview Press, 1994).

politically, socially and economically. Second, by pursuing this strategy simultaneously at a great number of locations all over the country, it becomes exceedingly difficult for the central state to create a unified opposition in public opinion to the secessionists which would secure the level of popular support and voluntary cooperation necessary for a successful crackdown.[33]

If and only if we succeed in this endeavor, if we then proceed to return all public property into appropriate private hands and adopt a new "constitution" which declares all taxation and legislation henceforth unlawful, and if we then finally allow insurance agencies to do what they are destined to do, can we truly be proud again and will America be justified in claiming to provide an example to the rest of the world.

---

[33]The danger of a government crackdown is greatest during the initial stage of this secessionist scenario, i.e., while the number of free city territories is still small. Hence, during this phase it is advisable to avoid any direct confrontation with the central government. Rather than renouncing its legitimacy altogether, it would seem prudent, for instance, to guarantee the government's "property" of federal buildings, etc., within the free territory, and "only" deny its right to future taxation and legislation concerning anyone and anything within this territory. Provided that this is done with the appropriate diplomatic tact and given the necessity of a substantial level of support in public opinion, it is difficult to imagine how the central government would dare to invade a territory and crush a group of people who had committed no other sin than trying to mind their own business. Subsequently, once the number of secessionist territories has reached a critical mass—and every success in one location promoted imitation by other localities—the difficulties of crushing the secessionists will increase exponentially, and the central government would quickly be rendered impotent and implode under its own weight.

INDEX
Compiled by Richard Perry